The Saga of Lucien L. Nunn and Deep Springs College

Portrait of L.L. Nunn by Pat Bagley.

THE SAGA
of Lucien L. Nunn &
DEEP SPRINGS COLLEGE

REVISED EDITION

L. Jackson Newell

FOREWORD BY WILLIAM T. VOLLMANN

The University of Utah Press
Salt Lake City

Previously published as *The Electric Edge of Academe: The Saga of Lucien L. Nunn and Deep Springs College*. Revised paperback edition 2025.

Library of Congress Cataloging-in-Publication Data
Names: Newell, L. Jackson, 1938- author.
Title: The Saga of Lucien L. Nunn and Deep Springs College. Revised edition / L. Jackson Newell; foreword by William T. Vollmann.
Description: Salt Lake City : The University of Utah Press, [2025] | Includes bibliographical references and index.
Identifiers: ISBN 9781647692797 (paperback) | ISBN 9781647692803 (ebook)

For EU safety / GPSR concerns:
Email: gpsr@mare-nostrum.co.uk

Physical address:
Mare Nostrum Group B.V.
Mauritskade 21D
1091 GC Amsterdam
The Netherlands

Cover photograph: Deep Springs Valley with the Sierra Nevada Range on the western horizon. Photograph by L. Jackson Newell.

Poignantly, I pay homage to my late wife, historian
Linda King Newell (1941-2023), who joined me in ferreting out
the documentary evidence on which this story rests, critiqued each chapter as I
drafted it, and gamely indulged my devotion to this project for nearly a decade.
Her presence is revealed throughout this work.

To my children, Heather, Eric, Jennifer, and Christine, and grandchildren,
Lydia, Lila, Drake, Sydney, Benjamin, William, Nathan,
Ezra, Elise, Micah, Nicholas, and Sage.
To you I entrust my dreams of a more just and humane world.

CONTENTS

MAPS

FOREWORD

My friend Jack Newell has requested me to write a few words about his book on L.L. Nunn and the Deep Springs educational experiment.

Deep Springs was one of the great experiences of my life. I came to the college in dread of physical labor, because throughout my childhood, my bad eyesight and my love of reading had rendered me not just worthless but odious to most other boys. At Deep Springs I found that I could succeed in unskilled labor as well as many others, and even take accomplishment-pleasure in digging a ditch. A classmate of mine, Ben Campbell, used to say that the main virtue of Deep Springs was that it taught one how to fail. I certainly failed in many ways. But once I dared to emerge from my shy and privileged middle-class isolation, I learned that I could manage to do many things I hadn't ever done, and this lesson has never left me. I cherish the patient, kindly education that the ranch hands gave me. I learned that "student power" can mean something, and that many people (not all) will rise to the occasion when given responsibility, respect and trust. My current life brings me into almost daily contact with the homeless, and I find that the latter principle works as well with them as with anyone else. Sometimes my trust is abused by a methamphetamine addict; sometimes it is abused by my President. No matter; I try to keep on trusting when I can—but always to think for myself, another simple principle I learned from Deep Springs. I bore responsibility for the livestock I fed and slaughtered at Deep Springs. It was up to me to show prudence, competence, and humaneness. I try to do the same when somebody asks me to comment on the latest American drone strike in Pakistan (results: a dead al-Qaeda militant whom we have never heard of before—he might have been a threat—and seventeen or forty-one dead women and children).

Above all, Deep Springs taught me to prepare for a life of service. New students were sent a copy of the so-called "Gray Book," which contained certain sayings, letters, et cetera of the founder, L.L. Nunn. Many of his phrases sounded crabbed and crackpot-ish to me. His humorless elitism, his authoritarian streak, these were not only characteristic of his epoch; they were also qualities of the "Little Napoleon" himself. His gnomelike figure and his alleged pederasties made him all the odder. And yet there was something curiously impressive about the man. His tendency to elevate something as trivial as, say, a request to attend a dance into a grandly pointed prohibition against "entangling alliances" was laughable, but not entirely. He aimed to place a group of raw boys in the middle of nowhere, give them all the power and responsibility he thought they could handle (this to be adjusted upward or downward depending on what they did with it), and direct them to exercise it in the interest of higher principles. He was a mystic; he thought the desert had a voice. When I went out alone, I found that it does. He thought that a carpenter could be, simply by practicing his profession with "abundance of heart," as worthy a "Trustee of the Nation" as anyone. So do I. He despised materialism and commercialism. How many colleges and universities speak likewise? He gave me a free education; I didn't even have to pay for my meals. He never knew me and might have disliked the man I have become. I feel that I know him at least partially, through the Gray Book, and from that standpoint I admire him and feel grateful to him. He was not a genius, but something better: a man who devoted much of his money, and his poor health, to helping young men learn who they were, what they were capable of, and how they themselves might if they wished it help others.

L.L. Nunn deserves a biography of his own. Jack and his wife Linda have toiled over this project for a number of years. Thanks to them, that strange, obscure small man and the good he did will be better illuminated, and may even by affecting the mind or heart of some unknown reader bring about some new benefit.

William T. Vollmann
Sacramento, California

PREFACE TO THE REVISED EDITION

Times change. When the first edition of this book came out a decade ago, I thought the title, *The Electric Edge of Academe*, captured its nature as the blended biography of hydroelectric pioneer Lucien L. Nunn and the history of his most prized achievement, Deep Springs College. But with the proliferation of online classes in American universities, even those Massive Open Online Courses (MOOCs) that are beamed around the world, "the electric edge of academe" appeared misleading. Many readers stumbled over that title and told me so.

This revised edition appears under the previous subtitle alone: *The Saga of Lucien L. Nunn and Deep Springs College.* And a saga it has been. For over a century, Deep Springs has existed on the leading edge of undergraduate innovation, educational democracy, geographical isolation, and, more than once, extinction.

It is surprising that L. L. Nunn considered his founding of Deep Springs College the crowning achievement of his life. Earlier, he had pioneered the joining of Nikola Tesla's alternating current theories with George Westinghouse's manufacturing capabilities to produce hydroelectric power on a commercial scale—first at tiny Ames, Colorado, in 1891, then with a major breakthrough at Olmsted, Utah, at the turn of the century, and finally in constructing the mammoth Ontario Power Plant at Niagara Falls. No one contributed more than L. L. Nunn to the early development of electrical power to transform industrial production and everyday life.

Indeed, Nunn was also a bundle of contradictions. A visionary in spirit and action, yet fragile at his core, he championed the rights of marginalized people but bullied competitors who threatened his entrepreneurial ventures. A passionate believer in democracy, his authoritarian instincts sometimes undermined his educational principles. From beginning to end, however, Nunn was a compelling and charismatic presence whose contradictions often fed his mystique. His spirit was irrepressible and his ideas continue to inspire new reforms in undergraduate education.

Sometimes described as a perpetual experiment in higher education, Deep Springs itself has adapted and evolved as society and the environment have changed. When the first edition of this book went to press, the fate of a decades-long battle over the admission of women to the student body remained unresolved. The college had won a decisive judgment in support of coeducation from the California Superior Court in Inyo County, but the celebration ended abruptly when the two board opponents of the decision sent the case to the Appeals Court of California. More than a year later, that court found the Superior Court's judgment flawless. Still, the objectors appealed the case to the California Supreme Court. Year after year, Deep Springs cancelled its plans to recruit and select female candidates for admission.

Then, on June 30, 2017, on the eve of the centennial celebration of the founding of Deep Springs, with three hundred alumni camping at the ranch, board chair Dave Hitz received the long-awaited judgment from the state's Supreme Court. With two members recusing themselves because of ties with Deep Springs, the justices had accepted the decisions of the lower courts. Fittingly, the college would pivot to coeducation just as it launched its second century. The legal battle had been very costly, but the long-anticipated transformation could hardly have begun at a more opportune time. The college would launch its second century as a coeducational institution.

Veteran president David Neidorf guided the college through the transition with a steady hand, joining the student body in minimizing press and alumni visits so the newly integrated Student Body and resident community could establish healthy new patterns without external distractions. It worked, as the students navigated new challenges to communication and cultural adjustment with the intelligence and integrity Lucien Nunn always expected would arise when the stakes are highest and trust rules the day. Neidorf concluded his long and successful tenure as the leader of the college in 2020, handing the reins to the college's first woman president.

Anthropologist Sue Darlington arrived from a deanship at Hampshire College in Massachusetts. Her tenure was complicated by the Covid pandemic at its peak and two disruptive construction projects prompted in part by a modest expansion of the student body (from twenty-six to thirty members) associated with coeducation. Despite these challenging conditions (including no community dining hall for most of her tenure), Darlington's presence was felt over the din of conflicts with students and the community. Before her tenure was over, she had laid the groundwork for a $3,000,000 endowment gift, one of the largest in Deep Springs's history.

Behavioral and conservation biologist Andrew Zink accepted the presidency in the summer of 2023, after having managed a major research lab at San Francisco State University. He commenced his leadership following a gap of several chaotic months caused by his predecessor's earlier-than-expected departure. As decisive as he is humane by nature, Zink's tenure has been characterized by repopulating and reenergizing the staff and faculty, increasing the college's ongoing stewardship of Deep Springs Valley, launching new fund-raising initiatives, and strengthening science in the curriculum.

What of the transition to coeducation? Women are routinely elected to leadership positions within the student body (as chair/presidents, labor commissioners, trustees, and committee leaders), and they do the same share of garden, farm, and ranch work (including the sought-after and demanding summer cowboy positions) that students have always done. They have also succeeded and failed, just like their male counterparts, as they tackle the daily cacophony of challenges built into communal living in a strenuous physical and intellectual environment. Conflicts still rage over Student Body decisions, some of them as always over sex and gender, with no greater or lesser intensity than before. With coeducation, the college has doubled the talent pool from which it draws and deeply enriched the educational experiences derived from living, working, and learning in an intensely interconnected community.

Well into its second century now, the importance of Deep Springs College appears greater than ever. Its commitment to Deweyan democracy in educational practices, and its belief in preparing its students for service to society through diplomacy, education, journalism, science, and myriad other walks of life, is more needed and more vital than ever. Deep Springs prepares students to hear one another, to think critically, and act with each other's welfare in mind. No wonder CBS's *60 Minutes* recently featured Deep Springs as a beacon of hope in higher education. Perhaps it's no surprise that New Jersey's newly elected United States Senator, Andy Kim (DS'00), is an alumnus, that Raymond Jeanloz (DS'70) and Michael Stryker (DS'65) lead a list of alumni members of the National Academy of Sciences, and artist and urban planner Damon Rich (DS'93) is the latest of three alumni to win a MacArthur Genius Fellowship. Philip Kennicott (DS'83) and Zack Mider (DS'96) have won Pulitzer Prizes. William Vollmann (DS'1977) is a recipient of the National Book Award for Fiction.

A covey of new colleges is springing up based on L. L. Nunn's principles and what is commonly known as the Deep Springs model. These small but radical experiments are all committed to student engagement in every element of the school's operations and governance, high expectations for student performance, direct practical applications of student learning, and, notably, world views that integrate scientific and cultural knowledge. Democracy is a lived experience on these campuses. It is too early to know if these colleges will survive or thrive but, undeniably, Outer Coast College in Sitka, Alaska; Thoreau College in Viroqua, Wisconsin; Tidelines Institute in Gustavus, Alaska; and a half-dozen others are tapping Nunn's ideas and drawing on Deep Springs's experience to break new ground in twenty-first century higher education. This book, I hope, makes clear why the steady development of Deep Springs for more than a century provides inspiration, practical guidance, and some cautionary tales for those to come.

Remoteness and the resultant interdependence of neighbors in times of need characterizes life in these new learning communities, as has been the case at Deep Springs since Death Valley Scotty (and especially his patron Albert Johnson) pitched in to support L. L. Nunn at the beginning. From the 1970s to the early 2000s, this phenomenon took an unusual twist at Deep Springs. At that time, the best public transportation route to the college was to fly into Las Vegas, catch the Reno bus up US 95, and get off at remote Lida Junction. That's where a student or staff member picked up the travelers and drove them east across the desert and two mountain ranges to Deep Springs. But Lida Junction was also the site of the Cottontail Ranch, a licensed brothel in Nevada and the only habitation within twenty-five miles. Generations of students told of being scolded by other bus passengers for de-boarding at Lida Junction. Occasionally, when a blizzard prevented the Deep Springs van from making the connection on time, the madam offered shelter and food. When it closed in 2004, decades of alumni acknowledged this remnant of western "live and let live" neighborliness in a storm.

When I wrote this book a decade ago, I was daunted by the task of rendering an account true to the documentary evidence even when the story did not reflect well on the judgments of colleagues who preceded or joined me as players in the drama. I also experienced moments of realization that I had suppressed painful memories of my own mistakes in leading the college. Certainly, I worried that long friendships with other presidents, trustees, faculty, or staff would be lost or compromised because of what I wrote. And some were, at least for a time. Still, I felt that nothing less than an honest account of the college's history, as I strove to grasp it, was worthy of the institution to which I owed so much. I deeply appreciate the patience and forgiveness of any I may have offended.

INTRODUCTION

I noticed a small man come into the railroad coach and slip quietly into a seat, where he appeared to be thinking intently. One of the engineers remarked, "That is L.L. Nunn."

—Charles D. Walcott

This book illuminates the odyssey of Lucien L. Nunn by tracing the origin and development of his far-reaching ideas about society, technology, and education (chapters 1–3), exploring their flowering in his founding and early guidance of Deep Springs College (chapters 4–8), and then examining the plight of those ideas and the college he established when they were entrusted to others after his death in 1925 (chapters 9–16). The survival and further development of Deep Springs for nearly a century, through a succession of institutional crises and triumphs, has thrust Nunn's life force into the present. The saga is all the more intriguing because it has often been the Deep Springs students themselves rather than the trustees who have risen to defend Nunn's progressive ethical principles and radical educational methods.

L.L. Nunn personified the imagination, resolve, conscience, and, indeed, paradoxes of the Progressive Era in American history. Starting with little more than a quick and curious mind and more restless energy than his compact body could contain, he wandered the Northeast and Europe in search of truth and a mission in life. In his late twenties, he migrated west to test his mettle on the American frontier. Nunn struggled with repeated failures and disappointments en route to high achievements as a small businessman, mine operator, banker, newspaper owner, hydroelectric power developer, corporate leader, and, finally, educational innovator and college founder.

Constantly improvising, when his hydroelectric plants near Telluride, Colorado, faltered for lack of trained workers, he devised a plan to attract able young men and taught them on the job. Like John Dewey, he would use democratic educational methods to induce personal and social responsibility, but he chose to concentrate his efforts on the most promising young men he could find.

From his multifaceted Telluride beginning, Nunn's industrial enterprises spread throughout the West, reaching into Mexico and Canada, and eventually encompassing the installation (between 1903 and 1906) of the landmark Ontario Power Works at Niagara Falls. At the hub of his operations, the Olmsted Power Station in Provo Canyon, Utah, Nunn established an educational institute for his power company apprentices.

To extend his educational work, Nunn founded and endowed Telluride Association in 1911, establishing a scholarship house next to the Cornell University campus where his most able students could live when they left Olmsted and matriculated there. Telluride quickly became a self-governing, self-perpetuating scholarship-granting organization of about a hundred students and young intellectuals. After a period of personal preparation and further experimentation, he founded Deep Springs College in 1917, basing its educational program on democratic self-governance, personal responsibility, and study of the liberal arts and sciences—all designed to instill an ethic of service to humanity. He aimed to prepare genuinely free individuals who would commit their lives to the common good.

The story continues after the college's founding as an extension of Nunn's ambition. His progressive ideas faced one grave challenge after another. He loathed racial bigotry, religious fanaticism, political indoctrination, and fraud of any kind, each of which would worm its way dangerously close to the heart of his college during its first century. Like his robber baron contemporaries, Nunn was a ferocious competitor. But he was also a man of universal interests and sometime conflicting humane and ruthless instincts. The battles over his ideas were just being joined when Lucien L. Nunn drew his final breath at age seventy-two.

One of my challenges in doing justice to Nunn and his legacy has been to understand and explain why and how Deep Springs has remained loyal to its founder's vision while adapting successfully to a rapidly changing society. One clue may be found in the words of 1946 alumnus Park Honan when he reflected on the meaning of his education at the ranch: "Deep Springs means to discourage any passive attitude toward life, by which responsibility is allowed to go by default to those who always stand ready to seize it unworthily."[1] The college has had its share of unworthy aspirants and forgettable moments, but it adapts and persists because its perennial champions, the students and alumni, have been acculturated to adapt and persist.

Late in life, Nunn indulged few memories of past exploits and took little pride in his entrepreneurial triumphs. The only thing that mattered to him—and it mattered greatly—was Deep Springs College. Even Telluride Association, in which he had invested so much of himself and his resources, had become secondary. His Deep Springs legacy is both instructive and fascinating.

The California setting of the college, Deep Springs Valley, has brought such a democratic quality to the lives and learning of students that I have accorded it a special chapter (chapter 4). Nunn had developed a profound respect for the desert's solitude and deceiving expanse, even before he bought the site. This inspiring physical setting and the wild remoteness, he hoped, would foster contemplation, inspiration, even spirituality—and develop students' strength to face adversity, to combine self-reliance with community spirit, and to contend with powerful natural forces from blizzards and flash floods to handling animals large enough to do them in.

Deep Springs is the smallest, most remote, most selective, and certainly the most unusual liberal arts college in the world. With a student body of fewer than thirty members, its campus is an oasis at the center of a ranch with grazing allotments that spread over a quarter of a million acres of California and Nevada desert. Farm and ranch labor rival academic demands for students' time, and the college duels institutions such as Harvard, Caltech, and MIT to claim the most promising high school graduates. Deep Springs is at once a bold twentieth-century experiment in higher education and an evocation of the university's most ancient origins.

Medieval Italian universities such as Bologna and Padua began eight centuries ago when students formed self-governing guilds and hired master scholars to teach them. So serious were these young scholars that some forbade their favorite tutors to marry without permission, lest wedded bliss interfere with their teaching, and required them to post a bond before leaving town to assure their return. Deep Springs is, in a sense, a re-creation of these radical beginnings (minus the meddling in professors' personal affairs). The college works, sometimes brilliantly, because students are at the center of things again. It is a strenuous life, physically, intellectually, and emotionally.

A men's college since its founding, coeducation was an inflammatory issue after the 1960s. For many years, opening admission to women was supported by most students and younger alumni but opposed by a majority of older and more influential graduates. By the second decade of the twenty-first century, however, many senior alumni had reconsidered coeducation. The trustees of Deep Springs voted overwhelmingly to admit women in 2011, but there were two dissenters and they sought to block implementation in court. The legal battle continued for six years. A decision from the Superior Court of California on November 19, 2014, solidly supported the trustees' decision to admit women as well as men. The trustees' decision to embrace coeducation, and the controversy that followed, is detailed in the new preface.

Deep Springs takes sound principles of teaching and scholarship to their practical limits. Learning is stimulated by the need to solve problems and for the sheer joy of exploration and understanding. Students govern their own affairs and take the lead in choosing the faculty, designing the liberal arts curriculum, running the admissions process, deciding whether their peers should be invited to return for a second year, and writing and editing official publications. The students also cook many of the meals for the community, operate the library and bookstore, plant, weed, and harvest the garden, milk the cows, irrigate the fields, mow and bale the hay, herd the cattle, and operate the heavy equipment. They also do less romantic labor like washing dishes, making guest beds, cleaning toilets, and mopping floors—all tasks essential to the smooth running of any community.

Nunn gave students both power and responsibility. In the Deed of Trust, he charged them with observing two ground rules, known informally as the "isolation policy": no tobacco or alcohol (later interpreted to include mind-altering drugs), and no trips to nearby towns like Big Pine or Bishop for social encounters. Courageously, Nunn put the student body itself in charge of defining and enforcing these rules within the limits of law. Observance of this policy has varied widely, and abuses have not been infrequent. "The freedom that the students have possessed is not in contradiction to the purpose of Deep Springs," Nunn wrote. "It is a means of promoting it. I want students to know the eternal truths of the universe. But I want them to do more than know these truths; I want them to live them."[2]

The freedom Nunn granted students came accompanied by the responsibility to operate the largely organic farm and cattle ranch under the guidance of professional staff members and, later, a student elected as labor commissioner (or foreman). Students benefit from rare opportunities to understand the production of food and fiber, processes from which their contemporaries are almost completely removed. More important, perhaps, these agricultural operations are working laboratories, joining theory and practice in land stewardship and sustainable agriculture.

The admissions committee receives about one thousand complete applications each year. The number is relatively small for three reasons: (1) selection criteria are known to be stiff; (2) college life at Deep Springs is ascetic by any standard; and (3) applicants must write seven essays just to merit full consideration. Forty finalists are invited to spend three days at Deep Springs, usually in groups of three or four. During these visits, each one participates fully in the academic and labor programs. On their last day, they face their potential peers in an hour-long interview. After these visits, the student Applications Committee recommends about fifteen for admission. Of those who are admitted, almost all accept the opportunity and responsibility of membership in the student body. While no cut-off levels are set for standardized test scores or high school grade point averages, the average SAT score for those admitted is in the top two percent nationally.

About July 1 each year, these students join their second-year peers. Deep Springs never uses "freshman" and "sophomore" and, unlike other colleges, identifies alumni by the year they enrolled. For example, Charles Munford (DS'00) was admitted in 2000 (and "Mr. T," his potbellied pig, moved into the dorm with him). The college now attracts students from all over the world. Religious, political, and cultural diversity is especially central to this educational environment, and the contrasts within the student body are always strong. Sharp differences of opinion or judgment abound, but they are frequently buffered by spontaneous humor.

The purpose of Deep Springs is to prepare principled, capable, and sagacious leaders. When Deep Springers accept admission, they are expected to share fully in creating a robust and healthy community and enhancing the most comprehensive liberal arts education available anywhere. They are also expected to set self-interest aside and work unstintingly for the community's welfare. Students participate in virtually every decision that bears on their education, directly or indirectly, from academic policies and faculty and staff selection to budget expenditures and endowment holdings.

Nunn regarded his students as the "beneficial owners" of the college. No tuition and fees have ever been levied, despite some very lean years, making it clear that students are neither consumers (tuition-payers) nor honorees (scholarship recipients). To make his point even clearer, Nunn specified in the Deed of Trust that one of the nine trustees would be a fully empowered student member, embracing student participation in governance a half-century before the rest of higher education recognized its importance. When the trustees expanded their membership to thirteen in the early 1990s, they granted the student body a second seat, thereby enhancing rather than diluting the students' influence.

Graduates take with them an obligation to serve humanity, thus dispatching their debt to the college and embodying the essence of their extraordinary learning experiences. Most of them are accepted at schools like the University of Chicago, Columbia, Harvard, Stanford, U.C. Berkeley, and Yale. Over half eventually earn academic or professional doctorates.

The genius in Nunn's approach is that he did not define "service" or "community." Rather, each student, faculty, and staff member must hammer out a personal definition. Deep Springs' students, therefore, live and study with a consciousness that much has been given them and that even more will be expected of them. Their opportunity to attend Deep Springs is presented not so much as a gift but rather as evidence of personal promise that they should magnify to benefit others. Embracing that responsibility with an abundance of heart is the ethic of the college, passed down from the founder.

Most alumni have pursued careers in the arts, literature, sciences, and service professions such as medicine, law, and higher education. Many have been drawn to the Foreign Service. By 2025, the twelve hundred Deep Springs alumni (living and dead) included four Rhodes Scholars, three MacArthur Fellows, four U.S. ambassadors, and twelve Truman Scholars. Many alumni are highly involved in their local communities. Virtually all live with the verve L.L. Nunn hoped to inspire.

My experience with the college is long and varied. I was smitten by Deep Springs at age twelve when family friend Brandt Kehoe (DS'51) showed me photographs and told me about his experiences there. Four years later, high school classmate Bill Anderson and I sputtered across the eastern California desert in an old Chevrolet. Twenty-eight miles east of Big Pine, I turned down the narrow road marked "Deep Springs Ranch 1 Mile." Moments later we rumbled across the cattle guard onto the tree-shaded oasis of the cattle ranch. A circle of attractive, wide-eaved buildings nestled against the lush alfalfa fields and grazing cattle. Everything was alive and moving. This was my first look at Deep Springs, and my heart pounded in my chest. The next year I matriculated as a student.

I stayed at Deep Springs for what was then the customary three academic years (subsequently changed to two calendar years). How lucky I felt to live in such a stunning environment, but also to irrigate the fields, buck the bales, and ride the open range astride a good quarter horse—all as an integral part of my liberal education.

I finished my baccalaureate in American history at the Ohio State University, then earned a master's degree at Duke University in the same field. With my wife, Linda King Newell, I returned to Deep Springs and taught there from 1965 to 1967. A few years later, another stint at Ohio State produced my doctorate with a focus on the history and philosophy of higher education. After a post-doctoral fellowship, Linda and I, along with the first three of our four children, moved to Salt Lake City where I had joined the University of Utah faculty and soon served as Dean of Liberal Education. This post allowed me to bring my Deep Springs experience and philosophy to bear on a university-wide program that included designing and creating interdisciplinary, real-world–oriented "core" courses required of all undergraduate students.

Living within a long day's drive of Deep Springs, I was soon invited to serve as an academic advisor to the Curriculum Committee, the faculty, and the trustees. In 1987, I was appointed a trustee of Deep Springs and, in 1993, elected chair of the board. Seven months after I rotated off the Board of Trustees, I returned as the college's president, a post I held from 1995 to 2004. L.L. Nunn's unusual experiment in undergraduate education not only influenced my life for good but continues to energize my long career as a university professor.

I approached this book as a professor of the history and philosophy of higher education, having long concentrated my teaching and research on the life cycles of progressive colleges and undergraduate reforms in major universities. Why do some fine institutions like Black Mountain College in North Carolina (1933–1956) simply burn out? Why do others like the University of California, Santa Cruz (founded in 1965) surrender their distinctive characteristics and join mainstream higher education? Why do a few like Berea (1855), College of the Atlantic (1969), and Evergreen State (1971) succeed in renewing their resources while remaining true to their progressive heritage? I have repeatedly explored questions like these with my graduate students. The work of two seminars in which we addressed these questions is reported in *Maverick Colleges: Fourteen Notable Experiments in American Undergraduate Education.*[3]

Nunn lived his whole life on the edge of social convention and his entire entrepreneurial career on the cusp of technological and business innovations. The ultimate outsider as a gay man on the Utah and Colorado frontier, he earned respect from the western business elite and even Utah's Mormon hierarchy, while continuing to understand and empathize with those on the perimeter.

Equally edgy is Nunn's brainchild, Deep Springs College. For nearly a century, its educational program has pushed the limits of convention. Not only has it been on the leading edge of innovation, it is also on the margin of civilization—poised between two federally designated wilderness areas.

Finally, both the college and its founder teetered on the edge of extinction more than once. L.L. Nunn's life nearly ebbed away on several occasions from his young adulthood to his last great effort to secure the college. And Deep Springs has stared into the abyss more than once, only to step back and straighten up, stronger than before.

I wrote this book to take a place alongside two pioneering works about the long and bumpy history of progressive colleges in America. In *The Distinctive College*, a case study of Antioch, Reed, and Swarthmore, Burton R. Clark argued that the work of transformational leaders and the continuing successes of these colleges depend on the emergence of "organizational sagas" that perpetuate their daring and noble identities. These sagas shape the aspirations and steel the nerves of successive generations of alumni, faculty, and trustees—sometimes with "cultish overtones," as historian John Thelin observed.[4] Yet if these heroic legends fade, a distinctive college can lose its edge or expire, as did Antioch College (established in 1853) in 2008. Antioch's revival three years later tapped the saga initiated by Horace Mann and added a new chapter.

If sagas matter to reformist institutions, so do philosophical foundations and educational purposes. David Riesman and Gerald Grant argued in *The Perpetual Dream: Reform and Experiment in the American College*, that most attempts to improve undergraduate education only tinker with incremental changes.[5] Adding incentives for excellent teaching, striving to recruit more highly qualified students, or urging the creation of new courses may enliven programs of study but will not transform the student experience or prepare young people to meet new societal conditions.

What interested Riesman and Grant were the rare colleges that attempted "telic reforms"—alternative models of undergraduate education driven by a coherent educational philosophy.[6] Because "telic reforms could be thought of as counterrevolutionary, that is, as counter to the rise of research universities," they swim against the current. It is often academic outsiders or peripheral players who sense a critical need for new purposes and methods and muster the courage and resources to give them life. They see undergraduate study as an end in itself—resulting in personal enrichment and political, social, or aesthetic engagement—rather than as preparation for graduate school and professional life.

I am not the first to attempt a biography of L.L. Nunn and his telic educational endeavors. He had hoped that someone would write his story before he died, and he saved his correspondence and other records with great care. All of them. Even before he had founded Deep Springs, Telluride Association contemplated sponsoring and supporting such a book. A plan to commission renowned muckraking journalist Ida Tarbell to write that story after Nunn's death did not materialize. Instead, one of Nunn's protégés, Stephen A. Bailey, wrote a modest biography, *L.L. Nunn: A Memoir* (1933), dedicated "To the Members of Deep Springs Student Body and Telluride Association." The association reprinted the volume on its sixtieth anniversary, adding a thoughtful introduction by Scott McDermott.[7]

Another Telluride associate spent much of the 1960s and early 1970s writing a documentary history of Nunn and his educational initiatives. Orville Sweeting's manuscript "The Education Experiment of L.L. Nunn" topped 1,800 pages but was nowhere near publishable when he died unexpectedly in 1976.[8] His work, however, is an invaluable resource for historians, especially because Sweeting quoted many documents in full or in part that have since been lost.

In his ninety-third year, Robert Aird, an alumnus whose family enjoyed a close friendship with L.L. Nunn in Utah before he enrolled as a student at Deep Springs, wrote an illuminating remembrance of the founder and a short history of the college's first half-century. The trustees of Deep Springs published *Deep Springs: Its Founder, History, and Philosophy with Personal Reflections* as a paperback before Aird's death.[9]

Two other books about Nunn's accomplishments have appeared more recently. Alumnus Denis E. Clark (DS'69) culminated years of on-site exploration of L.L. Nunn's power business in *Telluride Power: A Brief Illustrated History of the Early Days*.[10] It is packed with historical and contemporary photographs and information. In 2000 Michael A. Smith published *The Students of Deep Springs College*.[11] While teaching at the college, he crafted two photographic character sketches of each student, accompanied by the student's brief personal statement. William T. Vollmann (DS'77) and I wrote short essays to provide context for Smith's photographic collection. Each of these works provided foundations for *The Saga of Lucien L. Nunn and Deep Springs College*.

Research took Linda and me across Nunn's America, from his birthplace in northern Ohio to his crypt in the mausoleum at Forest Lawn in Glendale,

California. A pilgrimage to Telluride, Colorado, enabled us to see Nunn's Alta, Ophir, and Gold King mines, his powerhouse at nearby Ames where the first long-distance transmission of electricity for commercial use took place, the bank he founded, and his stately home on the corner of Columbia and Aspen Streets. Next to it stands the Cornell House, an attractive dormitory for the students who worked in his first power plants.

I was unexpectedly inspired by what we saw in and around Telluride. We drove away with a new and brighter illumination of Nunn's entrepreneurial and educational exploits. Leaving Telluride, we toured the Glen Canyon Dam and Power Station with its twelve 345,000-volt transformers producing at capacity. From Ames, Colorado, to Page, Arizona, in a single day, we leaped three-quarters of a century of hydroelectric history. What a transformative power Nunn had set in motion!

The juxtaposition of the Ames and Glen Canyon hydro plants got me thinking further about Nunn's educational legacies. Has Deep Springs—as the accomplishment that brought L.L. Nunn greatest satisfaction at the end of his life—merely survived like the Cornell House in Telluride, Colorado, or has it influenced lives, or other colleges and universities, to anything near the degree that his technical and business innovations revolutionized the power industry? That question continues to drive my interest in the man and his college.

PART 1

LUCIEN L. NUNN
A PERSONAL ODYSSEY

An irrepressible innovator, Lucien Nunn, the eighth child of recent British immigrants, was born on an Ohio farm in 1853. He started two small businesses in his early teens, and found a spiritual guide in activist theologian Charles Grandison Finney, then a professor at Oberlin College. Never finishing high school or college, Nunn roamed Europe twice in search of truth and a mission in life. Still adrift, he studied law for a semester at Harvard, then headed west in 1879 to assay his grit on the Colorado frontier.

A dozen years later, L.L. Nunn became known around the world for transmitting high voltage alternating current from a hydroelectric plant he designed and built on Howard Fork to his Gold King mine high in the mountains above Telluride, Colorado. Over the next two decades, the diminutive Nunn became a larger than life innovator in generating and transmitting electrical energy and in developing a radically different model of industrial training anchored at his Olmsted, Utah, headquarters. Shifting his focus, Nunn capped his career as a champion and practitioner of progressive reform in education, founding Deep Springs College in 1917.

Lucien L. Nunn.

CHAPTER 1

THE DIMINUTIVE DYNAMO, 1853–1890

So live that when the storms of life shall sweep down and across your path striking fear, discouragement and despair into the hearts of the timorous, you may guide those around you by your moral sense.

—L.L. Nunn

"To reach the bedside of his dying son at Niagara Falls," the *Los Angeles Times* noted on July 4, 1905, "a special train bearing L.L. Nunn, president of the Telluride Power Company, is racing East over the Union Pacific this evening." A more detailed report in the *Salt Lake Herald* identified Nunn as "a Provo capitalist" who hired the special train to overtake Union Pacific No. 4 on its way east. The *Ogden Standard*, published in the Utah city from which Nunn's personal express train had embarked, identified him as president of the Salt Lake and Mercur Railroad, while the *Denver Post*'s account emphasized Nunn's Telluride Power Company connection but asserted that it was Nunn's wife who was gravely ill and that he was racing to Telluride, Colorado.[1] A few days later, the *Telluride Daily Journal* lampooned these stories by pointing out that Nunn, actually headed for Niagara Falls, was "a bachelor and never had a wife or son."[2]

Except for these crucial details, the other newspapers' descriptions of L.L. Nunn were all true. He was racing to the deathbed of a young protégé, Charles Frederic Hutton, who had been diagnosed with a rapidly advancing paralysis.[3]

Miriam Eliza Kendall, 1818–1885. Courtesy of Helen M. Heckman.

Charles Robert Nunn 1816–1896. Courtesy of Helen M. Heckman.

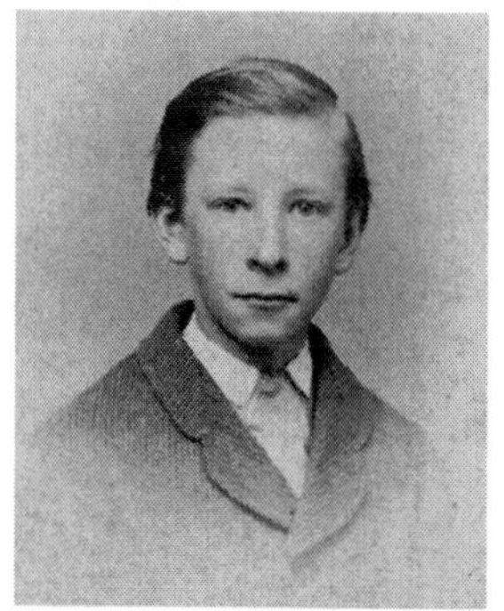

Lucien L. Nunn, age thirteen, when he lived with his sisters and studied at Linda Guilford's school in Cleveland. Courtesy of Helen M. Heckman.

He died before Nunn reached his bedside. Hutton, a brilliant young Montanan, had been a rising star in Nunn's Telluride Power Company.

Nunn was news because, still in his early fifties, he was already instrumental in replacing muscle power and steam with electricity in mining and industry. He was also experimenting with applying a potent blend of pragmatism and idealism to higher education. His storied career led from one quest to the next, beginning in Colorado. It had crested in Utah by 1905, expanded rapidly across much of North America, and landed him on a remote desert ranch north of Death Valley in 1917. There he devoted his final years to founding Deep Springs College, a little-known jewel in American higher education.

At the time of the train race, Nunn was scaling down his Colorado mining, banking, and real estate interests in favor of moving to Provo, Utah where he managed an expanding web of power stations and high-tension electric lines and got deadly serious about educational experimentation.

Lucien Lucius Nunn barely topped five feet one inch or tipped the scales above 118 pounds. With his piercing blue eyes, staccato voice, and perfect diction, he exuded energy and confidence. What he lacked in physical stature he more than made up for in presence. This was no accident.

L.L. Nunn's parents, Miriam Kendall Nunn and Charles Robert Nunn, emigrated from Suffolk, England, in 1851 and settled as farming tenants in Medina in northeastern Ohio.[4] As Baptist dissenters in England, they were seeking better opportunities for themselves and their seven children in the United States.

Their first American-born children, Lucien Lucius and his twin, Lucius

Lucien, were born there on March 16, 1853. Lucius died at age three, leaving Lucien devastated and vulnerable to bouts of loneliness and depression throughout his life. This death left Nunn the sole proprietor of their common initials, L.L., which he used as his signature and brand throughout his life.

Lucien harbored affectionate memories of his parents, his maternal grandmother, Mary Towler Kendall, and several aunts and uncles who also settled in Medina. An accomplished woman, Mary had attended her father's lectures at the University of Cambridge as a young adult and continued her intellectual interests throughout her life. She died while reading the New Testament in Hebrew, leaving a deep impression on Lucien, then age twelve.[5] Near his own life's end, Nunn wrote of his mother, Miriam: "To me the great evidence of immortality and better things is my mother's comprehensive and undying love. The absolute stability of [this] woman's philosophy, her faith, her devotion, her love—proof as it is against every form of attack—furnishes a final resting place for my tired and worn-out consciousness."[6] This sentiment was particularly touching for a man whose life rarely included comfortable, much less intimate, relationships with women outside his own family.

Except for lifelong closeness to his siblings, little evidence survives of Nunn's youth. He was twelve when the Civil War ended and Lincoln was assassinated. The war left every community short-handed, and farm children bore even more adult responsibilities than usual, often to the detriment of their formal schooling.

Nunn's industrious parents acquired their own farm near Peru, Ohio. Hard work, family cooperation, and education constituted primary values in their home, priorities drawn from previous generations. One forebear was a professor of medicine in Germany and another a Cambridge don. A landed family for generations, Robert William Nunn's (1778–1835) descendants believe that his profligate ways had exhausted the estate. His son, Charles Robert, sold the estate to pay debts and taxes, underwriting his family's passage to the United States with what remained.[7]

Lucien later told a nephew about leaving home at age fourteen "without ever having seen a railway or town of considerable size but fairly surging with ambition to be a factor in the world's developments and reckless as to personal results." Two sisters, Emily and Miriam, schoolteachers in Cleveland, provided a home and facilitated his entrance into "Miss Guilford's Cleveland Academy."[8] Lucien earned his keep by building chairs, tables, and beds for their home. "These two years, from fourteen to sixteen, constituted my only regular schooling," he claimed, although this story varied according to his audience.[9] He appreciatively quoted Guilford's insistence on personal authenticity: "It is what you *are*, my dear children, that is going to have its influence on those around you, not what you may *seem* to be."[10] Two of his academy schoolmates, Elton Hoyt and Ralph King, later became business partners of his in Colorado and Utah, and Hoyt presided at Nunn's funeral in Los Angeles six decades later.[11]

When Lucien finished his second year at Guilford's academy, his next older brother, Josiah, was matriculating at Oberlin College and his eldest brother, Fred, was doing business near Oberlin, an hour from Cleveland by rail. Lucien often shuttled back and forth among these four siblings.[12] At about sixteen, he joined Fred and Josiah in "Nunn Bros.," a bee-raising and honey extraction business. Unfortunately, a more experienced competitor patented their innovative extraction device.[13] Still, Nunn Bros. prospered, and Lucien learned how to borrow money, manage assets, and nurture a small business.

At the same time, his intellectual and spiritual predispositions quickened under the influence of the Presbyterian theologian and recently retired Oberlin College president, Charles Grandison Finney. As a charismatic young pastor in New York City, Finney had inspired many of the abolition movement's leaders. In 1837, he joined the largely abolitionist faculty at the Oberlin Collegiate Institute (renamed Oberlin College in 1850), founded in 1833 as the nation's first coeducational college. Finney enjoyed a distinguished career as professor of theology, founding editor of the *Oberlin Evangelist*, and a leading exponent of New School Calvinism with its emphasis on free will. His *Lectures on Revivals of Religion* (1835) was his century's definitive guide for revivalist ministers. Although Lucien did not enroll at the college, Finney took an interest in L.L., inspired Lucien's enduring admiration, and, more importantly, catalyzed his personal philosophy, upon which Finney bestowed a vocabulary and clarity. Finney inspired Nunn to read the *Edinburgh Review*, to muster both theology and reason to improve the human condition, and to see life as a test of will. Perseverance was the core virtue. Finney's was a theology of strenuous doing, rather than theological contemplation, and he launched the ambitious and impressionable Lucien on a quest to find moral order in the world and to live by its precepts. Nunn also internalized a style of intellectual and moral nurturance from the old gentleman that he later transmitted to his own youthful workers and students.

A few years later, sister Emily went to London to study under noted scientist Thomas Huxley, then serving chiefly on royal commissions. She was on her way to becoming Wellesley College's first professor of biology. In the meantime, sister Ellen committed her life to missionary service. These two marked the opposite poles on a continuum from science to religion, between which L.L. oscillated for many years.

Following his year in Oberlin, L.L. returned to the family farm near Peru. He and Fred profitably expanded their bee business and launched other agricultural enterprises. They lived simply and saved their earnings. In the fall of 1873, L.L. recalled the previous four years as "a season of personal adjustment with the world and several business ventures, the two largest being raising hedge for fences and bee culture. . . . Home finances were not pressing and our savings accumulated so that . . . when I was twenty years old, we considered our property worth about ten thousand dollars."[14] A single unit of their bee business in Henry County produced fifteen hundred pounds of honey that year.

At the urging of sisters Emily and Ellen,[15] L.L. and Fred entrusted their businesses to their parents and a beekeeping friend in Oberlin and set out for Europe. They traveled widely, finding inspiration in many cultures and traditions. "The trip stands out as a bright spot in my life," Lucien reflected decades later, "and the future at that time appeared an enlargement of that spot. Never since have mountains appeared so grand or lakes and valleys so calm and beautiful as those we saw on that trip. . . . Fortunate indeed were we to have caught this glimpse of a broader world, for troubles were near at hand."[16]

By the time they returned home, the nation was experiencing a financial depression, their bees, "which had produced us over four thousand dollars the season before," were wiped out by an unknown disease, and barbed-wire had replaced their hedge plants. As a final blow, "Fred's health gave way and I was left alone . . . with heavy obligations and practically no resources."[17] Lucien would not forget this lesson about new technology and rapid obsolescence, even as he launched himself at the financial challenge: "Failure to pay a debt seemed to me so horrible that my effort for [the next] two and a half years knew no bounds. Day and night I taxed to the uttermost my tenacious constitution, going without proper food and clothing, doing anything and everything to make or save a dollar which the stern principles of my father would permit, without once thinking of asking for assistance."[18] By the fall of 1876 his accounts were all clear.

Concerned about the interruption of L.L.'s education, Ellen paid for him to return to Europe, this time for a year of study.[19] He spent most of it in Germany near the University of Gottingen and the University of Leipzig, reading English translations of the texts of Continental thinkers and conversing with students about them. He became especially enamored of Johann Gottfried von Herder, social critic, philosopher, and disciple of Immanuel Kant, who had eloquently expressed unease at the rising tide of rationalism.[20]

Herder's claim that literary genius and great scientific talents are called forth by "the necessities of human existence," rather than being supernatural gifts, struck a chord in Nunn. So did Herder's effort to identify universal laws in human affairs comparable to natural laws in the physical and life sciences. But the "law" that struck Nunn deepest held that every human being must exercise "faithful obedience to an inviolable duty, to a truth felt in the inmost parts. It seeks not to investigate a thing about which there is doubt, but to do a thing about which there can be no doubt."[21]

Throughout his career, Nunn would admonish his colleagues and students to seek and live by "truths felt in the inmost parts." For Nunn, Herder provided an intellectual rationale for Finney's spiritual insights—that living well is a duty fulfilled only with struggle, self-discipline, and faith.

Decades later, Nunn commented to nephew Frank Whitman that this second European sojourn "cost less than three hundred dollars including passage both ways." Instead of formally studying, "I just read, thought, and grew. The horizon cleared, the problem of my life took form, my health came back and with the most complete contempt for any difficulty which could arise and with the feeling that success cannot be measured by locality or time but alone belongs to eternity and the universe I returned home to take up my work."[22]

This lofty self-report differs from that of a later business associate, Frank Noon. Noon met a lawyer in Chicago who had known L.L. as a student in Leipzig forty years earlier. What was Nunn like then? The attorney laughed: "His time was taken up with fighting the police and making love to German girls."[23]

When Nunn arrived home, the fall harvest was in "and there seemed nothing to do." He accepted fifty dollars from his patient father and went to Boston.[24] Taking odd jobs as a handyman, he read law with Henry W. Paine, including Sir William Blackstone's four-volume *Commentaries on the Laws of England* (1765–1769). Paine also shepherded Nunn into the Harvard Law School where he matriculated, funded by his older sisters, on February 4, 1879.[25] He proudly reported that his room became "much frequented by many of the foremost thinkers among the students."[26] He concluded his preparation for the practice of law later that year and returned to the family farm to help ease his parents' heavy summer load.

For intellectual stimulation, he joined the Antiliteral Class, a society of young intellectuals in nearby Mansfield. Twenty-year-old physician Charles D. Sain was secretary and M. W. McFarland was president. The constitution

Lucien L. Nunn, age twenty-five, when studying law at Harvard. Courtesy of Helen M. Heckman.

Paul N. Nunn, age twenty-five, when teaching school in Massachusetts. Courtesy of Helen M. Heckman.

declared its purpose: "to promote among its members: 1st. A general knowledge of standard literature, of history, fiction and poetry; 2nd. A knowledge of the recent discoveries of science, especially Biology; and 3rd. A knowledge of the latest hypotheses of philosophy respecting the science of Biology and unseen realities."[27]

Every several weeks, the group heard and discussed addresses given by scholars at nearby colleges. It was those "unseen realities," manifest by what L.L. called an innate "moral sense," that intrigued him. He enjoyed grappling with the conflicting claims posed by Emily's scientific knowledge anchored in the senses, Ellen's evangelical idealism, and his own mystical notion of an endowed conscience. For him, antiliteralism meant questioning both the literal meaning of scripture and also the rising tide of scientific knowledge.

Late in 1879, twenty-six-year-old Nunn went to St. Louis where he "spent the winter almost entirely" in its famous public library, "again broadening my horizon" and attempting to resolve paradoxes in his moral reasoning.[28] There he wrote "The Moral Sense," an essay he mailed to Charles Sain on March 18, 1880.[29] Sain read it to the Antiliteral Class on March 22 and also published it in the *Mansfield Herald* with correspondence "from the pen of Lucien L. Nunn, of Harvard College." The essay contrasts the rapidly accumulating scientific knowledge with the existence of enduring human consciousness. Consciousness, especially if properly nourished by education, experience, and religion, Nunn asserted, provides access to enduring truths like justice and mercy. The human universe is bound together by these principles, in support of which human beings must develop and exert their will. Nunn concluded: "So live that when the storms of life shall sweep down and across your path striking fear, discouragement and despair into the hearts of the timorous, you may guide those around you by your moral sense." This sentiment would provide the groundwork for the college he would found nearly four decades later. It also articulated an axiological foundation on which he built his career. Until his death in 1925, he kept the *Herald* clipping with other especially important documents in a scrapbook in his bedroom.[30]

Nunn's curiosity and facility with words and ideas set him apart at an early age, an achievement in itself since he read slowly, running his right index finger under each line. He cited a childhood eye injury and corrective surgery as the reason for this need.[31] Throughout his career, Nunn's aides and associates read aloud to him whenever possible, and he dictated virtually all of his letters. He acquired books across a wide spectrum of subjects, assimilated their major concepts, and then sought nimble sparring partners with whom to discuss the ideas. The cut and thrust of informed argumentation honed Nunn's thinking. His genius as an entrepreneur and innovator stemmed from this unique method of compensating for a reading disability, while his penchant for acting decisively on the insights he gained closed the loop between theoretical and practical matters.

Always conscious of his small body but instinctively ambitious, Nunn always admired Napoleon Bonaparte's reforming zeal, even though he was chagrined to learn that Napoleon was four or five inches taller.[32] To create a larger presence, L.L. resolved to make his speech and personal bearing extraordinary. Abraham Lincoln, whose presidency dominated L.L.'s childhood, also impressed Nunn with the power of language used well. Throughout his career, he consistently demonstrated his gifts for speaking persuasively and writing with unfailing literacy.

Lucien Nunn turned twenty-seven in the spring of 1880, having been schooled in the practical crafts of agriculture, carpentry, and small business and in the intellectual arts of moral philosophy and law. Although most of his siblings had pursued conventional academic degrees, then taken up business, education, or law, L.L.'s path to knowledge had been almost entirely self-directed. Perhaps the brightest, most imaginative, and most driven of the siblings, he had roamed restlessly through many pursuits, testing the moral and financial support of his parents and siblings. Despite mixed feelings, their loyalty to him endured throughout his life.

When the snow melted across Missouri that spring, Lucien Nunn accepted another $300 from his father and climbed aboard the train to Denver, just four years after Colorado achieved statehood.[33] In booming Leadville, he supported himself with carpentry odd jobs and forged a friendship with twenty-one-year-old Malachi ("Mack") Kinney. During a building suppliers' price war, Nunn purchased a dray of lumber from one proprietor, hauled it to another, and sold it for a profit. The two men used Nunn's earnings to construct a building, buy culinary utensils, and open the "Leadville Restaurant," to which hungry miners thronged for its two-bit suppers.[34] They soon accepted an invitation to move into Hill's gambling house, the premier gathering place in town, but the "Pacific Grotto's" fifty-cent meals were apparently more than the traffic would bear, and it flopped.

That fall, the two men set out in a spring wagon for Tombstone, Arizona, chasing rumors of a silver strike. Counter-rumors of Indian uprisings terminated their trajectory at Durango, Colorado, a town on the Denver and Rio Grande Railroad.[35] They bought several town lots for a few dollars each and began constructing doors and windows for miners' cabins. More ambitiously, they also built and opened a new restaurant that got off to a strong start with many regular customers, and a few who were curiously influential.

To sister Emily on February 10, 1881, Nunn described Durango's dangers: "I have seen a young man shot through and through with five balls, for no purpose or reason except that he refused to lend the ruffian $5.00. . . . I am right in the midst of it. Within the last two weeks I have had three balls pass close to my head. The danger is far greater than in an ordinary war. Last night the marshal of the town came in my place [the new Pacific Grotto] drunk & drew a revolver & commenced shooting out the lights." L.L. concluded that, if Emily would send him train fare ($110), he would return home "if I am not killed before help reaches me."[36]

A somewhat skeptical Emily queried brother Fred: "You see L wishes to come back—he puts the danger prominent so as to induce & I have no doubt he is [in] a rough place. . . . I think it may be a depressing place too—tho' I do not think one can tell much from his letters. Probably the most forcable [*sic*] reason for sending for him would be Mother's anxiety and ferment."[37] Compassionate but resigned, she commented: "I do not think he will change—do not think he can change. He is one of those strangely made pieces who work wrong because

Emily A. Nunn, who became a professor of biology at Wellesley College. Courtesy of Helen M. Heckman.

they are made wrong." She contemplated getting him care from a Yale physician but also hiring him to build her a cottage near the Oceanographic Institution at Woods Hole, Massachusetts, after which he would serve as its caretaker.

A week later, apparently based on a letter from L.L. that has not survived, Emily was "nauseated" by a new revelation:

> I have found sufficient reason for believing that the young man Lou took care of was himself. I was very much interested to know what ailed Lou at that time. It was mysterious to me and I had a passing wonder several times but was *quite* unsuspicious. I really did think that whatever faults Lou had, sensual indulgency [this word unclear] was not among them. I am afraid now that I was mistaken, indeed I really have no doubt. . . . Perhaps one may well let him be killed or not. When I think of his coming back to me now, I feel as if I could hardly stomach his presence.[38]

Emily now reflected on other behavior, including an unspecified case of "internal inflammation" that she now found suspicious. Their mother, described as anxious in her first letter, now felt that L.L. would not pull his own weight on the farm; and the other siblings "have all said they so wished he was back but its very [interesting] that no one wants to see him back enough to let him have money to come back on."[39]

Emily then quoted a more recent letter from L.L. in which he again hinted for money, describing his physical danger, but which she now found sinister: "I often wonder whether I shall escape knife and bullet until I have time to get away? What is more important—whether I shall have a moral nature left even if I should get off with my physical [self] as soon as possible."[40]

Emily's correspondence reveals no further specifics, but sexuality was clearly the issue. Her language suggests a venereal disease with its associations of family disgrace. But would Emily, then a professor of biology at Wellesley, be so repelled that she would prefer her brother dead? Homosexuality seems a more likely explanation.

At the Pacific Grotto, Nunn and Kinney's patrons included the Garret–Eskridge–Pruitt gang of thirty-eight men who dominated the district and threatened civic governance in Durango.[41] When a vigilante committee urged the partners to help bring the desperados to justice, they ducked out of town—according to their later account. But another possibility is that Lucien and Mack had been "outed" as homosexual partners. Such exposure may explain the marshal's inebriated harassment, and he may have tried to force the two into the danger of serving on the posse.

Neither Emily nor her siblings rescued L.L. Correspondence among Emily, Ellen, and Fred during this period shares a belief that they saw their younger brothers, Lucien and Paul, as irresponsible—unlikely to become self-supporting or responsible citizens.

Whether L.L. Nunn and Malachi Kinney fled Durango to avoid the gang war or were run out of town by bigots, they briefly considered a move to Santa Fe but chose Telluride instead—a tiny settlement of miners far more remote than the railroad town they were leaving behind. "We disposed our Durango interests at a loss," Kinney later wrote, "caused by giving credit too freely and feeding every man that came along 'broke.' . . . We traveled on foot, going by way of Silverton, Bridal Veil Basin and Pandora. . . . Reaching Telluride we pitched our tent, and soon found work, shingling a roof."[42]

The town of Telluride, initially known as Columbia, had just settled on its new name and the first streets were being surveyed that summer of 1881. High and inaccessible at 8,800 feet elevation, the mountains around Telluride had generally evaded earlier mining booms. Gold had been mined in the surrounding San Juan Mountains for about seven years, but now the Smuggler vein in the Marshall Basin north of town was showing promise.[43] The two partners bought a town lot for one dollar and built a ten-by-twelve-foot shack. "The roof was of boards and leaked, the sides were made by boards being put up & down like barn boards, there was no lining to the room so that the snow would blow in [on my bed]," L.L. wrote Ellen.[44] They hired out as carpenters.

In November, Lucien fell gravely ill with typhoid fever, an attack that lasted almost seven weeks. "I was reduced to a skeleton . . . too weak to lift my hand," he wrote. He lost thirty-eight pounds before his fever finally broke. Telluride had no doctors, so he prescribed his own medicines, which Kinney procured in Ridgeway, nearly forty miles north across the Dallas Divide. Nunn's mother wrote his brother Frederick, urging him to go care for his brother and to ship the body home if he succumbed.[45]

As he convalesced, Nunn longed to soak in a hot bath to soothe his aching body. As soon as he was strong enough, he and Malachi constructed a wooden frame, lined it with zinc-plated metal sheeting, piped it to a wood stove for heat, and reportedly enjoyed the first such amenity in town.[46]

Hardly a healthy place, Telluride (sometimes called "To Hell You Ride" by early residents) reeked from the hard bodies of men who worked long hours in the summer heat or winter cold, bunked in tight quarters, and paid scant attention to hygiene. Nunn and Kinney were soon hiring out their heated bathtub, building others, and earning a tidy profit. More importantly, it brought L.L. to the attention of many townspeople who admired his business sense and fell under what Kinney described as "his wonderful power of swaying men."[47]

On January 23, 1882, L.L. wrote an eight-page epistle to Fred. He still wanted to go east, but he radiated restored health: "Just eight days from the time I first sat up after the fever turned I did my first days work. It surprised me as well as all around me. I have never seen so rapid a recovery from such a very low state. . . . I am now in more perfect health than I ever remember being before." He had regained his lost weight and "hardly know what the sensation of tiredness is."[48] L.L. invited Fred to join him in opening a law office:

> It is folly for me to wait longer for I shall soon be old & have done nothing. I want to practice in the east but there is business here & here is a good place to commence & get experience & practice. . . . Were we here together we could gather around us in the form of books and journals the best minds of the past & present & could fit our selves for the highest place for which we are by nature fitted. . . . If you do not think it best to come I want to borrow your Law books & any other you may be willing to lend.

With pathos, he called this ambition "the last chance I shall have to rise above the common carpenter work at which I have been engaged during the last year." He confessed "a chilling fear."[49]

Nunn summed up his ambition in these words: "I long to be successful for the sake of others," he told Fred, referring to the debt he owed his parents and his desire to help younger brothers Urban and Paul. "Just by labor I have sent four dollars home in each letter for some time . . . but that will not pay the interest on what I owe. I must open broader fields through the law & that at once, *if possible.*"

In closing, he pleaded with Fred again to promptly ship the books he had stored in Cambridge, those in their parents' home, and as many of Fred's books as he could spare. "You know how necessary it is for me to have books. They are my moral & intellectual life. . . . You know that my task is as universal as knowledge itself & I must cultivate it if I would return East & Succeed."[50] Fred was so moved that he arrived in person, bringing the books with him. That summer, L.L. also welcomed his younger brother, Urban, who had an unspecified illness, and Charles D. Sain, the Antiliteral Class secretary, who had tuberculosis. They hoped to be restored by the mountain air and whatever care Lucien might provide.[51]

Meanwhile, Lucien and Malachi bought additional lots for a dollar apiece, built cabins on them, and rented or sold them to new residents. Nunn also purchased several prime lots on Columbia Avenue for ten to fifteen dollars apiece. He had longer-term ideas in mind. The partners opened "Nunn & Kinney" law offices, although Kinney had no legal training.[52] The two succeeded in this venture, with Kinney concentrating on other joint enterprises—especially developing commercial and residential properties in Telluride. They also procured land in or near the towns of San Miguel, Keystone, and Sawpit. With brothers Urban and Fred and a Mr. Stewart, L.L. launched a joint venture in ranching near Delta, Colorado, about eighty highway miles north of Telluride. Each partner purchased a quarter section (160 acres) of rangeland and built a cabin where the four properties intersected. Lucien's and Fred's cabins were so close to their property line that they joined them with a covered passage.[53] L.L. entrusted this operation to the others and returned to Telluride to manage his growing interests there.

Kinney praised Nunn's stamina and courage. He "would take trips on snowshoes over the mountains in the dead of winter that experienced old timers wouldn't think of undertaking."[54] He also coolly faced down a competitor supported by an angry crowd outside the Nunn and Kinney offices. The partners met him inside "with Nunn standing on one side of the room with two six-shooters strapped on and Kinney standing on the other side with two strapped on also!"[55]

In November 1887, after a seven-year partnership with L.L., Kinney moved to San Diego where he established a successful business. The two corresponded regularly although they did not meet again for many years.[56] Malachi reflected later on Lucien's determined optimism through their strenuous early years in Colorado—a very different portrait from that held by L.L.'s eastern siblings: "Lucien was an untiring worker. I remember his saying that work was the one cure for worry and grief. It was in this regard his panacea; for he never wasted time worrying over past mistakes or misfortunes. His mind was focused on the future, and he evinced unusual foresight. When our fare consisted of oatmeal, as it did for weeks on several occasions, he never failed to relish this frugal repast."[57]

Even before Kinney's departure, Nunn had begun focusing on mine management. He organized the Ilium Gold Mining Company, a placer operation, and quickly established himself as a resourceful operator. Over the next several years, he acquired significant interests in other placer and shaft mines in the mountains and valleys along the San Miguel River. His expanding operations paid off handsomely, especially after he enticed his brother-in-law, William Bird, who had a correspondence degree in homeopathic medicine, and his sister Miriam to leave Florida and join his management team in Telluride. Similarly, he enlisted Elton Hoyt and Ralph King, two boyhood friends from the Cleveland Academy, to help manage his sprawling interests. L.L. Nunn was becoming a dominant figure in the Telluride mining district.[58]

In 1888, Nunn established a new legal entity, the "Office of L.L. Nunn," an umbrella for his increasingly diversified interests.[59] Dismissing rumors of corruption involving William Story, a former U.S. district court judge for western Arkansas, Nunn appointed him as his chief partner. Story became Colorado's lieutenant governor in 1891 but later resumed his business association with Nunn in Utah. Nunn purchased a controlling interest in the San Miguel Valley Bank and launched the *Telluride Republican* to rival the *Telluride Journal*.[60] His strategy was to serve as the primary partner in joint ventures—thus magnifying his working capital while sacrificing little control.

On June 24, 1889, Butch Cassidy and three sidekicks pulled off their first bank heist, cutting Telluride's telegraph lines and robbing Nunn's San Miguel Valley Bank of more than $22,500 in hundred-dollar bills. As the story goes, L.L. leaped on his swiftest horse, Bug Juice, and gave chase. He quickly outdistanced the rest of the posse; but Cassidy doubled back, unhorsed the pistol-waving banker, and took his pearl-handled revolver—leaving Nunn unharmed for the posse to rescue. That is the myth. L.L. had indeed mounted his "fast and fiery bay" and galloped after the thieves, but he encountered a local rancher, Harry Adsit, along the trail and knew he was better equipped to pursue the outlaws. Nunn turned Bug Juice over to Adsit, and it was the rancher who suffered the embarrassment of being ambushed and losing his expensive sidearm.[61]

Nunn had much more at stake in Telluride than the cash he lost to Butch Cassidy. The mountains around the mines had been logged for building materials and fuel for the steam-driven stamp mills that crushed ore for gold extraction. Wildfires claimed what timber remained. Coal became the new fuel, but hauling it into the district by wagon was prohibitively expensive. Seizing the opportunity, Colorado railroad builder Otto Mears extended his rail line to Telluride,[62] but the coal still had to be hauled up steep mountain trails by mule. At thirty-five to fifty dollars a ton at the railhead, coal was not the hoped-for solution. Mining profitability hung in the balance.[63]

Management became anxious, labor grew restless, bankruptcies loomed, and Nunn's bank teetered. Then St. Louis entrepreneur James Campbell, who held the dominant interest in the Gold King Mine, invited Nunn to take over as his manager—remarking that L.L. was either an idiot or a genius.[64] The proposition was risky for both parties, because Campbell was deeply indebted to the San Miguel Valley Bank. Nunn demanded a significant ownership stake in the Gold King and got it. This partnership began in the early 1890s and would benefit and torment both men for decades.

Nunn loved to celebrate his successes. When he learned that Benjamin Franklin Butler, the eighty-two-year-old Civil War Union general, former member of Congress, and recent Massachusetts governor, was coming to Telluride on a much-ballyhooed western tour, he arranged to host a dinner party at his well-appointed home. The guest list included local authorities and power brokers, as well as General Butler's impressive entourage. *Boston Herald* journalist Thomas Kirwan, who was covering the general's trip, enjoyed reporting on the dessert course: "The Chinese cook brought in on a tray what seemed to be a pudding. It was shaped like a conical cannon shell, and was about four inches in diameter, and about seven or eight inches in height." The tray was garnished oddly with gold ore "and many of the guests looked at it curiously." Finally, one of them "put his hand under the tray, and a look of surprise appeared on his face that was comical to see. It was so heavy that he could barely raise a side of it from the table with

Telluride, Colorado, Main Street, 1892. Courtesy of Deep Springs Archives.

his hand. Then others tried it. . . . [T]he pudding was made of gold!"[65] The bullion weighed between thirty and forty pounds with an estimated value of more than $6,000.[66] After sampling Telluride's saloons and gambling houses, L.L. gave General Butler a tour of the Gold King Mine the next day.

Through the winter, while the other Telluride mining operators wrung their hands and weighed their options, Nunn traveled to Chicago, New York, and London in search of capital, technology, and talent to solve the power problem. Everywhere he went Nunn explored possibilities for more efficient, less expensive ways to drive his stamp mills. He kept thinking about the water flowing abundantly out of the Silver Mountains near the Gold King Mine.

He knew hydraulic principles from managing his placer mine at Ilium, so developing a hydro generator seemed feasible. But transferring electricity several miles had never been done. Nunn investigated cable drive, but its expense and maintenance appeared prohibitive. He also considered a pneumatic system using pipes, similar to George Westinghouse's 1869 patent for compressed air brakes for railroad trains; but its performance over a distance of several miles was problematic.

Thomas Edison's pioneering use of direct current (DC) for lighting intrigued him. Could it also power machinery? Direct current could not be transmitted more than a few hundred yards without significant loss of power, even with very thick copper wiring. Early in 1881, however, the Salt Lake Light,

Heat, and Power Company built a large brick power station in the heart of downtown. It had four steam boilers that drove a 150-horse-power engine. The engine drove three electrical generators. This plant had the capacity to electrify the central downtown streets and businesses in Utah's capital, but only within a radius of about a half mile. It was the fifth city in the world to be electrified (after London, New York, San Francisco, and Cleveland).[67] In 1883, Cornell University began offering courses in electrical engineering, but they focused entirely on direct current technology.

With this background, on May 21, 1890, L.L. wrote his youngest brother, thirty-year-old Paul ("P.N."), then a Massachusetts science teacher and school principal, urging him "to learn all he could, as fast as he could, about electricity for power purposes and instructed him to [come] to Colorado to report his findings."[68] P.N. resigned his job, ran a thorough study, and went to Pittsburgh to consult with George Westinghouse whose engineers were experimenting with alternating current (AC). While offering a few pointers, Westinghouse showed no interest in working with a couple of novices in Colorado.

P.N. and L.L. both knew the distance limitations of direct current,[69] so they studied Nikola Tesla's 1883 invention of the alternating-current induction motor. With AC induction motors and the much higher voltages made possible with AC transformers, might long-distance transmission of electrical power be achievable, and would it be commercially viable? The thirty-seven-year-old L.L. resolved to gamble on this emergent technology, based on Tesla's experiments and Westinghouse's interest in developing alternating current systems.[70]

CHAPTER 2

RISING WITH POWER, 1891–1912

To free the rich from the bondage of their riches and the poor from the bondage of their poverty . . . that is the work.

—L.L. Nunn

Armed with P.N.'s detailed report and the fruits of his own inquiries, L.L. Nunn resolved to make his own pitch to George Westinghouse in Pittsburgh in the autumn of 1890. To the inventor-entrepreneur and the directors of the Westinghouse Electric Company, Nunn proposed a partnership that played on Westinghouse's bitter rivalry with Thomas Edison—whose wealth and reputation turned on the continuing dominance of his direct current systems. Until this time, lighting constituted electricity's sole commercial application.

Historian Orville Sweeting offered this account of Nunn's pitch to Westinghouse:

> After explaining the situation and outlining the chance for a breakthrough in power development, L.L. placed on the conference table in Pittsburgh $100,000 in gold coin (which represented the total output of the Gold King mill for the year), and is said to have put the proposition to Mr. Westinghouse somewhat as follows: I am ready to wager $100,000 gold on the success of our proposed

> venture into alternating current power development, if you will wager an equal amount in the time and experience of your staff in manufacturing the needed equipment.[1]

Westinghouse took the challenge and agreed to build a groundbreaking AC generator and electric motor. "Call it a grandstand ploy if you like," Sweeting continued, "but the old man was sincere in risking everything on a venture into hydroelectric power at Ames, Colorado."[2]

While capturing the drama, Sweeting's account played loose with facts. The "old man," L.L. Nunn, was just thirty-seven. And, in 1890, when gold was valued at $21 per troy ounce, $100,000 in gold weighed 262 pounds, hardly a parcel Nunn could have slipped onto the table. Nor would he have risked carrying $3.5 million (today's value) in cash on a rail trip across the country. As a banker, he had better options. For his part, George Westinghouse invested at least $25,000 of his own money in the venture when his board of directors chose not to underwrite the project. There is also evidence that Nunn offered to put up $50,000 if Westinghouse would match him and his company's time and materials—totalling $100,000.[3]

Before winter snows descended on the Telluride district in 1890, Westinghouse had delivered a single-phase, 133-cycle alternating-current generator and a matching electric motor, both rated at the prescribed 100 horsepower. It was the highest voltage generator ever built and the largest electric motor of its time. Operating without transformers, this initial system would generate, transmit, and apply electrical energy at an astonishing 3,000 volts.[4]

L.L. orchestrated the project, and P.N. served as chief engineer. Their workers built a frame powerhouse for the generator at Ames, where Howard Fork empties into the South Fork of the San Miguel River, about eleven miles southwest of Telluride. A 4,000-foot steel penstock leading up Howard Fork Canyon provided 320 feet of head above the six-foot diameter Pelton water wheel. Two and a half miles away, at an elevation of 12,000 feet in the Silver Mountains, crews installed the Tesla-Westinghouse electric motor in the Gold King stamp mill. Workers were instructed to string the copper power lines as straight and tight as they could for fear that the unprecedentedly high-voltage current might not negotiate abrupt turns. Experts had warned that a lightning bolt might shoot forward at the first bend—presenting the sort of deadly peril that Edison claimed alternating current posed.

Blizzards, freezing temperatures, and ice delayed the experiment until summer; but on June 21, 1891, with the Pelton wheel screaming at the prescribed speed, L.L. Nunn nodded to a trusted technician to throw the big knife switch. As the brass blade began to close, a blinding bolt of electricity arced nearly six feet across the narrowing gap. Once secure, however, the high voltage current surged through the wires. Seconds later, workers up at the Gold King telegraphed excitedly that the Tesla motor had sprung into action.

The generator ran continuously for over a week. No one welcomed the task of opening the knife switch, fearing that it would produce an arc like the one that occurred when they closed the connection. In fact, the arc flashed as expected, but it continued to buzz across the gap. Fortunately, Nunn's technicians discovered that they could quell the arc by waving a felt hat through it.[5]

In just over six months, L.L. Nunn had pioneered the world's first long-distance transmission of electric energy for industrial use. The astonishing news spread across America and Europe almost immediately. This breakthrough, which separated the use of electrical energy from its power source, would quickly revolutionize industrial production throughout the world. At home, the cost of power for the Gold King Mine dropped from $2,500 a month to $500.

Even so, Nunn's readiness to begin extending power from Ames to other sites for other uses got him into local trouble. When his crews erected poles for stringing wires from the Ames power plant to his home in Telluride, city authorities saw threats to public safety and apparently heard the cries of potential competitors. They cut down the poles that were within municipal boundaries and forbade Nunn or his company "to erect any poles in, or stretch or string any wire or wires across any street, avenue, alley or public place within . . . the Town of Telluride."[6] The controversy over rights of way raged for weeks, but Nunn ultimately prevailed. His ownership of the *Telluride Republican* served him well.

The International Electro-Technical Exhibition in Frankfurt-Lauffen, Germany, featured even greater developments with three-phase, 15,000 volt, AC power in the summer and fall of 1891—although they were experimental demonstrations rather than commercial applications. Others duplicated Nunn's feat in California and Oregon.[7] They would all claim to have been the first, but L.L.'s "significant achievement," physicist Robert Sproull recently stated, "was to show that AC was as safe as DC and to clear the way for rapid development of high voltage AC systems, with multiple generating stations, transformers, long lines, and multiple users."[8] Over the next few years, Nunn was able to expand these hardware applications with bold financial arrangements to create a new industry. "The key element was the transformer," Sproull explained, and this technological innovation was made possible by the use of AC current.

Ames Power Plant, 1891. Courtesy of Deep Springs Archives.

Pinheads operating 3,000-volt AC generator at Ames, June 1891. Courtesy of Deep Springs Archives.

"[It] liberated the line voltage, which could be raised to hundreds of thousands of volts, from the generator voltage, that had to be held down to voltages like 3000 for the sake of safety and efficiency in the generator windings."[9] At the consumer end, voltage could be stepped down again to just 220 or 110 V for safe application.

Nunn was more concerned with the commercial development of hydroelectric power than bragging rights. His prodigious energies and talents shifted decidedly from mining to hydroelectric power and long-distance transmission. At first, Nunn's burgeoning electricity business flourished as part of the San Miguel Consolidated Gold Mining Company; but five years later, he gave electricity its own Telluride Power Transmission Company.[10] Following reorganization and consolidation with other Nunn power projects, this enterprise would become the Telluride Power Company at the turn of the century. Along the way, the San Miguel Valley Bank also morphed into the First National Bank of Telluride, housed in an impressive new stone edifice, with former Arkansas judge William Story as president and L.L. Nunn as vice president.

Nunn exuded optimism as he described his growing business empire in a long letter to the president and manager of the *Telluride Journal* in March 1892. When the editor tried to remove a controversial section about Nunn's plan to electrify the city, he published it in his own *Telluride Republican* on March 10, 1892:

> I am now manager of, with individual interests in, the following properties: The Ilium, comprising seven mining claims and a ten-stamp mill; the Gold King, with the most complete forty-stamp mill in the State of Colorado; the Turkey Creek, embracing fifteen claims, with a ten-stamp mill and a Huntington mill of about the same capacity; the Prospect Basin, embracing five claims and having a ten-stamp mill; the Golden Group, including twenty-one claims in all and a ten-stamp mill; the Power Plant at the junction of Lake and Howard's Forks of the San Miguel river, from which point we propose transmitting by electric currents sufficient power and light for all of the above mentioned properties. My idea has been to consolidate all of these interests in one company, capitalized at $15,000,000, with full expectation of putting the stock at par.[11]

Less than thirteen years later, the *Telluride Journal* would report that L.L. Nunn was a millionaire, one of two in the county.[12]

For a short period, Nunn confessed, he dallied with "dreams of opulence, yachts, and Mediterranean villas."[13] But the voices of Charles Grandison Finney and Johann von Herder came back to prick his conscience, prompted, perhaps, by sobering productivity forecasts at his mines. If persistence, self-denial, and ingenuity had brought him such success, then perhaps the best way to remind himself regularly of these virtues was to nurture them in others. He began to experiment seriously with linking two deep-running passions: technological innovation and industrial education.

Starting back in 1891, Nunn made a deliberate effort to recruit and train exceptional young men to run his power stations, initiating this effort at his Bear Creek mine high in the mountains south of Telluride. He tried hiring electrical engineering graduates from Cornell and Ohio State, but quickly found that they were ill prepared to work in remote areas where constant improvisation was necessary to keep a power station running.[14] They knew little about the new AC technology that, particularly with the single-phase current used at the beginning, required complicated maneuvers to start the induction motors and keep components of the system synchronized.[15]

Nunn's apprentice laborers, whom he chose with the help of his widening network of business and personal associates, were known as "pinheads" from the beginning. The traditional explanation for this term is that he kept track of their movements among his power stations with colored pins on a map.[16] But senior staff found "pinheads" the perfect putdown for the precocious young men joining their ranks. The apprentices themselves embraced the term as a badge of honor. To house the pinheads, Nunn built an attractive residence to serve as a school, dormitory, and social gathering place next door to his own home on Columbia Avenue in Telluride. And to inspire them with new technology, he wired the structure for AC electric power—possibly the first private residence in the world to be illuminated in this way.[17] This well-appointed home also featured beautifully designed inlaid hardwood floors and woodwork.

The house became known as the "Cornell House" because its earliest inhabitants were student interns from Cornell University. Local newspapers occasionally reported on social events there such as a concert by the Glee and Mandolin Club, followed by a Dutch lunch.[18] On another occasion, the *Telluride Journal* reported that "Nunn's boys" invited about twenty young people to their house for "an evening with music, social conversation, cards." The décor drew editorial comment: "The commodious rooms were profusely decorated with cut flowers, mostly American Beauty roses."[19]

L.L. Nunn as a leading figure in Telluride following his early success with hydroelectric power. Courtesy of Helen M. Heckman.

Cornell House in Telluride, Colorado. Photograph by author.

Nunn's bank in Telluride, Colorado. Lucien L. Nunn Papers, #37-4-1770. Division of Rare and Manuscript Collections, Cornell University Library, Ithaca, New York.

Nunn's ambition soon outgrew southwestern Colorado. He dispatched trusted agents like J. B. Bailey to scan the Intermountain West for potential dam sites for power plants. Their reports highlighted possibilities in Utah Territory, where high mountains, heavy winters, mining, railroads, and a growing population combined to create ideal conditions for hydroelectric power development. Nunn filed for water rights on the Provo River in October 1894, proposing to build a dam and power plant.[20] He made an almost simultaneous claim on the Logan River to the north and the Hercules Power Plant there became his first to produce electricity in Utah in 1896.

His task proved difficult in Provo Canyon, where the Denver & Rio Grande Railroad challenged his proposal to build a dam at least sixty feet high that would flood its right of way through the canyon. Recent memories of the 1889 Johnstown Flood, which had killed 2,200 people, put public opinion on the railroad's side. The controversy went all the way to the Utah Supreme Court, where the railroad prevailed.[21] The Nunn brothers scaled back, planning a much smaller dam and reservoir that would not impinge on the D&RG's right of way. But they feigned lack of interest in the project for a time, as a ploy to sway public sentiment their way.

Business and political interests in Provo were not unaware of the benefits of electric power for their community, an attitude sweetened by Nunn's pitch to provide street lighting for the city. They urged him to proceed with the revised plan. Satisfied, the brothers resumed construction on the dam, flume, and power plant. As they had done at Ames, L.L. served as general manager and P.N. as chief project engineer. The site became known as Nunns Station, or simply "Nunns." A road sign and public park still mark the site along U.S. Highway 189 through Provo Canyon.

Telluride Power hired the J.C. Watson & Brothers Company to haul the huge generator components from the railhead up the canyon to the construction site. The Westinghouse Electric armature and lower magnet alone weighed over sixteen tons, and the whole generator may have tallied fifty tons. When the equipment arrived by rail, Telluride Power and Watson Brothers had a bitter dispute over the already-signed contract. The Watsons knew that they alone could do the job and refused to start work until their demands were met.

Nunn would not be bullied. He dispatched his most trusted crew to the Watsons' equipment yard in the dark of night. They commandeered the heavy transporters and moved the generator components to the site without being seen or heard—returning the Watsons' equipment before dawn.[22] Nunn savored the uproar generated by the discovery of the heist, the Watsons' rage, and the press coverage. The controversy ended when county officials excused Telluride Power for its appropriation of the trucks and pointed out that the Watsons had been at fault for refusing to honor their contract.[23]

Despite legal and construction delays, crews finished work on Nunns Station and it initiated service in January 1898. Now using three-phase technology, the generators produced between 1,500 and 2,500 horsepower, charging a thirty-two-mile power line to the primary customer, Captain Joseph DeLaMar's Golden Gate Mine in the mountains west of Utah Lake. These high-tension lines were by far the longest attempted anywhere, and they required exceptionally high line voltage—40,000 volts—to make the transmission economical. By a factor of three, this was the highest voltage industrial service at the time.[24] The power lines were so "hot" that current sometimes arced to the cross arms on the power poles on foggy or rainy days, setting them aflame. In fact, this operation necessitated a major new round of engineering innovations, not only for more effective insulators but also for better designs for transformers (to step voltage up for transmission and down again for use at the receiving end), and for cooling mechanisms, switches, and transmission cables. All of these tasks, of course, called for more sophisticated technical and managerial training for the work force.

This plant became Westinghouse Electric's showpiece. Its design, equipment, and operation were world class. Two of Westinghouse's best engineers, Ralph D. Mershon (who later developed electrolytic capacitors essential to radio production) and V. G. Converse, came out to work on the station. Converse opted to stay with Telluride Power after the project was completed and invented the familiar pyramid-shaped glass "Provo Insulator" to prevent the corona of high-voltage current from torching power poles.

To serve powerful Utah Valley business client and aggressive mining entrepreneur Jesse Knight, Nunn constructed a twenty-six-mile cross-line that ran south across the desert from his Mercur trunk line near Fairfield to Knight's mines in Eureka, the hub of the Tintic Mining District. Nunn's rates were steep, so Knight decided to build or buy several small power plants of his own. When his crews began installing power poles for a direct line to his Tintic operations, Nunn realized that Knight's wires would have to cross Telluride's lines.[25]

The rivals met. Nunn claimed he could bankrupt Knight's investment in the power business if he did not abandon his plans for the Eureka line. Knight replied: "You couldn't break me at anything."[26] His workers soon planted their poles on both sides of Telluride's line, preparing to string their wires. L.L. was told (incorrectly, as it turned out) that Knight had put his poles inside L.L.'s right of way. He dispatched a crew to chop down Knight's poles. In the furor that followed, Knight proved that his poles were outside Nunn's easement. The mining magnate reset his shortened poles and strung the wires under Telluride's lines. The triangle pattern of power lines they had created—from Provo to Mercur to Eureka and back to Provo—actually benefited both parties by providing an alternate route for current if any sector of the grid failed.

Having gained mutual respect in this showdown, these two maverick visionaries—the Mormon entrepreneur who violated his culture's prohibition on mining and the freewheeling outsider with the audacity to compete with the Mormon establishment in Provo—made peace with one another. This rapprochement could not have happened without the assistance of Latter-day Saint apostle (and soon-to-be U.S. senator from Utah) Reed Smoot, and the senior LDS apostle (who also happened to be president of the Utah Light and Power Company), Joseph F. Smith.[27] These and other Mormon leaders had come to respect and admire L.L. Nunn. Their intercession over the next half-dozen years enabled Telluride Power to hammer out contracts and cooperative relationships with many rival power interests. Nunn and Senator Smoot (who served in Washington from 1903 to 1933) enjoyed a close and mutually supportive relationship until Nunn's death.[28]

Meanwhile, Nunn pushed ahead on another front. Early in 1898, he petitioned the Salt Lake County Commission for permission to run an electric rail line from Salt Lake City to the booming Bingham Mine camp in the southwest corner of the valley. They agreed, and Nunn organized the Salt Lake & Utah Valley Railroad Company, an electric interurban line to link towns from Salt Lake to Provo.[29] This electric passenger service did not materialize.

In 1902, the *Telluride Journal* announced that power from Nunn's Hercules generating station near Logan had been joined with the Telluride Power Company's service to form a continuous 150-mile circuit from Logan to Provo. "The merging of the two currents will make the Telluride Company's service one of the best and most reliable in the world . . . and by carrying it to success Mr. Nunn . . . has accomplished a feat that will give him world-wide fame."[30]

A year later, L.L. Nunn celebrated his fiftieth year in style. He and P.N. began work on their contract with the Ontario Power Company to build a power plant on the north side of the Canadian Falls at Niagara. They served as the general contractor, having no stake in the plant's ownership or operation of the plant once it went on line. The project, by far their largest, dragged on until 1906, due primarily to protests over visual and environmental issues that required substantial redesign. P.N. moved to Niagara to supervise construction. L.L. worked chiefly by remote control from the West; but the Union Pacific's express line passed through Salt Lake City, making frequent eastern excursions pleasant.

Though these rail trips were long, they came at little expense to Nunn. A few years earlier during an annual round of contract talks with Joseph DeLaMar about the power contract for his mines near Mercur, DeLaMar had threatened Nunn: Telluride Power must reduce its rates or the Golden Gate Mine would fire up its newly acquired steam generator. The conversation, according to Sweeting, unfolded as follows:

> L.L. appeared unruffled and quietly replied: Fine, fine, but then there are other subjects to discuss also, such as freight rates for machinery and other materials such as coking coal from Salt Lake. De La Mar and his partner were baffled and asked what the connection was between these issues. L.L. informed them that he also owned the Salt Lake and Mercur Railroad. His two adversaries expressed disbelief . . . for they well knew the churchmen in Salt Lake who owned the railroad. Sensing a bluff, they challenged Nunn by asking how long he had owned the railway. L.L., with a characteristic flair for the dramatic, slowly withdrew his watch from a vest pocket, glanced at it, and replied, "Oh, about 36 hours."[31]

Nunn had gotten a tip concerning DeLaMar's strategy, made discreet inquiries about the railroad's solvency (which was not good), and then made a low but successful offer. Not only did his prime Mercur customer agree to Telluride's prevailing rates, but L.L. became a railroad owner with reciprocal travel privileges on any other line he wished to use. Union Pacific executive Edward H. Harriman, however, refused to reissue Nunn's annual pass after the first year or two because, he explained, the UPRR owned thousands of miles of track and the Salt Lake and Mercur claimed only twelve. L.L. responded: "M[r]. Harriman, the Salt Lake and Mercur may not be as long as the Union Pacific, but it's just as wide."[32] The pass was his.

E. H. Harriman would become a major investor in Nunn's enterprises. No stranger to Utah, he also bought a controlling interest in Salt Lake City power utilities and electric streetcar services in 1906. He soon made them models recognized around the world. Following a conversation with Nunn about the possibility of using electric engines on his major railroad routes, he wrote to their mutual friend, Charles D. Walcott: "I like your friend Nunn. He has imagination."[33]

Although Harriman died in 1909 and the Salt Lake and Mercur dissolved in 1914, Nunn enjoyed the use of these annual railroad passes—nearly fifty of them—to the end of his life.[34] This free travel enabled him to stay in almost constant motion. Without a wife or children to anchor him, he often maintained secondary residences close to his projects and lodged in strategically located hotels across the country—as the letterheads and return addresses on his correspondence reveal.

As demand outstripped capacity at Nunns Station, Telluride Power began constructing the Olmsted Power Station, a much larger facility at the mouth of Provo Canyon, three miles downstream. It began operating in April 1904 and rapidly became known as a world-class facility. With three 3,600-horsepower turbines and their generators operating at 44,000 volts, it served mines and communities across Utah. This station, with its original generators, has been in constant operation for well over a century and, with a fourth generator added in 1917, is now used as a training facility for Rocky Mountain Power. It ranked as Utah's fourth largest hydroelectric plant in 2014.[35] Nunn named this station for one of his most promising young engineers, Fay D. "Fred" Olmsted, who died of tuberculosis shortly before the power plant went on line. The spacious and attractive site became the hub of Nunn's power business as well as his emerging educational endeavors.[36]

For nearly twenty-five years, his primary residence had been in Telluride; but with the construction of the Olmsted Station, Nunn moved there to a lovely Craftsman-style residence in 1903, sharing it with P.N. and his wife, Agnes. Seven miles down Academy Avenue from Olmsted, in the center of Provo's growing business district, they established Telluride Power's new headquarters.[37] On June 8, the *Telluride Journal* reported: "The furniture and equipment of the large residence of L.L. Nunn is being packed up preparatory to shipment to Provo, Utah." In parting, Nunn ordered a new picket fence for the property and "extensive repairs and renovations" so that Stephen A. Bailey and his family could move in and enjoy it.[38] With Addison Wrench, junior partner at Nunn's bank, Bailey remained behind to manage Nunn's Colorado banking and real estate interests, with which he had assisted since 1889. Three decades later, Bailey would write Nunn's memoir.

Utah's more central western location had exerted a strong pull on Nunn, but he had also gotten a shove from Colorado. In 1899, Arthur Collins, the operator of the Smuggler-Union Mine, had dictated new labor contract terms using the fathom system, which replaced hourly wages with an output measure. Two years later, when Collins reduced the pay rate per fathom, the union miners

Olmsted Power Plant, Provo Canyon, Utah. Nunn's home is center left. Courtesy of Deep Springs Archives.

Looking west, downstream, and featuring the Institute Building, top left. Courtesy of Deep Springs Archives.

walked out. Collins hired scab laborers, prompting 250 armed union members to confront the scabs at the mine entrance. Management apparently fired first, but after several volleys, three scabs lay dead in the tunnel.[39] The remaining scabs were ushered out of town, and union laborers resumed their posts with improved wages. Collins was buying time. When the Smuggler-Union advertised again for nonunion laborers, Arthur Collins received his reward from the muzzle of a shotgun thrust through a window at his home.[40] Governor James Peabody declared martial law in Telluride and sent five hundred members of the Colorado National Guard. Violence continued, the martial law order was intermittently canceled, and peace was not restored until the spring of 1904.

Nunn traveled in and out of Telluride often during these years. The violence unnerved him, but he did not engage in the mine owners' antilabor frenzy. Addison Wrench, however, worked behind Nunn's back with the unsavory new Smuggler-Union manager, Bulkeley Wells, to plot against the Western Federation of Miners.[41] Aware of Wrench's scheming and appalled by the breakdown of civil authority, Nunn was glad to leave Telluride behind.

Moving to Utah was also prompted by Nunn's imaginative experimentation to solve the shortage of skilled labor in the power industry. Could traditional distinctions between labor and management be blurred? Might ambitious and talented young men serve as apprentices for two or three years at modest pay while receiving educational benefits to fit them for broader careers? He now had in mind something far greater than his earlier plan. Next to his Olmsted Power Station in Provo Canyon he constructed a stately, three-story "Quarters Building" to house his pinheads, and an equally impressive four-story "Telluride Building" southwest of it with classrooms, laboratories, and offices.[42]

He soon offered free room, board, and study space to professors on sabbatical leaves from their universities. In exchange, they would tutor his young workers in physics, engineering, and electricity. Then, while the Olmsted station buildings were still under construction, he formally organized the Telluride Institute.

In the autumn of 1904, Nunn hired forty-one-year-old Ernest A. Thornhill, a Phi Beta Kappa graduate of Harvard College, to teach at Olmsted. Nunn was especially impressed that Thornhill had earned a master's degree under John Dewey at the University of Chicago. Recently married to Lida Connale, Thornhill gradually took on other responsibilities for Nunn, including directing the educational program at Olmsted and institute branches associated with Nunn's other power stations at Telluride, Colorado; Bliss/Boise and Grace, Idaho; Norris, Montana; Logan and Beaver, Utah; and the Ontario Power Project in Canada.

Nunn's home at Olmsted. Photograph by author in 2011.

Original 44,000-volt, 3,600-horsepower generators still operating in 2014. Alumni Vern Penner, Jack Newell, and Rick Coville in foreground. Photograph by Linda K. Newell.

Each pinhead signed on for a three-year program. The first year required eight to twelve hours of daily labor at one of the remote power stations to acquire "the power of continuous application [by] absorbing much of the spirit of the actual search after principle and in many instances [to] develop an enthusiasm rarely found among the ordinary students." Their labors included maintaining waterways and penstocks, operating power stations, assisting in laboratories, calibrating instruments, and working in machine shops, carpentry mills, and foundries.[43]

Rotated to a different power station for their second year, students worked five hours a day (the whole morning or afternoon) and devoted the balance of their time to coursework and study. Then, at the Telluride Institute at Olmsted for their third year, students received "resident scholarships" without work assignments and were "released from the rigid discipline and control" to study under the general direction of Thornhill (now enjoying the title of dean) and company research staff. The research arm of the Telluride Power Company was critical in its commercial successes. Nunn depended on it to maintain the company's competitive edge, and this strategy pervaded his management philosophy. "At Olmsted," he wrote, "only freshman and sophomore training is given undergraduates—all other work there being post-graduate or research work."[44]

After completing their third year in the program, the highest achieving students received scholarships to continue their studies at a university. He admitted students "naturally qualified for the professions" and continued to support them according to their progress. Thornhill developed a curriculum designed to prepare pinheads for admission to the nation's top universities. Nunn instructed him to keep schools with emerging electrical engineering programs in his students' minds. These included Cornell, Harvard, the Massachusetts Institute of Technology, Ohio State, and Yale. The Telluride Institute awarded each graduate a renewable annual scholarship of $450–$600 to continue his education at one of those universities—or another of his choosing. Each pinhead who received support was expected to "apply himself industriously as a student of . . . literature, philosophy, and science."[45] The list of scholarship recipients soon went on for pages and included Alma Richards, Utah's first Olympic gold medalist who won the high jump event at Stockholm in 1912.

Clearly, Nunn's educational vision was shifting from engineering and management training toward the arts and humanities, and from labor supply issues and labor-management relations to civic leadership and what Nunn referred to as "the moral order of the universe." His own years of study came to the fore. The *Mansfield Herald* clipping of "The Moral Sense," still in his desk drawer, demanded a fresh reading. Yet as his interests expanded, so did demands on his time. Recognizing P.N.'s early experience as an educator, L.L. invited him to join in overseeing Dean Thornhill and the institute program.

The visionary L.L. granted a large measure of autonomy to the pinheads at each of Telluride Institute's field schools and began to refer to those who came to Olmsted as "the Student Body." Wherever his students were, he expected them to cooperatively work, study, and govern their own affairs. The more tangible and complete the responsibility given them, Nunn reasoned, the more they would learn about leadership and the better they would understand the needs of others and the demands of citizenship. All of this would make them better humans, whether or not they came back to his employ.

Generating electricity now became a secondary interest. Nunn was consumed with expanding his plan for building character and cultivating leaders. The Telluride Power Company produced electricity at a profit, but it also generated dollars for his research and educational experiments.

A year after formally establishing the Telluride Institute, Nunn met Charles D. Walcott, then a scientist with the U.S. Geological Survey and soon to become Secretary of the Smithsonian Institution (1907–1927). Walcott described his first encounter with Nunn in 1905:

> Coming down from Strawberry Valley, Utah, . . . with a party of Reclamation Service engineers, I noticed a small man come into the railroad coach at a way station and slip quietly into a seat, where he appeared to be thinking intently, not paying attention to anyone. One of the engineers remarked, "That is L.L. Nunn." I had heard of him in connection with the Telluride Power Company and the Telluride [Institute].

Walcott took a seat next to Nunn and introduced himself. The two engaged immediately in a spirited conversation. Seeing an opportunity, Nunn interjected: "I should like very much to have you stop overnight at Provo so that we can talk over . . . a project that I am working on in connection with the training of young men and boys."[46] This encounter would pay rich dividends for both men over the next twenty years.

Nunn's old friends in Telluride, where he visited often on business, noted the fluidity of his movements. "Time was when Mr. Nunn made his trips from, instead of to Telluride," one of the papers reported, "but time and good fortune have changed that, and while many less fortunate than he, still count our nine months winter and three months late in the fall, he can go whither he wants and find a climate to suit him."[47] Several years later, the *Telluride Journal* reported: "The Nunn Party arriving from Provo, Utah, Monday evening missed connections with the regular train at Grand Junction . . . and chartering a special, overtook the train at Montrose before it pulled out for Telluride. Time is money for Mr. Nunn and he never wastes it."[48]

L.L. pushed forward with diverse capital ventures. In 1907, with his junior business partner Addison Wrench, he launched the Federal Heights residential development in Salt Lake City, near the University of Utah, apparently naming its most prominent street for his new friend Charles D. Walcott. When the infrastructure was complete, Nunn enlisted twelve of his best students over the summer to sell lots there—reserving four prime lots for himself.[49] He also purchased a Ford dealership in Provo and began constructing new power plants independent of the Telluride Power Company in Utah and Idaho. Residential demand for power was mushrooming with the growing popularity of electric stoves, refrigerators, and other appliances. As the power business became more complex and competitive, so did Nunn. The value of his personal stake in the Telluride Power Company alone was about a million dollars.[50]

In 1907, L.L. and P.N. contracted with Nunn's old business partner, James Campbell, to build a power plant to support a gold and silver mining operation at Lluvia de Oro in Chihuahua, Mexico. The project required great effort, including construction of a riveted steel, forty-foot *amphibious* river boat to negotiate the Fuertes River on ten-day voyages to ferry supplies and equipment for the project. Nunn designed this unusual craft himself.

Nunn's many interests and responsibilities began to weigh him down. He could no longer shake off the chronic bouts of exhaustion mixed with discouragement and spasms of acute loneliness. Nunn's resilience flagged. He seemed to be aging prematurely. A lifelong bachelor, he had embraced work as his partner a quarter-century earlier. Balding, road weary, and suffering an impoverished emotional life, L.L.'s weight dropped from his normal 118 pounds to just over 100. His romantic idealism failed him, too; his hydroelectric innovations and entrepreneurial triumphs provided scant solace.

His burgeoning enterprises, especially the Ontario Power Company's project at Niagara Falls, had stretched his management style to the limit. He felt like a martyr, outworking everyone around him and taking care of many, while being criticized for failing to maximize Telluride's stock dividends. Meanwhile, the myriad personal loyalties on which he relied to keep his businesses rolling were wearing thin.

Ontario Power Plant at Niagara Falls early in construction, January 1905. Lucien L. Nunn Papers, #37-4-1770. Division of Rare and Manuscript Collections, Cornell University Library, Ithaca, New York.

Nunn's reputation for bigheartedness was legendary, and he kept careful records both of his personal generosities and of his company's investments in junior managers and pinheads.[51] The line separating these two types of disbursement was not always clear, given the personal nature of his management style. When the 1907 banking crisis put the squeeze on profits everywhere, Nunn's business partners began to see his commitments to the Telluride Institute and company education as needless and wasteful ventures. As pressures mounted on his business model, his intensely personal style of leadership caused some to suspect favoritism as well.

Nunn had always preferred the company of men and did not seek women as companions except within his extended family. He remained close to his sisters, and his nieces and grandnieces loved him and the attention he lavished on them. "Uncle Lu" was their favorite uncle. Instinctively keeping his emotional distance from those outside the family, Nunn found in the structure and formality of business dealings or philosophical conversations a mode in which he flourished. Here his perfect diction, air of command, and theatrical flair enabled him to compensate for his short stature and uncertain social skills. These characteristics kept almost everyone at bay, but men slipped through his protective screen more easily than women, and young men most easily of all.[52] With a few of them, Lucien Nunn enjoyed unguarded interludes of emotional intimacy.

Nunn's contemporaries seemed to regard his intense same-sex relationships within the nineteenth-century romantic ideal of hearty men empowered by bonds of affection and camaraderie. This brotherhood archetype, with experienced veterans mentoring eager understudies, found expression in all-male boarding schools and colleges, and in military training. YMCA programs even promoted it at the time (though eschewed it later), and it was an element of frontier culture.[53] With no children of his own, Nunn's deep devotion to the welfare of young men was also viewed as redirected fatherliness.

Even those who reported intimate experiences with Nunn when they were young looked back later without judgment. Paul Ashworth, one of Nunn's protégés, wrote unselfconsciously about an interview with Nunn when he was in his late teens. At the end of the conversation, he reported, "I got up to go home but he insisted that I phone Mother that I would spend the night at his place. . . . He took me upstairs into a large bedroom, showed me the bathroom, where I might have the rare pleasure of a shower, handed me a long white starched night-shirt, and left. I took the shower, went to bed and to sleep. Sometime later, he came to bed with me—a most unexpected honor! But he was such a restless bedfellow that I didn't get much sleep!"[54]

Without further explanation and apparently with no further contact of this kind, Ashworth continued his larger narrative about working with Nunn as an employee and Telluride Institute participant. Their correspondence from that era reveals mutual respect but no particular intimacy.

From time to time, Nunn had become noticeably infatuated with other young men. He first met Addison Wrench, a shoe store clerk in Utica, New York, about 1888.[55] L.L. immediately took the twenty-year-old under his wing, employed him as a clerk at the San Miguel Valley Bank, and subsequently invested enormous energy in a plan to develop Wrench as a showcase for his budding educational ideas. The two enjoyed an emotionally intimate and affectionate relationship.

Despite their deep bond, Wrench did not fully embrace the plan Nunn laid out for him, which included an education at Colorado College followed by a grand tour of Europe on his own. When Addison fell in love with Utica schoolmate Minnie Wood, Nunn was genuinely tortured. Writing Nunn of his plans to marry her, Addison confided: "I love you both dearely, and when with one alone I want the other. I will not be absoloutely hapy until I have you both, and I sometimes think perhaps, that will be my punishment, to be parted from one or the other." He continued, "Oh Nunn, it is horriable . . . . I could not live without her and not happily without you."[56]

L.L. Nunn's Enterprises in the American West.

Although shaken severely, L.L. recovered from this blow, accepted the invitation to attend the wedding, and picked up the tab for what became Utica's social event of the season, sentimentally cherishing a souvenir piece of their wedding cake until his death.[57] He also underwrote the newlyweds' subsequent European tour and Addison's education at Oberlin College. Wrench rose to become Nunn's partner in banking and real estate, a relationship that survived even Wrench's scheming against Nunn's interests during the Telluride labor troubles.[58]

Nunn also yearned for other young men serially until his death at seventy-two. Attaching a handwritten personal note to a letter to young associate Ray Fruit on December 9, 1915, he confided: "It is midnight but I will write you a few words personally before retiring. What I have to say I cannot dictate. I want to tell you how your letter of Nov. 12th brought a big lump in my throat by indicating that you had given me what I have longed for—your affection. That letter and your photograph are always with me and do much to make life seem worthwhile."[59]

We will never know the full story of Nunn's emotional affinity for young men or the extent to which he acted on his longings. Many years later, Parker Bailey, son of one of Nunn's managers and his first biographer, wrote Sweeting: "I hope you will grin aloud at the disclosure of my first recollections of remarks about L.L.'s so-called deviant propensities; it was during my grade school days in Salt Lake City that I heard scraps of light conversation between my mother and Mrs. J. B. Bailey . . . to the effect that L.L. was 'forever getting crushes on pink cheeked hotel bellboys.'"[60]

Nunn's brother Josiah (J.J.) believed that the death of L.L.'s twin at age three left him with what Parker Bailey characterized as an "inveterate fellow-boy-longing" caused by the "trauma of his infantile grief."[61] Dr. Robert B. Aird, whose father had been Nunn's personal physician in Provo, discounted L.L.'s proclivity for young men and saw romantic interest in Nunn's financial support of Jesse Knight's niece, Estella Maud Knight, when she matriculated at Oberlin College.[62] Undeniably, this support was generous; but Nunn was then in his late forties and Estella was still in her teens. After graduating from Oberlin, she married one of Nunn's younger associates, William Biersach, in 1901.

It seems likely that Nunn's severe depression in 1904–1905 reflected at least in part his dwindling hope of sustaining any intimate relationship in his remaining years. Whatever the case, several observations are warranted. First, Nunn made no secret of his special affection for a few of his male protégés, being scrupulous to the end about preserving virtually all of his personal correspondence. Second, if the close associates who viewed his personal papers after he died had found any romantic letters to women, they surely would have preserved them.[63] Third, there is little or no evidence that Nunn was the object of destructive rumors about his sexual orientation in Telluride, Provo, or Salt Lake City, where he was highly respected by business associates, Mormon Church officials, and fellow members of the most exclusive social club in Utah, the Alta Club.[64] Finally, although students in Nunn's later educational ventures—Telluride Association and Deep Springs—often remarked on his emotional attachment to one or more of their peers, and cracked an occasional joke about why these students were granted scholarships, virtually all of them held L.L.'s character, intellect, and achievements in highest esteem. Lucien Nunn's sexual orientation mattered little, if at all, to the students, pinheads, or business associates with whom he interacted. Decades later, the recorded memories of some of these men reinforced this conclusion.[65]

Nunn's midlife crisis may have been intense, but it subsided as he channeled his energy into the Telluride Institute and subsequent educational endeavors. These projects commanded his attention and inspired him to regain his health and marshal his strength. At the same time, he would soon confront major new setbacks.

James Campbell, his business partner since 1890, and the other dominant stockholders in Telluride Power Company, had been very critical of Nunn's decision to build the elegant Quarters Building for the Telluride Institute. Nunn's expanding social and industrial vision meant nothing to these investors when they were hit with enormous losses in the Panic of 1907. Telluride Power was becoming an increasingly important element of Campbell's portfolio, and he demanded maximum profits.

In 1908, Campbell launched an open attack on Nunn's character, management practices, and support of the Telluride Institute program. "I hope to see this property run on business principles rather than for the benefit of friends and favorites," Campbell wrote on September 8. "I have too much real money invested, to sit by quietly and let you run it in the interest of the Institute and your friends."[66] Campbell's attacks escalated, and he accused Nunn of using the institute as a front for diverting company funds to his personal use.

In the bitter, four-year struggle that followed, Campbell first charged Nunn with fiscal mismanagement and launched a special company investigation.[67] Particularly painful for Nunn was the fact that a few of his oldest and most trusted business associates, including legal counsel Fred F. Steigmeyer and banking partner William Story, sided with Campbell. When the directors' audit committee cleared Nunn of all charges, Campbell prepared to sue Nunn for mismanagement.[68]

Two models of capitalism were squaring off here. One was arguably the best of the old style, the other emergent and impatient. Although Nunn's means were often cutthroat and clearly elitist, his ends appeared to be consciously moral. He envisioned business as the backbone of a new, more enlightened and prosperous way of life for all. Campbell did not quibble with Nunn's business practices, but he eschewed responsibility for anything beyond company profits, stock dividends, and, apparently, personal wealth. P.N. saw these differences clearly and identified loyally with his brother's philosophy. Never as dramatic as L.L. but solid and well informed, P.N. astutely penetrated to the core of Campbell's complaint and told him bluntly on December 4, 1908: "L.L. is a producer, you essentially an acquirer. L.L. is less concerned in the mere letter of law or technical justice than broadly regardful of the spirit of fairness and good faith. You have accepted conventional standards, have total disregard for sentiment in business. . . . L.L. inspires trust, the trust of the dying, seeking care for the estate of a widow, the morals of a son or the honor of a daughter."[69]

Despite P.N.'s loyalty, however, he suffered almost unbearable stress while defending L.L.'s management practices and personal reputation against Campbell's attacks. In a long letter to L.L. on New Year's Day, 1909, less than a month after his ringing defense of L.L., P.N. vented his long-simmering frustrations to L.L. at being exploited "like a clerk."[70] From 1895 to 1900, he wrote,

> I was actual Chief of the electrical department, created it and managed it . . . established the practice now dignified in the Institute, gave their electrical training to Woodhouse, Bacon, Blaney and Suhr, and time has proved that in spite of inexperience and hardship I did well. Then you, with scarcely a word, swept it from me, sent me to Logan as superintendent, then to Provo. . . . From a position of creative leadership successfully filled, I was supposed to "do as I was told" and given authority only when required in emergencies.[71]

P.N. continued with several pages of relentless particulars, then summarized: "You say of yourself 'I can't stand criticism' and then criticize others indiscriminately and mercilessly." He continued: "Your associates are not held in their jobs by advantage or preoccupied love of their work, but by the magnetism of your wonderful personality, bordering on, if not actually, hypnotic in nature." Worse, P.N. accused, "they can't leave you. Your smile, your handshake, and your frown carry more weight than all the intellectual processes of a decade." He found it sinister that L.L. used his charismatic power "incessantly" to control others. "The effect on the force and manhood of those governed is not good," he continued. "I know what it is. For years it controlled me. . . . And I, more than anything else in life, want to make my 'home' both personal and professional . . . within the organization of the Telluride Co., the Institute, and your personal circle; but I cannot return to the conditions of the past . . . or stifle my manhood in the uniform of an 'office boy.' . . . This cannot continue. You must decide and permit me a resting place."[72]

L.L. did not change, but P.N. returned to his spirited defense of his brother. His loyalty—and his resentments—persisted. The clash with Campbell and emotional distance from P.N. took a further toll on Nunn's health. He began withdrawing from the Telluride Power Company, given the stress it represented with both men, but pursued his educational agenda with renewed vigor.

Nunn had established a Telluride Institute branch in Ithaca, New York, two years earlier in 1907. It was his first pedagogical venture not dependent on a power plant. He chose Ithaca because of its proximity to Cornell University and the pioneering hydro-engineering research being conducted at waterfalls adjacent to the campus. He purchased a house at 508 Stewart Avenue as a home for advanced pinheads studying at Cornell. Checking in on this Cornell Branch (or Cornell Institute as they sometimes called it) periodically, Nunn became friends with recently retired Cornell president and celebrated intellect Andrew D. White and its current president, Jacob G. Schurman.

In midsummer 1909, Nunn used his budding friendship with White to pour out his dream of creating a largely independent college associated with Cornell, in a relationship like the British residential colleges at Oxford and Cambridge. Nunn's model, however, would educate only juniors and seniors. They would matriculate, taking Cornell's curricular offerings but conducting research independently—choosing their own projects and pursuing them without formal oversight from faculty committees.[73] L.L. Nunn saw this plan as uniting the best of the British residential college and the German-style research university, thus creating a new kind of undergraduate education in America.

On July 14, Andrew White noted in his diary his conversation with Nunn and one of his students: "Talk was general and I found Mr. N. very thoughtful and farsighted. He believes, so says his companion, in confining universities to university work with Junior [class status] beginning."[74] American higher education was forming battle lines between those who wanted universities to emphasize liberal education for all undergraduates, while others argued for America's maturing universities to concentrate on in-depth study at the upper division and graduate levels. Nunn clearly aligned himself in his Cornell experiment with noted economist and social critic Thorstein Veblen who sought to forge American universities into research institutions with minimal responsibility for undergraduate education.[75]

Supported by White, Nunn successfully negotiated with President Schurman for a lot at 217 West Avenue in the campus's southwest quadrant to house the "secondary branch" of his educational system.[76] Once again, Nunn would hover over every detail of planning and constructing. Its design echoed the lines and scale of the Olmsted Quarters Building.

Quarters Building at Olmsted. Lucien L. Nunn Papers, #37-4-1770. Division of Rare and Manuscript Collections, Cornell University Library, Ithaca, New York.

Telluride House at Cornell. Lucien L. Nunn Papers, #37-4-1770. Division of Rare and Manuscript Collections, Cornell University Library, Ithaca, New York.

Shuttling back and forth between the East and West, Nunn made sure he was in Utah on January 1, 1910, to host a lavish New Year's party at Olmsted. The *Telluride Journal*, which continued to follow his business and social events, gushed that this gala was "one of the greatest functions of its kind Utah has ever seen." The 257 guests included stockholders, company officers, engineers, division superintendents, subordinate officials, and "their ladies." The gathering began at two o'clock in the afternoon and the program included a reception, dinner, speeches, dancing, and other entertainment. "Several who were among the fortunate guests, say it was the grandest and happiest event of their lives."[77] The paper editorialized: "From an intimate friendship of nearly thirty years with Mr. Nunn, and familiarity with his humor and traits of character, the *Journal* has no hesitancy in saying that none of the guests enjoyed the affair as sincerely as did the host." The article then waxed even warmer:

> It is characteristic of Mr. Nunn to regard every individual connected with the great enterprise of which he is the head, from the highest official and most scientific engineer to the most menial employee, perhaps excavating a flume with a pick and shovel, with a kindly personal regard akin to the interest which the average man takes in the welfare of his brother. Were it possible he would enjoy nothing so much as gathering this vast army of employees from a half a dozen states around him for a big dinner. But of course that is out of the question.[78]

This lavish celebration kicked off a roller-coaster year. By mid-May, Nunn had signed off on architectural plans for what he now called the Telluride Institute House at Cornell. The grand building with room for nearly forty residents became a statement of purpose, permanency, and intent, inside and out. When classes opened in the fall, his students moved in from Stewart Avenue. Their scholarships included not only the posh quarters at Telluride House but full tuition, fees, travel costs, and a personal allowance—$250 a year for juniors and $350 for seniors.[79] Residents of the house would include advanced undergraduates, graduate students, company employees participating in research at Cornell, and distinguished guest scholars from around the world. President Schurman was so impressed that he remarked to L.L., "I expect more from that house than from any other building on the campus."[80]

Such sentiments were gratifying, certainly, but the battle for control of the Telluride Power Company still hung in the balance and Nunn hastened to put his personal assets out of Campbell's reach. At the height of the summer of 1910, he summoned fifteen of his best students and most trusted advisors to Olmsted to draft a constitution for his proposed Telluride Association. After nearly a month, they had rough-draft by-laws for a student-dominated organization independent of Nunn's control—to which he could transfer the bulk of his personal resources on short notice. The threat to his fortune still seemed distant, but he took solace in laying the groundwork to protect it. As winter approached, however, L.L. again found himself emotionally and physically spent.

On a train rumbling west toward Salt Lake City, on November 6, 1910, he scribbled P.N. a note, uncharacteristically describing himself as "utterly cast down, and utterly unrecognized, alone. Not one act of my life is favorably remembered."[81] Two doctors in Chicago had just diagnosed him with pulmonary tuberculosis in an advanced stage.[82] They warned the driven fifty-seven-year-old to slow down and enter a sanitarium to extend his life beyond a year or two. Nunn went directly to a southern California facility, committed himself, became exasperated by the confinement, and returned a week later to Utah to take stock and nurse his failing health. The year ended as somberly as it had opened grandly.

Nunn's worsening health and struggles with Campbell not only drove him to act decisively on his educational plans, but his antagonist's tactics provided additional impetus for placing moral philosophy at the center of his educational design. He might lose his fight for the company, but he resolved to create a generation of disciples who would carry forth his passion for a more enlightened society.

L.L. never regained his previous physical vigor, but the grim diagnosis focused his efforts as never before. From 1911 forward, Nunn defied his disease and walked a tightrope between strenuous exertions to achieve his final purposes and recuperative respites. On the straightforward advice of his personal physician and devoted friend, Dr. Eugene Fuller, Nunn built critically needed recesses between the seasons of intense expenditures of energy. These included a leisurely Hawaiian vacation with Senator Smoot and several members of Congress, a sojourn in a New Mexico sanitarium, and occasional interludes on the California desert.[83]

Meanwhile, Campbell's position had hardened and he announced his aim of "bringing the little fellow to his knees."[84] While Nunn was traveling east by rail across Wyoming the last week of April 1911, accompanied by long-time Ohio friend and business associate Albert M. Johnson, their train made its scheduled stop in Cheyenne. U.S. deputy marshal Thomas Clarke boarded the train unobtrusively and traveled more than a hundred miles to serve a subpoena on L.L. Nunn in his home state. The Union Pacific tracks slanted briefly across the extreme northeast corner of Colorado at Julesburg. The marshal located the private stateroom where Nunn and Johnson settled for the journey. "Just before the train crossed into Colorado," according to one account, "Mr. Nunn left Mr. Johnson and entered the toilet room. Mr. Johnson clicked the latch behind him and settled down for an afternoon nap."[85] Moments later, Clarke began beating on the door, proclaiming his authority, and demanding to see Nunn. When Johnson explained that Nunn was not in the room, the deputy threatened to break down the door. Johnson opened it a crack. The officer thrust the subpoena through the door, whirled around, and hurried off the train before it left the station.[86]

Although the subpoena may not have been legally served, Campbell, buttressed by allies William Story and Fred F. Steigmeyer, had filed suit against Nunn as the Telluride Power Company's general manager in the U.S. District Court of Colorado on April 26, 1911. The charges included eighteen years of mismanagement, misappropriation of funds for personal use (as much as a half-million dollars), and mishandling water and water rights. Especially important was Nunn's decision to build the Institute and Quarters buildings at Olmsted to house the Telluride Institute. Story had convinced Campbell that the institute was a front for "looting" the company.[87] They also accused the Nunn brothers of costly hydraulic engineering miscalculations that assumed "you have a Niagara River to deal with."[88] The trial opened promptly a month later in May 1911 and, including appeals, lasted fourteen months. The *Salt Lake Tribune* covered the trial in detail.[89] Utah's other newspapers covered the issue, too, typically pitting local hero L.L. Nunn against the bully tycoon from St. Louis.

Nunn knew he had to win this battle for control of the Telluride Power Company if he hoped to see his expanding educational ideas come to life. He promptly converted the Telluride Institute into the Telluride Association, which he entrusted neither to the power company nor to himself. He called upon his institute students at Olmsted and those at the educational branches associated with his scattered power plants to elect representatives for a convention, which opened on June 26 and closed July 11. Nunn presided over the representatives—about eighty-five young men and trusted Olmsted associates. He prepared an ambitious agenda focusing on the draft constitution he had refined since the previous summer. This legislative body debated, revised, and eventually approved the document—thereby launching Telluride Association and empowering its predominantly youthful membership.

"The purpose of the Telluride Association," the constitution's brief preface began, "is to promote the highest well being by broadening the field of knowledge and increasing the adoption of the rule of conduct of those truths from which flows individual freedom as the result of self-government in harmony with the Creator." Nunn's budding institution mirrored the academic spirit of its time in American higher education. Six months earlier, the University of Chicago had similarly proclaimed its purpose in the context of founder John D. Rockefeller's vision: "As the spirit of religion should penetrate and control the university . . . it will be proclaimed that the university in its ideal is dominated by the spirit of religion. All its departments are inspired by religious feeling and all its work is directed to the highest ends."[90]

The Telluride Constitution prescribed that "all [the association's] branches shall preserve inviolable a democratic form of government. No class or other artificial distinction shall be tolerated." Further, all scholarships should be awarded on "individual merit alone, determined without undue weight being given to scholastic attainment." Elected officers were to include a chancellor, dean, president, vice president, business manager, treasurer, and secretary. In practice, one or both of the first two offices went to a seasoned professional, while the rest devolved upon younger members.

Early in its proceedings, the convention elected 98 members, made provision for up to 135, and designated 13 members-elect whose memberships would become active on their fourteenth birthdays. The latter included but was not limited to the sons of prominent Nunn associates. Among the regular members were such younger associates as Paul Ashworth, Robert Fairbanks, Frank Noon, Carroll Whitman, Merrill Wrench, Parker Bailey, all three of Charles D. Walcott's sons, and two of L.L. younger brothers—but not P.N. Though he feigned ambivalence, Nunn was easily persuaded to accept his own election as a member. Along with his 1880 essay "The Moral Sense" and a few other treasured documents, L.L. Nunn kept a copy of the Telluride Association Constitution among his most precious possessions.

To underwrite this new governing body, Nunn had transferred a substantial portion of his personal fortune—$488,320 in stock certificates—to six interim trustees of the association, with a promise to add another $150,000 as soon as the Telluride Association ratified its constitution.[91] This action showed his passion to protect his educational plan, even if Campbell won in court. Nunn was confident of his ability to continue controlling these resources as the dominant member of the association.

Court proceedings dragged on while tongues wagged at the Alta Club. Bragging rights and, more significantly, fortunes teetered. Finally, on June 19,

1912, the U.S. District Court dismissed all charges against Nunn.[92] He was in Chicago that day, but his trusted associate, Stephen A. Bailey, dispatched a telegram: "Decision on demurrer . . . received this morning. Court sustains entire demurrer in elaborate opinion on ground of laches, indefiniteness and lack of equity. Court says nothing left to amend and dismisses bill." L.L. answered: "Yours. Incredible. Thanks. Nunn."[93] The judge opined that the Telluride Power Company had thrived "through the loyalty, industry and ability of the said L.L. Nunn and his associates. [Nunn has] served the company at a merely nominal salary, and if the Telluride Power Company were to lose the services of said L.L. Nunn the company would suffer irreparable loss and injury."[94]

In fact, the company did lose his services less than six months later. In a surprising development, on November 22, 1912, Nunn, Campbell, and the other owners sold the company, with its five generating plants and extensive distribution system in northern Utah and southern Idaho, to the newly formed Utah Power and Light Company, a subsidiary of the Maine-based Electric Bond and Share Company (EBASCO). At the time of the sale, L.L. Nunn owned over 40 percent of Telluride's million-plus shares. Campbell, Telluride Power's president, held less than 25 percent of the company stock, while P.N. Nunn owned about 5 percent. It was a bizarre conclusion to L.L.'s long battle with Campbell and his two decades of devotedly building and managing the company.[95]

But it was precisely the right time for the sixty-one-year-old L.L., who could now turn his waning energies to education, with the independence and financial liquidity to do as he pleased. EBASCO invited Nunn to serve as its vice president and to invest in the company's new stock, but he turned down both opportunities.[96] He did, however, continue to build new power plants and to manage those that he had held outside Telluride. Diesel-powered generators enabled him to expand beyond hydro sites.[97] In 1918 Nunn brought these interests together as a new Telluride Power Company. It remained intact until the late 1950s, when Utah Power and Light purchased it.

Free of intense pressures for the first time in decades, Nunn's health took an upswing. Although he continued to move about constantly, he kept his primary residence in Provo, and his dream took shape: He would devote the final years of life to founding a "primary branch" or junior college that would give students a foundation in the liberal arts and sciences and upon which they could build his secondary branch or upper division unit, the Telluride House on the Cornell campus. A letter in his own hand to the first group of his students who attended Cornell affords a rare glimpse of his vibrant idealism:

> Lessening man's toil by the use of a wire in lieu of transporting coal in sacks over steep trails on pack trains is but one of many results already accomplished. To raise man's efficiency—to reduce man's toil—to give him time and means to love his family, his country, and his soul is the work to be accomplished—through science—through society—through government. To free the rich from the bondage of their riches and the poor from the bondage of their poverty that the soul may receive its own. Not by revolution, not even by struggle but by investigation—thought, truth, that is the work.[98]

L.L. Nunn's contemporary, Henry Adams, lamented their era as one wandering between two worlds, one dead and the other powerless to be born.[99] For all of Lucien Nunn's foibles and frustrations, the little dynamo would engage himself in one final effort to shape the future.

CHAPTER 3

IN THE SPIRIT OF THE TIME

The British Empire has been founded, maintained and developed by a specifically educated class of men, who, consciously or unconsciously, have been trustees of the Empire.[1]

—L.L. Nunn

Higher education dominated Nunn's thoughts as his most eventful year, 1912, wound down. Now describing himself as "a builder of men," he had divested himself of nearly half his fortune, founded the Telluride Association, sold his controlling interest in the Telluride Power Company, and walked away from managing that sprawling enterprise. At age fifty-nine, he had cleared the decks in preparation for a new challenge. But he also lived under the shadow of a death sentence from the tuberculosis eating away at his lungs. This often-fatal disease remained treatable only with rest, healthy habits, and a dry climate.[2]

Operating without much of the extended corporate team that had always surrounded him, Nunn still owned and managed several power plants, distribution lines, and other enterprises. To raise cash for reinvestment in education, between 1913 and 1915 he sold the Idaho unit of the Beaver River Power Company, the First National Bank of Telluride, and other real estate and electric operations in Colorado. He wrote to Charles Walcott on April 5, 1915: "[I have] never worked harder in my life than during the past six months. . . . It has required unusual work to keep up our income."[3]

New business development had long driven his daily routines, but Nunn's intellectual interests reawakened. He ordered the remainder of his library and other personal effects to be shipped from Telluride to Provo[4] and sought out leading educators and philosophers with the same zeal that had driven him toward pioneers of electricity. His timing could not have been better. Reexamining education was on the national agenda.

Nunn remained convinced that the mushrooming scientific and technical advances of his time had outpaced the progress of human wisdom, leaving society at the mercy of its own creations and citizens unable to govern themselves. He felt peculiarly empowered when he reflected on his early Colorado experiences. There, his survival had turned daily on his improvisational skills, practical wisdom, and ability to team up with others.

Like his notable contemporaries, Theodore Roosevelt, Owen Wister, and Frederic Remington, the eastern-bred-and-educated Nunn had gone west to test his mettle on the frontier. Writing about this group of men in his 1987 essay, "The Intellectual Origins of L.L. Nunn," Ken Hovey (DS'62) noted that the "escapist always took books along with him and intended to stay away temporarily, typically two years."[5] For L.L. Nunn, like his political, literary, and artistic peers, this free and strenuous "initiation into manliness" shaped his being. Unlike these notable figures, however, Nunn did not return to the East.

As he took stock of his life, infused constantly with thinking *and* doing, idealism and practical challenges, he wanted to see another generation of young men grow in similar soil and in the same spirit that had nourished his own youth. It was no surprise, Hovey noted, that Longfellow's "My Lost Youth" was one of Nunn's favorite poems.[6] Nunn viewed his own sometimes callous and narcissistic style selectively, but it was the more selfless part of his character that he wished to perpetuate.

Important influences on L.L. Nunn's developing educational philosophy were the utopian ideas in the European literature classics on his own bookshelves. His love of such works as Sir Thomas More's *Utopia*, Shakespeare's *Love's Labors Lost*, and John Milton's short essay "Of Education," Hovey argued, filtered into his thinking.[7] The values and perspectives of the Renaissance era, so dear to Nunn, shone through.

Thomas More based *Utopia* on reason, assuming that human nature is fundamentally good, but he also acknowledged human vulnerability to selfishness. More's solution was to control narcissism through education—education, that is, that elicits self-control, respect for others, and sacrifice for the good of the whole through the study of philosophy and literature and the engagement of both mind and body. Farm work ensured the latter and bound More's colony together without glaring disparities in wealth or power. From such schooling, he believed, an enlightened few might arise who would govern wisely as Platonic philosopher-kings.

In *Love's Labors Lost*, Shakespeare frames an educational plan that eerily foreshadows Nunn's developing plan. Here the monarch of a mountain kingdom sets out to create a legion of superior leaders by removing them from ordinary distractions (including women) for three years and challenging them with privation, exertion, and demanding studies. Removed from worldly temptations and faced with great expectations, the young cavaliers were free to find and struggle along their own paths to wisdom.

For Nunn, the model might have been compelling, but not for Shakespeare. The Bard condemned the King of Navarre's courtly school as a failure. But "it is the esthetic rules," Hovey argued, "rather than the errant men that are condemned, for the rules are exposed to be contrary to nature."[8] Even so, Shakespeare's final judgment may have ruled differently on the value of asceticism, for, in a later utopian play, *The Tempest*, he suggested that a period of self-denial would strengthen and purify a man, and prepare him to govern himself in harmony with nature and society.

These fictional creations appeared to resonate with Nunn's personal story and what he had learned from two decades of power plant-based experimentation with education. In short: start students at an early age, present them with practical challenges that require imaginative thinking, cultivate intellectual curiosity with Socratic teaching in small groups, and encourage the development of moral sensitivity by granting them solemn consequential responsibilities.

Nunn's potent ideas coincided with a propitious point in American history. He mirrored many of the values of the Progressive Movement, but he quarreled with it as well. He was not favorably inclined toward the labor movement or public control of natural resources, both of which had, on occasion, crimped his industrial style. But he shared with Progressives in general, and with President Theodore Roosevelt in particular, an imperialistic predisposition, a belief in the elevation of civilization by education, and a devotion to vigorous living. Heroic efforts by the few, they both believed, could elevate the nation.

Nunn found the Progressive Education movement, only loosely associated with Progressivism in politics, more to his liking. Tracing its roots to French philosopher Jean-Jacques Rousseau, German thinker Friedrich Froebel, and American pragmatist John Dewey, this early twentieth-century movement sought to induct students into a democratic society through character education, reforms in industrial training, and instruction anchored in experience. "Education is a social process," Dewey wrote, "education is growth; education is not a preparation for life but is life itself."[9] Schooling and living should be integrated naturally, not sequenced so that one became the precursor to the other. For Dewey, who published his influential *Democracy and Education* in 1916, democracy ranked as a "primary ethical value." Students were to learn the ethics of citizenship in a free society by living these virtues from elementary school forward.

These ideas developed during the first decade and a half of the twentieth century in response to the continuing growth of industrialization, the rising tide of immigration, and the emergence of big cities in America. But they gained additional traction when World War I descended over Europe in 1914, prompting a new examination of democratic values on this side of the Atlantic. Many leading intellectuals joined Dewey in public discourse about the purpose and methods of education in a free society. The *Atlantic Monthly* and *Harper's Magazine* carried often-impassioned articles by nationally prominent writers like Abraham Flexner, Howard Warren, Henry S. Canby, John Erskine, and Alexander Meiklejohn—most of whom were driven to launch notable educational reforms or experiments to showcase their ideas and test their viability.

Flexner, revered for having revolutionized medical education, went on to envision a national resurgence by stimulating critical thinking, real-life engagement, and social opportunities for all children. He articulated these ideas in "A Modern School" and, with some fanfare, founded the experimental Lincoln School in New York in 1917.[10]

At Princeton, Howard Warren pioneered one of the world's first psychological laboratories and at once began to examine educational practices. Writing about the importance of academic freedom for both faculty and students, he concluded a 1914 *Atlantic Monthly* article with Lord Adam Gifford's statement when he endowed the renowned Gifford Lectures in natural theology: "The lecturers appointed shall be subject to no test of any kind, and shall not be required to take an oath, or to emit or subscribe to any declaration of belief . . . provided only that . . . they be sincere lovers of and earnest inquirers after truth."[11] This bold sentiment became a foundation of academic freedom.

Like minded, Nunn had sought to negate his own influence on students, declaring: "Again I say cut me out. Do not use my name. Refer no one to me for any cause. Establish the work on broader lines than individual plan or purpose, always having in mind that the benefits ultimately should go to the world and not to a class, to the end 'that government of the people, by the people, for the people, shall not perish from the earth.'"[12]

Even more important to Nunn was John Erskine, professor of literature at Columbia University, whose reform agenda would result in Columbia's general education movement. In "The Moral Obligation to Be Intelligent," delivered to the Amherst College (Massachusetts) Phi Beta Kappa Society,[13] Erskine lamented the disintegration of coherent curricula and shared learning attributed to Harvard's adoption of the elective principle a generation earlier. He sought to restore the coherence of undergraduate studies and intergenerational learning through reading and discussing classic texts.

Erskine's passion was to wrest great books from their captivity by elite programs and literary specialists, whom he outraged by freely recommending translations to make foreign language works more accessible to students and his requirement that all undergraduates at Columbia become familiar with classics of history, philosophy, literature, and biography. Erskine prevailed over his critics, and his faculty colleagues in 1920 approved his two-year General Honors course. For several decades, this curriculum served as a bellwether for reform in American higher education.

Erskine's plan was a throwback to the early liberal arts college, privileging the shared experience in reading Western classics over Dewey and Warren's faith in individual discovery, freedom, and societal engagement. Nunn pondered these two sides of the curricular divide. Could two such contrasting philosophies be combined? After all, they shared a common aim of restoring ethical maturation to a rightful place alongside intellectual development in the college experience.

Through his connections with Cornell University, well before he built Telluride House on the campus, Nunn had become friends with another of the leading figures on the higher education landscape, Cornell's founding president and later U.S. minister to Russia, Andrew Dickson White. In 1896, White had published *A History of the Warfare of Science with Theology in Christendom*, meticulously chronicling the rise of science since antiquity and Christian authorities' persistent opposition to its findings.[14] Nunn was no stranger to this issue, having ridden the crest of scientific and technological advances in electricity, nor, despite his intuitively religious character, did he harbor theological assumptions that complicated his embrace of rationality. He admired White personally and professionally, and their rapport helped secure the unusual physical and institutional niche that Telluride Association and its house on West Avenue came to occupy at Cornell.

Not only was Andrew White talking excitedly about the Telluride Association on his campus, but word was spreading more widely, too. Citing U.S. Senator Reed Smoot, the *New York Times* reported on December 20, 1914: "L.L. Nunn, a wealthy citizen of Utah, was watching the proceedings of the Senate from a gallery yesterday when his attention was attracted to the alertness of one of the pages . . . Clyde S. Barley [*sic*]." Nunn swiftly inquired about the fourteen-year-old's character "and decided to pay his expenses for a four-year course at Cornell University." Citing Senator Smoot as its source, the article continued, "Mr. Nunn is now paying the way of nearly fifty boys through Cornell."[15]

Alexander Meiklejohn inspired Nunn—and gave him more to think about—than any other educator. A generation younger than L.L., he graduated from Brown with both academic and athletic laurels, earned his doctorate in philosophy at Cornell, and joined Brown's faculty where, at age twenty-nine, he became dean of the school. He accepted the presidency of Amherst College twelve years later. Like other reformers, Meiklejohn lambasted the fractured liberal arts and sciences curriculum and championed academic freedom for students and professors—including college presidents.[16]

Meiklejohn sought to demolish barriers between the college and its surrounding communities. One tactic was to send professors to teach their courses in local textile mills and farmers' grange halls. To the chagrin of Amherst's alumni, he even resisted the growing professionalization of college sports by refusing to hire full-time football and basketball coaches.[17]

Meiklejohn's tenure as Amherst's president, 1913–1923, nearly matched the span between L.L. Nunn's founding of the Telluride Association and his death. Throughout that period, Amherst's leader commanded national attention, and Nunn followed his every move. When L.L. decided to launch his own school, his vision of the right leader followed closely what he had learned by observing Meiklejohn's direct style and urbane philosophy. When, after fourteen years, Amherst's trustees could no longer tolerate Meiklejohn's adventurous leadership, he founded the notable Experimental College at the University of Wisconsin in 1927. *Time* magazine featured him on the cover of its October 1, 1928, issue as "Wisconsin's Meiklejohn." The Experimental College folded after five years, due to the Depression, but Meiklejohn continued to write and teach into his early nineties at the University of California, Berkeley. He visited Deep Springs College in the 1930s.

Antioch College in Yellow Springs, Ohio, had implemented many progressive ideas since Horace Mann founded it before the Civil War. So important did Mann rank service to humanity that he exhorted his first graduating class in 1859: "Be ashamed to die until you have won some victory for humanity."[18] The openly experimental school nearly perished in the early twentieth century. However, it experienced a renaissance under Arthur E. Morgan starting in 1920 and attracted much attention for combining work and study through its cooperative education plan. While Morgan was president, he also founded the Association for the Advancement of Progressive Education. Nunn's own youthful experiences at Oberlin College with its long history of integrating labor and academic study doubtless made him regard Morgan's experiment attentively, even though it had long since drifted toward a mainstream emphasis on academic excellence alone.

Another notable influence on Nunn's educational philosophy was British entrepreneur and African imperialist Cecil Rhodes. Born the same year as Nunn, Rhodes lived a strenuous life in the service of the Crown, the Empire, and his own wealth. The two men shared a powerful cocktail of ambition, competitive energy, and high idealism about public service and devotion to country. Rhodes died in 1902, leaving a will that endowed the Rhodes Scholarships at Oxford University.

This news coincided with Nunn's movement toward transforming his scattered power plant-based schools into the multilayered system that culminated in the Telluride Institute at Olmsted. Rhodes's vision of service to humanity, especially through Anglo-American institutions, and his drive to groom bright young men to become future leaders, remained prominent in Nunn's thinking to the end of his life. If Meiklejohn became the archetype for future leaders of his college, Rhodes provided Nunn with a social and educational vision on which he drew increasingly to shape his own legacy.[19]

The Lucien Nunn of myth was a solitary genius who converted decades of experience in educating his power plant pinheads into a radically innovative liberal arts college. He did, indeed, use that experience as a touchstone against which to strike the outpouring of progressive thought about education in the early twentieth century. But he had also thrust himself into the rapidly evolving controversies surrounding the aims and methods of undergraduate education, mastered the contending precepts, and identified with and learned from the leading thinkers and actors of his time.

Nunn's educational philosophy snapped into focus after he exited from the Telluride Power Company. Without the Olmsted campus and his other power

Students with L.L. Nunn (top, center) in front of the Brady House, Boise Branch, 1914. Lucien L. Nunn Papers, #37-4-1770. Division of Rare and Manuscript Collections, Cornell University Library, Ithaca, New York.

Beaver River Power Station near Beaver, Utah. Photograph by author.

station schools at which to culminate his pinheads' education, however, his system fell into disarray. An exception was his Beaver River Power Company, operating about twenty miles east of Beaver, Utah, and 155 miles south of Provo. Nestled in a narrow, forested canyon, the buildings were compact and sparse by Olmsted standards. It was here that L.L. moved the hub of his educational program and concentrated his most promising students.

Knowing the site would be inadequate for maintaining a primary branch feeder school for Telluride Association, however, Nunn had already resolved to build a new hydro unit in Idaho where the Malad River pours off a plateau and into the Snake River near Bliss. Construction proceeded throughout 1912 with two teachers assigned to tutor the young laborers.[20] These men also strung high-tension lines ninety-five miles northwest to serve the burgeoning power demand in Boise.

Having set a lofty standard with the construction of the Telluride House on the Cornell campus, Nunn sought a place of comparable dignity for his primary branch in the West. When Idaho's former governor James H. Brady won election to the U.S. Senate in 1912, Nunn arranged to lease the stately Brady House at 140 West Main Street in Boise.[21] The well-placed red brick Victorian home with spacious porches, ornate hand-crafted woodwork, and sunny rooms housed about twenty students in the spring of 1913, and L.L. Nunn entertained local, state, and national dignitaries in a revival of the splendid style characteristic of the height of his Provo years.[22]

While this Boise Branch possessed the requisite aesthetic and social trappings, it lacked the substantial labor base necessary to support his educational method. The Bliss plant was a half-day's travel away and too small to provide realistic labor opportunities for the students. The receiving end of the transmission line in Boise was not much more than a demonstration site. Nunn sold this power operation early in 1915, returned the house to Brady, and moved the remaining students to Beaver.

Bolstered by the influx of new blood from the north, the Beaver Institute students wrote and edited volume 1, no. 1 of *The Harlequin*, 160 pages of prose and poetry, which they released in typescript in April 1915. The work reflected an impressive array of talent, intellectual ferment, and discipline.[23] Beaver provided ferocious winters, strenuous work, and serious academics. It had all the elements Nunn sought, yet the scale was small and conditions Spartan.

During this period, Nunn maintained his stately home in Provo (as well as the modest place at Olmsted) but continued to dart about the country. Telluride Association offered him lodging at its house on the Cornell campus if he wished to "pursu[e] scholarly purposes."[24] He appreciated but did not accept that invitation, but he did like to drop in unannounced there and at his western branches.

By 1916, however, Washington, D.C., had become his focus. For two decades, L.L. and P.N. had built many of their dams, flumes, power stations, and transmission lines on public property. In 1914, the federal government sued the Beaver River Power Company and L.L. Nunn, challenging "the right of the power company to occupy and hold possession of lands within a national forest reserve for the development and transmission of hydroelectric power, without having obtained permission from the Interior Department and the payment of rental."[25] At issue were buildings, transmission lines, and over six miles of flumes that carried water from upstream diversion dams to powerhouse turbines. The government also filed suits against Utah Power and Light Company (UP&L), implicating Nunn because he had developed those works prior to selling them to UP&L. The government sought injunctions against the continued occupancy and use of its lands without complying with rules issued under the governing statute. It also sought compensation for past occupancy.

The multifaceted case had worked its way up through the U.S. District Court of Utah and the federal Circuit Court of Appeals, attracting a great deal of attention from western interests. The defendants argued, among other points, that Utah and the separate states possessed authority to control public lands within their boundaries, based on an 1866 federal law. The prosecution countered that legislation in 1896 handed that authority to the Secretary of the Interior on behalf of the federal government.[26]

Both sides appealed to the U.S. Supreme Court, which heard the case on October 11–12, 1916, but did not render its decision until March 19, 1917. The defendants, with *amicus curiae* support from Utah and four other western states rich in public lands, argued for a narrow view of the property power conferred on Congress by Article 4 of the Constitution.[27] This article, the defense argued, would allow the states to employ the power of eminent domain—exercised here by the public utilities empowered by the states—over federal property not being used for governmental purposes. The Court rejected that argument speedily and without dissent. Further, it found little merit in the defendants' argument based on a series of statutes that allowed for private use of federal lands, though clearly not for the production and transmission of electric power. The Court upheld the Interior's argument for the 1896 statute. Predating all of the power facilities at issue, this law dealt specifically with hydroelectric works on public lands, specified criteria for authorizing developments, and required official permission. The defendants had filed no applications for permission.

Finally, however, the defendants argued that the government could not deny them their continued use of the public lands because they understood that they had been given permission to do so by unnamed officials and employees and by the failure of the government to do anything to stop construction of the hydro plants. In response, the Court enunciated a principle, sometimes harsh in its effects, for which the case continues to be cited—namely, that the government is not bound by representations, actions, or inactions by its agents that are not sanctioned by law.[28]

Though this case preoccupied Nunn for two years, the adverse resolution had little practical effect. As the Court said, citing one of the briefs, the principal object of the suits was to test the defendants' claims. If they did not prevail, the defendants could either qualify under the 1896 statute or move their works off public land. The choice was easy. Nunn and the other defendants compensated the government for their past illegal occupancy in an amicable settlement. Although Nunn had invested a great deal of time and energy in defending his position, this setback, like others he had suffered, was not crippling.[29] The settlement amounted to little more than a slap on the wrist and modest payments for using the land from that time forward.

Nunn's frequent sojourns in Washington, D.C., opened a new door for his educational experimentation. Dissatisfied with both Beaver and Boise as long-term sites for his primary branch and knowing how rapidly the power business was changing, he determined that he could educate his future leaders better in an agricultural setting than in continuing his pinhead arrangement. Following Telluride's 1914 Convention, Nunn asked a few trusted members of the association and several seasoned power company engineers—a group that included Sidney Walcott, J. C. Miller, W. W. Clark, and W. D. Alexander—to search for a suitable location. He imposed no geographical exclusions on where to look, but he also cautioned, "We must be conservative as no line of activity offers such excellent chances to lose money."[30]

A logical possibility was a section (640 acres) of wooded ranch land located two miles west of Delta, Colorado, part of which Nunn had owned since 1886 and all of which was available to him now for seventy-five to eighty dollars an acre. One of his company superintendents, J. B. Bailey, visited the property, judged it suitable, and immediately requested money to secure water rights.[31] Nunn equivocated, deferring to his advisors at Telluride Association. They deemed the site less than ideal for agriculture and urged him to sell the land.

Nunn's interests seemed to be elsewhere anyway. Some of his advisors had recommended Texas, and Nunn reported on February 21, 1916, that he was traveling there "to attempt to purchase a part of the King Ranch for a primary branch."[32] From his diesel generating plant in Teague, Texas, he wrote Charles Walcott: "I am more relaxed than I have been for several years, and am loafing to my heart's content."[33] Nunn bid on a nice parcel but found the land too expensive and the Southwest generally too hot and dry for year-round outdoor labor. He seriously investigated another recommendation—a ranch in Nevada's Ruby Mountains—but ultimately rejected it along with pricy sites in California and the Pacific Northwest. He was not willing to jeopardize the educational component by overspending on the site.

At the behest of Charles Walcott, in the spring of 1916, L.L. drove up California's Owens Valley from Los Angeles in an open, air-cooled Stanley automobile owned by one of his trusted power company engineers, Otto Suhr. With them were the head of Nunn's legal team, Harold Waldo, and Walcott's son, Sidney, a member of Telluride Association. Bound for Deep Springs Valley, northwest of Death Valley, Nunn wanted to see the big ranch in Deep Springs Valley then owned by Arthur L. Stewart.

Charles Walcott had been one of the first natural scientists to study the area, conducting fieldwork in the White Mountains in 1894 and returning two years later with Frederick V. Coville to examine the Inyo Range.[34] He had been especially struck by the beauty and unusual morphology of Deep Springs Valley. In 1912, Walcott had brought his family west to visit L.L. at Olmsted,[35] and the two friends had conversed about L.L.'s need for a new campus. Walcott proposed a ranch in Deep Springs Valley, but only when Nunn's need became acute did he investigate it.

But how did he know the Deep Springs ranch was for sale? Lewis Payson, who owned property in Deep Springs Valley and dabbled in ranching and mining, had corresponded intermittently with Walcott since the 1890s, but both Lewis and his brother George had died by 1909. The tip may have come through one of their relatives, but a more likely source would have been Albert M. Johnson, the Chicago millionaire investor in Nunn's enterprises and long-time friend who was establishing a desert retreat in the north end of Death Valley. Using a roustabout cowboy, prospector, and promoter, "Death Valley Scotty," as his front, Johnson would later build the well-known Scotty's Castle in Grapevine Canyon—about seventy miles southeast of Deep Springs. There is also a plausible story that Owens Valley rancher Archibald Farrington, the new owner of the ranch, had serendipitously met one of Nunn's aides in a San Francisco barbershop.[36]

Upon seeing it, Nunn was smitten by Deep Springs Valley. He immediately tendered Farrington an offer; but larger events had turned unexpectedly in Farrington's favor, and he decided to hold onto his property. Disappointed and feeling increasing pressure to keep his plans rolling, Nunn turned quickly to another alternative. His junior colleagues and partners at Telluride Association, led by Gilbert Miller and Sidney Walcott, presented him with a sophisticated set of recommendations in a "Report on Virginia as a Home for the Central Branch of Telluride Association."[37]

Noting a variety of possible sites in North Carolina and Virginia, they found special merit in a run-down plantation once owned by Edgar Allan Poe's foster father. Nearly thirty-five hundred acres of overgrown farmland, it was located on a promontory along the south bank of the James River near the town of Claremont.[38] The area had never recovered from the devastation of the Civil War. The central parcel of six hundred acres featured vistas across the James River toward Williamsburg.[39] They recommended its immediate purchase from "A. J. Arrington, a merchant and mill owner." They also drafted a layout for the campus, arranging the buildings around a spacious green. Architectural designs and building specifications for a community of thirty to forty students, plus a substantial faculty and staff, rounded out the proposal.

According to this plan, the Claremont facility would become the home office of Telluride Association as well as the campus of the new primary branch of Nunn's overall plan. The Telluride House at Cornell would become secondary, indeed, a satellite branch for the final phase of the educational program. The Telluride committee foresaw an expansive labor program—timber harvesting, orchard management, truck gardening, peanut farming, animal husbandry, meat production, and a dairy operation. Telluride would acquire its own riverboat to ferry fruits, vegetables, and dairy products daily to markets in Richmond and Norfolk. Nunn bought the farm.

Although the "Telluride Institute of Virginia" at Claremont was not formally chartered until January 1917, Nunn ordered the old mansion to be renovated by early autumn 1916. The first week of November, thirteen student members of Telluride Association arrived in Claremont by train from the recently sold Beaver River plant.[40] At least six others arrived from the East and Midwest in a second wave. Veteran Nunn assistant Frank Noon had arrived with the initial group to find that virtually nothing was ready. No new buildings had been erected, the labor program began without direction, and classes opened with just one teacher.

In early November, Nunn, by now known affectionately as "the Old Man," moved down from Washington, D.C. Three weeks later, he was gone, leaving behind him a mixed message. Although the muggy climate exacerbated his asthma, it was not the cause.[41] Rather, as he wrote the Committee on Organization at Claremont, "I left because your members knew the intensity of my desire that they should progress along certain lines of conduct and because they ignored my wishes and left me for the pool room and the gossip of a little provincial town from which they would receive nothing worthwhile."[42] Although his pique at being ignored is obvious, he then flipped the message, saying that the students would try to please him as the one providing their scholarships rather than accepting the full weight of orchestrating their own affairs and governing their own conduct.

Mansion at Claremont, Virginia, 1916. Courtesy of Deep Springs Archives.

The students, all between ages seventeen and nineteen, came from all over the nation. Chester ("Chet") Dunn, an Indiana native, had a stellar record as an athlete, student, and leader—and had a phenomenally high IQ score.[43] At Beaver, he had ranked fourth overall among his peers, who included Ed Meehan of Illinois, Arthur A. ("Cy") Ross of Idaho, H. B. Dinkel of Louisiana, Allan Curtis of Washington, D.C., and F. E. McCarty of New York. This Claremont student group also included Ray Fruit, Clyde Bailey, and Bruce Simmons, three young men who held a special place in Nunn's affections. Fruit chaired the Committee on Organization for the new school.

The two had been in contact since 1915, when Nunn eloquently confessed his emotion at receiving a warm letter from Fruit, a recent high school graduate at the Boise Institute. Nunn had personally nominated Ray to the Telluride Association at Cornell and, when the association rejected him, L.L. resigned in protest. His power play worked. The Convention "confessed its error," Sweeting reported, and "L.L. remained a member . . . , but his faith in the good judgment of the Association had been deeply shaken."[44] Even so, he had embraced the association's grand plan for Claremont and committed himself to make it work.

Clyde Bailey was the Senate page who had come to Nunn's attention two years earlier. It is not known how or when Nunn first met Bruce Simmons.

However, in the spring of 1916, when Simmons was a private in training at a U.S. Army base in southern Arizona, Nunn had made strenuous efforts to arrange a three-day furlough for him while L.L. was in nearby Nogales on business. So intensely did Nunn want this time with Simmons that he prevailed upon Utah governor William Spry and U.S. Senator Reed Smoot to appeal directly to the secretary of war. Smoot explained that the secretary was presently out of the city, then followed up a week later, informing Nunn by telegram that the secretary of war "does not feel it advisable to take exception favoring private Simmons."[45] Even so, when the young man's enlistment ended late in 1916, he joined the student body at Claremont. So open was Nunn about his longing for Simmons's company, and so unconcealed was his quest to free the young man from duty in order to be with him, that it is impossible to overlook the straightforwardness with which he displayed his affectional preference.

Claremont opened as "a preparatory and collegiate" institution under the auspices of the Telluride Association, but the association formally granted L.L. Nunn authority to operate the school. He expected deference and received it, but he became increasingly locked in an internal struggle between his instinctive need to dominate and his earnest desire to grant the students responsibility and freedom. His professional staff suffered from this ambivalence as well, often not knowing how much authority they had or how much to exercise in managing Nunn's schools. Ernest Thornhill, former education director and dean at Olmsted and Beaver, had once again uprooted himself to move to Claremont to supervise and set the academic program in motion. He hired Professor C. O. Jandl and a "Professor Jones." Several black servants, including a cook and a maid, who had worked for the previous owner, prepared and served meals, cleaned house, and did laundry.

The challenge of launching the proposed agricultural system was very different from managing a western power plant. No one knew how to jumpstart the ambitious farm labor program, but there were thousands of trees to be cleared from the fallow fields. The students wielded axes and two-man bucksaws on the swampy ground day after day. Uninspired by months of monotonous work through the soggy winter, their attitudes on academic studies also soured. On January 17, a scant two weeks after the school received its Virginia charter, Dean Thornhill reported to the Committee on Scholastic Standing that the students were lazy and argumentative. "Some are effeminate instead of manly," he wrote. "Some are using profanity, vulgarity, slang . . . instead of decent English." Further, they were "coming to morning classes half-dressed, with shoes unlaced, and with slippers on; they loll in chairs, stretch, yawn and elevate their feet."[46] In fact, a few had already abandoned Claremont. Thornhill commended only six students, Chet Dunn among them, for being "earnest and persistent . . . on the right track and getting somewhere."

Nunn was now spending most of his time at Hotel Westminster in Los Angeles to be close to his physician and friend, Dr. Eugene Fuller. He craved news about Claremont but often balked at what he heard. Ten days after Thornhill's exasperated report, Nunn shot back in a letter to the students, beginning mildly enough that "the chaotic condition" was normal at the outset. When daily routines fell into place, the situation would improve. He was upset, however, that some of the stronger students were among those who had left. "I regret to say they are not members who could best be spared," he wrote.[47]

Receiving no response from either the student body or Thornhill, Nunn bypassed his academic dean and instructed Jandl to "write me of the conditions once a week. Write me from your inmost heart, not empty formal reports . . . based on your effort to arouse the lethargy around you."[48] The next day, February 4, long before Jandl could have received this plea, Nunn dictated a four-page single-spaced tirade to the "Gentlemen" of the student body. He rethought this venting and emblazoned "Not Sent" across the top before filing it away. In this missive, he told them that they had better get serious if Claremont "is ever to be known as anything but one of the many theoretical experiments of the Utopian type that have found a premature grave. . . . If your organization is to justify its existence every member must regard himself as an active, and I may say a very active portion of the administration."[49] Nunn chided them for their lack of gratitude and spelled out the dimensions of this opportunity: "We must bear in mind that our educational project is not an entertainment, but it is an effort devoted solely and exclusively to equipping men to meet with success in their mature lives."

A few days later, he wrote a more temperate letter, calling upon the students to understand that "you are not only your own legislators, but you are your own administrators. There is no chief executive possessing sole and arbitrary authority over you." Enunciating a favorite principle, he continued, "The discontented are those who are not in harmony with the task. . . . They are willing to step in and harvest the benefits of membership, but they rebel when they are called upon to perform their duties."[50]

The possibility that his grand final experiment might fall stillborn haunted Nunn. On February 20, less than two weeks later, he wrote the students with a pathos that must have stunned them:

> Since the crisis of your affairs, disorganized mobs of thoughts and emotions have taken possession of and run rampant throughout my being. The days have been filled with suffering and the nights have brought no relief. From sheer exhaustion I fell into a troubled sleep and dreamed a dream which was not all a dream. I visited again the scenes of my activities. The power plants of which I had been so proud were dilapidated and abandoned. The waterways had fallen down. The transmission lines lay on the ground. The magnificent reservoirs contained only a vast mass of decaying fish. The massive walls which once entrapped and quieted the turbulent waters of Niagara were in ruins. Dazed, but not daunted I turned to the greater work only to find that the Association had failed ignominiously and the Institute had long since been forgotten. . . . Then I awoke drenched in sweat. Oh, yes, I have suffered and you have suffered but do not think I have not been a companion in your suffering.[51]

Regaining his decorum, Nunn then emphasized the group's responsibility for self-governance. "The pernicious notion that the individual must police himself," he wrote, "is repugnant."[52]

These emotionally intense missives were playing out against troubling external events. That spring, the U.S. Supreme Court ruled against L.L. Nunn and his codefendants over their use of public forestlands, and World War I casualties were mounting higher. German submarines were tightening a noose around Britain, imperiling the delivery of U.S. aid. The United States had not yet entered the war, but "L.L., always an Anglophile, was devastated by the progress of the war in Europe . . . and took an increasingly pro-British posture," Sweeting reported. Nunn's politics were revealed by his collection of "pamphlets and broadsides . . . favorable to the Allies and highly uncomplimentary to the Central Powers."[53] The scales tipped when the U.S. State Department aroused American anger and fear with its release of the decoded Zimmermann Telegram. This diplomatic dispatch revealed Germany's invitation to Mexico to join the Central Powers, offering Arizona, New Mexico, and Texas as prizes if the United States were defeated.

Meanwhile, members of Telluride Association seemed blithely unconcerned. Coupled with his disappointment over the students' lack of commitment to genuine self-governance at both Cornell and Claremont, Nunn became increasingly agitated about the association as a whole. Just a week after the Zimmermann incident, Nunn wrote Telluride member Oliver Clark in Ithaca asking if conditions had not "grown so alarming that it is best to consider either disbanding the Association or fundamentally changing the character of its government? I would greatly appreciate your spontaneous opinion on this subject; so please write me at once without waiting to 'think it over' and again after you have thought it over."[54]

Despite Nunn's resignation from the association to protest its rejection of Ray Fruit and despite his current misgivings, he had embraced the association's grand plan for Claremont and committed himself to make it work.

At least three alumni of Nunn's educational programs reported later that he settled claims by young women in Claremont who had been impregnated by his students. No record remains of the financial arrangements necessary to resolve these cases, but there is no doubt that these affairs stuck in his craw. Nunn could sometimes overlook youthful shenanigans, but he was bitter about how easily the students had been lured from the lofty purposes for which he had assembled them.[55]

The international crisis so much on Nunn's mind intensified when President Woodrow Wilson's cabinet voted unanimously in favor of declaring war on the German empire. Young men across the nation began to volunteer for the armed forces and the trickle became a flood with Congress's Declaration of War on April 6, 1917. This wave of patriotism, coupled with continued student malaise at Claremont, prompted over half the student body to enlist. The recruits left almost immediately. The Claremont Institute virtually collapsed, although its doors remained open for another month.

On May 8, J. E. Meehan, president of the student body at Claremont, advised Nunn of the following resolution: "Whereas, Telluride Institute of Virginia, having discontinued its educational work, and intending shortly to disband, therefore, Be it resolved, that all property held in the name or administered by it, revert to the grantor, Mr. L.L. Nunn."[56] Nunn embraced this development with mixed emotions. After all, the students were serving their country, a value basic to his philosophy.

For a much more substantial reason, however, Nunn was not despondent at Claremont's closing. In December 1916, only a month after it opened, he had written Charles Walcott: Claremont had "possibilities," but "[they are] not such as there is in the west. Nothing has yet been determined in reference to Deep Springs Valley."[57] Two months later, in early February 1917, Nunn learned that Farrington might be interested in selling his Deep Springs ranch after all. Nunn resolved to acquire the property as quickly as possible, moving this time without Telluride.

Local newspapers reported as early as March 1 that E. P. Woodhouse, a company manager for L.L. Nunn, had been talking with Farrington, and that he had paid a second visit accompanied by Nunn's chief legal counsel, Harold R. Waldo, "for the purpose of examining the title to the ranch and ascertaining if it was all clear."[58] Westgard Pass was closed by deep snow when Waldo arrived, but he persevered with the help of the county sheriff who arranged assistance. "At the toll house," he later recalled, "we hitched on a team in front of the car and the fellow driving the team sat on the hood. It might have been a little warm, even on a cold day."[59] Successful in this effort, the meeting with Farrington proceeded as planned. The legal barriers also proved surmountable, and the local newspaper reportedly confidently: "In the transferring of this large ranch, one of the largest good stock ranges and farms in Inyo county has changed hands."[60]

In typical fashion, however, Nunn was thorough and systematic. He already had a team working behind the scenes on every angle of the purchase. His young personal assistant, Bruce Simmons, got involved in the acquisition along with Woodhouse and Waldo. Nunn's brother-in-law, William W. Bird, began working to secure all available water rights in Deep Springs Valley, causing another six weeks' delay.

Nunn had apparently chosen Simmons to help with the Deep Springs assignment because he thought his youthful presence might soften Farrington. Waldo was clearly the chief negotiator, but the three men made an effective team. Finally, most of Farrington's property in Deep Springs Valley changed hands in transactions dated April 11 and 12, 1917. Simmons was listed as the new owner of one significant parcel, but he transferred it to Nunn within days. In all, Nunn became the owner of about three thousand acres in Deep Springs Valley, including the home ranch with water rights on Wyman Creek in the northeast quarter, the spacious pastures with multiple springs located around the north shore of Deep Springs Lake, and Antelope Spring in the southwest quarter of the valley.[61]

Local curiosity abounded concerning Nunn and his reason for buying the ranch. "Purchaser of Farrington Ranch Will Make Model Farm," read a June 21 headline in the *Inyo Register*, which reported that Nunn "arrived at the ranch last Sunday from his Utah home, and with him were nine young men students."[62] His purpose, the story continued, was "to make extensive improvements and changes in his newly acquired California holdings." The ranch was to be "put under a high state of cultivation and a variety of crops grown." In addition to raising blooded stock, the report continued, "other ideas will be

Hauling the library and furniture across Nevada to Deep Springs, 1917. Courtesy of Deep Springs Archives.

carried out." The farm operation was to be expanded from 160 to 360 irrigated acres and "a hotel will be erected sufficiently large to care for 200 guests."[63]

Chet Dunn, who had first studied at Beaver Branch, was one of two students assigned to remain in Virginia long enough to close the operation at Claremont, sell the property, and ship all the furniture, equipment, books, and art across the country.[64] Even as Nunn looked ahead, he insisted that Dunn and his companion continue their studies while they dismantled the school. He sternly instructed: "No more girls are to be brought to the house nor is the Ford to be used by you for your own use. I am requesting Prof. Jones to inforce [*sic*] the strictest discipline and secure at least double the results scholastically that would ordinarily be expected."[65]

Ever resilient, L.L. Nunn had awakened from his Claremont nightmare with his larger dream undamaged. Now he felt even greater urgency to launch the Deep Springs program. At its convention that summer, the Telluride Association endorsed Nunn's new primary branch. Led by L.L.'s nephew, Carroll Whitman, its members voted to place "all the Association's resources at Mr. Nunn's disposal."[66] It was as though nothing had changed, yet everything would be different. Especially the fortuitous place. And Nunn knew this was truly his last chance.

CHAPTER 4

A FORTUITOUS PLACE

Deep Springs Valley

The desert has a deep personality; it has a voice; and God speaks through its personality and voice. Great leaders of all ages from Moses to Roosevelt, have sought the desert and heard its voice. You can hear it if you listen, but you cannot hear it while in the midst of uproar and strife for material things.

—L.L. Nunn

The sun seems to rise in the west at Deep Springs, not because time runs backward here but as a function of the unique morphology of the valley. The modern ranch and college sit tight against the mountains on the eastern edge of the valley, keeping it in the morning shadows until the day is well along. At dawn, however, the sun bursts brilliantly against the snow-capped 14,000-foot Sierra Nevada peaks that fringe the skyline over Westgard Pass and gradually creeps down their faces before bathing the west side of Deep Springs Valley in morning light. The long shadows from the steep escarpment behind the college then shrink as sunshine gradually approaches the alfalfa fields and finally illuminates the ranch and college buildings. Now, as in the distant past, all eyes are drawn to the west in the morning and return there in the evening when dramatic sunsets and lenticular clouds frequently loom over the Sierras.

This place would account for much of the success of Nunn's educational dream. Deep Springs Valley has left an indelible imprint on the character of every student

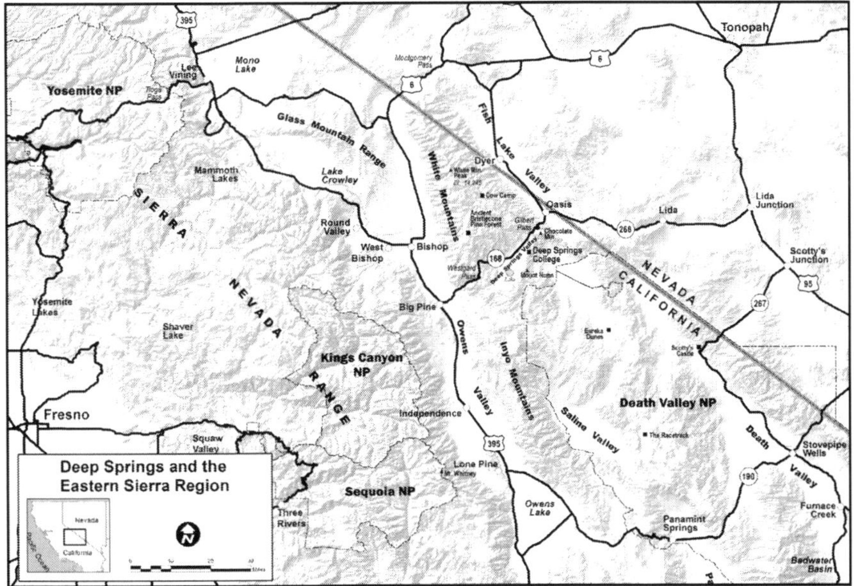

Deep Springs and the Eastern Sierra Region.

who has descended Gilbert Pass or Westgard Pass since 1917. The geography, the climate, and the many people who had inhabited the valley before the students' coming, as well as the artifacts, ruins, and mines, have settled in the memories of those students. This extraordinary place has shaped and reinforced the philosophy, ideals, and practices central to the success of L.L. Nunn's final project.

At a floor elevation of 5,200 feet, Deep Springs Valley is a little over thirteen miles long and two to five miles wide. Manhattan Island could be dropped inside it. The valley stands out on topographical maps because it slants decidedly northeast, somewhat counter to the slightly northwesterly bias of the valleys around it. Chocolate Mountain (also known as Piper Peak and Piper Mountain) looms over the northeast corner—aptly named for the dark brown volcanic rock that flows down its slopes.

Deep Springs is on the western edge of the Great Basin, an arid region that sprawls between Utah's Wasatch Mountains and the Sierra Nevada Range of California. This vast area encompasses most of Nevada as well as parts of California, Idaho, Oregon, and Utah.[1] The three distinguishing characteristics of this "basin and range country" are a seemingly endless succession of elongated valleys and mountains, a paucity of rain and snow, and an absence of outlets to the sea. Although precipitation is normally sparse in the valleys, deep snowfields in the mountains gradually melt throughout the spring and summer to

Deep Springs Valley from Gilbert Pass. Photograph by author.

nourish an array of verdant plant and animal life along streams and around springs.[2] The rest is desert, strewn with bunch grasses, indigo bush, salt brush, white sage, and, in wet years, wildflowers galore.

Deep Springs Valley is a true "basin" encircled entirely by the towering White-Inyo Range to the west and north and an unnamed branch of that range that encloses the east and south perimeter. The White-Inyo Range is a single geologic formation about ninety miles long. The northern section is the White Mountains while the southern half is named Inyo, the Paiute word for "dwelling place of the Great Spirit." Westgard Pass (elev. 7,313), through which California Route 168 threads its way east from Owens Valley to Deep Springs Valley, divides the range in half.

A salina (or playa) occupies the southeast corner of the valley—a sterile salt flat surrounding a briny pastel lake barely a foot deep.[3] What little rain and snow that falls within the valley's 220-square-mile catchment area either runs to this concentric fried-egg-shaped formation or evaporates trying. As recently as fifteen thousand years ago, a lake filled Deep Springs Valley; Soldier Pass was the spillway through which it overflowed into Eureka Valley to the east.[4]

The valley takes its name from a series of springs that feed fresh water into several ponds at the base of a valley-long earthquake fault where it passes east of the lake. The deep springs, which emerge beneath and around the ponds, are known as Buckhorn Springs. The most prominent surface outlet, slightly to the north, is Corral Spring. It sustains a generous stream that runs year-round across the salty marsh to the lake. Scattered across the north side of the playa are several freshwater wetland patches known as the Bog Mound Springs.

Over millions of years, the Deep Springs Fault has dropped the east side of the valley about 5,000 vertical feet. Geologists believe the last major earthquake occurred about two thousand years ago, leaving a 40-foot escarpment that is clearly visible across the alluvial fans that sprawl out onto the valley floor from the canyons at the south end of the valley. Geologists have also traced this fault under the upper or north end of the valley, running almost directly beneath the ranch and college. A parallel fault runs the length of the valley on the west, with a 1,400-foot vertical displacement—only about one-third that of the east fault. Alluvial fill from the higher and wetter White-Inyo Range obscures the more recent escarpment. Together these geological down-thrusts have created a deep and steep-sided valley. Sediments from the erosion of mountains on both sides are estimated to be 750 feet deep at the north end and up to 2,400 feet in the center of the valley. Saturated with water over time, this voluminous mass became a significant aquifer.[5]

A large wave of exposed white rock known as the Poleta Folds erupts from the alluvial fan on the southwestern edge of the valley. This tortured formation in half-billion-year-old rock reveals the effects of unfathomable heat and pressure over geologic time. In addition to anchoring local points of interest, these unusual folds have become a regular stop for geology fieldtrips staged by universities from across the continent.

To the west, the 14,000-foot Sierra Nevada peaks rising nearly two vertical miles above Owens Valley are the cause of the extreme weather patterns affecting Deep Springs. When the prevailing winds coming off the Pacific Ocean reach the Sierras, the moist air must rise to surmount the peaks. In doing so, it cools and drops much of its moisture as rain or snow, generally leaving the terrain east of the mountains with meager leftovers. What moisture the Sierras don't wring from the clouds is claimed by the Inyo-White range, which crests at 14,246 feet at White Mountain Peak. At Deep Springs, where weather records have been kept since 1948, precipitation averages only six inches a year, although it can vary widely from one year to the next.[6]

Unusually wide variations in daily temperature have not made life easy for inhabitants, ancient or modern. Day and night temperatures often differ by 40 degrees Fahrenheit on the valley floor. Dry air does not retain heat as well as humid air, and the sun's radiation strikes the ground directly in desert country, heating it during the day but leaving it unblanketed by the trees and grasses of wetter climates. Hundred-degree days and sixty-degree nights are common at Deep Springs in summer, and the pattern persists with 40-degree days and zero-degree nights in winter. These wide variations leave only about 130 frost-free nights—a short growing season.

No one has captured the spirit of this "Eastern Sierra" region better than Mary Austin. "This is the country of three seasons," she wrote in *Land of Little Rain*. "From June on to November it lies hot, still, and unbearable, sick with violent unrelieving storms; then on until April, chill, quiescent, drinking its scant rain and scanter snows; from April to the hot season again, blossoming, radiant, and seductive . . . the land sets its seasons by the rain."[7]

Tree-ring scientists have reconstructed precipitation and temperature data across the Southwest that go back over ten thousand years. The twentieth century was cooler and wetter than the two previous centuries (1700 to 1900). In fact, it was the wettest century in the last millennium. A recent warming trend reflecting global climate change is apparent. Precipitation levels have decreased significantly since the late 1980s.[8]

Agriculture in Deep Springs Valley, like other basins of the Intermountain West, depends on irrigation. After a heavy winter, the spring snowpack at the headwaters of Wyman Canyon has been as deep as eight or ten feet and the stream will run fast and deep.[9] Wyman Creek can run briskly into the northwest corner of the valley and flow five or six miles across the flatlands before disappearing into the sandy soil. In these years, it discharges enough water to irrigate 120 acres of alfalfa at Deep Springs Ranch all summer.[10] But if the snowpack is sparse following a dry winter—or two or three—the stream may be little more than a trickle and will peter out almost entirely by midsummer.

As early as 10,000 years ago, the first humans began casual passage through the area and left traces of their brief sojourns. About 4,500 years ago their numbers grew and their culture morphed into a more complex social and economic structure. They developed limited residential patterns coupled with high mobility for hunting and gathering in the Owens Valley lowlands. At the higher elevations, hunting camp artifacts dating back four millennia reveal only sporadic summer use. More extensive seasonal camps began to appear in Deep Springs Valley about 3,000 years ago.[11]

These ancient people relied on at least a hundred species of plants and animals for their food, clothing, and shelter. Gophers, mice, and packrats were as important as antelope, deer, and mountain sheep. At some point, the residents began a simple form of wild crop irrigation to expand the marshes and increase the growth of edible plants.[12] Piling rocks, logs, and brush in the water courses

Petroglyphs on boulder in Wyman Canyon. Photograph by Linda K. Newell.

between the springs and the lake, they forced the life-giving water to spread out over the lowland.

An amphibian species that is found only in Deep Springs Valley, the black toad, or *Bufo exsul*, continues to live in the natural marsh areas at the south end of the valley.[13] Prolific and active during the spring breeding season, these toads and their eggs (which are strung together in transparent tubes) also provided a seasonal source of protein.

In the autumn, large family groups assembled to celebrate the summer's harvest and cooperate in driving jackrabbits, cottontails, and antelope into V-shaped traps to harvest their meat and pelts. These times were marked by dancing, feasting, and sacred rites. Afterward, they dispersed to scattered camps for the winter.

Early human inhabitants left enduring markings on rock formations throughout the area. Their petroglyphs (figures chipped or etched into the patina on rock surfaces) and pictographs (figures painted with dyes onto absorbent rock) survive on canyon walls and boulder-strewn slopes rising above the valley on its western side. At the mouth of Wyman Canyon, running parallel to the creek's north bank, are three large boulders several hundred feet apart decorated with petroglyphs on their south faces. Some figures are stylized human or animal forms, while others resemble lightning bolts or may be abstract images. Anthropologists do not agree on whether these complex clusters celebrated events, signified sacred spaces, provided directions for hunters, or were decorative art.

Above today's ranch is a small birthing shelter tucked into the rocks on a northeast-facing slope. In a scramble of large boulders, one large slab leans against another, forming a small cave-like room, hardly big enough for two people to sit. Here native women found privacy and shelter from the elements to give birth, evidenced by two images painted with rust-colored pigment. One of these is a standing figure with legs parted and blood flowing. The other appears to be a child wrapped on a cradleboard.

Three Paiute groups clustered around the White Mountains. In addition to the Deep Springs band, the Fish Lake Valley group lived north of Deep Springs over Gilbert Pass, and the Owens Valley group, the largest of the three, resided to the west over Westgard Pass. They identified themselves as the Nimi or Numa—quite simply "the people."[14] Members of the Deep Springs group referred to their valley as Patosabaya and themselves as the Patosabaya nunemua.[15] Noted anthropologist Julian Steward (DS'18) demonstrated that the Owens Valley Paiutes, comparatively few in number and restricted in geographic range, were at the center of a linguistic and cultural dispersion that affected American Indian language development throughout the Great Basin.[16]

About 600 A.D. these Paiutes acquired the bow and arrow, a much more maneuverable and precise instrument than the hand-thrown spear and atlatl.[17] With the additional food made possible by this new technology, the human population surged. This boom, however, occurred just when long-term precipitation levels were falling. As pressure on food sources mounted, Paiutes dispersed into less hospitable areas to sustain themselves. Year-round occupation of traditional summer encampments in Deep Springs Valley now became the rule. The Deep Springs band also began to establish summer-long hunting camps in the alpine zone high in the White Mountains. Remnants of their temporary shelters are still visible at elevations as high as 12,000 feet.[18]

At the newly important higher elevations, a previously ignored food became a dietary staple. Rich in protein and fat, pinyon pine nuts were abundant. Mixed with juniper trees, pinyon pines blanket most slopes between 6,000 and 9,000 feet elevation.[19] Gathering and extracting pine nuts from their cones, and storing them for later processing into meal, became an autumn ritual. It began when the cones were mature but still closed, green and sappy. If not harvested at this point, the cones would open and begin to drop, giving birds and rodents a competitive edge. The Paiutes heated the sticky cones over hot embers to pop them open and release the seeds.

When Europeans first entered the region, Deep Springs Paiutes lived in family clusters numbering twenty to thirty individuals, moving from camp to camp within the valley. There are at least six identifiable village sites near the lake (three to the east and three to the west), three more around Antelope Springs in the southwest quarter of the valley, and four near the mouth of Wyman Canyon.[20] On the valley floor, families dwelled in low, thatched conical structures, fifteen to twenty feet in diameter. In the higher pinyon woodlands, they took shelter in simple gabled log structures covered by pine boughs.[21]

Even as Paiute settlements within the Deep Springs basin became permanent, these villagers ranged fifty or more miles to find pinyons that bore good harvests. They also traded over broad areas for items not available locally. Their greatest need was for obsidian (volcanic "glass") to make projectile points, knives, and scrapers.

A gender-based division of labor prevailed among these people, with women as gatherers and men as hunters. Metate stones for grinding seeds are scattered throughout the valley. Projectile points and obsidian chips still litter the ground around the remnants of their stone hunting blinds near springs and marshes.

The permanent residents of Deep Springs Valley may never have exceeded thirty to sixty individuals at a time, but a population of about two hundred adults is essential to maintain tribal prohibitions against incest.[22] Deep Springs Paiutes, therefore, often found their mates among neighboring Paiute villagers in the Owens and Fish Lake Valleys. They did not have horses until white explorers and settlers introduced them. They were initially more likely to eat them than ride them.[23]

Spain laid claim to North America's far west in 1767, but ceded the entire region to Mexico after its successful revolution of 1822. In 1829 Peter Skene Ogden of the British Hudson's Bay Company led an expedition to the Eastern Sierra region in search of furs. Joseph Walker followed five years later with a group of adventurers and returned in 1843 with the first wagon train to traverse the Eastern Sierras en route to the greener pastures of California's Central Valley.[24] Two years later, he accompanied John C. Frémont and Kit Carson on an expedition to map the Owens Valley.

War broke out between the United States and Mexico in 1846 and ended two years later with Mexico ceding all of its territory north of the Gila River to the United States. The U.S. Congress moved quickly to organize the Territory of California. With the discovery of gold at Sutter's Mill in January 1848 and the resulting rush of forty-niners seeking instant wealth, California secured an inside track to statehood.

Because word had spread among the gold seekers that the central Sierras presented travelers with an impenetrable wall, the forty-niners either swept south through Las Vegas or north over Donner Summit. Just one errant wagon train attempted to cross Death Valley. An immigrant party with two wagons, however, entered Deep Springs Valley from the north. The travelers were out of provisions, but the Paiutes offered them food and invited them to lay over briefly at the lake to refit and resupply. An early winter marooned them, however, and starvation soon threatened everyone. When the Paiutes took stock of their dwindling reserves, they concluded they must kill their unbidden visitors to assure their own survival. After the bloody massacre, they buried the dead and burned the wagons. Wagon wheel rims, cooking pots, and tools that could not be destroyed were also buried to obscure the evidence. The secret was kept for decades until two curious Paiute boys asked their aunt about a strange metal object they had found. She grabbed it angrily, then reconsidered, and told the story from her childhood about the wagon party, the first "boxes on wheels" she ever saw, and the near-demise of the Deep Springs Paiutes themselves.[25]

Meanwhile, the Mormons, who had arrived in the Salt Lake Valley in 1847, claimed an expansive homeland for themselves. Brigham Young had petitioned Congress to create the Territory of Deseret, which encompassed much of the American West. This bold proposal incorporated almost all of today's Nevada, most of Arizona, a slice of western New Mexico, and nearly half of California, including a generous stretch of the Pacific Coast from Los Angeles south beyond San Diego. Deep Springs Valley and all the White and Inyo Mountains lay within Deseret's boundaries. This audacious "State of Deseret" existed as a claim for two years until, on September 9, 1850, Congress created the Utah Territory—a mere fragment of Brigham Young's plan. That same day, California became the thirty-first state to enter the Union. Deep Springs Valley was tucked just inside its east-central border.

Frémont returned to the Eastern Sierras on his fifth and final expedition in 1853–1854, approaching it from central Nevada across what was until recently the secret Air Force base Area 51. He traversed Lida Pass and descended into the south end of Fish Lake Valley. The explorers had become cavalier about recording their observations by this stage, making only sketchy notes, but they probably crossed Gilbert Pass into Deep Springs Valley (where their scouts would have seen signs of water) on their way to Owens Valley. If not, they followed a torturous route south, exiting Fish Lake Valley's natural drainage into waterless Eureka Valley, and then passing into and through inhospitable Saline Valley. There they would have scaled the Inyo Mountains to reach the lower end of Owens Valley.

Within five years of Frémont's passage through the area, two groups of Europeans began trickling into Owens Valley. Miners in search of gold and silver wandered down from the Comstock region near Reno, while others pushed up from the south.[26] Cattlemen, too, drove livestock into Owens Valley from both ends, drawn by the lush feed along the Owens River and the demand for beef in the mining camps. Both industries spilled into Deep Springs Valley almost immediately.

Prospectors began scouring the canyons and ridges of Deep Springs Valley, and land speculators developed a scheme to capitalize on the hubbub over mineral wealth. News of gold in streambeds (known as placer deposits) on the eastern slopes of the White Mountains enticed a group of miners to leave their prospect near Aurora, Nevada, in 1861. Among them were William Roach, Dan Wyman, James S. "Scott" Broder, and brothers Al and William Graves. They surveyed a town plat on Cottonwood Creek in the southwest corner of Fish Lake Valley, naming it Roachville. Across the ridge in Deep Springs Valley, they laid out a site for White Mountain City at the mouth of what was known as Wyoming Creek by some and Guymas, Guimas, or Clear Creek by others. The miners honored one of their own by casually changing the name of the stream to Wyman Creek for Dan Wyman. These towns were planned as outfitting stations for the miners.

Government officials organized the Big Springs Voting District for the residents of White Mountain City and its environs, and on August 16, 1861, just two weeks before the general election—at the "request of one or two signatures"—they established a polling place in Deep Springs Valley. At stake was a state senate contest between Joseph Cavis of the Union Party and Leander Quint, a Union Democrat. B. K. Davis, a Breckenridge Democrat, and Republican Nelson Orr vied for the new state assembly seat. When the ballots were tallied, Quint and Davis won.

The defeated Orr sensed foul play and appealed to election authorities. Returns showed 521 ballots from the Big Springs District, with only a single Republican vote among them. Noticing other problems, Orr decided to visit Deep Springs Valley. He found several people living on small farmsteads and a few prospectors at White Mountain City, bringing the population of the whole precinct to "only a handful." The situation screamed "rigging."

Requesting that they be seated, Orr appealed to the assembly and Cavis to the state senate. An official investigation ensued, but the ballots inexplicably disappeared in transit to Sacramento. One witness testified that, when he looked over the list of voters, he "was struck with the familiar appearance of some of the names, and finally ascertained that they had been copied from the passenger list of the steamer on which he had come from Panama to San Francisco." Both houses of the legislature concluded that the Big Springs election returns were fraudulent and reversed the outcome.[27]

White Mountain City limped along for several more years. Samuel MacVickar still held the office of mayor in 1864. That same year, Governor Frederick Low appointed a notary public for White Mountain City, and a former deputy surveyor of Santa Cruz County opened a mining agency there.[28] Even so, the town died an early death; few references to it appear in state or local records after 1864. Except for crumbling rock foundations and a rough stone smelter, White Mountain City passed ignominiously into history.

In 1862, a small band of Indians from Nevada began threatening miners in Roachville. Chief Joe Bowers, head of the Deep Springs Paiutes, interceded on behalf of the whites, but said he could not guarantee their safety. He urged them to move to a safer place, which they did. Bowers, who was born in Deep Springs Valley and lived there most of his life, befriended other miners, too. Known as a peacemaker in the region, he worked to avoid bloodshed between his people and the newcomers. He later served as a U.S. Army guide at Camp Independence. One writer said of Bowers: "He was no traitor to his people. They knew how he felt; he had explained to them his views, pleaded [and] warned and expostulated; and when he refused to fight, his . . . followers felt the moral excellence of the man, and respected his command."[29]

When an early and severe winter settled over the region, however, food became scarce. Some Owens Valley Paiutes helped themselves to the settlers' cattle. One rancher retaliated by killing an Indian who, he said, was driving one of his animals away. The Paiutes exacted revenge by killing and scalping one of the Graves brothers who had just left Deep Springs. Tensions soared on both sides, but good sense prevailed and both groups agreed to talk. Three chiefs signed a treaty with their mark as did a dozen settlers. At least two of the miners from White Mountain City—Dan Wyman and the remaining Graves brother—were among them.

One signature was absent, that of Joaquin Jim who headed a Paiute band near Mono Lake and had no use for reconciliation with, much less submission to, the white intruders. Hostilities broke out again, and a local war ensued. Captain Moses A. McLaughlin, a notorious Indian hater, commanded the U.S. Army troops stationed at Camp Independence. McLaughlin's men overwhelmed the remaining Paiutes in the summer of 1863. On July 11, they forcibly marched 1,000 of them in the scorching heat from Camp Independence to the

San Sebastian Reservation, near the abandoned Fort Tejon, two hundred miles south. About 150 died on the trail. Within months, most of the captives had escaped and returned to Owens Valley.[30]

The Deep Springs band did not share the fate of their Owens Valley counterparts. When they received word, apparently from Joe Bowers, that the soldiers were coming to get them, the natives stored supplies in a small cave on the mountainside about two hundred feet above the valley floor. The cave's mouth is so well hidden that one can walk within twenty feet of the opening and not see it. When sentries saw the soldiers entering the valley, the Paiutes hid in the cave. From their secure perch on the steep slope, they watched as the frustrated soldiers pillaged their stripped-down settlement.[31] Concluding that the village was abandoned, the soldiers left empty-handed.

Early in 1864, three miners named Crow, Mathews, and Byrnes staked a claim on Bitterbrush Flat in the northwest corner of the valley. They named their mine Cinderella and, by summer's end, had dug a sixty-foot-deep shaft that yielded silver ore assayed at seventy-five dollars a ton.[32] The three men were aware that a group of Paiutes, most likely the same Nevada group that harassed the Roachville miners, had been watching them. On friendly terms with members of the Deep Springs band, they were not concerned. But on the evening of November 1, Mathews returned to their cabin to prepare dinner. A Paiute man and woman appeared at the door and asked for food. As Mathews turned to help, the man pulled a pistol and shot him. The bullet entered below his temple and exited through his lower jaw.

Still conscious, Mathews grabbed his gun and fired as the intruders fled. At the mine, the attackers shot Crow and threw his body down the shaft. Byrnes, who had been working at the bottom of the mine, tried to protect himself as the Paiutes rained bullets down—wounding him in both arms. Finally, they pulled up the rope ladder, leaving him to die.

When Mathews was certain the intruders had left, he stumbled to the work site to find Crow and Byrnes. He could not call out because of his wound, so Byrnes assumed the footsteps above him where those of his enemies and lay still on the floor of the mine. Mathews could make out two motionless forms in the fading light and concluded that both his partners were dead. He started out for Owens Valley on foot to get help for his grievous wound. Mathews walked for two days before reaching the Owens River. While trying to quench his overwhelming thirst, he fell into shallow water, loosening the blood clot from his mouth and throat. Now able to utter sounds, he attracted the attention of a passing rider, who took him to a nearby ranch. His benefactors fed him through a cow horn and nursed him back to health, but he never regained intelligible speech.

Meanwhile, Byrnes passed a sleepless night in the mine. At first light, he heaped rocks on Crow's body as a makeshift grave. About mid-morning he heard footsteps above. To his relief, Joe Bowers peered over the cusp of the mine. Without a rope, however, he could not rescue the stricken miner. Joe poured some water down to Byrnes and promised that he would return with help. It took Bowers five days to walk to Big Pine and return. The rescue party hoisted the starving, dehydrated Byrnes to safety but left Crow's decomposing body buried in the mine.[33]

Water rights in the arid West were far more precious than land and a constant source of strife among settlers. In February 1869, James M. Sullivan claimed 160 acres "for agricultural purposes" in Deep Springs Valley about a mile below where Wyman Creek courses from the mouth of the canyon. He also filed for "five hundred inches of water of said Creek" where it flowed through his property.[34] Five hundred inches of water is about 42 acre-feet or enough to irrigate about forty acres of cropland.

On this site is a one-hundred-foot-square stone enclosure with walls four to five feet high. Curiously, a long "tail" wriggles eastward from the corner farthest from the only opening. Those who knew about this structure generally assumed it was a corral, possibly associated with the White Mountain City development. It appears to have been on Sullivan's claim, however, and some believe that he hired Paiute laborers to build the structure for his sheep operation. Sullivan also lined the irrigation ditch with flat rocks to prevent his share of the creek's water from disappearing into the sand.

Lt. D. A. Lyle of the ambitious Wheeler Survey Expedition traveled through Deep Springs Valley in July 1871. Lt. George Wheeler detached Lyle and fourteen other men from his main party to take a separate route from their camp in Meadow Creek Canyon (north of Belmont, Nevada) to Camp Independence, where they rendezvoused with Wheeler's main party fifteen days later. Lyle and his men were charged with inspecting agricultural, mining, and other activities along this route. In Fish Lake Valley, Lyle reported that "hay, barley, oats, and potatoes [were] being produced in abundance" in irrigated fields. At the south end of the valley, they found Piper's Ranch (later Oasis Ranch) to be "the most important one, perhaps, in the valley." It had several hundred acres of cultivated land, irrigated by the waters of Cottonwood Creek. He also noted that "a good wagon-road connects Piper's Ranch with . . . Deep Spring Valley."[35]

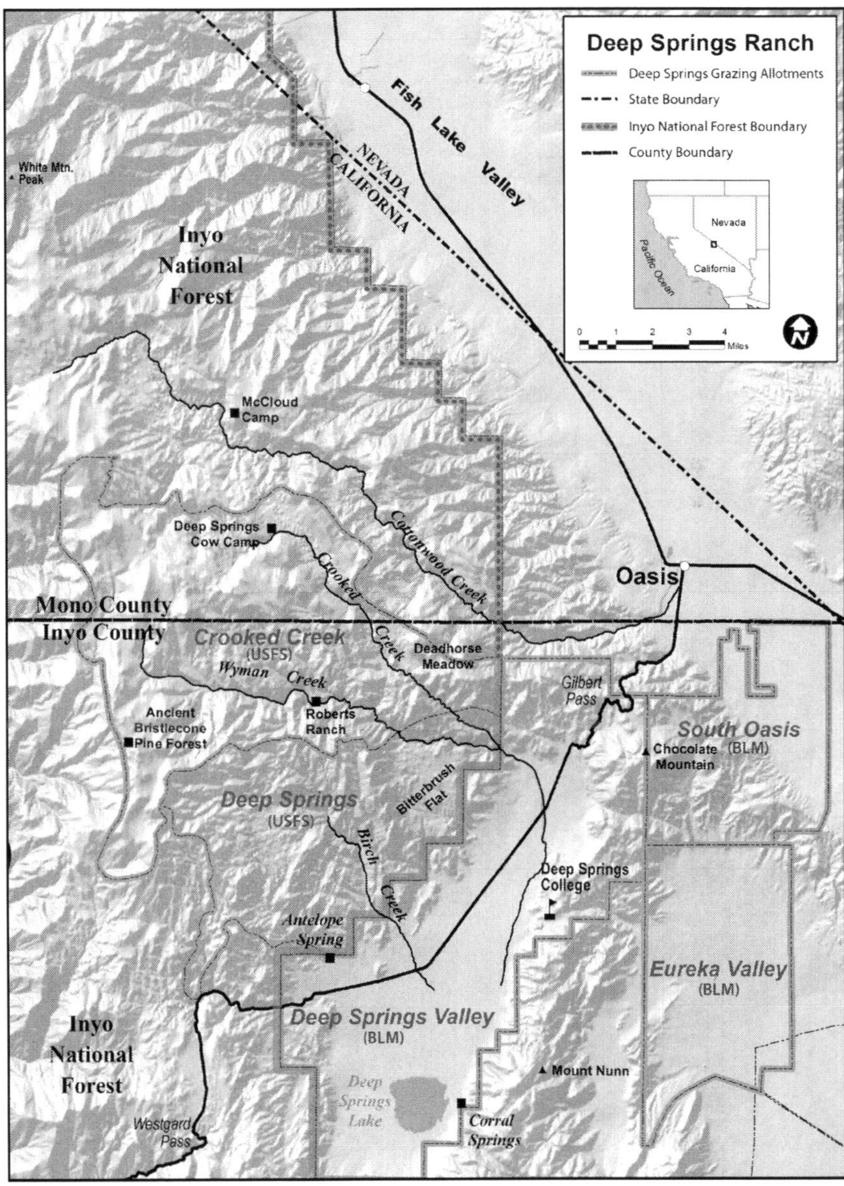

Deep Springs Ranch.

Lyle and his men crossed Gilbert Pass to enter Deep Springs Valley, "a small interior basin . . . inclosed [*sic*] by two spurs of the White Mountains which fork at the upper end of the valley and join again at the lower end." Around Deep Springs Lake, he noted "three small lakes, a salt marsh and several springs, some . . . being sulfur springs."[36] They found an abundance of grass around those springs, but observed that the "remainder of the valley is covered with sagebrush, growing in a deep, sandy soil."[37] He failed to mention Joe Bowers, his Paiute band, or Sullivan's ranch and ditch.

Lyle observed two silver-bearing veins along the western foothills of the valley. At a higher elevation, he reported a similar vein that ran on an east-west axis. The surveyors identified six mines in the valley—five active and the abandoned Cinderella Mine. They reported that miners had sunk a deep shaft several years earlier, but "were killed or driven away by the Indians." The other five mines were being worked with minimal to modest success. Most had not recovered their expenses, and none did better than to keep hope alive.[38]

One processing mill, situated by the ponds at the lake, operated in the valley. This five-stamp operation, run by Samuel McMurry,[39] had "one settler . . . and a smelting furnace which cost around $10,000 to build. It could process four tons of ore a day at a cost of $50 a ton." Lyle noted that the nearest railhead was 180 miles away in Wadsworth, Nevada, northwest of Reno, so shipping costs would take another big chunk of potential profits.[40]

Lyle and his men left the valley on July 14 or 15, traversing a "very good natural pass" which was not negotiable by wagons. A wagon road to Deep Springs, however, was under construction from the Owens Valley side of the mountain. That road opened ten days later, taking a somewhat parallel route north of Lyle's path.[41]

The need for a good wagon road had become more apparent as ranching and mining activities increased in both Deep Springs and Fish Lake Valleys. In the late 1860s, soldiers from Camp Independence had built a road south of the natural boundary between the White and Inyo Mountains. It probably joined today's State Route 168 two miles below the top of Westgard Pass.

On December 28, 1870, Scott Broder (one of the original miners from Aurora who had built White Mountain City in 1861), W. A. Greenly, and T. J. Hubbard petitioned the county for a permit to build a toll road between Big Pine and Deep Springs. The Deep Springs Valley Company would construct and maintain the road. With one hundred investors providing capital stock of $10,000, the three petitioners constituted the board of directors.

Two miles below the top of the pass, they blasted a new route through a deep V-shaped canyon previously blocked by a natural buttress of solid rock. Known as the Narrows, the new passage was just wide enough for a wagon to squeeze through. Although engineers would widen the Narrows slightly over the years, even today two vehicles cannot pass where the road slices through the rock.

Toll House Spring, 1916. Eastern California Museum, Independence, California.

The developers built a board-and-batten tollhouse at a small oasis two miles below the Narrows where Batchelder Spring (later known as Tollhouse Spring) provided a reliable source of water for domestic use, shade trees, an orchard, and a garden. A pipe carried water to an open concrete trough by the road.[42] On July 24, 1871, brothers Scott and Louis Broder began collecting tolls at this welcome oasis. A team and wagon could pass for a dollar, a horseman for 25 cents. Travelers also paid 50 cents for each additional draft animal, 12½ cents per pack animal, 10 cents for loose stock, and 5 cents each for sheep, goats, and swine.

On March 26, 1872, an earthquake, later estimated at 7.4 on the Richter Scale, devastated the region. It was comparable in violence to the San Francisco earthquake of 1906, though less devastating to life and property because of the thinly populated area. The epicenter near Lone Pine dropped a hundred-mile-long block of granite rock twenty-three feet straight down at the base of the Sierra foothills. It leveled fifty-two of the town's fifty-seven buildings, killing twenty-seven people.[43] The *Inyo Independent* reported over a week later that in Deep Springs Valley "one house was thrown down, and one person . . . slightly injured. This is much better news than we expected to hear from the place where there were a number of persons living in stone houses."[44] This would not be the last earthquake to shake the inhabitants of Deep Springs Valley.

That same year, thirty-six-year-old Irish immigrant Nathan Gilbert secured a patent on flat ground about four miles downstream from the mouth of Wyman Creek, now part of Deep Springs Ranch.[45] He also claimed the creek's waters for agricultural purposes, placing him at odds with Jim Sullivan. After ten months of strife, they agreed that there was enough water to go around. Gilbert bought half of Sullivan's share, enough to insure adequate water for his crops. At the bottom of the page recording the transaction is Gilbert's terse statement: "I hereby forbid all persons [from] interfering with or in any manner trespassing on my rights to the aforesaid water under penalty of the law."[46]

In 1873, just four years after staking his own claim, Sullivan sold Gilbert "two certain ranches with water privilege on Wyman Creek and Sullivan's Ditch" for $200.[47] Gilbert extended the ditch an additional three miles toward his main ranch, lining much of it with stone. A decade later, this water project appeared on maps as "Gilbert's Irrigating Ditch."[48] Over the last century, flash floods surging out of Wyman Canyon have obliterated any sign of cultivation that Sullivan may have done on his property. Portions of the ditch, however, and the crumbling remains of stone buildings still dot the area.

By this time, only twenty-three Deep Springs Paiutes still lived in the valley, with about a hundred in Fish Lake Valley and a thousand in Owens Valley.[49] The Deep Springs families wintered either along the eastern edge of Deep Springs Lake or at the mouth of Wyman Canyon. In mild winters, some also stayed in the area of the Roberts ranch farther up Wyman. The village at the mouth of Wyman Canyon had a sweathouse, and the group at the lake maintained another. These lodges had ceremonial uses, but they also served as general headquarters and doubled as dormitories when visitors came. The Wyman Canyon group sometimes hosted the annual six-day fall festival. At other times, the gatherings took place in Fish Lake Valley near Oasis.[50] Although Joe Bowers was the chief of the Deep Springs band, he was often absent from the valley, particularly during the Indian wars. At these times, the leadership fell to Joe's cousin, Big Mouth Tom, chief of the Fish Lake Valley Paiutes.

When Joe Bowers returned to Deep Springs in his later years, he and his wife scratched out a living on land they irrigated around Antelope Springs, still looking out for his Paiute followers. When smallpox devastated residents of the Owens Valley in 1876, Bowers grasped the saving power of vaccinations against the disease and sought help for his people. He traveled to Camp Independence where he persuaded army physician Washington Mathews to come to Deep Springs and "scratch" his people.[51]

Around 1878, Byrnes, whom Bowers had rescued from the Cinderella mineshaft, returned to Deep Springs and decided Antelope Springs would make a good home. The ungrateful miner ran Joe and his family off their land. Incensed, the chief went to Independence and reported the incident to his

Anglo friends there. Fourteen of them rode to Antelope Springs where they ordered the interloper to leave, threatening his life if he returned. The men also made a pact to provide Joe with the supplies he and his family needed to augment his monthly six-dollar pension as an army scout. They lived up to their promise.[52] The run-in with Byrnes prompted Joe to file a legal claim on Antelope Springs.[53]

About this time, John B. Hiskey and several partners founded the Lida Milling and Mining Company that operated near the boomtown of Lida, thirty-five miles east of Deep Springs. Their mines produced rich ore, but there were no mills close by to process it. They began looking elsewhere for milling opportunities and found them in Deep Springs Valley. They leased the water-powered mill at the old White Mountain City site from the failing Deep Springs Mining and Milling Company and hauled their ore to it using heavy-duty wagons pulled by twenty-two-mule teams. The first month of milling produced $6,000 in bullion. To accommodate an increasing ore supply, Hiskey installed a 12-horsepower engine, which he scavenged from a steam-vibrator threshing machine. Still the mill works could not keep pace. When the lease ended, Hiskey did not renew it.[54]

Two circuit-riding preachers traveled the toll road from Bishop to bring religion to the inhabitants of Deep Springs Valley during the 1870s. Pastor Andres Clark had established a Baptist church at Bishop Creek, and Reverend E. H. Orne founded a Methodist church in Independence. They preached alternately at Gilbert's ranch to the dozen or so residents of Deep Springs Valley.

The 1880 U.S. Census identified Nathan Gilbert as an unmarried forty-seven-year-old with three miners boarding at his ranch. One, Lewis M. Payson, was a miner and married, but his wife did not appear on the record. She was probably at their home in Big Pine. Two of Payson's mining partners were also on the list, Morgan S. Byrne and Samuel S. Chalmers. Several other residents of the valley—all single males—were listed as miners. The census listed Joe Bowers, then fifty-two, as a laborer living with a forty-five-year-old wife. Instead of her name, the census taker wrote "Woman." A note by each of them read "can not read or write."[55]

In 1884, the *Inyo Independent* carried an article praising Bowers for his many accomplishments and sterling character:

> He has always, and does now, command veneration and respect by a force of character which at times . . . rose to moral grandeur. . . . To gracious courtesy he opens his heart with honest delight. [He possesses]

Joe Bowers, Deep Springs Paiute Chief (circa 1884). Eastern California Museum, Independence, California.

> great intellectual strength, as well as moral power. . . . Bowers moved among [his people] a towering and beneficent spirit, directing and caring for them with a fatherly consideration . . . and he has still a handful of devoted followers, to whom his word is law.[56]

Joe Bowers died at Deep Springs sometime after 1905. He rests in Big Pine's cemetery under a headstone inscribed "Joe Bowers, Indian Scout."

Lewis Marshal Payson arrived in California from New York in 1849.[57] In 1866, he appeared as a registered voter in Inyo County and again in Fish Lake Valley in 1871. According to these early voting records, he was married, five feet eleven inches tall, gray-eyed, and a machinist by trade. For a while he hauled ore at Cerro Gordo while his eleven-year-old daughter kept house for him. By 1879 he and his partner, Samuel Chalmers, were working the Trade Dollar Mine two miles northwest of Antelope Springs in Deep Springs Valley. The two men shared a cabin at Sam Spring (named for Chalmers), and renamed their mine Gibraltar.[58] He made "quite a fortune in the '70s," even though he lost it later.[59]

Samuel P. "Jack" Roberts started searching for riches in the upper reaches of Wyman Canyon in the late 1870s. By 1880, Roberts's ranch and "pottato" patch, located about eight miles up Wyman Creek, already served as a reference point for other claims. He developed the productive Index Mine on the ridge to the south of his ranch. This rocky backbone appears as Pine Mountain in various land transactions of the era, but it would eventually be called Roberts Ridge.

Roberts formed partnerships with a variety of friends and began staking water and mining claims on the western slopes of Deep Springs Valley. In 1880 alone, he filed ten claims on water sources, usually parcels of a few acres.[60] John Chastain, however, owned the major spring feeding Wyman Creek and ran a mine and mill there.[61] Roberts persuaded him to sell this spring, several mining claims, and part of his ranch for $12,000, "the ranch being in the vicinity of the old Pine Mountain mining camp and furnace near the spring."[62] This spring gushes forth about fifty yards down the canyon from the dilapidated power-line cabin and adjacent board-and-batten cabin known simply as "Roberts" today.

In the summer of 1881, Roberts built a diversion dam just above the departure point for Gilbert's ditch. Gilbert filed an injunction against him, saying that, for "a long number of years," he had been the "owner of and entitled to the use . . . of 500 inches of the waters of Wyman Creek." The court ordered Roberts to pay Gilbert $23.80 for damages. These long-time neighbors salved their wounds and resumed their peaceful relationship.[63]

Nathan Gilbert applied and received a U.S. Post Office permit on May 31, 1881. His fourth-class postal unit called the Gilbert Post Office survived only eight months. Meanwhile, he expanded his ranch acreage and mining interests. He had purchased James M. Sullivan's holdings on Wyman Creek for $200 in 1873, then made a whopping profit when he sold most of it in 1880 for $6,800. Over the next sixteen years, he acquired three parcels of public land adjoining his Deep Springs Ranch for a total of 277 acres.[64]

Jack Roberts remained busy mining, while also attempting to lure investors to the Deep Springs Mining District. He was encouraged by the Carson and Colorado Railroad's completion of a narrow-gauge line in 1884 that ran from Belmont, Nevada, across Montgomery Pass and down the Owens Valley to the north shore of Owens Lake. The train was nicknamed "The Slim Princess." The *Inyo Independent* reported that when the new rail line opened, S. P. Roberts had several tons of ore ready for shipment.[65]

Another *Inyo Independent* article that year carried the byline "SPR," no doubt Samuel P. "Jack" Roberts. It was an unabashed promotion designed to lure speculators to the Deep Springs Mining District. Roberts could have written this account of a trip from Owens Valley to Deep Springs without leaving his tack shed. He described a pleasant outing with companions. Their first stop was at Toll House Spring, where they found Mr. Ashmore to be "an agreeable and accommodating gentleman to the traveling public. . . . He can always spare a little hay and grain to the tired and fagged-out teams that wish to camp for the night." The trip across Cedar Flat and down Payson Canyon culminated with "a splendid view of a part of Deep Springs Valley, the center of one of the richest and most valuable undeveloped mineral countries west of the Rocky mountains, and within 20 miles of the railroad, free, pure air, healthful climate and magnificent scenery."[66]

Stopping at Antelope Springs, the mythical party treated themselves to "a beverage that Nature has designed for all living things." The enthusiastic SPR declared this site a perfect setting for a mill or furnace to process ore being mined nearby. Before the end of that year, the *Inyo Independent* reported that Samuel and Jonathan McMurry, father and son, had constructed a furnace at Antelope Springs. Further, "Payson & Chalmers [have] six to ten tons of good smelting ores ready for the furnace."[67]

From Antelope Springs, Roberts described the view east across the lake. Ponds and sloughs around the springs "swarm with ducks and geese and other waterfowl in the Fall, Winter and Spring." To the north and east of the lake lay rich meadows, promising "150 to 250 tons of first quality hay every season."[68] Three years later, Jonathan McMurry sold these 400 acres at the lake to Nathan Rhine for $5,250.[69]

From the springs, Roberts could also see a ranch about six miles northeast—a little more than halfway from Antelope Springs to Gilbert's Ranch. The road to it was flanked by sagebrush and abundant bunchgrass, excellent feed for the "sleek, fat cattle" they observed. This ranch straddled today's State Route 168 and ranged east to the midvalley windmill. In the late 1990s, the California Department of Transportation found remnants of an orchard and other lingering signs of cultivation on this site.

Roberts wasted little ink on Gilbert's Ranch, reporting only that "man and beast can be accommodated [there] with the best the country at present affords." He then resumed his narrative in Wyman Canyon at his own ranch, describing "a magnificent spring, the head of Wyman Creek." Scattered nearby were the remnants of the abandoned Pine Mountain mining camp with its smelting furnace, which "stands as a monument of by-gone days."[70]

The travelers continued over the White Mountains until they hit the Black Canyon wagon road on the western slope. There they encountered men with heavy wagons hauling logs—most likely from Bristlecone pines at that altitude—for use on the railroad. Descending Black Canyon, they returned to

Cabin at Roberts Ranch, Wyman Canyon. Courtesy of Denis Clark.

Owens Valley.[71] After this journalistic effort to boost interest in the area, Roberts busily acquired additional land and water rights, especially in Wyman Canyon.

Another settler, Edwin M. Crocker, started acquiring land in Deep Springs Valley in 1887, beginning with 440 acres on the north and east shores of Deep Springs Lake. When he died in 1898, apparently without a will, his son, James C. Crocker, bought the lake property at public auction for fifty dollars. It passed through various family hands, eventually belonging to another son, Edwin A., and his wife, Ida, who became close friends of Lewis Payson. In the meantime, George Payson, a Civil War veteran, joined his brother Lew at Antelope Springs in 1890. Younger than Lewis by six years and single, he was a machinist by trade.

When L.L. Nunn's long-time friend and confidant Charles Walcott traveled to the White Mountains to conduct field work back in 1894, he enlisted Lewis Payson as his local guide. The two became friends; and when Walcott returned in 1896 to study the Inyo Mountains, he again called on Payson's knowledge of the region.[72] Walcott was struck with the beauty of Deep Springs Valley and would later share his enthusiasm with L.L. Nunn.

On May 18, 1905, Nathan Gilbert sold his most lucrative mine, the Boomerang, for \$6,500 and the core of his Deep Spring ranch for \$8,500 to Amos W. Broughton, who immediately transferred the contract to W. W. Broughton (probably a son or brother). W. W. then assigned the property to the G. A. Lathrup Company.[73] Lathrup soon fell behind on its payments and Gilbert repossessed it. In the meantime, Gilbert had sold other Deep Springs properties to the Crocker brothers, Fred and Ed, for $7,000. On June 28, 1906, the Crockers also purchased the parcels Lathrup had defaulted on.[74] With this last transaction, Gilbert abandoned Deep Springs after nearly five decades, though his name lingers on the pass leading to Fish Lake Valley. The summit of Gilbert Pass affords a stunning view of the ranch he once owned in the valley he loved.

The Payson brothers mined and farmed together until January 1907. After visiting Lewis in Big Pine, George set out on foot for his cabin at Antelope Springs—a foolish decision given the weather, the twenty-mile distance, and the elevation of Westgard Pass. As he ascended the pass, one traveler offered him a ride, but he refused, replying that he had walked the distance many times. The next day he was found lying face down in the snow, frozen.[75] Lew Payson sold the Antelope Springs property to Stephen G. Gregg, then bought it back three days later for $1,000 as a life estate. Upon his death, it passed to Luretta Crocker, the three-year-old daughter of his good friends and the new owners of the Deep Springs Ranch, Edwin and Ida Crocker.

The Crockers kept the unified ranch property just eighteen months before selling it to Arthur L. Stewart for $22,500 on April 1, 1909. The transaction included not only the 560 acres of the Deep Springs ranch property, but 760 acres of pasture at the lake and 60 acres in the middle of the valley, totaling 1,380 acres.[76] In an odd turn of events, Lewis Payson sold the Antelope Springs land again, this time to Stewart for five dollars. Three weeks later, the Superior Court of California ruled that Payson could not sell the land to Stewart but that Stewart could buy it from Carrie Crocker, young Luretta's guardian. This he did.[77] Lewis Payson left Antelope Springs for the last time on May 1, 1909. He died a week later at the age of eighty in the Crockers' home in Big Pine. Payson Canyon above Antelope Springs, through which most travelers enter and leave Deep Springs Valley, bears the name of these brothers. But the death of the Payson brothers did not end the Payson family saga in Deep Springs Valley. Lewis Horton Payson, the long-estranged son of George Payson, was unaware of the sale of the Antelope Springs land and assumed he had inherited the property. Before he died in 1945, he willed it in good faith to his daughter, Mary Payson—setting the stage for a future confrontation in the valley.[78]

During this time, other interests were crowding Jack Roberts's Wyman Canyon enclave. On June 18, 1906, the *Inyo Register* reported: "At Camp Roberts two new electric power lines now pass over the ruins of an early smelter." These

33,000-volt transmission lines belonged to the California-Nevada Electric Company and carried energy from a hydro facility, Plant 4 on Bishop Creek, to the stamp mills of a mining operation near Round Mountain, Nevada. The lines snaked up Silver Canyon from Owens Valley, angled down Wyman Canyon, and then tripped across the north end of Deep Springs Valley, exiting over Gilbert Pass.[79] A company lineman would live in a cabin next to Roberts's place for the next five decades. When silver prices plummeted in 1893, Roberts had sold half interest in some of this property for five dollars. In 1907, he peddled other mineral interests to the Golden Gate Mining Company.[80]

After nearly forty years of speculating, mining, promoting, and living in Wyman Canyon, Jack Roberts sold his remaining interests in 1916 and moved to Bishop. On March 1, 1917, the *Inyo Register* published this account of Roberts's death at age seventy-nine: "For more than half of his life a picturesque character in the vicinity of Bishop, [Roberts] blew his head off with an automatic pistol. He fired two shots almost instantaneously and one of the bullets crashed through a neighbor's bedroom and nearly took another life."[81] The irrepressible entrepreneur's one-room cabin near the spring that is the source of Wyman Creek is still used by deer hunters, as a retreat for Deep Springs students who are seeking a few days of solitude, and as a way station for Deep Springs cowboys as they drive cattle to and from the summer range in the White Mountains.

Roberts's passing marked the end of a colorful era. From the time the first miners entered Deep Springs Valley, around 1861, until World War I, scores of other seekers followed. At least thirty productive mines turned a profit for their owners, with names like the Copper Queen, Druid Valley, Trade Dollar, Red Bird No. 1 and No. 2, Boundary Gap, Green Apple, Mollie Gibson, Snow Goose, Fountain Head, Index Hill, Bull Domino, Banner, and others. Gold, silver, and lead were the most lucrative ores. These abandoned mines are often marked by deep shafts that plunge straight down or by tunnels that snake hundreds of feet into a mountainside and branch into a labyrinth of passages. Remnants of old cabins, mine works, and abandoned equipment—even an occasional box of old dynamite—are still discernible on some sites. In addition, more than sixty-five prospects pock the slopes and ridges around the valley where the miners achieved nothing for their labors except blisters on their hands and dust in their lungs.

Inyo County records also show more than forty water claims filed on springs and creeks that drained into the valley. Some were for livestock and agriculture, but most served mining, milling, smelting, and domestic purposes. Many were claims on the same water. Between 1871 and 1884, six different people filed for rights to Antelope Springs; and between 1880 and 1914, over a dozen people filed on the waters of Wyman Creek—either the springs that fed it or the creek itself.[82]

The toll road between Big Pine and Deep Springs, labeled Highway 63 initially but later designated State Highway 168, became an important link between the Owens Valley and Nevada. Owens Valley citizens petitioned the county in 1909 to make further improvements on the road up "Gilbert Hill" near Deep Springs. A recently established weekly stagecoach run brought the rough condition of the road to the attention of passengers and public officials.[83] In 1913, the Inyo County Board of Supervisors purchased the Big Pine–Deep Springs road.

Another toll road soon opened, direct from Bishop to Deep Springs. It followed the Silver Canyon trail from the town of Laws, a few miles north of Bishop, to the top of the ridge (over 10,000 feet elevation), then descended through Wyman Canyon into Deep Springs Valley. In summer, it offered a shorter route east for some Owens Valley residents. But the road down Silver Canyon was treacherously steep and very difficult to maintain. Even so, entrepreneurs kept it open until 1921.[84]

These developments all fed into the ambitious "Good Roads" movement that began early in the second decade of the new century. The Lincoln Highway, conceived in 1912, became its signature project. Seeking to make transcontinental auto travel feasible for ordinary people, boosters scouted possible routes. Soon, using a colorfully written guidebook, a motorist could drive from New York's Times Square to Lincoln Park in San Francisco on existing roads—only half of which were improved. Running parallel to this development, the Automobile Club of Southern California (ACSC) proposed a "Bullion Road" to link Los Angeles with the Lincoln Highway at the central Nevada town of Ely. The toll road between Owens Valley and Deep Springs fit perfectly into the ACSC plan.

The projected route through Deep Springs Valley led east over Soldier Pass, easily the lowest point on the rim of the valley, only 500 feet above the floor. A U.S. Army contingent had blazed this trail years earlier and, to the uninitiated, it appeared to be a plausible route. But not only was the descent extremely steep, it also opened into one of the driest and least hospitable valleys in America—Termination Valley, later named Eureka Valley. This idea was jettisoned in favor of the existing route over Gilbert Pass.

In 1913, the year the Lincoln Highway was dedicated, A. L. Westgard of the American Automobile Association led a group of twenty-two cars carrying sixty-three people west across the United States from Indiana. The caravan's goal was to test a route to Los Angeles using existing roads. When the citizens of the Eastern Sierra heard of the plan, they persuaded Westgard to take the Bullion Route through Deep Springs Valley, entering over Gilbert Pass and exiting up Payson Canyon to Big Pine. He agreed. The locals were so excited to have this caravan pass through their area that they changed the name of the old Deep Springs Toll Road to Westgard Pass. Later some of those same citizens questioned the renaming. "We regret," one account stated, "that it has not retained its old name, 'Deep Springs Valley Toll Road,' or have been named to honor Major Harry C. Egbert who was instrumental in having it built, or Scott Broder, who actually built the road."[85]

The Midland Trail, a project of the National Highway Association, hoped to challenge the Lincoln Highway by building on the Bullion Road plan to link Philadelphia to Los Angeles. It, too, followed existing primitive roads through Nevada, wending its way through Ely, Tonopah, Goldfield, and Lida. After passing into California near the Oasis Ranch, the route zigzagged up Gilbert Pass. The 1916 guidebook described this portion of the route: "To the summit is about 3 miles, thence down into Deep Spring Valley by way of Deep Spring Ranch where water, meals and lodging may be had. The road now follows southwesterly along the western side of Deep Spring Valley, bearing to the right up Payson Canyon for the crossing of the White Mountains."

While the *Midland Trail Tour Guide* made interesting reading, the route never caught on. When the American Automobile Association got into the act, it opted for a route that skirted north of the White Mountains over Montgomery Pass. It became U.S. Highway 6, running from the tip of Cape Cod in Massachusetts to Bishop. It remains the nation's longest federal highway.

World War I quashed the highway boom of 1916, but gave birth to another kind of development. Lead and silver prospecting and mineral extraction picked up across the West. Demand mushroomed for potassium compounds used in the manufacture of gunpowder, glass, and soap. On the north edge of Deep Springs Lake, a potash and potassium nitrate salts operation owned by California Alkali (later the Inyo Chemical Company of Detroit, Michigan, and then Standard Potash), initiated dredging operations. By 1920, it employed dozens of workers who were housed with their families in five cottages, a bunkhouse, and a community center along the shore. Using a huge dredge, workmen constructed a two-foot-high dike and broad ditch inside the natural perimeter of the lake to impound incoming spring water and seasonal storm runoff in the marshes outside the lake. Once the lake itself dried out, workers began stripping

Potash Extraction Works, Deep Springs Lake, 1919. Eastern California Museum, Independence, California.

Deep Springs Ranch, 1916. Courtesy of Deep Springs Archives.

the minerals from the surface and processing them in a large building west of the settlement.[86]

An aerial photograph taken in 1947 shows the entire dike still intact, and a chain of artificial lakes around its perimeter.[87] The ghost of the huge barge-like dredge and the cement foundations of the structures are still visible in the crusted white salts. The dirt road over which trucks hauled the minerals across the valley to meet the highway leading to Westgard Pass was, and is, impassable during every spring and after storms in any season.

In the six decades since European Americans began settling in the Eastern Sierras, most Paiutes in the region adapted more fully to the emerging capitalist economy than those in Deep Springs Valley—with mixed consequences. The diseases inadvertently introduced by white settlers, together with the bloody "Indian Wars" of the 1860s and 1870s, decimated all Paiute populations in the area. By 1917, ambitious ranchers, miners, and entrepreneurs, backed by the earlier presence of federal troops, had prevailed in the Eastern Sierra culturally, economically, and politically.

Thus, four men—Joe Bowers, Nathan Gilbert, Lewis Payson, and Jack Roberts—shared the valley for nearly five decades, guiding it through the transition from native to immigrant cultures. They left enduring marks on its land and history while maintaining ties of mutual respect. With the passage of another century, their rich legacies have been largely forgotten, even though they set the stage for the unique destiny of this high desert valley.

In 1913, the year the Westgard party passed through the valley, the ownership of the complex of properties associated with the Deep Springs Ranch passed from Arthur Stewart to prominent Bishop resident Archibald Farrington. Stewart had bought the ranch from the Crockers in 1909. "Uncle Arch," as he was often known, was seventy-one and had been single for many years. He owned mines in Death Valley and a ranch in Owens Valley, but his new spread at Deep Springs was widely regarded as one of the premier hay and cattle operations in the Eastern Sierra. Farrington's mines were producing enough lead and silver to give him a comfortable living, but age was having its way with him.[88] He had known about the eccentric entrepreneur L.L. Nunn for some time. The little man had poked temptingly around Deep Springs Valley in spring of 1916 and had even tendered an offer for the ranch. With the United States being sucked into the vortex of war in the spring of 1917, it was time to rekindle L. L. Nunn's interest.

CHAPTER 5

DAWN AT DEEP SPRINGS, 1917–1925

Gentlemen, "For what came ye into the wilderness?" Not for conventional scholastic training; not for ranch life; not to become proficient in commercial or professional pursuits for personal gain. You came to prepare for a life of service, with the understanding that superior ability and generous purpose would be expected of you, and this expectation must be justified. Even in scholastic work, average results obtained in orinary school will be satisfactory. The desert speaks. Those who listen will hear the purpose, philosophy, and ethics of Deep Springs, for it will need no prodding from teachers or superintendents to produce superior results in all departments.

—L.L. Nunn

In June 1917, Herbert Reich sped toward Cornell University, parked his motorcycle in front of the physics laboratory, and dashed inside. His older brother there had urged him to consider enrolling a year early, suggesting that he might qualify for a unique scholarship. Herb went to Telluride House, liked what he saw, and proceeded to New York City for an interview with L.L. Nunn.

Reich found the sixty-four-year-old Nunn more interested in talking about his plans for Deep Springs College than Telluride Association. The interview seemed to go well, and the two men, both physically small, saw eye-to-eye as they parted. Reich went home to Staten Island and wrote a required application essay on one of the following topics mailed to him from Provo, Utah, by Frank Noon: "Obedience vs. Initiative as a Basis for Compensation," "Vanity vs. Self-Reliance as Factors of Success," and "Tabulation and Graphic Expressions in Practical Life."[1] After submitting his composition, Herbert waited

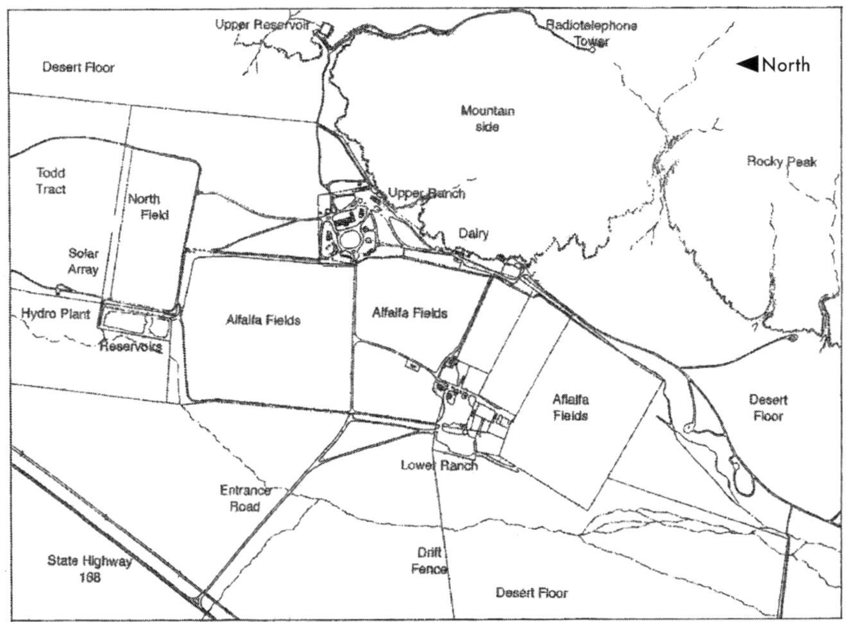

Ranch and Alfalfa Fields.

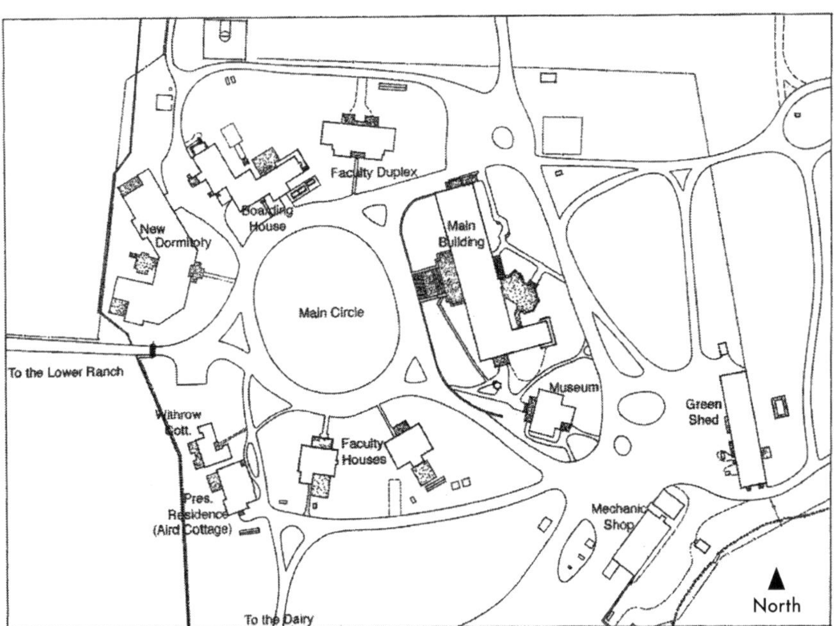

College Buildings around the Circle or "Upper Ranch."

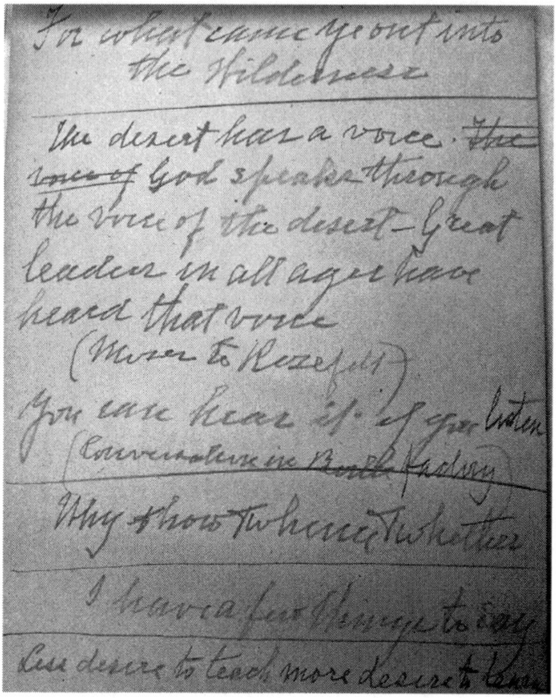
For what came ye out into the Wilderness

The desert has a voice. ~~The voice of~~ God speaks through the voice of the desert—Great leaders in all ages have heard that voice
(Moses to [illegible])
You can hear it if you listen
([illegible])

Why? Whence? Whither?

I have a few things to say

Less desire to teach more desire to learn

First draft of L.L. Nunn's often quoted admonition to the student body. Lucien L. Nunn Papers, #37-4-1770. Division of Rare and Manuscript Collections, Cornell University Library, Ithaca, New York.

anxiously for Nunn's response. Hearing nothing by midsummer, he resolved to settle for admission to Cornell University. With luck, he might live at Telluride House. Still, he could not get the romance of Deep Springs out of his mind.

Meanwhile, rumors spread that Telluride House was going to be closed, at least temporarily, and turned over to the university as an officers' club for the U.S. Army's military training program there.[2] But just after Labor Day, Reich received a telegram from Nunn inviting him to be one of ten students in his charter class at Deep Springs.

Wearing a new wool suit and carrying a single bag without so much as a blanket tucked inside, Herb Reich boarded a train in Grand Central Station and rode to San Francisco. He changed trains for Los Angeles, transferred again to the line running north to Owens Lake, and finally hopped onto the narrow-gauge Slim Princess that took him to Zurich—a railroad station on the Owens River two miles east of Big Pine, California.[3]

Zurich railroad station near Big Pine, California, circa 1917. Courtesy of Deep Springs Archives.

Original ranch buildings. Courtesy of Deep Springs Archives.

After a long wait on the platform, Chet Dunn, who had recently arrived from Claremont, rumbled up in Deep Springs' three-ton FWD brand truck, greeted Reich brusquely, and pointed to a pile of cement sacks. The two young men heaved the heavy load into place, and then Dunn astonished Reich by manually cranking the big engine to life. The heavily laden vehicle with its young driver and passenger struggled up the long, unpaved grade to the Toll House. They paid the transit fee, refreshed themselves and the truck's radiator at the spring, and then continued up the serpentine route to the summit of Westgard Pass. There, they tipped precariously down the long, curving grade that followed the dry streambed through Payson Canyon and into Deep Springs Valley. After the arduous mountain crossing, Reich's first view across the desert floor at twilight struck him as utterly stark and serene.

At the ranch, Dunn wished Reich happy birthday—he turned seventeen that week—and showed him to an unclaimed cot under the cottonwood trees by the ranch house. One of his new classmates grabbed a saddle blanket and tossed it to him. Reich drifted off to sleep, exhausted and exhilarated. The jarring reality of his arrival, though widely varied in detail, was shared by his classmates and would be echoed as a rite of passage by generations of Deep Springers all the way to the present.

Reich awakened to the stunning beauty of the Sierra Nevada Range across the hay fields, close-cropped from the season's third cutting. Most of his classmates were already there on neighboring cots, but all faculty members and Nunn were still in transit. Several board-and-batten sheds and a modest ranchhouse stood in the shade of the large cottonwoods. One small building with a tent attached served as the kitchen for two Chinese cooks, and the ranch house doubled as the dining room and community hub. A temporary office occupied another old shed.

The stone walls of the campus's spacious Main Building had risen to full height, but the rafters had not yet been set in place. With its low roof and spreading eaves, it was to become one of the largest examples of Frank Lloyd Wright–inspired Prairie Style architecture.

The college, even its physical plant, existed chiefly on drawing boards and in Nunn's mind, which was busily turning over a host of questions. Claremont had been a bitter disappointment. Would these students take his expectations and their responsibilities more seriously? And since the labor program at Claremont had never progressed beyond tree clearing, could he actually design an agricultural labor program to ground his educational vision? Could he attract outstanding teachers and build a sterling academic program in such an isolated place? To whom might he turn for on-site leadership to provide the adult models he believed his students deserved? Unlike his strategy at Claremont, Nunn intended to live at Deep Springs with its promising dry air as long as he could.

For eight years, Nunn gradually shaped his educational program, articulating his "three pillars": labor, academics, and student self-governance. The students during those early years were not only its beneficiaries but its cofounders.

Nunn captured his program's principles in his 1923 Deed of Trust and related documents, building on the ideas, responses, and participation of his

Upper Ranch around Circle, circa 1925. Courtesy of Deep Springs Archives.

early students. He set up his experiment in democratic education so that both his legacy and its participants would continue to shape it.

That first autumn, labor dominated the project. Stonemasons, carpenters, laborers, and the students swarmed over the site. The Main Building would house the library, classrooms, college offices, dormitory, guest rooms, post office, and a combination living room and meeting hall. Three other buildings were also under construction: a boarding house (with a large kitchen, butcher shop, dining hall, and living quarters for staff), a cottage for the dean, and a mechanic's shop. Wartime demands for military housing, munitions factories, and war machinery made building materials scarce, encouraging creative scavenging. All the structures, for example, were built of rough-cut local stone. The architect, remembered as "Mr. Leper"[4] (probably William H. Lepper of Salt Lake City and Chicago), initially provided general direction for Frederick W. Kropf, the superintendent of construction. Kropf, Nunn's trusted colleague, had built power stations and other facilities in Utah. His skilled masons and carpenters, also veterans of these earlier projects, provided a solid core of expertise.

In his rush to open the school, Nunn left them free, providing little more than a floor plan and exterior elevation for each building. No two buildings on the campus turned out alike in masonry, carpentry, or engineering, despite a general resemblance and common use of native stone.[5] Until winter slammed shut the building season, Kropf's team, working generally from April through October, took nearly eight years to complete the original ten buildings. They included a very large construction staging shed (the "Green Shed"), a second staff cottage, the dairy barn, a new ranch house, and a utilitarian museum and laboratory building.[6]

Deep Springs marks its beginning, not with the immersion in manual labor that began when students arrived in September, nor with the convening of classes in January 1918, but with the first official meeting of the Deep Springs student body. On the Sunday evening following Thanksgiving, having waited until their final member was in residence—Lucien L. Nunn himself—the body convened for business. "As time passes," he had reflected in an undated document, "I am impressed with the feeling that I should be a member. . . . Even though I may be older in years, I have a good deal more youthful poetry left in me than many of the boys."[7]

This yearning assertion expressed his largely unconscious compulsion to direct the course of events. With Nunn voting, the eleven men resolved: "That those present at the meeting constitute what is to be known as the Student Body of Deep Springs to be governed by Robert's Rules of Order."[8] They elected Ed Meehan, who had transferred from Claremont over the summer, as chair. The second order of business was to declare their purpose in language that did not have the ring of teenage voices: "To promote the highest well-being in harmony with the Creator."[9]

Meehan and Chet Dunn had been members of the Claremont student body. The remaining eight came from other Nunnian enterprises, were referred by L.L.'s Utah associates, or were fresh L.L. discoveries. Most were from the West. All ten had written challenging essays and survived face-to-face interviews with Nunn, their personal visions ignited by the promise of sharing that articulated by L.L.'s strong sense of mission. This initial class may have been recruited hurriedly and haphazardly, but Nunn called on his broad network of influential friends around Washington, D.C., to help him find promising students. The number admitted in these early years would vary from two to ten annually, but the total did not exceed twenty counting first-, second-, and the occasional third-year student.

Within a few days, Meehan wrote authoritatively to Dean E. A. Thornhill, who was not yet in residence: "Mr. Nunn has been here for a few days, and seems to feel that with the progress which has been made lately on the buildings and general work here, that we will very soon be in shape to begin school work. . . . In the light of these recent developments, it would seem that you will soon be with us to begin the year's work."[10]

One element of Nunn's program—isolation from social and commercial distractions—was not possible during the school's early years when construction workers outnumbered students almost three to one. So did farmworkers

Paiute "Captain" Harry in 1917. Courtesy of Deep Springs Archives.

Deep Springs Mary at camp near ranch gate. Lucien L. Nunn Papers, #37-4-1770. Division of Rare and Manuscript Collections, Cornell University Library, Ithaca, New York.

and ranch hands hired to perform duties that the students would soon be expected to master and pass along to their younger peers. Nunn hired laborers from neighboring valleys and paid them the going rate of twenty-five dollars a month. Some were also members of a multigeneration Paiute family that lived in one of their traditional transitory encampments along the streambed about a hundred yards west of the lower ranch gate. The aging patriarch, known then as Indian Harry or Captain Harry, had a bad elbow from a horse accident, but he was still a competent irrigator and he tinkered at odd jobs. His wife, Mary, and one of their daughters provided kitchen and laundry services for the community. Nephew Joe helped irrigate the fields.

Beyond Deep Springs' perimeter, a score or more of lonely gold and silver prospectors picked and shoveled exploratory pits and shafts in the rocky hills around the valley. The potash extraction crew and their families clustered on the north shore of Deep Springs Lake.[11] The rough and dusty road from Deep Springs to Big Pine saw a daily procession of automobiles, ore haulers, supply trucks, and farm machinery. Deep Springs Valley was never more alive with human activity, nor has it been so heavily populated since. Fewer than two hundred people would not ordinarily constitute a crowd in a valley of fifty square miles, but Nunn lamented the busyness, and worked to reduce it.

Nunn targeted the potash extraction works for removal, especially after he learned that one of his ablest students, Herbert Reich, had been sneaking away in the evenings with his ukulele to serenade the foreman's daughter—seven miles away. The operation finally shut down for economic reasons in 1923.[12]

As students acquired the necessary skills during the first year or two, they replaced most of the hired hands on the ranch. That first autumn, however, deciding where and how to employ his ten students presented a challenge. Neither Nunn nor anyone else then at Deep Springs had braved a winter there. Local people had warned him, however, and he felt intense pressure to act quickly. Academic work could wait. Indoor kitchen and dining facilities must be ready before the stormy season, and his young scholars needed to be moved indoors from their tents. Students, therefore, worked on construction that fall, roofing, wiring, plumbing, and painting alongside the hired laborers. Nunn decided to pay his students $12.50 a month for twenty to twenty-four hours of work a week, the same hourly rate earned by his fulltime laborers.

Crews enclosed the library wing of the Main Building just before Christmas 1917, and students crammed themselves into the space designated for the library. They heated it with a hand-made wood stove fashioned from an old steel barrel and doubled up in beds for lack of space for more.

Over the holidays, Nunn's academic mainstay, Dean Ernest Thornhill, his wife, Lida, and their ten-year-old daughter, Virginia, moved into the lone faculty cottage. This cottage next to the Museum was designed as a duplex for Nunn and one of his sisters, possibly Ellen; but when she did not take up residence at Deep Springs, Nunn turned the cottage over to the Thornhills and developed a suite in the Main Building for himself.[13]

One professor arrived before New Year's. He bunked with some of the laborers in staff quarters in the back of the boarding house. Classes would commence in January. Students arose with the sun, no strain during the long nights of winter, but evening study time was essential.

The Main Building was completed early in 1918 and Nunn settled into a suite on the east side, next to the Main Room, or "Big Room" as students then called it. His quarters included a combination sitting room and office with fireplace, bedroom, and private bath. Over the next few years, he divided his time between Deep Springs, various Los Angeles residences, and a spacious rented home on Dolores Street in San Franciso where he avoided the summer heat.[14]

Although high-tension power lines snaked across the north end of the valley to a gold mine near Round Mountain, Nevada, Nunn opted to provide power with a diesel-fueled Fairbanks Morse engine and generator bolted to the shop floor.[15] A student was assigned to start it at dusk each evening by warming the glow plugs with a blow-torch, then jumping on the cast-iron spokes of the five-foot-diameter flywheel to set the engine in motion. This task terrified student Henry Hayes, who could all-too-vividly imagine his foot slipping accidentally through the iron spokes and pulverizing his leg.[16] Turning the machine off required only the flip of a switch, which cast the community into darkness at 10:00 p.m. After several years of struggling with this system, Nunn connected the ranch to the power grid—possibly because the potash works at the lake needed power and joined Deep Springs in the expense of tapping into the main lines.[17]

Initially the community used Wyman Creek water directly from the irrigation ditch for drinking, laundry, and bathing. The cooks used water from the same source for cooking and washing dishes; but after a student drank from the ditch below the stock pens and contracted typhoid fever, L.L. built a sand trap along the ditch about halfway between the mouth of Wyman Canyon and the highway. He piped it the remaining three miles to the ranch with surplus pipe that P.N. had found in the Nevada mining town of Goldfield. This was "the only pipe that L.L. could afford at the end of the war," one alumnus recalled. "It was a four-inch tin sort of pipe, quite thin, and it was shallowly buried."[18] Gravity fed water to the ranch with sufficient pressure to push it up to a large wooden storage tank on the hillside above the garage.[19] A student "water boy" cared for the system.

Maintaining the community's utility infrastructure has been a feature of the labor program from the beginning, providing an awareness of services and conveniences taken for granted by the general public. Freezing and thawing attacked P.N.'s pipes even before the end of the first winter, with students improvising ways to fix them. Nothing seemed to work well or last long until state-of-the-art redwood stave pipes bound with spiraling galvanized steel wire were purchased and buried deeper than the old sections. Once all ten thousand feet of the line were installed, the system served until the 1960s. Its gradual deterioration, however, provided problem-solving challenges for subsequent generations. Meanwhile, irrigation water continued to flow most of the distance from Wyman Creek in the open, stone-lined ditch that Jim Sullivan and Nathan Gilbert had built between 1869 and 1875.

The four buildings around the circle were heated by hot water from a central coal-fired boiler in the basement of the Main Building. Insulated pipes ran underground to circulate the water to radiators in the other three buildings. Nunn had to relearn the lesson of his early Telluride years, however, when the price of transporting coal from distant sources proved prohibitive. Pinyon pine was plentiful, so Deep Springs switched to cordwood cut and hauled from the White Mountains by local Paiutes. After their services proved pricey, student woodcutters assumed the responsibility with six or more assigned to the job in autumn and spring. During the severe winter of 1921–1922, Jim Holmes, by then serving on staff, wrote Nunn that a foot of snow had fallen overnight, the mercury hovered at twelve degrees below zero, and draft horses were dragging vehicles over Westgard Pass. Still, the supply of wood was holding up—"between thirty and thirty-five cords of wood for the furnace," even though none had been added since before a Christmas storm.[20]

Henry Ford began mass-producing farm tractors the same year that Nunn founded Deep Springs.[21] The high cost of powering machinery with gasoline at Deep Springs proved daunting, however, because the fuel had to be shipped in barrels by rail from Los Angeles to Zurich, and then loaded on the FWD truck for transport to Deep Springs. Nunn preferred using teams of draft horses that would "burn hay grown on Deep Springs' fields." Beyond the economics of his decision, he believed that harnessing and driving draft horses required skill, intelligence, and patience, quailites worth developing in students.[22]

Henry Hayes and Jim Mansfield later reflected on the talent required to use teams in all the work of "hauling, plowing, harrowing, cutting, mowing, raking, all those things that are necessary to the operation of the ranch."[23] Getting up early and going down to the corrals "on a very cold windy morning . . . to harness [the horses] was a rugged part of the working experience. The only trouble with the horses was that most of the students . . . were city slickers, who had never before seen a workhorse. . . . Runaways [by draft horse teams in harness] were fairly frequent. We had to recruit a whole new company of guardian angels to handle the situation, and by and large they did quite well."[24]

Ranch manager A. L. "Bert" Woodhouse supervised student labor at the outset, which also became an issue. The student body lobbied to elect its own "labor commissioner." Shortening the workweek from twenty-four to twenty hours and allowing a student to supervise labor challenged Nunn to shift the paradigm he had lifted from his power plant days.

Herb Reich, writing his parents during his third and final year at Deep Springs, captures the range of students' labor experiences and the difficulty of counting hours. His activities included overhauling two gasoline engines, irrigating alfalfa fields, chopping down willows to clear irrigation ditches, pitching hay, hauling manure, feeding cattle, wiring new buildings, running the power plant, herding cattle, pulling a cow out of a mud hole, and making shopping trips to Big Pine and Bishop for the community.

Gathering rock for masonry to build the dairy barn became another of Reich's jobs. For two weeks in February 1918, he and Merrill Wrench rolled rocks down the slope above the construction site. The two were so tempted by the prospect of sending a teetering car-sized boulder down the mountain that they fashioned levers from timbers, liberated it, and watched with delight as it crashed down the steep pitch and "ended its spectacular descent in the middle of the road" where it rested until the following June.[25] They finally had to dynamite the boulder, then dug holes to bury the chunks that were still too large to move. Soon after completion of the dairy barn, Herb served as one of two dairy boys whose "job consists of milking, separating churning, cutting meat and chopping wood."[26]

The academic program was the last of Deep Springs' three pillars of education to be put into place that first year. Curiously, none of the students remembered much about it in their later years. No faculty who had taught at Claremont the previous spring was invited west. Dean Thornhill, however, taught an English course while Paul Cadman "taught pretty much everything else."[27] As Nunn saw his full program begin to unfold in January 1918, he told the students, "The time will come, when it will be considered an honor to have been one of the first members of the Student Body.

. . . [You] are setting precedents for the organization."[28] It was those precedents that interested him most.

By autumn 1918, three professors were in place. Herb Reich wrote home: "In addition to the required Public Speaking and College English, I shall be taking Calculus and second-year Latin."[29] Public speaking and composition, Nunn believed, were essential to the preparation of future leaders whose precision and felicity of expression, like his own, would magnify their leadership potential. He attended public speaking every Monday evening when he was at Deep Springs but assigned Ernest Thornhill, the course's perennial teacher, the responsibility of critiquing the speeches. From 1917 to the present, public speaking is required of every student every semester, and writing instruction remains mandatory for first-year students.

By 1920, one semester's class schedule included twelve courses: science, great men/historical biography, English, public speaking, French II and III, Latin II, Spanish II, German, calculus, solid geometry, and elementary math.[30] This curriculum was heavy on languages and literature, strong in mathematics, and weak in science. The arts were completely missing. A tally in Thornhill's handwriting showed all eighteen students enrolled in the first four courses listed, nine in solid geometry, seven in Spanish, six in French, and the rest scattered thinly among the other classes. Only one student took calculus. A year later, courses were added in geology and physics, and a "General Lecture Course," consisting of two lectures a week, rotated among Otto Suhr (geology), Ernest Thornhill (philosophy of life), and three other faculty members whose lecture topics were not listed in advance. On his occasional visits to the ranch, trustee Frank Noon lectured on "Generals Grant and Lee."

Nunn found an ingenious way to supplement this lopsided academic program. The Chautauqua movement of the early twentieth century had brought major speakers, musicians, and culture to rural America, including Russell Conwell (who gave his "Acres of Diamond" speech at least five thousand times), William Jennings Bryan, and John Phillip Sousa.

Deep Springs' early curriculum featured a series of short courses, much like the Chautauqua program, offered by prominent scholars who would spend a week to a month in residence. Each would give a series of addresses in the Main Room and then engage the students in structured discussions. Many of these intensive courses on world events, American history, or political science were informative and stimulating, while the regular faculty framed continuing conversations around these lecturers, using their own assignments and class sessions.[31]

Six years into its existence, Deep Springs' academic program under Thornhill's direction and with Nunn's encouragement was attracting nationally prominent visitors to stimulate and inspire the student body. In 1924–1925, student George Lyon described this system: The lecture system . . . , of having a lecturer up here for a week every month, is being followed this year. In October we had . . . Dr. Flewelling, professor of philosophy at the University of Southern California, and editor of "The Personalist." His evening talks centered about the dramas of doubt in which he took up Prometheus Bound, Job, Hamlet, Faust, and Brand. . . . Our second lecturer, Dr. Klinberg, is head of the Department of History at the University of California, Southern Branch [now UCLA]. He is full to overflowing of his subject, believes in making history interesting. . . . The general subject of his talks was, the European background of American History.[32] Flewelling and Klinberg were both in the midst of truly distinguished careers.[33]

Nunn did not want the confines of the classroom or the ranch to limit the students' education. Acting on his suggestion, they organized their first motor trip to Death Valley for a semester break in 1918. Herb Reich described their hair-raising adventure in a light-hearted letter to his parents: One morning, "the truck went only a few feet until both left wheels sank up to their hubs in mud. It took us six hours to get it to firm ground. Shortly thereafter we experienced a sand storm with wind so strong that we could lean against it without falling. We spent the night only a short distance beyond the mud hole." He summarized triumphantly: "It is quite a thing to be able to say 'I have been through Death Valley in a truck.'"[34] This strenuous and unpredictable Death Valley trip was to become an annual event, invariably requiring wit and grit. A staff or faculty member typically went along.

Though pleased with this adventure, Nunn framed it in economic terms for the students. Careless treatment of vehicles and machinery had "cost more than $10,000 during the two previous seasons." By eliminating this "routinely accepted waste" of resources, the students could "spend more on instruction and educational work, such as the trip through Death Valley taken by practically the entire Student Body during the Easter vacation of 1918."[35]

Early on, Nunn realized that his personal fortune could not sustain the college, but he refused to scrimp on expenditures for aesthetics. From the outset, he wished to create a fine residential environment that would inspire students with lofty thoughts and fire them with pride of ownership. Midway through the first year, Reich wrote, "Three women arrived this week to do the cooking and waiting of tables. We got out all the china, silver, table-cloths, and napkins and are now eating in style. The food is much better and eating at covered tables in the new dining room is much more pleasant."[36] The student body further rose to the occasion by accepting Dean Thornhill's instruction "that every student must wear a coat to meals and especially to the evening meal and to come properly combed and washed."[37]

Returning to Deep Springs after Christmas on January 11, 1919, Reich wrote in a similar vein, "I was surprised to see the improvements. . . . The reception room in the Main Building has oriental rugs, tapestries, pictures, and fine furniture. It compares favorably with the living room at Telluride House."[38] Ranch work and desert living might be means to build ingenuity, endurance, and character, but for Nunn they were not ends in themselves. The aim was to build character and intellect, which also required art, beauty, and sensitivity to the finer things in one's culture. To lead with vision, he believed, his students needed to develop across the breadth of their potential.

Taking up Nunn's challenge of stewardship for their fine property, the student body established the labor position of orderly (janitor), soon added a second, and eventually a third. Problems persisted, stemming from constant "roughhousing" among the students and "chooching" (their own term for blowing off steam), as well as from deficient janitorial skills. Along with these duties came the flag ceremony, the twice-daily raising or lowering of the colors on the flagpole in the center of the circle accompanied by a student bugler trumpeting reveille and taps.

The influenza pandemic reached Deep Springs in the autumn of 1918. In less than two years, it would kill over 650,000 Americans and an estimated 50 million people worldwide. Students Cabot Coville and Harvey Gerry both caught it but survived. Deep Springs' Greek immigrant irrigator was not so lucky. Coville remembered later that he and Mansfield "were doing just everything we could for him, taking advantage of our temporary immunity and keeping him fully isolated. There was no chance of taking him to town, it was beyond consideration."[39] Instead, the two immune students isolated their patient in an outbuilding at the lower ranch and took turns nursing him around the clock. One day Coville "arrived to take my period with him but Harvey told me he'd just died."[40] Traumatic as this event must have been within the small community, it marked the limit of the epidemic's reach at Deep Springs.

Important in protecting the students' general health, no doubt, was their robust diet and outdoor life. In addition to their daily labors, the students set out on frequent weekend hiking and climbing trips into the White Mountains and Sierras, also exploring the valley itself on foot or horseback. As the weather

Students driving teams pulling Fresno scrapers to dig lower reservoir, 1919. Courtesy of Deep Springs Archives.

warmed in the spring of 1919, every Sunday afternoon the students harnessed a four-horse team to a Fresno scraper and worked on dredging out a swimming pool over ten feet deep and outfitted with a platform and diving board.[41] So valuable did it become for impounding excess irrigation water that the ranch manager commandeered it for farm use, while allowing swimming to continue.

Competitive sports also played a role in student life. The first year, Chet Dunn chaired the Student Body Football Committee that supported Walter Welti's request for five dollars to purchase a ball. The next Thanksgiving, the students divided along east-west lines and played without pads on an alfalfa field—the beginning of an annual tradition. In the 1922 game, Henry Hayes's left arm was "badly dislocated by a tackle by, of all people, Bob Aird," his future brother-in-law.[42] The always-serious Nunn chose not to make an issue of this annual event, but he did object with heavy-handed sarcasm when the students built a tennis court on the largest open space remaining around the main circle of the campus: "I am not objecting to any young man putting his entire heart and soul into playing marbles or jumping around like a monkey on a tennis court but . . . it ought to be possible to find sixteen or eighteen young men in this whole land who do not care for such things but are preparing to be trustees of the nation."[43]

Word reached the ranch in 1919 that miners in Goldfield had discovered new gold deposits, and prospectors in Deep Springs Valley spoke of their promising silver strikes. As a result, Reich told his parents, "prospecting fever has hit the school." He and Julian Steward lost no time in staking seven silver claims on Soldier Pass.[44] They mined nothing but stories that they would tell for many decades.

Julian Steward had another experience at Deep Springs that shaped his choice of career. He befriended and took a serious interest in Captain Harry and his family, the Paiutes who lived and worked at the ranch. When Harry died in 1920, his wife, Mary, led the family in the Paiute tradition of burning all his possessions and the camp itself. Julian watched with conflicting emotions—torn between respecting the age-old tradition and wanting to rush in and save the baskets, pottery, blankets, and implements from the mounting flames. When the smoke cleared and the ashes cooled, Mary left Deep Springs to live with her daughter in Owens Valley. Steward felt a keen sense of loss with their disappearance from the Deep Springs community, something that prompted him to became one of the twentieth century's most influential anthropologists. Many of the notable theories for which he became known sprang from first-hand experience with this Paiute family.[45] Steward maintained his ties with "Deep Springs Mary" or "Mary Harry," as she was later known, and returned to interview her years later when he conducted research in Owens Valley.

Julian Steward and Windsor Putnam completed their studies in the early summer of 1921, planning to continue their education at the University of California, Berkeley. They stayed a few extra weeks after classes ended to help with the haying and prepare for a final adventure. In late June, they packed two burros with their bedrolls, belongings, and supplies and set out on foot, leading the animals. For the next fifteen days, they snaked up and over the White Mountains, through the Sierra Nevadas, and across California's San Joaquin Valley to San Francisco, a distance of nearly three hundred miles.[46] Their memorable—almost symbolic—passage back to "normal" life set a standard that others would occasionally seek to match.

Leaving with a flair was one thing, but where did Nunn find such students in the first place? The majority were recruited from what he termed "high grade material" based on their high school achievements, prominent families, or a blend of the two. Some, like Chet Dunn, Herb Reich, Simon Whitney, and Julian Steward, were a product of Nunn's wide network of associates, including Telluride Association; but others arose from a particularly fruitful hub surrounding Smithsonian Secretary Charles Walcott in Washington, D.C. After the first several years, Walcott's circle of intimate associates, all with intense interests and expertise in the natural sciences, became known as the

L.L. Nunn on Main Building porch, 1918. Courtesy of Deep Springs Archives.

L.L. Nunn, seated center, with community on Main Building porch, 1918. Courtesy of Deep Springs Archives.

"Washington Twelve." Deep Springs quickly acquired the reputation as their sons' most desirable college.

Walcott had been devoted to Nunn's educational vision since they had met on a train in 1905. His son, Sidney, participated in founding Telluride Association, served as its first president, and played a prominent role in the search for the Deep Springs property. The first year, students from this Washington group included Carlyle Ashley, Sherlock Davis, and Jim Holmes. They were followed by Cabot Coville and Harvey Gerry the second year, and, in following years, the three Mansfield brothers—Harvey, James, and Robert—whose father was one of Walcott's close associates.

In addition to these well-connected and high-achieving East Coast recruits, Nunn also expedited the admission of the sons of old friends and business associates, such as Merrill Wrench, John Olmsted, Henry Suhr, and Robert Aird. Some struggled to keep pace while others proved entirely worthy of the opportunity. Robert Aird, for example, came from a prominent non-Mormon family in Provo, Utah. His father, John W. Aird, was Nunn's personal doctor, physician and surgeon for employees at Nunn's Olmsted Power Plant, and an investor in Nunn's Utah enterprises. John's wife, Emily McAuslan Aird, was a civic leader who later served two terms in the Utah legislature.

Young Robert apparently planned to go to the University of Utah like his siblings, but Nunn wanted him at Deep Springs. He interviewed Robert and one of his friends in the spring of 1921, but only Aird got the nod. Bob stalled, reluctant to go without his buddy. Tired of waiting, Nunn wrote his father in mid-August. "To get right down to tacks, I want Robert to go to Deep Springs, provided that it is the right place for him."[47] After enumerating the many reasons he considered Deep Springs the superior choice, he encouraged John to have Bob consider his points "carefully and thoroughly and then talk them over with you." Nunn continued: "We all know, that the spirit of the age is both commercial and materialistic. In that sense it is atheistic. Deep Springs is theistic, spiritual." He pressed harder, "Its purpose is the promotion of well-being, it is not limited to the well-being of a nation, or even of mankind, but to the sentient universe. It does not prepare a young man for the most effective method of strife which our commercial system demands as a means of success." Impressed by Nunn's high-flown appeal, at the eleventh hour, Dr. Aird persuaded Bob to try Deep Springs for a year.[48] Robert's life would be woven into the fabric of Deep Springs for nearly eight decades.

In addition to these common sources of student admissions, it seemed that every class included a student who resonated with Nunn personally. He welcomed them aboard with little regard for their scholastic qualifications. These students were rarely able to compete academically with their peers, but they were usually accepted as having a place in the community.[49] Occasionally the object of humor and dubbed "Top Boys" or "Nunn's Boys" behind their backs,[50] some of them grew beyond their initial status (about which they may not have been aware) while others continued to occupy an important place in Nunn's private life and personal legacy.

Two students illustrate this phenomenon. Bruce Simmons, who had come first to Claremont then helped secure Deep Springs Ranch, was a participant during the college's opening months. Somewhat older than the other students, he opted to leave before the student body convened in late November. Simmons "didn't have anywhere near the qualifications academically that others did," Carlisle Ashley recalled candidly, but he "was really much closer to L.L. Nunn than most of the other students. . . . I don't think this is quite a fair word, but Bruce was very solicitous, let's say, of L.L., but he had that kind of a nature anyway, so I don't think it was anything more than that."[51]

The second case was Wallace Cook of Salt Lake City, to whom Nunn granted provisional admission in September 1920. Two months later, Nunn dictated a letter to him about college business but signed it warmly, "Your friend, L.L. Nunn."[52] Before Cook returned to Deep Springs in the fall of 1921, Nunn dictated a short letter, "Come back as soon as you can. . . . I am just aching for an opportunity to beat you up."[53] Two months later, he wrote privately in longhand, "My dear Wallace: Just a Christmas greeting from your old 'pard.' Affectionately, L.L."[54] After completing his studies at the college, Cook served as Nunn's personal secretary until L.L.'s death.[55]

At the least, Nunn's multifaceted admission system assured that the earliest student bodies possessed cultural, geographical, intellectual, and other diversity. Nor were highly qualified candidates in short supply. "I never had so difficult a task to keep within the limit of the number we can take," he wrote John Aird at the same time he was pressuring Robert to attend in 1921. "I have had to reject many admirably suited to this place, . . . because of the great number of applications."[56]

From the beginning, students and alumni were keenly aware of Nunn's double—even triple—standard for admission to Deep Springs. Until at least 1923, the final selection rested on Nunn's personal choices; and although he often found superbly talented young men, his judgments were anything but systematic. Although the number of students never approached the ideal of "at least thirty carefully selected young men" that Nunn earlier envisioned, his admission system seemed to be working.[57] Within a couple of years, however, Nunn had little energy left for recruiting. The entering class of 1923 dropped to six, and then to only two in 1924. One was Henry Suhr, the son of his business manager.

A schism opened early between two factions within the student body. They labeled each other "the Brains" or "Do-gooders" on the one hand, and "the Roughnecks" on the other, signaling either their presumed intellectual savvy or practical know-how. Both struggled for supremacy within the student body and for Nunn's attention. The Brains, who were led initially by Ed Meehan and Chet Dunn, appeared to get the upper hand.

Cy Ross (DS'19), one of those pushed to the periphery as a Roughneck, later claimed that as Nunn approached death in 1925, he confided in him: "Cy, now that I'm coming to the end, I'm seeing that I trusted the wrong people, I wanted you to know it. See, Bruce Simmons and Eddie and Chet . . . now, they were good people, don't get me wrong, but the roughnecks . . .,' he said, 'it's taken me years to find out.'"[58] Although this second-hand statement was not completely coherent, Ross claimed that Nunn had finally realized that the Brains had "pulled the wool over the old man's eyes."

It is not clear what favors or advantages the Brains received as a result of capturing Nunn's approval; but in a small, isolated community, the mere sense of being in the inner circle would have been reward enough. Whatever the merits of Ross's recollections, schisms had started as early as Claremont and would surface repeatedly throughout the college's history.

Oddly enough, given Nunn's highly personalized recruiting, he preferred to deal with the student body as a group. But sometimes he could not refrain from meddling in the selection of student leaders. An example with far-reaching consequences unfolded in September 1922. Jack Laylin, Nunn's favorite student, had been given special responsibilities during his second year, including the coordination of student labor. Bob Aird, a year behind Laylin, had dutifully completed his first year without falling under Nunn's spell and had even complained to Nunn about mediocre classes and humdrum ranch work. When Aird returned for his second year, he let it be known that he would like to serve as student body president.[59] But Nunn persuaded Laylin, then entering his third year, to run for the office.

When word spread that Nunn was attempting to influence the election, the student body elected Aird in protest. "Mr. Nunn was quite upset by this," Aird remembered, "and I was called to his room that same evening. He charged me with playing politics and it became obvious that I was about to be the recipient of one of his most artful 'lacing down' outbursts."[60] Aird endured the outburst, basked in his duly elected position, and eventually came to revere both Nunn and Deep Springs. The competition with Laylin, however, prompted resentments on both sides that would reverberate through college politics for decades to come. Aird later claimed that Nunn created the student office of labor commissioner as a consolation prize for his defeated rival, but his chronology was off. Laylin had already performed those duties on assignment from Nunn.[61]

Student body politics and Nunn's ill-concealed preferences for his favorites complicated the most sensitive of Deep Springs issues—reinvitation. From the beginning, Deep Springs scholarships were awarded for one year at a time. Continuing membership in the student body rested upon positive reviews and formal renewal. Nunn eschewed this level of internal management, but he expected Dean Thornhill, Business Manager Suhr, and the faculty to make difficult judgments whether or not the student body accepted responsibility as part of its duty to be self-governing.

Wrestling with this dilemma as early as 1919, student Jim Holmes appealed to Nunn for direction. Nunn responded immediately with guidelines. First, he warned, "the older and more mature members" tended "to 'eliminate' or crowd out the younger and less mature" ones because "the younger ones are not up to the proper standard."[62] This sort of dismissal, Nunn warned, "will never take place so long as I control the situation"—a revealing statement in itself—because "youth, inexperience or necessity for special care will not be regarded as reasons for elimination. . . . Once started, there would be no place to stop until the number was reduced to one who thought himself superior to all the rest."[63]

Conceding the need for judgments, however, Nunn counseled: "The development of a desire within to do right is one, probably the most important of the principal functions of the student body. Do not attempt to correct too many small matters, do not nag."[64]

Here Nunn spoke in the constructive voice that he hoped would prevail in student evaluations. His patience with students' inexperience and irresponsibility shone through again and again, not only in governance, but also in other areas of college life. His anger and frustration might boil over one day, but the utmost equanimity would follow on the next. Beneath it all, he was animated by an almost inexplicable determination that his final strenuous effort would endure, knowing that these were the last students he could influence personally.

CHAPTER 6

THE VOICE OF THE DESERT

The few have often come out of the wilderness—the eternal silence of the desert. This is not a fanatic life of asceticism but a short season of preparation for the work of the few, the great work—the heavy toil of leadership.

—L.L. Nunn

At Deep Springs, the romance of desert solitude floats serenely above turbulent natural forces that can turn moments of quiet contemplation into life-threatening emergencies. Human inhabitants must learn to adapt and be patient, and young blood ups the ante. The "voice of the desert" beckons, but the need to improvise is ever-present where help of any kind is an hour or more away. When the passes are blocked by winter storms or the roads are washed out by summer flash floods, the community may be almost completely on its own for days or weeks.

One of the educational benefits of Deep Springs' setting has been the constant presence of practical problems that must be solved just to live in reasonable safety and comfort. The well, storage tank, and treatment plant must be maintained or the community is without water; the cows have to be milked on time twice a day or there will be no dairy products for the kitchen. When things break or go wrong, they usually have to be fixed without dialing a plumber or calling an auto repair shop. Even the telephone system must be maintained by the college itself and there is no back-up; cellular signals do not reach the college buildings.

These conditions dictate that staff members—for instance, the cook, the farmer, the mechanic, or the office manager—can achieve a level of respect that rivals or exceeds that accorded to the faculty. These employees possess skills on which everyone else relies for basic needs. An integral part of the social and cultural fabric of the community, they work in plain view, teaching and modeling for students the skills that they, too, must learn to fulfill their own responsibilities.

For students who arrive believing that their academic gifts equal universal competency, Deep Springs offers lessons in humility. When, for example, the ranch manager, astride a galloping horse, snags the rear hooves of a running calf with a lariat and brings the young animal to an abrupt halt, students' jaws drop. The rich and varied lives of many staff members also give some of them a natural wisdom that students notice. While this term did not come into use until after Nunn's time, it is perhaps no coincidence that the adults at Deep Springs later came to be known collectively as "the stafulty."

One such staff member was mechanic Martin Sachse. An immigrant from Germany, he apprenticed as a Mercedes automobile mechanic before enlisting in the German army in 1914. Rising quickly, he became a World War I bomber pilot, flying ninety-two missions over France before being shot down. He survived the crash and, despite serious injuries, saved all but one member of his crew, for which he received the Iron Cross. After the 1918 armistice, his brother Richard sponsored Martin's move to the United States.

Sachse recalled that a friend "introduced me to a real millionaire, a Mr. Nunn, who hired me to work and teach machine shop at his school at Deep Springs, a very good place for a foreigner because here I could take part in the classwork of the students and attend the lectures [in the] evenings."[1] He moved into a "cabin" beside the chicken coop and started work in 1920.

Sachse's work ethic was infectious, as was his thirst for knowledge. He enrolled in as many classes as his time would allow and mastered English with remarkable speed—owing, in part, to student Bob Aird, who said he taught Sachse English while Sachse taught him auto mechanics. His job, however, involved more than fixing vehicles. "I had charge of all the machinery, plumbing, heating and electrical installations, also the upkeep of trucks and cars," he remembered. "I liked the place, the people, my work and also the money I could save. . . . I was furnished room and board, my laundry was taken care of and I needed no car of my own."[2] At twenty-nine years of age, however, Martin realized that, if he wished to marry and have a family, Deep Springs offered bleak prospects. He resigned his job in 1923 and moved to Los Angeles.

After a year of frustrating temporary jobs, Martin met Kate Park. A nurse, she had served in France during the war and then worked with a health organization in Mexico. "It was about this time," Martin recalled, "that [I] was asked by Mr. Nunn . . . to go back to the school. Things were going badly there and he made me feel that I was needed."[3] Sachse bargained with Nunn. He planned to marry that summer, he explained, so he would consider the job only if Deep Springs built them a house of their own. Nunn agreed, and Martin proposed to Kate that afternoon. She accepted, and they planned a summer wedding.

Sachse returned to Deep Springs alone on January 4, 1924, but in a series of love letters to Kate, written between early January and the end of July, he provided an unparalleled portrait of student life and labors, communication and transportation, ventures into Death Valley, and institutional governance. Mail left Deep Springs on Mondays, Wednesdays, and Fridays. Martin posted letters to Kate at each opportunity.[4]

"Arrived at Zurich at noon yesterday," he wrote in the first of these letters, "and the stage took me over and landed here at 4 o'clock, shortly before sunset. Having had a hearty welcome, I took possession of my old dear little cabin, which [I found] in comfortable condition. Nothing has changed in the least up here." He would shortly remark, however, on his feelings about the spring branding of new calves: "The air is full of moaning of the new branded cattle. To me it seems cruel, to hurt these dumb animals in such a way for the sake of commerce which means dirty dollars."[5]

Later that month he lamented, "There is no loafing at all around here. Work outside until sundown and after eating, going to class or talking to the boys separately, writing letters and paying a little visit or receiving a visitor to our community. I have read hardly anything since I came up, and played the zither but once."[6] He wrote Kate about separate conversations with Frank Noon and Harold Waldo concerning the residence Nunn had promised for them. "The plans we have made in regard to our house are not altogether satisfactory [to these men]. The trustees are quite different from Mr. Nunn, but we will fix up a neat little house just the same. . . . You can trust me."[7]

On March 2, excitement burst from the pages of Martin's letter: "Mr. [Albert] Johnson came in last night [from his place in Death Valley] with three cars. . . . He brought with him his secretary . . . and an architect, a real one and a famous one, too." The unexpected guest was Frank Lloyd Wright, then fifty-seven, survivor of a sex and murder scandal in his studio, founder of the Prairie

Style school of architecture, and well known for such dazzling works as Falling Water, Unity Temple, and the Robie House. Sachse seized the moment and asked Wright to design the house that Nunn had promised him and Kate. "Mr. Wright has promised to send me some plans of modern, convenient little houses which would be constructed in harmony to this desert valley and have the features necessary for this country in regard to sandstorms, heat and cold."[8] Later he told Kate how Wright envisioned houses of the future: "lots of windows, little windows all around the walls, close to the ceiling for ventilation and light through reflection on the ceiling."[9] Wright began sketching a design even before he and Johnson left for Death Valley.

Martin was not the only one impressed by Wright's lectures at Deep Springs. Student Harvey Mansfield recalled that "Wright was bubbling over with enthusiasm at how his Imperial Hotel in Japan had survived the great Tokyo earthquake" of September 1, 1923, a catastrophe in which more than 140,000 people died. Other students thought Wright was so egotistical in telling this story that they learned little about his architectural ideas. Dean Thornhill's teenage daughter, Virginia, noted: "Frank Lloyd Wright . . . attended my father's evening Bible class and they got in a big dispute about something. . . . I can remember him with his cape, very striking character."[10] Nunn and Wright mixed it up rather vigorously as well, with religion being the point of contention.[11]

Albert M. Johnson had retained Wright to design a castle for him in Grapevine Canyon, with Death Valley Scotty, his old friend, entertainer, and huckster fronting as the prospector-who-made-it-big. Thus, it would become known as Scotty's Castle. In the end, Johnson's wife, Bessie, insisted on replicating the stucco walls and red-tile roofs that characterized Stanford University, her alma mater. Johnson hired another architect.

Just a month after Wright's visit to Deep Springs, Sachse accompanied the students on their annual Death Valley trip. He kept a daily log, which he mailed to Kate upon their return. It began: "Tuesday, April 1, got up at five, loading of bedrolls and canvases, breakfast at 6:45, leave at 7:30, one Franklin [automobile] with Mr. Suhr and his son and three boys [students], one Buick with [Wallace] Cook and four other boys, and FWD truck with myself, Don Falconer and the rest of the boys, I think 12, besides our supplies, bedding and other things," including 110 gallons of gasoline, 15 gallons of motor oil, and 70 gallons of drinking water.[12] They made fifty miles that day, getting stuck twice in the mud and snow on Lida Pass.

The next day, they threaded their way "over bad and sandy roads" through Grapevine Canyon where they stopped at Scotty's Ranch. "I was very much

Perspective for the Martin Sachse House, Deep Springs, California, 1924. Frank Lloyd Wright: © 2014 Frank Lloyd Wright Foundation, Scottsdale, AZ /Artists Rights Society (ARS), NY.

astonished to see Johnson's doings in Death Valley," he wrote. It will have "huge houses, an enormous garage, a boarding house with dining room for at least thirty people, a nice swimming pool, [and] one large two-story house with lots of windows and large rooms." Johnson was also building a residence for himself and Bessie, and promised to put up another for Kate and Martin if Sachse came to work for him. Martin declined. He explained to Kate about his disappointment over the Deep Springs house plan: "Mr. Wright never did send me a plan and it looks as if Johnson had told him not to [because he assumed I would be moving there]. We shall get along without him all right." Wright completed the drawings as promised, but Sachse never saw them.[13]

The Deep Springs caravan continued south, assisting other motorists with broken springs and stalled engines along the way. Describing that leg of their journey, Martin wrote: "Today hotter than h___ in summertime. . . . To watch the boys in their enthusiasm is a treat itself. Have had good meals so far. I'd never made a trip before where I did not have to work after we got into camp. Should like to do something, but there are three for almost everything that's to be done." The next morning he wrote, "We almost turned over. Went up a steep grade along the side of a sandhill when the whole bank gave way and the truck slid sideways down. Most of the boys turned pale, but then we built a new road for nearly two hours. You see we have all kinds of fun."[14]

The Deep Springs contingent proceeded through the town of Beatty and on to Rhyolite, finding a single prospector where twelve thousand people had lived twenty years earlier. With strong winds whipping a snowstorm down on them, they slept in the shell of the deserted railroad depot. After a good camp dinner, they generated their own entertainment with the "boys singing and playing mandolins, everybody happy." The snow was too deep to move the next morning, so the travelers laid over and were given better shelter in a church the second night. Continuing down to Furnace Creek Ranch the following day, they found it "inhabited by Mexicans and Indians, no white people," and savored a good swim in the mineral pool before an evening around a campfire "singing and playing, telling stories and jokes, [and] having a fine time."[15]

With trepidation, they approached Salt Creek Crossing about twelve miles north of Furnace Creek—a stretch of about "500 feet of mud and clay, like you never saw in your life." Unloading the truck, they began using it to haul loads of rock to build their own road through the sinkhole. Still, the truck repeatedly sank to its hubs as the students stuffed armloads of sagebrush under the spinning wheels. "More rocks, more sage brush, shoveling, pushing, pulling with block and tackle, four chains on four wheels and out we went about 4 o'clock."[16]

The trip continued in this fashion for several more days, eventually taking them south to Trona and then back through Owens Valley and over Westgard Pass. "Many hardships together," Sachse reported, "but beautiful scenes and deep impressions of the mountains and the desert left in our minds and partly on film."

By mid-summer Nunn had a simple board-and-batten house built for the Sachses with a volcanic rock fireplace in its living room. Set just south of the ranch house, it had a second bedroom where a corner porch had been planned. Kate requested this room. She wanted a bedroom of her own, she explained, because Martin often arose early for work and she didn't wish to be disturbed. Martin was perplexed but agreed.[17]

The couple wed in Los Angeles the first week of August 1924. After the evening ceremony, they boarded the train for Lone Pine, arriving in the wee hours of the morning. They switched to the Slim Princess the next morning, bound for the Zurich depot. Kate got her introduction to the high desert: "It was all freight cars except for one chair car with kerosene lamps, wood stove and ancient wooden benches to sit on. As we rattled through the desert . . . dust seeped in through the cracks in the windows and doors." Reaching Zurich, they "were happy to see the director of Deep Springs [Otto Suhr] and his 1913 Franklin."[18] Martin continued: "Before we settled down for good, we spent a week's honeymoon at a little shack [Roberts's cabin in Wyman Canyon] high in the mountains."[19] They remained at Deep Springs for six years, during which Kate bore two daughters. When the older daughter, Heide, approached school age in 1930, the Sachse family relocated to Kerby, Oregon.

In addition to the culture and conditions Sachse described, student body minutes reveal conflicts over internal and community issues ranging from "stamping out vulgarity and profanity" and lateness in getting to meals to marking laundry improperly and shooting guns around and toward buildings. Shooting nongame animals also became a problem along with "washing clothes in drinking water." Errant students were dealt with by criticism, censure, and the temporary suspension of their student body membership. Censure brought humiliation, but suspension placed a student outside the body politic. The student body elected a sergeant at arms to confiscate the guns of students who used them carelessly and reprimand others who practiced their roping skills by lassoing the ranch's pigs, goats, or each other. Sensing the danger, Nunn asked one of the carpenters to build a large gun cabinet in the Main Building hallway so that dorm rooms would be free of firearms.

At Telluride House, Claremont, and Deep Springs, Nunn consistently admonished his students to avoid alcohol and tobacco. He assumed students knew the detrimental effects of the former but explained in some detail what he believed to be the consequences of smoking. Tobacco "destroys the moral sense," he wrote, "the ability to reason clearly and correctly, and injures the judgment of the members in their life work."[20] What worried him most, however, was the element that had hastened the collapse of Claremont: the "social distraction" presented by young women in neighboring towns.

The student body soon dubbed this three-point code the "Isolation Policy," and it later became known as the "Ground Rules." In the beginning, however, it neither merited a name nor attracted much fanfare. While there was plenty of drinking and smoking among construction workers at the ranch, early alumni recalled that "no one smoked" among the student body, nor did they drink, because, as Herb Reich recalled, "It was illegal."[21]

Nearly all the students, however, dreamed of making contact with young women in Bishop. Nunn, who admired daring and improvisation, could tolerate some youthful rambunctiousness, but he drew the line at guarding the social isolation he believed essential to the success of his educational plan. "Last Sunday," the Student Body formally wrote Nunn on April 1, 1919, "we had as our guest Mr. Summers of Bishop." He "remarked that we had a wonderful place in which to hold a dance, and suggested that we entertain. He offered to attend to the bringing of our guests from Bishop in autos with chaperones."[22] The student letter continued, "No definite arrangement has been made, of course, and we are anxious to get your opinion of the matter." The letter was dated April 1. The students knew Nunn's love of British traditions, but if this was a joke he played along.

From the Hotel Westminster in Los Angeles, Nunn replied: "I have no doubt that your judgment as to the matter is the same as mine, namely that such an affair is not to be thought of for one moment; that 'entangling alliances must be avoided.'"[23] The dance did not occur, but the student body came back about a year later with a related proposal. Six students wanted to take the Deep Springs' Ford sedan to Bishop for Easter vacation.

This time, Nunn responded both thoughtfully and thoroughly. "I shall not arbitrarily veto the action," he wrote, "but to the extent that you respect my opinions you cannot but think ill of such a plan. You know how I feel about establishing social connections in towns near the ranch. You know to what extent I have gone in order to prevent such social connections." He continued, "I must find in the Student Body a more responsive attitude toward my views . . . if I am to have great confidence in the wisdom of your body." Nunn invited "those who feel that they must spend a part or all of their vacation in a town or city to come here or go to San Francisco. . . . I will give them a cordial welcome and endeavor to make their stay enjoyable and profitable . . . [but] I certainly cannot consent to the ranch Ford being used in any such manner as the request implies." His signature was very bold, twice normal size, and underlined.[24]

Nunn wrote again three days later. This letter revealed the anxieties he suffered over deep divisions within the country, the battle over the League of Nations, and the recent collapse of President Woodrow Wilson's health. "The ship of state is rocking in the storm," he wrote, "with insufficient and unstable ballast." He then responded to criticism "as to whether my membership in these two bodies"—Telluride Association and the Deep Springs Student Body—is "consistent with their general purpose and plan." His answer:

> I am a student; more than ninety percent of my time is given to progressive education; to the acquisition and utilization of knowledge. I am in absolute sympathy and living in conformity with both the purpose and the plan of those organizations. My every commercial interest is dedicated to their development. I certainly am eligible and I am loyal. Under the circumstances, it is proper that I speak as freely in reference to the conduct of any member of your organization as it is the practice and duty of you gentlemen to speak in your sessions.[25]

He continued: "The above naturally leads to the subject about which I wrote to you a few days ago. . . . Individual freedom of both thought and action is one of the corner stones [of Deep Springs], but individual freedom consists in 'forestalling restraint with self-restraint.'" Annapolis, West Point, and the "higher grade private institutions," he said, controlled students by rules and regulations, whereas at Deep Springs natural barriers coupled with student self-governance were expected to assure a purer devotion to lofty purposes. As for meeting girls, Nunn concluded, "Visiting in the surrounding towns should not be permitted and it is your duty in the exercise of the authority given you to control it." He signed with strokes only slightly less emphatic than those of his previous letter.

The student body responded the following week, explaining that, after several long meetings and by a slim majority, it approved the following policy: "Although the Student Body feels it inadvisable for the ranch to incur social obligations in this vicinity, it nevertheless believes that the execution of this principle can be most effectively handled by personal self-restraint. Through this self-restraint and through the check which the Student Body possesses in controlling the conduct of its members by individual criticism, the Body undertakes to keep the institution's local social connections within narrow limits."[26]

Matching wits with the band of promising young men he had chosen to educate for leadership, Nunn was not faring as well as he wished. The students had left loopholes to do as they pleased, individually or collectively, while trying to sound cooperative and hoping that their benefactor would be satisfied by their use of high-sounding terms like "personal self-restraint" and "individual criticism." Nunn was not beguiled, nor were the students any more comfortable exercising control over each other than they were in being managed by him.

Spring seemed to be the season for crossing swords and Nunn started early in 1921. For months, he had been irritated by student laxity in caring for the ranch's resources and in carrying out their duties. He assembled a list and, typically, the more riled up he became the larger his handwriting and the bolder his strokes. The words cascaded down the yellow sheet of paper in a crescendo of intensifying magnitude:

> Liberty, majority no right to arbitrar
> [control(?)],
> personal protection against
> majority
> Office Work
> Tools &c,

Three students prepare to fertilize the vegetable garden with cow manure, ca. 1934. Courtesy of Deep Springs Archives.

Roughhousing
No attention to callers
Trying to please instead of telling the truth
Care of books
Filthy condition of dairy[27]

Nunn had been making other lists that included mishandling the work horses, carelessness that resulted in broken wagon tongues and hay racks, broken hay forks, losing shovels and other implements, the misappropriation of college towels and linen for personal use, and disrespect for the buildings and grounds. "The control by the Student Body has been in many important respects worse than a joke; it has been a farce," he had written to the students back when the third year began in September 1919, "resulting not only in complete failure to broaden the conception of responsibility but, what is worse, has calloused those perceptions."[28]

The students smarted at these charges of personal irresponsibility. What happened between late September when Nunn prepared his missive and January 20, 1920, when they responded, is not clear, but presumably they held a number of formal meetings to debate the accusations. In a letter that has not survived, but which Nunn quoted in his response, they contested his judgment: "We hold that the student body as an organization is not responsible for equipment unless this responsibility and authority that goes with it, have been definitely delegated to us." Nunn, who was traveling, fired back four days later, addressing his letter to "Simon N. Whitney, Sec'y of the Deep Springs Student Body":

> Replying to your letter of the 20th. The student body must acquire authority by wise conduct. There are comparatively few instances in the world's affairs where authority antedates responsibility and control. . . . The student body is responsible for the conduct of its members and its members can and should care for the tools except where such care is absolutely beyond their control. The power to control is the necessary condition to moral responsibility.[29]

Apparently Nunn considered the subject closed by his dictum.

The next issue was a student resolution asking that the labor program be reduced to five days a week. Nunn was then in residence and his typed, three-page, single-spaced response encompassed almost the entire range of his perspectives on the student body's place in the scheme of things at Deep Springs. His opening salvo was quick and direct: "Your resolution assigns no reason for granting the request contained therein. Your request is denied."[30] He continued: "Your members came with the understanding that they possessed superior ability and purpose and this understanding must be justified. Average results obtained by ordinary schools will not be accepted as satisfactory at Deep Springs. . . . You are less anxious for the truth and more hungry for authority than any of your predecessors. The time has come to call a halt."

Asserting a dual perspective, Nunn described only two paths open to "intelligent beings": (1) devotion to the right, meaning "the well-being of the universe," or (2) "devotion to the self and . . . selfishness or self-interest," which is a "state of rebellion against the right, against moral principles, against the moral order of the universe." This dualism, he asserted, "favors no special creed. It is equally adapted to every form of theism and Deep Springs is a theistic institution."

The next two pages of Nunn's long letter contained his response to the students' claim that he had first granted them the authority of self-governance, then eroded that authority. After his harsh beginning, he presented a confession of pathos, obviously with the intent of triggering the students' feelings of guilt: "I am talked out, I have given you the very best within me and it has been disregarded." They had been acting like ordinary students, he charged, rather than the very few he had "selected from the hundred million people of this country as the best material out of which to make public servants and trustees of the country's welfare."

In the balance of this letter, Nunn pursued his thesis that power must be earned through the exercise of responsibility. When the students mismanaged the Boarding House, he had had to appoint a staff member to restore order. When dairy production dropped by half and the milk and cheese were tainted, the students also lost the right to manage it. So, what did the student body have a right to control?

> It has authority over the conduct of its members and the right to increase that authority to an absolutely unlimited extent. . . . It even has the right to see that wood be provided the cook without requiring her to tramp around and beg the one whose duty it is to see that she is supplied with it. . . . It has a right to see that four hours honest full measure of the time of each student is devoted [daily] to outside work.[31]

After rounding out a long list of other responsibilities over which the students could earn authority, Nunn stated that the student body "still has the right to regain all that control which it has gradually lost by reason of insufficient attention. It seems hungry for authority but its careless and inefficient exercising of it has brought about the present crisis." He concluded that "this criticism is not personal" but is directed to the Student Body as an organization." If the students will "recognize the necessity of radical improvement [and] will pledge their utmost . . . to meet the requirements . . . and request a reconsideration of the order issued last Saturday, their request will be considered."[32]

Within twenty-four hours, all seventeen members of the student body had signed the following statement: "We, the undersigned members of the Student Body, acknowledge that we have been at fault, and pledge our utmost endeavor to secure radical improvement and to meet the requirements of the purpose of Deep Springs, as opposed to self; and petition for a reconsideration of the order issued last Saturday."[33] Nunn granted the students' request for a five-day work week and student conduct improved, but he harbored no illusion of having achieved a permanent solution. He understood that such fraught negotiations were part of an important, natural process.

Dean Thornhill, already regarded as stiff and even prissy, also felt the sting of the students' restiveness. After eavesdropping on a student body meeting in the Main Building one evening in February 1924, Martin Sachse wrote Kate:

> Student Body meeting is not over yet and there is a lively discussion and almost a revolt toward the dean, who handed out the credits for the first half of the term. The credits have never been so poor before. The best boys have gotten only 85 points, while the lowest one, 50. . . . The dean explained that the scholastic work was not so unsatisfactory, but the general behavior [was]. Too much newspaper reading, Victrola playing, fooling around and other things which are improper for Deep Springs boys.[34]

Duels with the student body continued. Early alumni remembered Nunn dealing almost exclusively with the students as a body rather than with individuals. Carlyle Ashley (DS'17) characterized him flatly: "He was not a teacher."[35] He rarely engaged in face-to-face discussions with the student body or addressed the community as a whole, held a question-answer session, or even presented a proposition or complaint within the bounds of formal debate rules. Instead, he would write letters or memos—often long ones.

Was Nunn too physically weak to engage in the vigorous repartee so characteristic of his style in the bloom of his career? Had his ego become so fragile that he could not risk the embarrassment of losing an argument? Or did he choose to communicate in writing because he saw these manifestos and dicta as producing an enduring record of his ideas and expectations? Ashley was certain that Nunn's overarching purpose was to empower the student body as a self-governing entity.[36] But Nunn appeared deeply ambivalent about how much authority students should have in managing the college and ranch. On the one hand, alumnus Bob Gatje (DS'42) paraphrased Nunn's philosophy succinctly as: "Give young people more responsibility than they can be expected to handle and they will grow into the job."[37] On the other hand, if students did not handle their responsibilities well, Nunn punished them by withdrawing some of their authority.

The student position of labor commissioner is a case in point. Nunn had not envisioned or desired a student foreman (later called "labor commissioner") who would assign students to jobs and oversee their work, but he still accepted the students' proposal for it and appointed the first foreman, Jack Laylin. When things fell apart under Laylin's successor whom Nunn had also appointed, he minced no words in returning the job to the ranch manager. This cycle occurred at least once more during Nunn's life, leaving the student body without its own foreman when he died.

In writing about the role of the director of the college, while trying to recruit his prime candidate for the position in 1919, Nunn had stated:

> Deep Springs is not and cannot be a democracy. The youth and inexperience of the students require a guiding hand. A student body should be given much responsibility and authority and would be a great help to "The Man." This has been wonderfully demonstrated the last two years at Deep Springs. The students have had a keyed-up interest in affairs and have executed their trust beyond the accomplishments of any superintendent.[38]

The students, he continued, recognized "that the enterprise is for them and they have been frankly loyal to it," but cautioned, "They have always understood that they are acting under authority" of the director. It is not clear that the students shared Nunn's interpretation, given the mixed messages he had given them over the past two years. He was clearly shaping the picture of the college to attract the director that he wanted; but the letter shows that his sense of balance between adult control and student authority remained fluid—even contradictory—during his final years.

Whatever his capacity or style, Nunn was clearly working out his *modus operandi*, just as the students were adapting to the high expectations thrust upon them. Significantly, they did not seem to resent Nunn's moralizing or become bitter over his authoritarian spasms. They respected him enormously and sought to please him, but they also found relief from the pressure of his intensity through humor. They entertained themselves especially with wry references to the "MOU," their shorthand for Nunn's hallowed concept of the "Moral Order of the Universe."

Comic relief and occasional high drama defused community tensions and spiced ordinary routines. When Death Valley Scotty passed the ranch en route to Owens Valley, he unfailingly indulged his trademark egoism. Friends visiting Kate and Martin Sachse remembered that, when Scotty reached "the top of the ridge that separated Deep Springs Valley from Fish Lake Valley he would turn on a siren, [and] everybody on the ranch would stand by to greet him, for he always managed to come at meal time."[39]

Other travelers passing through Deep Springs Valley sometimes stopped at the ranch if they needed gas, radiator water, or emergency repairs to their vehicles. In the fall of 1923, three brothers drove in from Big Pine and created quite a stir. Weeks earlier they had made national news for a daring attempt to rob an Oregon train, the Gold Special, believing that it carried a half-million dollars' worth of the precious metal. They set their ambush and succeeded in stopping the train inside a long tunnel; but in their attempt to open the sealed mail

Death Valley Scotty at his castle in 1926. Courtesy of Deep Springs Archives.

coach with dynamite, they overestimated the amount needed and blew up the entire car, killing the federal employee inside. In the mayhem that followed, they shot and killed the train's engineer, brakeman, and another employee, then escaped into the mountains.

The three had been on the lam for many days when the sheriff in Big Pine received a report that they had been spotted heading up Westgard Pass. He rang Deep Springs to warn the community of their coming. Enthralled, the students watched the trail of billowing dust rise behind the car as it sped across the valley and then, to their amazement, turned onto the ranch road. Once inside the gate, the three asked casually if they could purchase gasoline and dinner. Knowing that the sheriff was assembling a posse, the students and staff saw the merit of accommodating the bandits and thus delaying them.

Harvey Mansfield and another student took the three visitors to the shop for the gasoline, which at the time had to be siphoned from a large barrel into a five-gallon can. When the brothers were looking out over the valley to see if they were being followed, the students put a half-gallon of water in the container, topped it off with gas, and poured the mix into the car's tank. After a nervous but uneventful dinner, the infamous trio got back in their car and set out for Nevada. They sputtered to a halt within sight of the college, then jumped out and dashed away, disappearing into the gathering darkness. The next morning, the sheriff's posse followed their footprints and apprehended the men near the crest of Gilbert Pass.[40]

Juxtaposed to the drama and intensity so typical of community life, the "Voice of the Desert" became the phrase that captured and idealized the experience of Deep Springs' isolation. Unlike the dramas that were constantly thrust upon the students, however, listening to the voice required a conscious effort to step out of the frenetic stream of events in the tiny community.

Students have always been drawn away from the ranch buildings to toss their blankets or sleeping bags on the sand for a night's rest under the Milky Way, to take a long, lonely walk at dawn or dusk, or to make room in their schedules for solo weekend hikes or camping trips, simply to drink in the beauty of their surroundings and ponder the life they wished to make for themselves.

A powerful attraction became the truly remote and enormous Eureka Valley sand dune, visible looking southeast from the ridge behind the ranch but accessible only after a day-long cross-country hike without a water source or by driving more than a hundred miles on primitive roads. Climbing the 650-foot-high dune by the light of a full moon, sliding down its face naked for long stretches and then sleeping on its flank in the warm desert air became a ritual savored and repeated by virtually all Deep Springers. For some, experiences such as these were primarily physical adventures, but others came to know them increasingly as opportunities for self-reflection or spiritual exploration.

This facet of education at Deep Springs College, of course, has been known by each student in his own way. Few, however, have passed through the school without being touched by the many hours or days they spent wandering in solitude. By whatever name, these respites have often provided a spiritual dimension or added an occasional life-changing epiphany for those who came to prepare for lives of leadership and service.

Did the place L.L. Nunn chose for his final project truly reinforce the educational recipe he had striven so long to perfect? It would be quite a stretch to imagine a better fit than Deep Springs Valley.

CHAPTER 7

IN PERPETUITY?

Deep Springs has worked very imperfectly. I have never been satisfied with it, and I hope that the Trustees will never be. But . . . I shall keep driving home to you gentlemen, even if it takes my dying breath, that the purpose of Deep Springs is the education of promising young men for unselfish service. The freedom of the student is the greatest means to that end.

—L.L. Nunn

As Nunn faced the nearing reality of Deep Springs without his leadership, his values seemed to crystalize, with some becoming more radical and others more orthodox. Among the factors shaping this process was an invitation from the editors of *Marquis Who's Who in America.* They wrote to "Professor L.L. Nunn" in 1922, wishing to include his biographical sketch in their forthcoming edition. He was not inclined to respond. P.N., however, was always eager to advance his brother's reputation and drafted a statement on his behalf. In forwarding it to L.L., he noted the brevity of the draft he had prepared and expressed the hope that his brother would not object "to the implied connection between Deep Springs and the Association."[1] P.N. explained that the proper descriptor for L.L. would be "lawyer, executive, capitalist and educator," but he had to choose the latter because Marquis's would list only one field.

L.L. Nunn reading in car, circa 1923. Courtesy of Deep Springs Archives.

L.L. rejected P.N.'s draft, wrote a short account in his own hand—ignoring the prescribed form and format—and sent it directly to the editor with a rambling cover letter. Nunn would agree to inclusion, he said, only because "some persons of importance wishing to learn of my Deep Springs work, with a view of securing for a son or friend admission to Deep Springs, might find it convenient to obtain certain data from your work." Telling the editor that he knew his submission was "entirely out of place," he enclosed the single paragraph:

> Education: The Cleveland Academy, Cleveland Ohio. Universities of Gottingen and Leipzig in Germany. Harvard Law School. I still am, and for twenty-five years past have been, a trustee of the Marine Biological Laboratory of Woodshole, Massachusetts. I am a member of the Board of Custodians of Telluride Association (Collegiate), Founder and Director of Deep Springs (Preparatory and Collegiate). Religion: Orthodox. Preference, Episcopal. Activities: Educational. Since retiring from active executive, legal, and engineering work ten years ago.[2]

Nunn did not appear to care that his submission was rejected. Even so, it reveals how completely he had abandoned his previous identity as an entrepreneur. In listing his religion as "Orthodox. Preference, Episcopal" he also acknowledged his conservative shift away from the unorthodox Christianity, even deism, of his early and middle adulthood. This movement had occurred gradually and did not seem to be prompted by a single event or insight.

Framed by the chain of events associated with the *Who's Who* episode were three elements of Nunn's final push: the rising conventionality of his religious sentiments, the growing forthrightness of his embrace of religious diversity, and an underlying desire that both of these values be honored by those to whom he would pass Deep Springs. These themes would manifest themselves in the founder's final efforts to set the course for Deep Springs beyond his own life.

At Deep Springs, Nunn provided the Episcopal *Book of Common Prayer* for Sunday services in the Main Room. Yet he hired Lutheran minister Ludwig Thomsen to teach in 1919; and in an era when both Catholics and Jews were regarded with suspicion by the dominant Protestant culture, Nunn remained steadfast in seeking to educate his students through an inclusive curriculum. In the spring of 1922, he called at the Santa Barbara home of prominent Catholic theologian Thomas Ewing Sherman. Sherman later recorded: "[He] invited me to give some talks to the pupils of Deep Springs," but "on my suggesting a few of my subjects, he tartly snapped, 'These are nothing at all. You are a Catholic priest,—I want you to talk about religion.' But your school is not Catholic, and you are not," came Father Sherman's reply. "That has nothing to do with it," Nunn retorted, "I invite you as a priest. Come and talk about religion." Sherman reflected later: "He impressed it upon me that he knew religion to be an essential element of education, and that the Catholic religion was a great one; though our country, as he thought, is not ripe to receive or accept it. Frank, candid, brusque, sincere he was in every utterance."[3]

Sherman lectured at Deep Springs regularly, and typically Nunn "gave me his own handsome suite of rooms, attended all the lectures, and made no comment of any kind. This was characteristic. He left me entirely free."[4]

After he attended Claremont and then led the entering class at Deep Springs, John E. ("Ed") Meehan returned to Cornell and completed his degree. Some Telluride members looked askance at Meehan's Catholicism and castigated Nunn for underwriting Meehan's education to become a priest. Nunn addressed the 1923 Convention by letter: "I have heard that criticisms have been made by a good many of the preferment [support] given to one preparing for the priesthood. Why, my dear associates, that occupation affords opportunity for the very highest form of actual service to mankind. . . . I beseech you to cleanse the Association from all spirit of opposition to such dedication of one's self." Concluding, Nunn wrote, "May the 'God of our Fathers' be with you. Your devoted member, L.L. Nunn."[5] Nunn's principled stand should have surprised no one at Telluride. Nearly a decade earlier, he had excoriated its members when they sought to expel Jewish music student Hyman Deutsch from Telluride House because one of the three arguments by which they found him an unworthy member was his race.[6]

The orchestration of college and ranch affairs was anything but smooth during the early years, partly because Nunn micromanaged but did it mostly from Los Angeles. Dean Thornhill showed little interest beyond the academic program. Nunn had also hoped to rely on A. L. ("Bert") Woodhouse, an early pinhead, who first managed the ranch. He and his wife lived in the new stone cottage west of the Thornhills. With no tangible experience in agriculture or education, Woodhouse appears to have had little effect during his few years at Deep Springs.

Otto B. Suhr, who also began as a pinhead, went on to graduate from the Colorado School of Mines in 1895. An engineer, he played a central role in building the Ontario Power Plant at Niagara Falls. At Deep Springs, he oversaw construction and managed the business side of the college, and he came closest to having general responsibility when Nunn was not in residence. Nunn appointed him director in July 1918, then let this title lapse, only to revive it—and then repeat the cycle.

The *Telluride Newsletter* printed a report from Deep Springs in 1924 which began: "This year, for the first time, we started out with a Director at the helm. Mr. Suhr . . . has helped greatly in coordinating the different branches of the work here."[7] The fact that the report's author was Otto Suhr's son, first-year student Henry Suhr, may have exacerbated the situation, but Nunn was clearly displeased by the public reference to the senior Suhr as "Director." His irritation revealed his own reluctance to surrender personal control, especially to anyone less than a distinguished progressive educator.

Nunn thought briefly about appointing his veteran assistant, Frank Noon. Noon was chancellor of Telluride Association (1913–1924) and did double duty very briefly as director of Deep Springs; but, like the other three, he failed Nunn's test for potential leadership. Indeed, Thornhill, Woodhouse, Suhr, and Noon were all bland compared with Nunn, and none had earned stature outside his realm.

Students regarded Thornhill as humorless and his wife, Lida, as domineering, although they liked the couple's preteen daughter, Virginia. They never warmed to Woodhouse and his wife, but respected the tall, gaunt, and reserved Suhr as a sturdy, practical man. Though firmly committed to Nunn's plan, he seemed preoccupied with prospecting in his 1913 Franklin automobile, eventually staking multiple claims in the Deer Creek drainage near Crystal Peak. Still, Suhr was an admired and interesting presence, though not an inspiring one. The gangly, neatly dressed Noon floated in and out of Deep Springs, failing to impress students or faculty.

To find a visionary leader for his students, Nunn knew he had to look further afield. Furthermore, despite his sentiments about democracy and liberty, he rejected consensus in favor of the "Great Man" model in which he, the first "Great Man," would be followed by a hand-picked understudy who would encapsulate his own virtues.

Nunn had expressed these concerns to Charles Walcott back in the summer of 1918:

> I wish you would come out and see this place . . . and tell me what to do with it before it is too late. . . . It should not be left under the Association for several years to come, at least. It should have three unusual men as instructors, and at least one should be more interested in the spiritual than the material, and certainly the guiding spirit [of the leader] should realize the emptiness of personal accumulations. . . . If I could only find the right man.[8]

Walcott said he was in no position to help. His youngest son, Stuart, also a member of Telluride Association, had been killed on the Western Front the previous fall. The senior Walcotts were still staggered by their loss.

Nunn, who turned seventy in the spring of 1923, had been wrestling with the succession problem for five years, but now a particularly "bad spell" with his health brought new urgency.[9] He permanently reduced his travel, rarely visited Deep Springs, and concentrated on two urgent tasks: appointing a board of trustees and crafting a deed of trust to serve as the governing manifesto for the college. Harold Waldo recalled that Nunn "felt he ought to have a separate organization," not linked to Telluride, but he "didn't want to incorporate because that [would] put it under a great deal of State supervision."[10]

Puzzlingly, there is no evidence that he tried to enlist as trustees some of the period's towering educators and intellectuals: Charles Walcott, Frederick Coville, Alexander Meiklejohn, even John Dewey, all of them healthy and active. "As so many strong men have shown," former Deep Springs president

Chris Breiseth would reflect, "there's a mixture of respect for people of real strength and independence as well as a reliance on yes-men. . . . L.L. had more than his share of both. He really was attracted to students who were strong and independent—who were leaders. He also had the Frank Noons and others who very much were there to do his bidding."[11]

In appointing the board, Nunn opted for loyalty over strength, tapping mostly those within his immediate entourage or family. They included the steadfast treasurer of his commercial empire, William Biersach; his business troubleshooter, Frank Noon; the veteran dean of his educational endeavors since the Telluride Institute at Olmsted, Ernest Thornhill; his business manager and construction supervisor, Otto B. Suhr; University of California economics professor (who began his career teaching at Deep Springs) and officer of the San Francisco Stock Exchange, Paul F. Cadman; his nephew and upstate New York attorney, Carroll N. Whitman; his brother and business partner, Paul Nunn; and his legal counsel since 1911, Harold R. Waldo of Salt Lake City.

Nunn obviously sought balance, choosing two educators (Cadman and Thornhill), two lawyers (Waldo and Whitman), two engineers (P.N. Nunn and Suhr), and two businessmen and financiers (Biersach and Noon). Oddly, he appointed them for life. Did he lack confidence in the college's long-term prospects? Did he wish to lock in a weak board? He may have thought that an "Articles of Confederation" strategy would prevent anyone from aggregating enough power to corrupt his plan.

Alone among the eight, Waldo combined the qualities of unimpeachable integrity, high professionalism, and widely recognized competence with a pure dedication to L.L. Nunn's educational methods and ideals.[12] Inexplicably, none had contributed in any way to the vigorous national conversation about educational reform that had consumed Nunn. Only Cadman had academic credibility, and only Waldo enjoyed Nunn's unreserved respect. From the outset—and this was revolutionary—the ninth member of the board was to be a representative elected by the Student Body.

Nunn assembled a quorum of this group—those available in Los Angeles—on the evening of May 15, 1923. (Absent were Cadman, P.N. Nunn, Whitman, and the Student Body representative.) He presented a six-page draft of his trust instrument for Deep Springs, enumerating six terms and conditions. He had framed the constitution for Telluride Association, so his experience and ideas shone through, but Waldo crafted the legal framework and provided most of the language. Recent alumnus and future American diplomat Cabot Coville (DS'18), then serving as Nunn's personal secretary, did much of the legwork.

The group elected temporary officers, after which Harold Waldo read the Deed of Trust draft aloud. The new board approved it unanimously and witnessed Nunn's signature.[13] Without fanfare, they then arranged for the orderly conclusion of Deep Springs' academic year, assigned Biersach to attend to finances, noted a problem with the mail route, and adjourned the meeting. With the acceptance of this unrecorded deed, the real property of the ranch and college, and the responsibility to manage the institution, now rested in the trustees' hands.

Waldo had the Deed of Trust vetted by the law firm of Chickering and Gregory in San Francisco to assure conformity with California law.[14] When the board convened again on June 25 in Provo, Utah, Nunn did not attend, taking the position that he was an "advisor" only.

He was very much present, however, in a letter that Waldo had instructions to read aloud to the board. One item of business Nunn dealt with firmly—dispatching rumors that his grant of authority was revocable. He noted that since the organizational meeting at his place the previous month "I am very much worse; that is, very much more uncomfortable and my brain very much more muddled."[15] He continued, "Let the trustees understand that I have delivered the deed beyond my recall." He also seized the opportunity to clarify his educational philosophy. After saluting Thornhill for his disciplined management of the academic program, he switched gears, cautioning that Thornhill

> is not a profound scholar in ethics, philosophy and spiritual work. Going further, I have never agreed with him that the best way to establish character was by stimulating and disciplining the mind in technical subjects. There is a field that such work does not enter. . . . I think the main growth of character has been stimulated within the Student Body. I hope the Student Body will always accept guidance but that no theorist or creed devotee will have the power to bully it. I hope the board will always protect the Student Body and that it will not leave the work of protecting it to any who may be appointed by it as instructors, executives, or general representatives of the Board.[16]

This philosophy of education harkened back to his prized 1879 essay, "The Moral Sense." His warning that the board was duty-bound to assure that "no creed devotee will [ever] have power to bully" the Student Body would reverberate in one of these trustees' minds—his nephew Carroll Whitman—thirty-six years later, and save the college.

Nunn's unease with his chosen board came to a head early, when they elected Frank Noon as chair. Writing to the trustees after receiving this news, Nunn announced crisply: "I told Mr. Noon when he was here that I was sorry he did not decline to be the president of the Board and that I hope he will resign in Mr. Waldo's favor at the next meeting. . . . Moreover, Mr. Noon's declared policy against my ideas of student authority make it particularly important that he should not be president of the Board."[17] Noon stepped aside reluctantly and the trustees elevated Waldo. This issue would resurface long after Nunn's death.

Attending the June 1923 meeting was Jack Laylin, the first student trustee. The board approved Nunn's recommendation that ten second- and third-year men be invited to return the following year, leaving room for eight first-year recruits in a student body then planned to total eighteen.[18] Three new students were admitted on the recommendation of Cadman and Coville with Noon and Thornhill finding the other five.

Two faculty members, identified in the minutes as Falconer and Knopf, received extended contracts, but the recently appointed ranch manager, a Mr. Osgerly, resigned. Board members expressed hope that alumnus Chet Dunn, a recent Stanford graduate, might come back to manage the ranch, but he declined. Doing business as the Deep Springs Trust, "the trust estate" arranged to deposit its funds in any of four banks on which Treasurer William Biersach could draw to pay operating expenses. Nunn promised to make deposits "in cash and securities."[19]

As the trustees considered a director for Deep Springs, they listened to Waldo's reading of Nunn's composition "The Man Required for Deep Springs."[20] The leader, he wrote, "should be a careful student of affairs, conservative and slow to make changes in the present institution, which has grown up during practically half a century and which is the embodiment of the truest democratic spirit." In addition to possessing executive and financial management skills, the director "should be a great student himself, finding much broadening . . . in the lives of men who have done things worth while. He should be a teacher from the abundance of his learning and enthusiasm, obtained from his own studies."

Rather than constantly residing at Deep Springs, the leader should frequently visit other universities, becoming "known as an educator and a writer and speaker on educational topics. He should return to Deep Springs and bring the best that he has acquired from the outside." These qualities, he concluded, should enable future directors to inspire students to develop "the highest type of ethical and religious character."[21] The statement incorporated many of the distinctive characteristics Nunn admired in Amherst's retiring president Alexander Meiklejohn.

Nunn's personal hopes centered on Lionel G. Nightingale, who had been centrally involved in founding Telluride Association and who had served as its president from 1913 to 1916. He had taken his leadership responsibilities seriously, conducting a comparative study of the "articles of incorporation, constitution and by-laws" of thirty-five of the foremost universities around the world.[22] He later served as a noncombatant army officer in World War I, assigned apparently to a nitrate production operation at Muscle Shoals, Alabama, which was powered by a large hydroelectric plant.[23] He returned to civilian life in 1918 at the rank of captain.

Nunn immediately offered him an invitation to become Deep Springs' director. He sent Nightingale an early draft of his "The Man Required for Deep Springs" and encouraged him to spend several weeks at the ranch to steep himself in the program. Nightingale did not visit or show much interest, but his Telluride credentials kept future trustees interested in him.

Nunn also tried to involve Morse A. Cartwright, an authority on adult education at Columbia University, whose scholarship would receive much attention in the 1930s.[24] Perhaps it was Nunn's failure to lure men of such caliber to Deep Springs that fueled his continuing criticisms of Thornhill, Noon, and others, but he also seemed blind to the difficulty of hiring an educator of real stature who would have to report to a board of much less distinction. Would an eagle come to roost in a sparrow's nest?

Between May and November 1923, Nunn worked diligently with Waldo to clarify and extend the already accepted trust document. On November 5, 1923, "The Deed of Trust of Lucien L. Nunn" became the college's legal governing document.[25] Many of Nunn's conditions would become hallowed principles, while others would take incongruous twists or become points of bitter contention.

The trust encompassed all college and ranch property including land, water rights, buildings, libraries, furniture, vehicles, farm machinery, cattle, horses, poultry, other livestock, and the registered "swinging T" brand. These resources were dedicated "to provide for and carry on educational work . . . for the education of promising young men, selected by said Trustees or as they may prescribe, in a manner emphasizing the need and opportunity for unselfish service."[26]

The eight trustees would serve without terms or limits; upon a member's death, resignation, or incapacity, a two-thirds majority of the remaining trustees "may appoint a suitable person as his successor." The only name given the school was "Deep Springs," but the board was empowered to adapt that title, alter the by-laws, and change other provisions "to secure the safe and convenient transaction of the financial and other [presumably educational] business of this trust."[27]

Unique for such a document, the students in attendance at any time were designated "the sole beneficiaries of this trust, constitut[ing] the Student Body, and are to be considered as the *beneficial owners* of all the property. . . . Therefore, it shall be the duty of said Trustees to accord the Student Body full right, power and authority of democratic self-government . . . including control of the conduct of its members and of the buildings used as students' dormitories and the power . . . to veto the dismissal of any member during the school year but not the power to dismiss any member."[28] These were and are unusual powers to be granted the students of any educational institution and they would be cited, tested, and contested throughout Deep Springs' existence.

As the beneficial owner, "the Student Body shall be entitled to appoint one of its members to act as the Student Body Representative" on the board, with full power to speak and vote in all trustee meetings and "be considered and counted as if he were one of said Trustees . . . except on matters involving the conveyance or transfer of . . . the property forming a part of the trust estate."[29] This exception recognized that students would be minors in the eyes of the law and could not legally transfer property. Nunn had explained to the students earlier that "you and your successors are the real owners of the property, the legal title to which is held in trust as a matter of convenience only, just as a minor's estate is held by his guardian until he has reached the age where the law assumes that he [can] handle it wisely in his own interests."[30]

Significantly, the unusual rights and powers granted to the student body were to be honored by the trustees in accordance with the "traditions and the ideals and policies . . . set forth in the correspondence and documents of Grantor." L.L. Nunn intended that his letters to the student body, in addition to the trust deed and other official documents, would become integral to the culture, lore, and traditions of the college.

During this period, Father Thomas Ewing Sherman thought L.L. "looked like [a] ghost, a shadow, a mere shell. [Still,] he would drag himself to the assembly room, fasten his eyes on me and keep them fastened through an hour's lecture, when I thought he was dying."[31]

The mile-high elevation of Deep Springs made it risky for Nunn to go there at all, and his presence in the community must have been something of a spectacle, even as its frequency decreased. Henry Hayes recalled that "Mr. Nunn always had with him at Deep Springs a large good-natured Swede named Olof Swenson, who served as nurse, valet, cook and dietician (Mr. Nunn always ate alone) and chauffeur. When Mr. Nunn was particularly tired or depressed Olof would pick him up and carry him from chair to chair, or to his car."[32]

Swenson often gave Nunn car rides up and down the valley in the evenings until he fell asleep. The road was unpaved and rough, so on the advice of an automobile dealer in Los Angeles, Nunn had purchased a 1922 Marmon Model 34 aluminum automobile, instead of his typical Buick, because its pneumatic tires were soft-riding. Even then, he asked that the tires be inflated only partially to make the ride even smoother. In her early teens, Virginia Thornhill occasionally accompanied Nunn and Swenson on these leisurely twilight drives. Years later, she would describe Olof Swenson as "Mr. Nunn's everything; he just took care of him like a baby."[33]

Nunn's pitiable physical condition swung his moods from temper tantrums to coolly rational moments. Bob Aird, as a student, once rode north from Los Angeles with Nunn. Angus McKay, Nunn's bookkeeper, did most of the driving. When the party stopped in Lone Pine for lunch, a solicitous waiter mistakenly assumed McKay was in charge. "It probably was a trivial mistake on the part of the waiter," Aird recalled, "but L.L.'s lacing down of the poor fellow was anything but trivial. He was an artist at it and . . . [the waiter] ended up in a most obsequious posture with much bowing and profuse apologies."[34]

For the most part, however, Nunn faced the reality of his condition with admirable courage and urged others to do likewise. He responded with brutal frankness to Lionel Nightingale's expression of hope for his improved health:

> I recognize the kindness in your wishing my recovery from my present sickness, but there comes a time in a man's experience when it is far kinder to him for his friends to recognize the seriousness of the situation and let him know that they recognize it. It is easy for those who wish to know that I cannot recover, that I am in reality a dying man struggling to adjust some matters before I go hence, so that the persistent purpose of my life is fairly protected. Wishes for my recovery have become nauseating. I am no coward, and with full realization of the awful solemnity of the change, I prefer to face it like a soldier rather than to attempt the hopeless task of escaping from it.[35]

Nunn confided in the student body early in 1925: "I am about to go hence, and indications are strong that Deep Springs will die with me and the most humiliating thought is that it will die before I do."[36] When he launched Deep Springs, Nunn believed he had the resources to endow the college in perpetuity. His confidence was shaken almost immediately, however, when inflation shot up over 15 percent in 1917 and stayed in that range for four years, followed by recession and stagnation of the U.S. economy during the final years of his life. The recession had made building materials and construction labor costs cheaper, which helped, but operating expenses climbed inexorably without compensatory revenue coming in from Nunn's investments. He was barely able to meet expenses; furthermore, when he died the cost of a director's salary would be added.

Nunn's personal resources were almost indistinguishable from institutional finances until the trust was approved late in 1923. By his own reckoning, however, it cost $40,000 to run Deep Springs for the academic year 1918–1919. Frank Noon reported expenses of $50,000 the following year.[37] These sums came out at about $2,000 per student, a figure Nunn accepted without either satisfaction or alarm. As the new trustees were taking hold four years later, they estimated income and expenses for fiscal 1923–1924 at $40,000. Income collected from Deep Springs securities would total $43,800 for that period, yielding a modest surplus.[38] Appropriations for the next fiscal year, Nunn's last, raised the budget to $44,950.

Still no director had been appointed, nor did the budget provide for one's salary. At Nunn's apparent urging, institutional fund-raising began. Fat envelopes bearing the greeting, "Merry Christmas, Compliments of Deep Springs, 1924," went out to friends of the college. They included eight student poems and essays and an artistic photograph of Yosemite taken on a student trip that autumn.[39] This effort apparently netted little beyond good will.

Only months before he died, Nunn personally directed what his colleagues described as a brilliant business transaction to sell the last of his electric utilities, the Natrona Power Company, a diesel-powered unit west of Casper, Wyoming. This action added perhaps several hundred thousand dollars in cash to his coffers, $221,000 of which apparently further endowed Deep Springs. It also liberated as much as $550,000 in Telluride-owned Natrona stock for the association's direct management.[40]

Nunn now called upon Telluride Association to assist Deep Springs. This matter was dicey because he had openly blamed Telluride Association members for the Claremont failure. For their part, Telluride leaders believed Nunn had been too free with their money in trying to make Claremont work.[41] This conflict had prompted Nunn to proceed alone in buying Deep Springs ranch and launching the college.

Nunn, however, had been motivated by more than pique. He had earlier told Lionel Nightingale that "Deep Springs should be the real institution—Telluride Association a graduate school, perhaps mainly devoted to diplomacy,"[42] so that the college "should not be left under the Association for several years to come, at least." Also significant was P.N.'s tiptoeing around Telluride when he drafted the *Who's Who* entry. Although L.L. continued his interest in and personal dominance of Telluride Association, Deep Springs was clearly his consuming interest and he did not wish it to be subservient to Telluride. He did have a way of playing his two institutions off against each other, but the final nod went to assuring Deep Springs' independent governance.

Telluride Association responded positively to Nunn's fund-raising directives, no doubt wishing to accommodate its benefactor but also aware that it needed but could not afford to build its own primary branch. In the June 1920 *Telluride News Letter*, Carroll Whitman, who was serving as president of Telluride Association, summed up the situation as Nunn doubtless wanted it seen: "If we are granted the further co-operation of the institution at Deep Springs, we need not worry about a preparatory branch, for that is the ideal establishment for our purpose."[43] With this interest in mind, Telluride Convention voted $10,000 to support Deep Springs for 1920–1921.

After a couple of years off to sort out its own finances, Telluride resumed annual allocations to Deep Springs in 1923 and continued to support it at about the $10,000 level until the early 1940s. Underwriting what was initially one-quarter of the college's annual budget constituted a very significant tie, of course, and Deep Springs' role in supplying about half the members of Telluride Association endured for decades.[44] This *quid pro quo* proved to be very much in the interest of both Nunnian institutions in the early decades. It would later ebb and flow, but never fade completely.

L.L. Nunn was buoyed by the recent return of a bull market as he entered his final months. Also giving him hope were his successes in bolstering the endowment, securing Telluride's cooperation, and the student body's holiday mailing—even though its material contribution had been small. Now Nunn turned to final instructions for the student body. He wanted to make two things clear. First, leadership in the service of humanity should permeate the culture of the college. Second, he wanted to emphasize the spiritual dimension of his educational method.

Nunn finished writing this formal statement, commonly known as "The Purpose" but originally titled "Children of This World," on December 30, 1924. He began with a jolting elitist statement: "It is a fact of social evolution that the few always dominate. This is because the mass is dull-witted, sluggish, incapable.... Only the few have the vision of the Divine plan and purpose.... These forerunners, pacemakers, who anticipate progress perhaps by decades are those who break the trails and point the way."[45] What falls to them, he said, "is the burden of leadership. . . . the consciousness of the call," although "acceptance of the calling to be one of the few is half of the labor accomplished." Nunn continued, "The purpose of Deep Springs is to help in the training of the few. It is to create an environment where young men of sound character may find religious influence which will help them build the character for full employment in the service of their fellowmen."

Turning to the method for training his few, Nunn addressed the trustees in emphasizing the vital role of free inquiry in developing both the intellect and the spirit through study of "the Humanities, the Sciences and all human achievement." The still unappointed "Man for Deep Springs" would be a "Guide," charged with creating a rich environment for refining character, sharpening minds, and invigorating bodies. Reading "the great masters" was essential and "in all this the student is left to discover and achieve from within."

Earning academic credits for transfer should not be the aim. No student should have "uppermost in his mind the fulfillment of stereotyped academic requirements for entrance to a given class, rank, or grade of a university. . . . In fact, many may stay the maximum period with true loyalty to the trust and profit to themselves, without making a single unit." The aim was to avoid the materialism of the day by building "whole lives—not one-tenth, or one-half or three-quarters."[46]

If others were to inquire about what was being accomplished at Deep Springs, he admonished, "there will be no pointing with the material finger to a fortune achieved or to a mechanistic invention." Rather, "the few have always had an abundance of heart and out of that abundance they have spoken. The developing influence of Deep Springs should make . . . that abundance coherent, and should bring it to expression."

Importantly, Nunn buffered his elitist paradigm by stressing that the few must rise on the merits of their own capabilities and ethical principles. He simply wanted to find those with the greatest potential and groom them with his extraordinary methods. Less predictable was the breadth of his conception of leadership. It could be manifest in any walk of life. "The abundance of heart may be evident in the blacksmith as well as in the great preacher or master surgeon. But wherever the heart is abundant there will be a leader no matter how great or how small the following. And the blacksmith or the teacher or the surgeon who fulfills in himself the Purpose of Deep Springs will be a good blacksmith, a good teacher, and a good surgeon, even as Christ must have been a good carpenter." This passage echoes Nunn's deeply embedded assumption that it is especially virtuous to work well with one's hands.

The strong religiosity in Nunn's closing statements and his vision that religious sentiment and academic inquiry were inherently compatible paralleled the era's prominent intellectual leaders. Charles D. Walcott addressed the American Association for the Advancement of Science as its retiring president the same week that Nunn completed "The Purpose." Walcott said, "I believe that a good scientist should be a good Christian and a good Christian should be a good scientist in his method and work, as both are seeking the truth and the fundamental principles underlying their respective fields of endeavor."[47]

Similarly, John D. Rockefeller's words are inscribed on a brass tablet at the entrance of the University of Chicago's Memorial Chapel: "As the spirit of religion should penetrate and control the university so the building which represents religion ought to be the central and dominant feature of the university group. Thus it will be proclaimed that the university in its ideal is dominated by the spirit of religion, and its departments are inspired by religious feeling and all its work is directed to the highest ends."

Despite his recent shift toward orthodoxy, Nunn's thought continued to be inclusive. "Knowledge is not wisdom," he believed, "for wisdom consists of two qualities, knowledge and action. The ancient East knew it better than modern Europe. Consequently the Eastern schools taught wisdom, the Western schools learning. If the prevalent question of the West has been: How much knowledge have you? the prevalent question of the East was: How are you using your knowledge, for good or evil? With this question the East stood more in touch with the divine spirit of the Universe."[48] He added, "If I must have common material in either line, give me character and purpose rather than intellect."[49]

By sidestepping what he saw as the traps of religious orthodoxy on the one hand or *Who's Who* forms on the other, Nunn fit awkwardly into his era. The world in which he had thrived had nearly vanished by 1925, yet the principles he championed seemed at once strangely archaic and oddly promising. The childless Nunn felt deeply that his legacy to the planet would be his college. Through it, he hoped his most important work would continue.

And his time had come. Almost. To protect charitable bequests from crippling taxation, California law required that a person survive six months beyond the date of filing his or her will. Although Nunn had executed his will in May 1923, conveying the remainder of his estate at death to the trustees of Deep Springs, he had more recently filed a codicil refining his instructions. It was dated October 1, 1924. He had to live until April 1 the following year.

By March 1925, Nunn was often too weak to rise from his bed at 867 Lucille Avenue in Los Angeles, but his friend of many decades, Dr. Eugene Fuller, supervised his care. Bottled oxygen kept Nunn going, and he controlled the petcock himself. For weeks, he slipped in and out of full consciousness. Frank Noon was at his beside in the wee hours of April 1 when Nunn asked about the date. "The first day of April," came the reply. Nunn responded: "The six months are up. That gives me great pleasure."[50] The following afternoon, with Olof Swenson, Estelle Knight Biersach, Frank Noon, and a nurse keeping vigil, his private secretary Wallace Cook out getting more oxygen, and his brother Paul racing to reach his side, L.L. Nunn rolled over on his side, tucked the corner of a pillow under his chin and slipped peacefully away.[51]

CHAPTER 8

NUNN'S TEMPESTUOUS WAKE, 1925–1926

"I should not want the contents of the trunk handled promiscuously or scattered about."

—P.N. Nunn

Informed immediately that L.L. Nunn had died at home on Thursday afternoon, April 2, 1925, the Deep Springs Student Body wired Wallace Cook the next morning at the Lucille Avenue address: "The Student Body desires an opportunity to participate in doing honor to our founder and fellow member should arrangements permit it."[1] They received their answer by telegram around noon on Saturday, April 3: "Funeral at house two o'clock Tuesday Interment Forest Lawn Glendale. Wallace Cook." The students and most other members of the Deep Springs community arranged quickly for their two-day trip to Los Angeles, some traveling by car, others by train.

The service at Nunn's home revealed the durability of his friendships. Elton Hoyt, a deacon in the Protestant Episcopal Church, presided over the gathering. He and Nunn had been classmates at the Cleveland Academy fifty-nine years earlier. Following the ceremony, the procession followed Nunn's remains to Crypt #1185 in the Forest Lawn Memorial Park mausoleum in Glendale. A few yards away, at the end of the Coleus Corridor, a stained-glass window portrays a ship at full sail and a verse from Alfred, Lord Tennyson's "Crossing the Bar":

Sunset and evening star,
And one clear call for me!
And may there be no moaning of the bar,
When I put out to sea.

Nunn had commissioned this art for placement near his crypt.

The autopsy report given to Wallace Cook revealed that Nunn died of bronchial pneumonia. The tuberculosis that had knocked out his left lung years before had caused it to atrophy.[2] To compensate, the right lung had expanded toward the empty cavity, pushing his heart out of alignment and twisting the aorta. Some scarring from tuberculosis remained in the right lung, but the disease itself was no longer active. No sign of sexually transmitted disease appeared, suspicion of which had horrified his older siblings in the early 1880s.[3]

Depending on where they were published, memorial tributes to Lucien Nunn featured different facets of his life. A *Los Angeles Times* article ran under the complicated headline, "Nunn, Long Ill, Dies at Home Here: Attorney and Mining Man Native of Ohio: Pioneer in Hydroelectric Work." After highlighting how he earned his money, the article noted that a "great part of his wealth was devoted to training young men through the Telluride Association and the preparatory institution at Deep Springs, Cal."[4]

In Utah, the Mormon Church–owned *Deseret News* featured a portrait of Nunn under the headline "L.L. Nunn Former Salt Lake Business Man Dies on Coast."[5] After listing his many entrepreneurial ventures in the state and his active participation as a member of the Alta Club, the obituary continues: "Although Mr. Nunn gained international recognition as the builder and engineer of the first power plant at Niagara Falls . . . , then the largest power plant in the world, he is perhaps known best in the intermountain region for his benefactions." The *Provo Herald* carried an article headed "Benefactor Closes Long Useful Life," with the subtitle: "Assisted Thousands of Young Men in Securing a College Education."[6]

In Colorado, a long *Telluride Journal* article, "Hydro-Electric Power Pioneer Dead on Coast," took pride in the fact that Nunn's meteoric rise had begun there and noted with satisfaction his distinctive contributions to education.[7] For its part, Telluride Association printed a solemn "death announcement" and mailed it in a black-bordered envelope to all its associates and contacts.[8] Receiving one of these, the Harvard Alumni Directory requested information from William Biersach on which it might base a tribute to Nunn's life and work.[9]

The most telling tribute to Nunn came from Charles D. Walcott, still Secretary of the Smithsonian Institution, in a letter published in the *Telluride Newsletter*.[10] After recounting their chance meeting on a train decades earlier, Walcott praised Nunn's constant devotion to "the building of character and the developing of men that would be of the highest service in all of the activities of life. This was his one real purpose that ran through and controlled his business, social and personal relations in life." Walcott admitted that Nunn had been disappointed by those of "large means" who had not chosen to help him advance his educational work, but he concluded: "Some of them thought that it was a dream that would end when he passed on and there would be no one to carry on."

Nunn was survived by four of his ten siblings. Paul (P.N.), the youngest of the brood, had been L.L.'s constant partner in business, engineering, and education since 1890 when he agreed to help investigate the use of hydroelectric power for the Gold King Mine. Josiah (J.J.), three years L.L.'s senior, had floated on the edge of Nunn's world; he had also studied law but abandoned it early to assist Lucien with the power company in Provo and pursue agriculture in Oregon. Both before and after his brother's death, J.J. served briefly as Deep Springs' ranch manager.

Sisters Emily Nunn Whitman and Ellen M. Nunn, who by their contrasting career choices had inspired Nunn as a young man to consider the alternative claims of scientific and religious knowledge, lived to see him migrate toward the latter. Each of them received a generous bequest from his estate. The irony must have been bitter-sweet for Emily, especially, who had stood staunchly by her younger brother, supporting his education at critical points in his early adulthood, but then had written him off as hopeless and perhaps better off dead during his rambunctious early years in Leadville and Durango.

Alumni remembered that Nunn's personal effects were left undisturbed for a year or more, both at Deep Springs and Lucille Avenue. Then, taken into custody were Jacques-Louis David's portrait of Napoleon Bonaparte, an original copy of Nunn's 1879 essay "The Moral Sense," a well-worn leather wallet tooled with a bold "LLN" monogram, a thick wad of passes for railroads from coast to coast, and a carefully preserved slice of wedding cake from the 1889 marriage of Addison Wrench, one of Nunn's earliest protégés, and Minnie Wood.[11]

The immediate effect on Deep Springs of Nunn's passing was minimal. He had not been there in the memory of any but a few third-year students, and his correspondence with the student body had dwindled away during his final year, which spanned the residency of the students admitted the previous autumn.

As he seemed to have planned it, Nunn's influence was now felt chiefly through his letters and the key documents he had drafted during his final two years. The older students could quote him to win arguments, but soon everyone had equal access to the "Old Man's" intellectual and institutional legacy on paper. Several of the more senior students and Dean Thornhill began to assemble the most important documents. Originally printed as "The Letters of L.L. Nunn to the Deep Springs Student Body," in one form or another this corpus has endured to the present as the "Gray Book."

Less durable and more difficult to pin down were Nunn's financial assets and liabilities, and the state of Deep Springs finances, at the time of his death. The best source is the "Return for Federal Estate Tax" that William Biersach filed for Nunn's estate a year after he died.[12] The gross value of the estate was listed as $462,914, of which $300,456 was earmarked as a bequest to the trustees of Deep Springs. In 2025 dollars, these sums would be roughly $8 million and $5.4 million, respectively. Nunn's generosity included members of his family. Bachelor nephew Carroll N. Whitman received the largest share at $15,000, although his brother P.N. and his wife, Agnes, received the same total, split $10,000 and $5,000, respectively.[13] Sisters Emily and Ellen inherited well over $10,000 each, although theirs came in combinations of real estate, monthly payments for life, and (in Ellen's case) the cancellation of a loan. Brother Josiah got $2,000, as did a sister-in-law and a brother-in-law.

Next came Nunn's close associates, with Frank Noon and William Biersach receiving $12,500 each. Biersach's wife, Estella, and their son, William Jr., received $5,000 and $2,500, respectively. Estella remained the only woman outside his family whose college education Nunn underwrote. For their willingness to continue his educational work at Deep Springs, an additional $5,000 went to four trustees: Biersach, Noon, Whitman, and Harold Waldo. Some of his personal aides over the years were also remembered, among them Bruce Simmons at $10,000, Wallace Cook and Olof Swenson at about $4,000 each, and Clyde Bailey and Bernt Olsson at $1,000 apiece.

In arranging the size of his various bequests, Nunn may have worked backwards from the $300,000 he wished to leave for Deep Springs. If this was the case, he had estimated his overall worth, deducted the large sum designated for Deep Springs, and then divided up the rest among the family members and friends he wished to benefit. This strategy seems plausible because his final bequest to Deep Springs made his lifetime gifts to Telluride and the college equal.

The estate tax filing helps to make this case. It claims that, in 1911, "deceased transferred property worth about $750,000 for the use of Telluride Association."[14]

Telluride also realized about $550,000 from Nunn's decision to sell the association's share of the Natrona Power Company just before he died, making it possible to peg his overall investment in the association at about $1.3 million.[15]

In Deep Springs' case, Nunn supplemented his 1923 property transfer of land, buildings, and financial assets to the trustees valued at about $600,000 with a 1925 gift of $221,000 (probably from the sale of his personal shares of Natrona) and $300,456 in his bequest to the college. These three contributions total $1.12 million. If he counted what he had personally put into operating Deep Springs at $40,000 per year, then Nunn's investment in the college would come out very close to $1.3 million. The equivalent value today would be at least $17 million.

The overall figure for Deep Springs squares roughly with the results of a November 1926 audit that identified college assets at $1,073,487—just $46,000 less than the sum of Nunn's three major infusions. Shortly after his death, then, the audit showed an endowment of about $750,000, plus land and water rights valued at $125,000 and buildings, library holdings, and farm equipment estimated slightly below $200,000.[16]

The battle over L.L. Nunn's historical legacy was joined even before he died. His closest associates, especially P.N., Frank Noon, and William Biersach, were determined to secure his reputation as a great innovator in electric development and higher education. The assiduousness with which he preserved his business and private correspondence only reinforced the widely held belief among his protégés that he hoped his biography would be written. Paul Cadman removed any doubt, confirming that Nunn "was very deeply interested and had already been corresponding with a number of people about it."[17] Less than three months after Nunn's death, Telluride established a committee "to collect all biographical material pertaining to the life and work of Mr. L.L. Nunn" and appropriated $1,000 to expedite the task.[18]

A year later, at its June 1926 Convention held at Deep Springs, the committee chaired by Elmer M. ("Johnny") Johnson reported that it had "sent out circulars and several hundred personal letters" requesting biographical information from Nunn's associates, relatives, "and even . . . humble laborers." It had also scoured newspapers published in the cities where he had lived and assembled a file of correspondence from "Nunn's friends—statesmen, scientists, doctors, ministers, financiers, laborers," and others. For all of this material, the committee had built "a complete card index of names and addresses for ready reference, all of which will be handed over to any person this Convention may designate." In the Provo-era files alone, Johnson reported, there were thousands of letters to and from Nunn. Further, "there is a trunkful of private correspondence in Mr. Nunn's

Los Angeles residence."[19] These documents and countless other letters and photographs were to "be available when called for by the official biographer."[20]

According to Johnson:

> If the biography is written now, it would undoubtedly be put in a safety deposit vault for a decade or two before publication because a true life of Mr. Nunn would doubtless have chapters decidedly unpleasant to living individuals. However, if the writing is deferred ten or twenty years, many of Mr. Nunn's older friends and associates with valuable and rich memories will have passed on. It is up to the Convention, however, to decide what it desires to do.[21]

Celebrated investigative journalist and Abraham Lincoln authority Ida Tarbell had also published an acclaimed *History of the Standard Oil Company* (1904). As early as 1916, the Telluride History Committee considered her a top candidate to author a book on Nunn's business empire and educational projects. Nothing came of that initiative, but Tarbell's name surfaced again in 1926 as Nunn's ideal biographer. Now in her late sixties, the time to engage Tarbell seemed opportune. Johnson petitioned P.N. to help set the process in motion.

P.N.'s anxieties boiled up as he thought about the contents of that trunk in L.L.'s house. It was not the reputation of Nunn's associates that occupied him. Rather, he did not want anything about his brother's personal life made public. In his 1993 "Prologue" to Stephen A. Bailey's *L.L. Nunn: A Memoir*, Scott McDermott masterfully knit together the next sequence of events.

> Without saying no, P.N. stonewalled the project. When Johnson asked to see the contents of the trunk, P.N. wrote on 24 March 1926, "Naturally many of the letters are of an intensely personal nature and I should not want the contents of the trunk handled promiscuously or scattered about." To take Johnson off the scent, P.N. repeated L.L.'s farfetched idea of hiring Ida Tarbell, "But I fancy she is not a cheap old girl," wrote P.N. His letter concluded ominously, "It is too early for a really truthful recital. It would create a storm of abuse."[22]

Even if Johnson had been unaware of Nunn's sexual orientation prior to this time, McDermott makes it clear that Johnson was no longer naïve. In his systematic effort to collect information about L.L.'s life, Johnson had recently received a response from one of Nunn's physicians, J. Walter Kean, who wrote that Lucien Nunn "was jealous of his friendships, with a strong sex complex, of a preference for young boys, giving as a reason his ambition to find and make a genius, and [eventually] thinking the only real genius in all history was Napoleon."[23]

The 1920s had brought a sharp rise in the acceptance of homosexuality in America's great cities, with avant-garde films and songs openly accepting same-sex attractions and challenging Victorian norms.[24] Conservative forces rallied vigorously to face down the new open-mindedness. At the same time, early studies of adult sexuality involving underage partners were raising disturbing questions about child abuse. In this milieu, P.N., Noon, and Biersach became alarmed that public knowledge of Lucien Nunn's more intimate relationships with young men could jeopardize his place in history.

With P.N.'s approval, Frank Noon had already destroyed much of L.L.'s carefully preserved correspondence. With new urgency, William Biersach apparently seized the trunk and finished the job. He later explained to Johnson that after "pawing over reams of letters, most of which were to or from the family or from people who are just names to us, I decided that their destruction would not be fatal."[25] Eight decades would pass before enough other letters of L.L. Nunn came to light to bring the picture into clearer focus.[26] In the meantime, speculation and rumors proved more damaging than the truth.[27]

Whatever one makes of Nunn's personal life, enough is now known for us to see a high-achieving man whose periods of loneliness and even self-doubt were intense, whose longing for emotional intimacy was rarely satisfied, and whose enormous energies and keen intellect were sharply focused. Unlike most of his contemporaries, that focus was neither on a spouse nor children, whom he never had, nor on himself. Instead, it was on a few grand ideas about labor and leadership and a morally ordered society. By the autumn of 1926, with his life stilled and well-meaning loyalists striving to lock their wishes for his image in others' minds, L.L. Nunn's tangible legacies, Deep Springs College and Telluride Association, were on their own.

PART 2

THE SAGA OF DEEP SPRINGS COLLEGE

Lucien L. Nunn's seventy-two years spanned from the Civil War to the Roaring Twenties—from the social and political upheavals of Reconstruction and industrialization to the "normalcy" of Calvin Coolidge's administration. While Nunn was a man of his times, he was generally ahead of them by an inch or a mile. To his last breath, he invested in the future. Deep Springs College is the most significant legacy he wished to leave. It is fitting, therefore, that this account of Nunn's life trace the extension of his work across what is now over a century of the college's existence.

Nunn conceived, founded, and endowed Deep Springs College, but its path would seldom be straight or smooth. While the strength of his spirit would continue to animate America's most unusual college, flaws in his judgment—especially about people—dogged the institution for five decades and troubled it for much longer. Yet Deep Springs' vitality today owes much to its unsettled past. The resilience of the college reflects the personality of its founder.

Deep Springs Valley and the Sierra Nevada Mountain Range in winter.

CHAPTER 9

THE SWAY OF AFFAIRS, 1925–1940

Lucien never found the Man for Deep Springs, though his brother . . . believed himself the man.

—*Orville Sweeting*

Two years after his brother's death, Paul N. Nunn was invited to address the American Institute of Electrical Engineers. The master of ceremonies introduced him with customary high praise, prompting P.N. to begin his remarks: "Most of the complimentary things and the particular esteem which attaches to the name do not belong to this Mr. Nunn. . . . They are due to my brother, the late L.L. Nunn. Had the decisions all rested with me, I should never have had the courage, the hardihood, the gambler's instinct and the nerve to have undertaken the many things my brother did. . . . I have been the engineer; he was the courage."[1]

Moving from a charismatic founder to prosaic successors is a tricky organizational maneuver, and this transition tested whether the trustees could guide the college along the knife-edge between blind devotion to the founder's words and losing sight of his radical vision. For the vast majority of progressive and experimental colleges in America, failure to negotiate that edge has spelled doom.[2]

The complicated relationship between the two Nunns, Orville Sweeting observed, continued after L.L.'s death: Lucien "never found The Man for Deep Springs, though his brother . . . believed himself the man." Across the thirty-five

Paul N. Nunn at Deep Springs, circa 1931. Courtesy of Deep Springs Archives.

years of their partnership, an uneasy truce existed between the brothers. "L.L. felt himself almost divinely inspired in his mission and had never fully admitted anyone into his confidence. P.N. felt ignored, his superior technical training deprecated, his ideas accepted and subsumed by L.L., who ostensibly shunned publicity but secretly enjoyed being in center-stage."[3]

While P.N. styled himself as his brother's natural successor, L.L. had done nothing to encourage this assumption.[4] Quite the contrary: "During the last months of his life," Sweeting wrote, "Nunn saturated his associate [Director Otto Suhr] with his deep fear that some masterful personality, possibly Brother P.N. or Dean Thornhill would get control at Deep Springs and run away with the institution."[5] As Nunn's anxieties mounted in May 1924, he minced no words in a letter to Suhr: "My feeling is that Dean Thornhill is a menace to the

PURPOSE . . . and that if he is not eliminated or most strenuously controlled, he will ruin the institution for all that I have aimed at for it. . . [H]e disregards entirely his *moral obligation* . . . as laid down by the founder."[6] After all, when left to their own devices, the board had elected Frank Noon as chair. Then, at L.L.'s urging, they replaced him with Harold Waldo. P.N. had never been in the running, but he would not rest, thus setting the stage for political intrigue.

L.L. had trusted Waldo. He admired his independence and knew that this colleague truly understood and embraced his educational philosophy and plan for Deep Springs. Waldo was not yet age forty. His legal practice was thriving; and, like Nunn, he was becoming a pillar among Salt Lake City's non-Mormon elite. A prominent Presbyterian and rising Masonic leader, he did not need Deep Springs. His ego did not require it, nor did he see it as a source of personal income.[7]

Among the seven other nonstudent trustees, two were blood relatives and the careers of five had been tied to L.L. Nunn. Four were in his employ when he died—Bill Biersach, Frank Noon, Otto Suhr, and Ernest Thornhill—and their livelihoods continued to be at least partially dependent on Deep Springs and Telluride Association. P.N. may have been living comfortably in retirement, but his ego investment in Deep Springs exceeded the others. Nunn's nephew, Carroll Whitman, developed a similar sense of familial entitlement although his legal career gave him independent means. Only one trustee, Paul Cadman, joined Harold Waldo in having no personal advantage to be extracted from his association with the college. Nor could Nunn have struck a more vivid contrast between the governance models of his two educational institutions. He had set Telluride in motion with a perpetually renewing youth membership but established Deep Springs under the leadership of trustees-for-life.

Thus, at his death, Nunn had failed to identify a leader to whom he wished to entrust Deep Springs, instead leaving it with a board whom he himself had appointed and whose longevity he had assured. It was a dangerous concoction. Further, the gaping chasm between L.L. Nunn's ideals and his board's provincialism became an echo chamber within which the college's fate would rattle for many decades. Given these issues, however, an enigma emerged early and persisted throughout its history: the college would continue to attract extraordinary students, admit them, and work its magic on their lives. Only in the worst of times have students suffered from the incompetence, nonsense, and chaos that repeatedly engulfed the adults responsible for the institution.

L.L. Nunn's notable end-of-life letters to the student body notwithstanding, he had lacked the energy to maintain the network of personal friends on whom he had depended to find outstanding recruits. As a result, the arrival of new students dropped from the usual ten per year, to six in 1923 and two in the autumn of 1924. The trustees were concerned—especially Thornhill and Suhr, whose livelihoods depended on the college—and they moved quickly when Nunn died. In the spring and summer of 1925, they rounded up a class of twelve to begin that September. Over the next decade, entering classes would oscillate between eight and eleven.

The student body quickly regained its three-year symmetry and the educational program successfully prepared students to qualify for junior standing when they transferred to Cornell or other universities. If students survived their first year and were invited to continue, they typically remained for the full six semesters, going home for one of the two summers and working on the ranch the other. Providing a labor team for summer haying and irrigating had become a student body responsibility. Third-year men enjoyed no special status formally but were often elected to key student body offices, served as mentors to their younger peers in classes and on labor assignments. These leadership roles became vitally important after 1925 when the students could look to few adults for insight or inspiration. Learning from able and inspiring peers has great potential everywhere in higher education, but it emerged in the late 1920s as a particularly important phenomenon at Deep Springs—and became an element of increasing influence.

Jim Withrow came to Deep Springs from Columbus, Ohio, in the fall of 1927 and quickly earned the respect of his peers and the adults in the community. The next spring, he initiated a discussion about reestablishing the labor position of "Office Man" with responsibility for the college's financial accounting. This idea was not far-fetched, because every student continued to be trained in double-entry bookkeeping to maintain his personal account. The student body backed Withrow's plan. Director Suhr and the trustees agreed to try it, but only if the candidate passed a summer accounting course at the University of Southern California.[8] All parties agreed, Suhr chose Withrow. Jim aced the course, and kept (or supervised others in keeping) Deep Springs' books until he left nearly two years later.

Otto Suhr trusted the students more fully than L.L. had, not only by supporting Withrow's important new role, but also by endorsing the student body's wish to create other new student positions, including community fire chief and curator of the museum and archive. Students responded favorably to the increased trust, taking initiatives for the larger welfare of the community. Another student-generated initiative created a Ranch Improvement Committee. Withrow recalled

Earle Henley doing laundry, 1933. Courtesy of Deep Springs Archives.

Frederic Laise milking, 1933. Courtesy of Deep Springs Archives.

that the students upgraded landscaping around the circle. "[We] put in the triangles, went out and got cactus [*sic*] and made the cactus gardens." "[We] also came up with the money to plant the trees which now obscure the view of the Sierras. We bought the cheapest trees that we could find that were supposed to be able to weather DS, which we called Chinese Elms."[9]

More important than these initiatives, students petitioned for the labor commissioner's position. Nunn had only occasionally used it to reward a particular student, but Suhr apparently believed that the student body was worthy of increased responsibility. He agreed to establish the labor commissioner position in 1927, and granted the student body the right to elect one of its own members to the office.

Third-year man Lee Davy became the first student-elected labor commissioner. His duties included assigning students to labor positions, preparing them for their responsibilities, supervising their work, and disciplining or reassigning those whose performance fell short. Over the years, labor commissioners have also been responsible for coordinating closely with the ranch manager to accomplish the ever-changing work of the whole college; but they have enjoyed some leeway in initiating and organizing work projects of their own.

As years passed, Davy and his successors presided over an increasingly complicated work program. Without L.L. Nunn to cover significant expenses from his personal resources, the college experienced increased financial stresses. In addition to the positions of labor commissioner and office manager, students assumed responsibility for the laundry. From this job arose the tradition of the "bone pile." Unclaimed or unmarked clothing was washed, folded, stacked neatly, and made available to other students for the taking. It morphed into a free flea market exchange, restocked regularly by those leaving the community.[10]

The dairy was also serious business, with two students milking ten to fifteen cows by hand morning and evening, making cheese, and churning butter. When the number of milk cows rose to eighteen, the labor commissioner assigned a third student to the job.[11]

Twenty or more acres of the farm were devoted to growing corn, which had to be chopped and blown into two silos to help feed the cows in winter.[12] In addition, a "chicken man" oversaw the poultry operation, a "feed man" (always a favorite job) cared for the goats, pigs, rabbits, sheep, and turkeys, and fed the bulls. Other students slaughtered and butchered these animals for boarding-house consumption. By 1937, the student body had also created the position of gardener to prune the orchard and encourage greater production of fruits and vegetables. The resulting surpluses, coupled with the always-bounteous dairy products, were sold in Big Pine and Bishop, providing welcome college income. Other student jobs have continued to the present, including the mechanic's assistant. This position shares responsibility for the maintenance, repair, and replacement of the farm machinery, trucks, and cars, electrical and water systems, and furnaces. The old heavy-duty FWD truck remained in regular service until 1927.

Farming with horse-drawn implements was slow and demanding, requiring attention throughout the daylight hours. As a result, schedules for classwork and labor were split, with half the students attending classes in the mornings and the other half in the afternoons. The labor schedule mirrored this pattern.

Nearing sixty, Dean Thornhill, whom one student described as "a little man, well built, mostly bald, and with a somewhat round face," continued to preside over the academic program.[13] He had divided his time with Telluride Association, where he had also served as dean since before Deep Springs began. But Telluride dismissed him in 1928, and despite his devotion and experience, Thornhill's weariness seemed to get the better of him. His role at the college did not expand; in fact, he passed the public speaking course on to a student committee. Students increasingly chafed under his leadership style, resented his supercilious correction of their written and spoken English, and secretly mimicked his British affectations. Nor did it help that students saw him as

Elmer M. (Johnny) Johnson, Telluride dean and Deep-Springs professor in 1934. Courtesy of Deep Springs Archives.

hopelessly dominated by his wife, Lida, a situation more evident now that their daughter, Virginia, had grown up and left home.

Although Thornhill's regular faculty appointees did not meet contemporary liberal arts college standards, he attracted many outstanding visiting professors, including alumnus Father Ed Meehan who taught on and off throughout the 1930s. Telluride's new dean, Elmer M. ("Johnny") Johnson became a perennial favorite. An authority on Joseph Conrad, he never completed his doctorate—for which his wife blamed Telluride. Johnny began making annual winter pilgrimages to Deep Springs to teach short courses on English literature, etymology, theater, and writing. His immediate popularity no doubt contrasted sharply with Thornhill's dwindling vitality.[14]

Johnson's importance to Deep Springs ultimately rested on his inexhaustible efforts to recruit students for the college. Throughout the 1930s and 1940s, he exploited his high school contacts, especially in Buffalo, Rochester, and

Chicago, to find more than a few of Deep Springs' most outstanding students. Among these were distinguished physicist and University of Rochester president Robert Lamb Sproull (DS'35), and Deputy United Nations Ambassador William J. vanden Heuvel (DS'46).[15]

Otto Suhr, always a bit awkward socially, rose and fell in the students' esteem; but he and his wife, Katherine, always made the students welcome at their home. Katherine Suhr frequently served tea, popcorn balls, or freshly baked cakes and pies after public speaking or student body meetings. Otto taught a geology course every year, about which Tom Fairchild wrote his mother: "This brings me to speak of Mr. Suhr. He knows the country very well, having been over it as school director, prospector, and mining engineer; so he was a great help in taking us places. Also he knows much about geology, and since we are all more or less interested in that subject, his knowledge is timely. To a certain extent, he was able to get in with the fellows as it may be expressed, but he never quite loses his embarrassment."[16]

As director, Suhr oversaw the whole operation at Deep Springs and made an annual swing around the country to recruit students from leading urban high schools. Admitting students had always been the director's responsibility, sometimes with trustee involvement; but in the spring of 1928, several third-year students asked Suhr if they might participate. They were responding to a controversy surrounding the recent admission of two students who had not done well. One was Otto's son, and the other was Trustee Biersach's son.[17] Suhr expanded the students' role in governance another step by inviting the third-year students to read the materials submitted by applicants and make recommendations. Nearly a decade passed before the student body established a formal Applications Committee with a spelled-out role in assisting the dean and director.

Suhr and Thornhill sparred increasingly over the expanding scope of student responsibilities and the proper balance among academics, labor, and governance. Thornhill sharply criticized what he considered the dilution of academic learning as student labor and governance responsibilities expanded. For his part, Suhr was unhappy with the quality of Thornhill's faculty and believed that Thornhill failed to appreciate the significance of empowering students.

A debate over the college letterhead highlighted their differences. L.L. Nunn had insisted that the only acceptable letterhead for the institution was "Deep Springs Preparatory and Collegiate." Within a few years, the students and trustees agreed on "Deep Springs," Nunn's designation in the Deed of Trust. The decision to omit "College" from the letterhead reflected the desire of Otto

Suhr and P.N. Nunn to emphasize the distinctiveness of Deep Springs' holistic educational philosophy. They wished to set it apart from other institutions of higher learning that focused more on scholastic progress and content mastery.

A more substantive manifestation of the growing schism appears in Thornhill's proposal to increase class-related work from five hours a day to eight, reduce labor from five hours to three, and cut back governance/community engagement from three hours to one.[18]

The resulting controversy energized Suhr who, with P.N.'s help, mustered the courage to release Thornhill from the deanship he had occupied in Nunnian schools for three and a half decades. P.N. Nunn reportedly mobilized support from reluctant trustees by offering to pay a new dean's salary.[19] A reading of Thornhill's cryptic reports to the trustees confirms that he had been disengaging for some time, so he did not resist strenuously when the separation agreement included a year's leave with full pay. Ernest and Lida Thornhill withdrew from Deep Springs in the summer of 1929, although he did not leave the board until his health failed in 1941.

Warren Kumler, formerly of Antioch College, joined the faculty when Thornhill left. After a brief test as an academic counselor and instructor of everything from philosophy to chemistry, the board appointed him dean. Drawing on his experience at Antioch, he sought to put "a greater burden upon the initiative and responsibility of the individual than ever before," including allowing students to choose the courses they wanted to take and to meet for classes whenever and wherever professors would agree to engage them.[20]

Kumler's curricular recommendations to the board were even more revealing of his laissez-faire philosophy: "Little attention should be paid to conversation, composition, and even grammar. . . . Spending [an] undue amount of time on these things serves principally to clutter up the student's brain with a lot of intellectual rubbish."[21] Suhr and the trustees were apparently so pleased to be rid of Thornhill that they tacitly accepted Kumler's initiatives, even though those who had been steeped in L.L. Nunn's passion for precision were uneasy with Kumler's approach.

The Great Depression forced college trustees everywhere to slice budgets, reduce faculty and staff positions, defer building and campus maintenance, and eliminate services. Some colleges closed their doors. The Deep Springs budget had already been cut severely; but in January 1932, Treasurer Biersach warned his fellow trustees that "income from securities and rentals was about $40,000 year in and year out" but he could not see more than $20,000 yearly income from these sources now.[22] Ranch income had been fluctuating between $6,000

Students planting potatoes, 1934. Courtesy of Deep Springs Archives.

and $15,000 a year. Ten days later, he wrote Johnny Johnson at Telluride: "Were it not for the $10,000 to $12,000 the Association supplied in recent years, DS work would have suffered and will suffer in future if that help or outside help is not forthcoming."[23]

With investment income dropping to half, the trustees had to slash college expenses from $54,000 during the 1931–1932 fiscal year to $27,250 for 1932–1933. Salaries and wages were gutted—from $25,000 to $11,000.[24] The student body debated whether its members should continue to receive the monthly payment of $12.50 that L.L. Nunn had specified as part of their training in fiscal responsibility. The trustees were divided but agreed to reduce rather than eliminate student payments.

Otto Suhr's salary, the largest single item in the budget, was vulnerable. Working behind the scenes with board allies, P.N. offered to serve as acting director without remuneration if they would convince Otto to step aside. Suhr read the signals and responded reluctantly when his fellow trustees voted "to relieve Mr. Suhr from duty as Director of Deep Springs as of April 1, 1932."[25] The settlement included a $1,000 separation payment, continued residence at the ranch, use of college vehicles until he and his family relocated, and paying off the mortgage on the Suhr residence in Glendale, California. The veteran director stepped aside, underappreciated and inadequately thanked for the competent service he had rendered Deep Springs and Nunnian education across his long career. The trustees then thanked P.N. Nunn for his willingness to serve. He seized the reins ten days later.

Although P.N.'s appointment helped keep the college afloat, it had negative repercussions for the school. Considering the students ungrateful and unruly, he had already established an adversarial stance. They promptly clashed over the outside parameters of student behavior that L.L. prescribed—abstaining from alcohol and tobacco, and eschewing social relationship with young women in Big Pine, Bishop, and beyond. Smoking would seem the least significant of these three issues, but fire safety is critical in a dry desert community far from help. Even so, the board and P.N. chose to define tobacco as a moral issue.

Jim Haughey (DS'30), who grew up in Kansas and thrived at Deep Springs, enjoyed smoking, as did many of his peers. When the trustees tried to crack down in the fall of 1931, the student body debated the matter at length. Among the issues considered were the morality of smoking, the trustees' right to make this decision, and whether L.L. had banned pipes and cigars as well as cigarettes. Some "felt that the [student] body had an inalienable right to smoke, from which no trustee's threat should frighten it."[26] Under pressure from P.N., the students vacillated throughout the autumn, but finally passed a motion in December that declared the issue "a matter of personal decision."[27]

Knowing that he would soon be taking charge, P.N. decided to make an example of the students who smoked. Jim Haughey remembered that P.N. arrived by limousine "the week before the Christmas holidays, called me into his office and told me, 'Well, get your things packed up and go home and don't ever come back.'"[28] Haughey reminded Nunn that, according to the Deed of Trust, the director could not make such a dismissal decision unilaterally except at the end of an academic year. Knowing the deed, Nunn had to agree, but he challenged Haughey to muster the support of his peers.

Jim took his case to the student body the night before Christmas break, after which most of his peers drove off to Big Pine to begin their travels home. Haughey stayed until morning, of course, to deliver the students' endorsement to Nunn. "Oh," P.N. replied, "that was just an oral vote. It is not in writing so it doesn't count."[29] Haughey left as ordered and did not return for seventy-one years.[30] P.N. had launched a fraught relationship with the student body.

While maintaining his home in San Diego, P.N. soon moved to Deep Springs and assumed responsibility for daily operations. He was seventy-one, portly, and partially deaf. Student Paul Swatek (DS'33) remembered Nunn's trustee visits as lackluster: he just seemed "crotchety" and "lectured sternly on everything." Jack deBeers (DS'32) recalled conversations as an ordeal: he always "leaned forward and tipped his ear trumpet in my direction." Jack would shout to help the old man hear, but P.N. did almost all the talking himself.[31]

P.N. savored living well on his accumulated wealth. A stately home overlooking San Diego Bay suited him perfectly. He owned fine cars, employed a chauffeur and flirted shamelessly with young women.[32] Grandniece Helen Heckman grew up nearby. Once, in her teens, she and a schoolmate visited P.N. early one evening. When they were saying goodbye, he asked if they would each like ten dollars to spend when they went out that evening. When they said "Yes!" he pulled the money from his pocket and offered it to them if they would lift their skirts and let him tuck the bills in their garters. Heckman still holds P.N. in contempt, but she remembers her "Uncle Lu" (L.L. Nunn) with affection, based on his genuine interest in her and her education and his kind regard for all members of the Nunn family.

With P.N.'s arrival at Deep Springs, a long-lived rumor came alive. P.N. drove in with Agnes, his wife of many years, and Jewel Hamilton, his mistress of many years. "Mrs. Hamilton" was a bit younger than Agnes but it required an act of self-control not to blink when she was introduced as the Nunns' foster daughter. Jewel's husband, a dentist, had died much earlier. P.N. had long-since negotiated a de facto divorce from Agnes, "refusing to touch her after their only child, Helen, died in 1897 at the age of six."[33] A niece remembers: "They carried the child's remains [from Telluride, Colorado] to Salt Lake City where she was embalmed and held in a mausoleum or their home in a glass-topped coffin for periodic viewing. When low lights and soft music no longer did the trick, they finally buried her." Although Agnes and Jewel amicably shared P.N.'s house, Deep Springs was not a welcome retreat for this ménage à trois—but P.N. had an agenda.

Three years earlier, P.N. had written a ten-page statement titled "What's the Matter with Deep Springs?" He addressed it to the student body, trustees, and leaders of Telluride Association.[34] Everyone seemed to bemoan the state of the college, he wrote. "Telluride Association consistently deprecates it," the student body threatens mutiny, Dean Thornhill complains constantly, and "several trustees have considered resigning because we are getting nowhere."[35] Independently, the students called the able Paul Cadman "the trout trustee" because he spent more time fly-fishing in Wyman Canyon than on college business when he came for board meetings.

The problem, P.N. argued, was that Deep Springs was surrendering its special mission, due to the benign influence of its friends and the board's lethargy and timidity. He scorned Telluride for paying Deep Springs to become its "training field" for new members. The association's generous annual gifts were diverting attention from the education the college provided students as an end in itself. The noble ideals of character development and service to humanity were being replaced, he said, with a narrow emphasis on academic knowledge. The cultivation of independent thought and the application of knowledge to improve civilization had both given way to a preoccupation with traditional subject mastery.

For their part, he asserted, the trustees had lost sight of the founder's distinctive vision of education. In their inattention to the Deed of Trust and other basic documents, they were allowing the college to revert to the mainstream university pattern, against which L.L. Nunn founded Deep Springs as a protest.

To make his case, P.N. cited an impressive array of authorities who were then among the leaders of undergraduate reform: Swarthmore's president Frank Aydelotte, Antioch's new leader Arthur Morgan, Harper's "Easy Chair" columnist William Howells, and rising intellectual star Bernard DeVoto. P.N. described the college as his brother's final but unfinished experiment. Its current custodians must understand and keep sacred the original ends, while continuing to refine the means and methods of education for better results.[36]

P.N. may have been angry, and his delivery anything but inviting, but Sweeting was mistaken when he labeled it a "diatribe." Nunn was onto something. Deep Springs would either hold fast to its distinctive mission or die a slow death. But it had to adapt. Clearly, P.N. had been preparing for years to seize the helm and steer the college back toward L.L.'s educational ideals. The students were awed by P.N.'s knowledge but irritated by his presumption, describing him derisively as thinking he was the "new founder of Deep Springs."

To his credit, P.N. was the only trustee who seemed to follow the national conversation about higher education, and his exposition about ideals was compelling. By this time, however, he lacked something that L.L. had had in abundance: resilience, if not patience, especially for dealing with rambunctious young men.

Six months after taking charge at Deep Springs, P.N. sent a dense four-page report to Chairman Waldo "and other interested trustees." He had found the place "running very smoothly although expensively and in a perverted direction."[37] The students, he believed, had become "too literal" in interpreting the Deed of Trust and L.L.'s "grandiose" language. In their focus on the rights and liberties the founder had granted them, "they had become utterly subversive of his purpose."[38] Their "spirituality," he believed, had given way to arrogance, laziness, and selfishness. His concern over the students' spirituality had been heightened by student body discussions about abolishing the tradition of student-led Sunday services.[39] Over a year earlier, Tom Fairchild had written his mother that P.N. "was rather discouraged about the lack of interest in Sunday services, and that he thought the boys were becoming atheists."[40]

Nunn reported some progress in getting the students' attention, however, and he hoped his new dean, Walter Crawford, would help him turn things around. Crawford, a counseling psychologist who had taught in Chinese mission schools, had most recently headed an elite boys boarding school in Washington State. The two men found leadership more difficult than they had anticipated. P.N.'s report had described the precipitous decline of education and culture in America. Wondering if "L.L. [was] a visionary idealist who has put his Trustees afloat in his little craft, in a current too swift and powerful for their little power plant, only for them to be swept away into the oblivion of futility! I'm merely asking, not answering. I'm tired."[41]

After this fiery beginning, P.N. seemed deflated. He tried to get Crawford to accept overall responsibility at Deep Springs so that he could return to San Diego. "Meanwhile," he reported to the board, "things are going to the devil. That you don't see it means nothing. . . . We are training these boys amid surroundings . . . which exemplify sloppy, shiftless get-by disorder destructive to the very elements of character which we prate of building."[42] Driving his harangue, no doubt, was Nunn's anger and anxiety about the likely election the next week of Franklin Roosevelt, whom he saw as the harbinger of doom for American values. This outburst was the first shot in a struggle that would shape trustee attitudes for nearly thirty years.

Drained, but not yet willing to relinquish control, P.N. succeeded in getting Crawford to accept the position of dean-director but convinced the trustees to bestow on himself the new title of "Executive Trustee." He, Agnes, and Jewel then moved back to San Diego where he directed college affairs, by design or default, by remote control. Then, in one of those strange flip-flops occasionally displayed by P.N. and his nephew Carroll Whitman, he addressed the student body constructively shortly after FDR's election. His remarkably farsighted political and economic commentary, titled "That New Social Order," analyzed the rise of technology and its implications for labor, democracy, and the distribution of wealth.[43]

From the outset, Crawford appeared to be overwhelmed by Deep Springs, so consumed with guiding the students, P.N. complained, that he had no time left to help run the college. Servile and compliant, the new director's strenuous efforts to please Nunn earned him nothing but contempt. He fared little better with the students, who narrowly defeated a motion to express to the board their disapproval of Crawford.[44] Crawford broke under the pressure and willingly moved aside when the board asked Lawrence Kimpton to take charge as acting dean in 1936.

Kimpton had come to teach at Deep Springs with his wife, Genevra, the previous year. Holding two degrees from Stanford, he had just completed his Ph.D. in philosophy at Cornell. He had become aware of Deep Springs through friends at Telluride House, and probably had no other job prospects as the depression ground on. The man stood six feet two and a half inches tall, weighed well over two hundred pounds, and came across initially as a gentle Saint Bernard. He "was very suave," Bob Sproull remembered as a student. "His appearance, his bearing, his vocabulary, everything, everything was—I shouldn't say contrived—but planned."[45] The twenty-six-year-old dean brought long-overdue academic professionalism and high scholastic standards, teaching his philosophy classes well. However, he seemed aloof from the community. Sproull saw him as currying favor with the trustees, whose leadership abilities were disintegrating. Capitalizing on an engaging personal style and deft political skills, Kimpton took advantage of the board's exasperation with P.N., whose credibility and strength were waning. At Kimpton's appointment, Trustee Biersach had written him: "I wonder if P.N. will be able to stir up enough members to back him up in his vindictiveness. We in high places better be prepared in our own minds for retirement or to scrap for being retained. I don't know what's his & others objectives—except to *rule* without opposition. These are my confidential thoughts & I wish you'd so regard them."[46] Kimpton negotiated this political minefield skillfully. The board soon put him in sole charge as both director and dean.

Optimism abounded despite the continuing austerity of the economic depression. Students responded positively when Kimpton encouraged their increased engagement in governing the college. In the spring of 1937 alone, the student body formed a committee "to help the dean secure a faculty for next year," undertook a comprehensive study of the aging heating system, and collected bids for the installation of a new one. They investigated options to replace the worn furniture in the Main Building, took money from their savings account to print additional copies of the *Letters of L.L. Nunn*, made plans to publish the first directory of college alumni, and formed a committee to "meet with Dean Kimpton, the faculty, and [the ranch manager to] decide which men are to return to Deep Springs the following year."[47] They thus laid the foundations for what became the Student Body Curriculum Committee and the Re-invitations Committee. The Applications Committee was now functioning by name.

Kimpton, unlike the carping P.N., also manifested a high tolerance for youthful high jinks. Francis Tetreault wrote his mother about a weekend "crash," the slang term for a party:

> At our crash last Saturday, I took a huge picture of LL off the wall and danced around with it. This was true sacrilege, but it was funny. In his day old LL didn't even allow the profs to have their wives on the ranch, they had to leave them in town. And here his predecessors [*sic*] were dancing with *women* on his rugs in his living room and with his picture. It actually resembled a very small brawl except that the lecturer and the teacher were there all along as chaperones. Larry [Kimpton] and the other teachers went down to their own cottages so they wouldn't have to testify against us.[48]

The students' mood could hardly have been more different than during P.N.'s domination. But the students were also sensing the practical limits on what they could do. A year later, the student body president started a discussion among his peers, then reported to the board: "Just because the field of student body responsibility has expanded in the past two years to the enhancement of the prestige of the Student Body does not necessarily mean that to be an effective Student Body we must continue to expand our authority. On the contrary, the opinion has often been expressed that student body authority and responsibility has reached its saturation point, that the Student Body has all on its hands that it can take care of."[49] It was a surprisingly mature self-evaluation.

Despite the economic strictures, Deep Springs continued to weather the Depression surprisingly well. On the revenue side of the ledger, ranch income did not drop like investment income when bonds were in default and stocks no longer paid dividends. Rather, it constituted a critical and rising source of income. Further, Telluride Association continued its annual $10,000 support as it had since the mid-twenties. Faculty and staff were already paid significantly in direct services, including free or nearly free housing, utilities, and meals. At the same time, the college itself was insulated from the shortage of essential goods because it produced its own meat and dairy products and many of its own fruits and vegetables. The use of wood for fuel and draft horses for farm work were also positive economic factors. Robert Aird, who was a student in the 1920s and director in the 1960s, later concluded that, "but for the farm and ranch, Deep Springs would have soon closed." He was probably right, not so much because of the income from the hay and cattle operation but because the

ROTC, Deep Springs style. Students leave for a weekend desert trip as World War II storm clouds gather. Deep Springs future president John "Buzz" Anderson is at the wheel. Courtesy of Deep Springs Archives.

school produced so much of its own food and energy.[50] Deep Springs has never been as self-sustaining as it was in the 1930s.

Roderick J. MacKenzie, a highly regarded Colorado cattleman and brother-in-law of Harold Waldo (chair of the trustees) joined the staff as ranch manager in March 1933. Behind him was solid experience in advising the trustees on ranch and farm practices during the drought years. Surprisingly, he, Kimpton, and the board tackled renovation and planned new buildings even as the Depression wore on. They converted furnaces to oil, installed the first water treatment facility, renovated the dormitory, built a concrete block bunkhouse by the orchard at the lower ranch, and constructed a spacious stone and wood frame horse barn with a haymow. They also began raising money to build a faculty duplex between the Boarding House and Main Building.

An unlikely prompt came from landscape artist Christian Midjo. Described as having "a wobbly temperament," he joined the faculty as a visiting professor from Cornell in 1938, loved the place from the outset, and goaded the students, administration, and trustees on many fronts. Midjo succeeded in getting them to redecorate the Boarding House and Main Building, volunteering design ideas and color schemes. Four of Midjo's paintings of the desert land and sky are on permanent display in the Main Room at the college.[51]

Beyond the ranch gate, the pace also quickened. California assumed ownership of the road from Big Pine to the Nevada boundary about 1930 and launched a seven-year project to survey, grade, and pave what became State Highway 168. The new road no longer swept past the ranch entrance gate and skirted along the western edge of the alfalfa fields, but followed a straight line down the center of the valley. In May 1933, the California Transportation Department established a maintenance station two miles north of the ranch with one house and four tents for staff members. Deep Springs had its first perennial neighbors since Captain Harry's Paiute family had abandoned their settlement nearly two decades earlier.

The newly paved road cut travel time to Big Pine from two hours to one. The new highway made it feasible to haul heavier and more precarious cargo in and out of the ranch, expediting hay sales in good water years and hay purchases in poor years. This lifeline was all the more welcome because the Southern Pacific Railroad had recently closed its Zurich Station near Big Pine, making the overall transportation of goods to Deep Springs a longer haul.[52] The half-mile-long entrance road to the ranch gate was not paved until 1947.

The ranch flourished as never before. MacKenzie, a stout little Scotsman and skilled horseman, became an energetic and farsighted manager. His flamboyant wife, Evangeline, turned heads. Mac introduced tractor power, improved grazing practices, upgraded breeding protocols for the herd, increased the pregnancy rate, and leveled the fields for better distribution of irrigation water. For the first time in two decades, the ranch was again a state-of-the-art operation.

Back in 1931 when he was advising the trustees, MacKenzie had recommended acquiring the Crooked Creek grazing allotment north of Wyman Creek. Farmer Wallace Cook (DS'20), however, preferred to lease Roland Giroux's Bar Double 9 Ranch in Fish Lake Valley.[53] The "four years of extreme drought," he explained, had cut hay production from 350 to 500 tons per season to an abysmal 60 tons as Wyman Creek shrank to a trickle.[54] The ranch was already making expensive purchases of hay and grain for livestock, and this gap between production and consumption would only increase.

At the Bar Double 9, Cook explained, McAfee Creek flowed more plentifully than Wyman because its headwaters were on the slopes of White Mountain (elev. 14,246). Hay production could be much greater. The board opted to lease Giroux's ranch, and MacKenzie raised 700 tons of hay there the first year. With that success, the trustees authorized him to lease summer pastures in Long Valley

Evangeline MacKenzie and Ranch Manager Roderick MacKenzie, circa 1936. Courtesy of Deep Springs Archives.

north of Bishop, as well as Owens Valley pastures for winter use east of Big Pine. By the end of the decade, Kimpton expressed concern to the board that the ranch was becoming so large that it might overwhelm the academic program.

In June 1939, Ned Bedell (DS'36) wrote a report for the *Telluride Newsletter* that captured an emerging issue: "Ranch Manager MacKenzie has under consideration the purchase of a hay loader as a step toward the reduction of the large and expensive summer haying crews which have been necessitated in the last few years by the great increase in the amount of hay harvested."[55]

By this time, with deeper snow packs accumulating more reliably, the trustees had stopped leasing the Bar Double 9. Still, MacKenzie continued to make good use of the grazing allotments and leases he had secured for the college in Long Valley, Owens Valley, Fish Lake Valley, and Eureka Valley. The cattle herd, however, was not growing so much as it was being spread out for better forage, healthier conditions, and—the payoff—higher calf yields.

At a glance, the ranch ran more cattle in Deep Springs Valley during the 1920s and 1930s than it had earlier. The numbers are deceiving, however, because past trustees had counted mother cows and calves separately. In 1924, for instance, the herd was reported to number 480 "of which 280 are cows."[56] Two years later the count appeared to be up sharply at 740, but that number included only 290 cows, with 220 calves, and about 230 steers awaiting the annual sale.[57] During the MacKenzie years, when the ranch operation sprawled across five valleys, overall herd size increased to a reported 425 cows with 268 calves at the end of his tenure.[58] The grazing burden on Deep Springs Valley and the White Mountains did not increase.

Under federal grazing permit rules since the 1970s, a cow with a nursing calf has counted as a single "animal unit" and herd sizes have been tallied accordingly. With the exception of the MacKenzie years, then, Deep Springs' herd size has not risen or fallen significantly since the twenties, having remained in the neighborhood of 250 to 340 animal units. Associated with the perception of huge cattle counts has been the assumption that the Forest Service long ignored the threat of overgrazing. As early as 1931, however, Wallace Cook reported that the college's White Mountain–Crooked Creek range permit "calls for but one hundred fifty head for the summer and the Forest Service is quite insistent that we should not overstock the range."[59]

The academic program benefited greatly from Kimpton's growing national network of prominent educators. He attracted not only competent regular faculty but also put together a series of vigorous guest lectures. "Visitors and lecturers have been numerous recently," student Ned Bedell wrote early in 1939, with an average of one lecturer for every two weeks. "Dr. Alexander Meiklejohn, progressive educator and former president of Amherst College and of Wisconsin Experimental College," he wrote, was the most recent lecturer.[60]

With eerie prescience, in April 1938 the student body resolved: "That future Sunday Service meetings should be constituted along ethical rather than religious lines."[61] For all the recent progress at Deep Springs, troubles were bubbling up. Charles Collingwood, the future CBS News foreign correspondent and protégé of Edward R. Murrow, had enrolled at Deep Springs in 1934. Brilliant but insecure, and emitting more than his share of pheromones, he reportedly assuaged his precarious ego with sexual fantasies and occasional encounters.[62]

During his third year, Collingwood struck a chord with Genevra Kimpton. The two of them indulged in a brief affair, but Larry Kimpton and Evangeline MacKenzie were similarly engrossed.[63] Evangeline could handle a horse with authority, a skill that would prove convenient for remote trysts. Mac MacKenzie was the odd man out, but he had been brewing a risky scheme of his own. Even so, Larry Kimpton and Evangeline MacKenzie's affair did not pass his notice. Alumni from the time remember a fiery exchange, even a fistfight, between Kimpton and Mac MacKenzie in the Boarding House one morning after breakfast.[64]

The ranch was more profitable than ever, but Kimpton began to notice that some cattle sales were irregular and that the herd count was off. Investigating quietly, he discovered that Mac was running a cattle operation of his own in Owens Valley—in violation of his contract with Deep Springs—and, more significantly, that his herd was mixing with Deep Springs' cattle on rangeland owned or leased by the trustees. The ranch manager was also selling cattle from both herds as his own, and then writing checks to Deep Springs for what he reported as the college's share of each sale. Kimpton realized that he had been snookered.[65]

If Kimpton's affair with Mac's wife was not enough to tie his hands for dealing with the situation, another factor came into play. MacKenzie's sister, Katherine MacKenzie Waldo, was married to Harold Waldo. Reporting Roderick MacKenzie's activities, therefore, would place Kimpton in the position of embarrassing his boss and enraging the husband of his mistress. Nor could such activities be kept from the community. Bob Sproull remembered the roiling gossip as an unexpected element of his education: "Stealing cattle, sleeping around. What do you want? I must say that it was more than just growing up in the Middle West. It was a different world from my standpoint."[66]

Kimpton initially opted to say nothing to any member of the divided board, but he began "rounding up steers and [pursuing] rustlers as well as other more routine duties."[67] Evangeline became his riding partner, playing both sides against the middle.

Nor was Kimpton above unsavory tactics of his own. Henry Hayes, who had entered Deep Springs in 1920 and was also an alumnus of Telluride Association, came back to teach English and French in 1938. He did well, earning the respect of the students and establishing rapport with Kimpton. When Henry and his wife returned from the Christmas holidays, however, Kimpton gave them a chilly reception. Apparently fearing that Hayes might become an inside witness of his affair with Evangeline MacKenzie and a possible rival for leadership, he told Hayes that the trustees would agree only to a much smaller salary than the one Kimpton had promised. Kimpton also "made a number of charges against me to the trustees," Hayes recalled, about which he remained unaware until much later.[68] Even worse, Kimpton involved the students, undercutting Hayes's authority and "appointing a two-man student committee to keep track of me when he was away and report to him." Both students, Hayes reported, "later apologized to me for their part in this distasteful affair." Hayes, whose unimpeachable reputation served him well throughout his life, concluded that "Kimpton's conduct toward me was quite unscrupulous, but I felt no good could come to Deep Springs from public charges and countercharges—particularly as the trustees were backing him blindly."[69] He took some satisfaction, however, in subsequent events.

Finally, in the summer of 1939, Kimpton was ready to act. He informed the board of MacKenzie's unconventional cattle operation. In violation of his employment contract, Mac had been running Deep Springs' cattle operations in Owens Valley and Long Valley entirely through his personal bank account. He billed the college for purchases, and reimbursed it for sales—all without documentation. Further, he was using pastures leased by the college for his own animals. Outraged and embarrassed, the trustees fired MacKenzie and hired a team from the prestigious accounting firm Price, Waterhouse and Company to investigate and report. The student body followed the case with enormous curiosity—especially when suspicions of brand tampering arose.

L.L. Nunn had personally secured Deep Springs' brand. His first of the three choices permitted on the brand application was for two capital "Ls" back to back—the "Double L." His second choice, which was granted, merged the letters as an upside down "T"—sometimes known as the "T Down." The brand is commonly called the "Swinging T" because, when applied to the animal's left hip, it appears to swing with movement.[70] Unfortunately, its simplicity made alterations relatively easy with a "running iron," the edge of a hot ring.[71]

On December 6, 1939, Price Waterhouse submitted its report to the trustees. They first castigated the college for inexplicably lax accounting, then charged MacKenzie with record-keeping failures worse than Kimpton's accusations, and concluded that he had bilked the college in a dozen different ways: brand tampering, bogus reporting, using veterinary and related services paid for by Deep Springs to service his own herd, and selling college cattle as his own.[72] As a result, the report concluded, the college had a shortfall of 585 cows over six and a half years. At a conservative average of $40 per head, the loss amounted to $23,600. The estimated damages were recalculated at $17,500; but after much wrangling among attorneys, during which Trustee Carroll Whitman's prosecutorial instincts proved more ferocious than effective, the parties agreed to settle for $8,000. Whitman amassed additional evidence in the spring of 1940, however, and MacKenzie agreed to pay $10,500 to put the case to rest.[73] Damages totaled over $400,000 in today's dollars, and the settlement exceeded $180,000. MacKenzie began dispatching his debt immediately and completed the task in about a year.

P.N. Nunn's star faded to a flicker after his failed attempt to dominate the board in 1936. Bordering on irrelevance for several years, he died on October 27, 1939, at age seventy-eight—just when the MacKenzie investigation peaked. Deep Springs sent a delegation of three—Kimpton, his assistant Armand Kelley, and student Francis Tetreault—to attend the funeral in San Diego. The *Telluride Association Newsletter* marked P.N.'s passing with a large photograph and small tribute.[74] Obituaries drew from a statement released by the family, which repeated the official line that P.N. had "married Agnes Aird Geddes, of Hoosick Falls, N.Y., who survives him, together with a foster daughter, Mrs. J. V. Hamilton. Their own child, Helen, born in 1891, died at the age of six."[75] After providing for Agnes and Jewel, P.N. Nunn pointedly assigned the remainder of his estate to Pomona College.[76]

Kimpton's star also fell. Carroll Whitman, sensing opportunity and power as the last Nunn in the Deep Springs constellation, had taken the lead in prosecuting MacKenzie, browbeating the manager's attorneys, and pushing the case to the limit. He had enough fury left over to go after Kimpton, faulting him for inattention to his administrative responsibilities and failure to report the scandal for at least two years. Other board members, apparently appalled by Whitman's savagery in pursuing MacKenzie, were tentative about supporting his assault on Kimpton.

In the spring of 1941, with the board equivocating, thirty-one-year-old Larry Kimpton scrambled to find options. And excuses. As he awaited the renewal of his contract, he hinted that Genevra's health had become a problem. When the board took no action, Kimpton addressed the trustees on May 22: "It is with real regret that I inform you herewith of my decision to resign my position as Dean and Director of Deep Springs at the end of this academic year. The decision certainly does not constitute a criticism of Deep Springs or its Board of Trustees; you have been very good to me and I have been very happy here. The decision has been forced upon me entirely by personal considerations." A sentence citing his wife's health follows, but Kimpton or someone else crossed it out. Noting that "I shall be living within 250 miles away," he offered his continuing support if called upon. "I believe," he concluded, "that I can say without any false pride that I return Deep Springs to you in better all around shape than when I took it over. I have made many mistakes here and I have done many things that I deeply regret. But, . . . Deep Springs is going uphill, and I sincerely hope that it will continue its ascent."[77]

Kimpton's well-polished resume never accounted for the next year of his life, during which he, Genevra, and their infant son, John, lived on her family's ranch near Reno. Two years later, however, after a year as dean of humanities at a state college in Missouri, he was managing the Metallurgical Laboratory at the University of Chicago. Within seven years, he had served a short stint as dean of students at Stanford University and ascended through two vice-presidencies at the University of Chicago, one of them as liaison with the Manhattan Project to create the atomic bomb. His academic career climaxed in 1951 when he succeeded Robert Maynard Hutchins as chancellor/president of the University of Chicago.[78] Kimpton reflected later that "Deep Springs was the most challenging and interesting experience of my professional life."[79]

The final casualty of the MacKenzie-Kimpton saga was board chair Harold Waldo. Mortified and feeling compromised by his brother-in-law, Waldo had recused himself from the MacKenzie investigation and settlement of charges. When the crisis passed, he insisted on resigning as chair, thus ending nearly two decades of patient and competent orchestration of the often-dysfunctional governing body. Fortunately, he continued as a member of the board. Ironically, Waldo's exit from board leadership would soon open the way for Frank Noon's ascendency.

For all of the chaos that swirled about them, the students of Deep Springs continued unfazed with their charge as "beneficial owners," learning from every opportunity, often from negative examples. As a retreat from the storms of community life, however, student body leader Jim Olin (DS'38) built a tiny one-room cabin high on the mountainside above the dairy barn where he routinely slept.[80]

Labor Commissioner Paul Swatek (DS'33) captured the persistent rewards of L.L. Nunn's educational plan as perfectly as any: "The complete life at Deep Springs—total participation—that was unique. There was no make-believe, no false fronts, no bluff. You knew your fellow students and they knew you. They depended on you and you wanted their respect." For example, "You are labor commissioner—an old hand—and you sell yourself and your ideas to your fellow students in this new responsibility." His example became the attractive and functional stone retaining wall across the front of the Main Building: "You bring the rock from the canyon over the pass, dig a foundation, mix the mortar, fit the rocks, and you've engineered something enduring."[81] Indeed, the wall he and his fellow students built remains in almost perfect shape eighty years later. What might have appeared to outsiders as crippling institutional relationships among faculty, administrators, and trustees often amounted to little more than annoying background noise, or wry amusement, to the students. Their culture and education just rolled on.

CHAPTER 10

FLOWERING AND ROOT ROT, 1941–1956

It is hard for me to restrain a feeling of contempt and condemnation for those who, having had remarkable educational opportunities, yet remain bound down by prejudice, bigotry, and religious fanaticism.

—L.L. Nunn

Anti-Semitism came to a boil in Nazi Germany in 1938 when Jews were banned from entering most professions. They were ordered to register with the police and carry identity cards at all times. These actions prompted Alice and Kurt Bergel to abandon their budding scholarly careers in Germany and flee to London. Two years later, they immigrated to the United States. "In the spring of 1941," Alice would later write, "we presented ourselves at a Teacher's Agency in New York in search of a job for the fall [and] met four or five [other] applicants for the teaching position at Deep Springs, for which Larry Kimpton was going to conduct interviews."[1] When he got to the Bergels, he hired them on the spot.

Alice had recently received her Ph.D. in Romance languages from the Frederick William University of Berlin and had been teaching there; but Kurt, who was nearing completion of his doctoral program at the same institution, was denied his degree, thanks to a new decree banning advanced degrees to Jews.[2] He left his homeland holding only a master's degree from the University of

Frankfurt. Also a gifted musician, Kurt opted to devote his career to the arts and humanities. Together, the Bergels would earn renown for their scholarship on Albert Schweitzer's life and work.[3] Prepared to teach languages, literature, and history, Alice and Kurt arrived at Deep Springs early that September of 1941 in the wake of Kimpton's awkward departure. This bright couple, still shy of their thirtieth birthdays, would become the departing leader's most important legacy to Deep Springs.

As the Bergels settled into the newly completed faculty duplex on the Circle, the trustees launched their search for a new dean-director while Kimpton's assistant, twenty-nine-year-old Armand Kelley (DS'30), who had been teaching economics and sociology, assumed administrative responsibility at the college. His blonde wife, Bunny, drew many favorable comments from students.

In 1939 the board had been enlivened by the first replacement of a charter trustee when Jack Laylin succeeded Otto Suhr, who had resigned because of failing health the previous year. An alumnus from the class of 1920, Laylin was still in his mid-thirties and a rising star in the Washington, D.C., legal community. He was the youngest trustee by far. Early in 1941, he was joined by Parker Monroe, P.N. Nunn's replacement. Monroe had been prominently involved in Telluride Association as one of its four finance committee members and was now a trust officer for the Carnegie Foundation.

Although the Japanese attack on Pearl Harbor was still months away in the autumn of 1941, apprehension swept across America as the Nazi military juggernaut engulfed Europe and London endured repeated bombings. Congress had initiated military conscription in the United States in the autumn of 1940. Worry deepened, both for students and their colleges.

When student Erik Pell came to Deep Springs in September 1941, he found a vigorous and adventurous community. He was also stunned to discover that "Dr. Lawrence A. Kimpton, who had interviewed me months earlier in Milwaukee and who had so greatly impressed me, was no longer Director."[4] Further, his peers "ascribed it all to the ineptitude of the trustees, most of whom were not held in high regard by the students." Coming from a Milwaukee public high school, Erik was awed to be just one of ten in the entire country granted such a unique educational opportunity.

Almost immediately, Pell found professors Kurt and Alice Bergel to be "inspired and capable teachers." They were already settling in for a long and fruitful stay, probably unaware that they were being paid much less than other faculty members. The entire faculty showed brilliance, Pell wrote, with "the most distinguished among them, perhaps because of his neat, white goatee," being Dr.

Allan Saunders who taught "political philosophy, with emphasis on the fascism and communism then rampant in Europe."[5] Unfortunately, Saunder's settling in had not been pleasant. The old and overloaded Deep Springs pickup truck that hauled the two thousand volumes of his personal library from Big Pine caught fire at the top of Westgard Pass and destroyed the entire collection.[6] He would receive a satisfactory settlement from the trustees and remain at Deep Springs for five years. Saunders eventually moved on to the University of Hawaii where he founded Hawaii's first chapter of the American Civil Liberties Union.

Among other faculty who enjoyed less esteem were Elizabethan scholar Robert Gorrell, a former Telluride Associate; Larry Wilkins, a science and mathematics professor; and Victor Church, a Utah State University geologist. Church seized every excuse to teach short courses at Deep Springs, leading students on outings to the Eureka sand dunes, the Sierra peaks, and the summit of White Mountain Peak. As had been the case for many years, Johnny Johnson's English composition course won high praise from students. Aspiring to become a chemical engineer, Pell loaded up on humanities classes his first year, planning to take laboratory science courses at the University of California, Berkeley, the next summer.

The farm and ranch enjoyed a bumper year in 1941, thanks to a huge snowpack in the White Mountains and the "laconic but capable cattle expert," Charlie Uhlmeyer, who had been hired as the new ranch manager. He and his cowboy baffled the students at roundups, consistently snagging the rear feet of bolting calves with their lariats. Cattle sales topped eight thousand dollars that fall, clearing a good profit for the college. Anticipating sharp price increases because of the war in Europe, the trustees bought a new sedan, pickup truck, baler, gasoline-powered backup electrical generator, and, for the first time, a power lawn mower to mow the expanded lawns planted on and around the Circle.

Pell's labor assignments beginning in September 1941 included raking, forking, and hauling away mounds of tumbleweed that the wind had piled high against the barbed-wire fences. Doing community laundry followed, then working in the mechanic's shop. There, he invented a clock-driven timer to turn the furnace on and off. This task required, he explained, "the fabrication of a sheet metal gear that drove a metal shoe around a wooden disc with a semi-circular trough containing mercury. When the shoe dropped into the trough, a circuit would be completed through the mercury to start the furnace."[7] The dormitory would now be warm before the dairy boys arose to milk the cows. Pell also initiated an effort "to widen the educative side of the work in the garage and machine shop, without sacrifice of practical value."[8]

The Japanese attack on Pearl Harbor rocked the nation, but its effects hit in slow motion at Deep Springs. A faculty member heard the news on the radio in Bishop that Sunday afternoon, December 7, 1941, and rushed back over the pass with the information. As the news spread throughout the community, there seemed to be few illusions. "We all knew in our hearts what this would mean," Pell wrote. "Americans, and in particular WE would now be called to join the fight that our European brethren were already waging. . . . There was no traumatic reaction. . . . Some of us may have been silenced by shock. . . . We all realized that this was something that could not fail to have a very, very big impact on each of our lives."[9]

One of the most immediate effects would be the end of educational deferments originally afforded by the Selective Training and Service Act of 1940, which required all men between ages eighteen and forty-five to enroll with local draft boards. Many of the students had registered before coming to Deep Springs, but neither they nor their slightly younger peers expected to be inducted until they finished college. The rules would change quickly now, and they knew it.

Rationing of vital materials such as gasoline and tires did not begin immediately, so the student body proceeded with preparations for its spring trip. Instead of going to the Grand Canyon as planned, however, they stayed closer to home, touring Death Valley from Ubehebe Crater to Furnace Creek. There they "managed also to sneak into the luxurious pool . . . where the few lovely young ladies had no objection to the presence of a few handsome young men."[10] Several students even rented golf clubs and played on the patchy course.

In the spring of 1942, the trustees picked Simon N. Whitney as the new dean and director, capitalizing on Telluride's willingness to pay part of his salary in return for his simultaneous service during the summer months as Telluride's dean. Si, as everyone came to know him, was a Deep Springer from the class of 1919 and a recent president of Telluride Association. An economist, he had earned his B.A. and Ph.D. degrees at Yale University. Along the way, Whitney had campaigned for Progressive Party presidential candidate Senator Robert Lafollette in 1924, served as an economist in the Anti-Trust Division of the U.S. Department of Justice, and in 1940 had joined an official delegation to Japan to explore the expansion of trade with that country. Less than a year before, he had married Eunice McIntosh, a Northwestern University graduate whom he had met on the ship home from Japan. When they arrived at Deep Springs, he was thirty-nine and she had just turned twenty-three.

Eunice, barely older than the students, naturally drew their attention. Well liked, though reserved, she loved classical music, prompting one student to

Dean-Director Simon N. Whitney with his wife Eunice in 1943. Courtesy of Eunice "Beth" Whitney Thomas.

write home that she "plays the piano notsogood, viola very good and French horn very good. Very nice."[11] Si was a voracious reader of the *New York Times*, *The Economist*, *Harpers*, and any other serious publication that reached Deep Springs. His "red aunts" kept him supplied with subscriptions to the *Nation* and *The New Republic.* He could be seen at the oddest hours strolling across the desert—or playing right field in a pickup baseball game—with his nose buried in a book. This absent-minded professor was also a natural teacher who engaged students at every turn. "He always treated me and my ideas seriously," remembers Mel Kohn. "He pushed me to examine my arguments—not, I came to realize, to convert me to his conclusions but to help me understand and defend my own."[12] Together with the Bergels, who possessed similar gifts, he would open the minds and raise the bar for a generation of students.

Whitney was not revered by all his students. Barney Childs (DS'43) called him "Wyman N. Shitney" behind the director's back, and Gerrard Pook (DS'43) still remembers a stinging experience. Whitney, walking by him and another student on the steps of the Main Building, asked if they would take a new abbreviated IQ test on the spot. They did. Whitney checked the results, looked up, and announced that the other student had scored higher, then glanced at Pook and muttered, "Just as I thought."[13] He then walked on, without discussion or explanation.

Trustee Carroll Whitman had urged the board to close Deep Springs for the duration of the war, pointing to the wholesale conscription of eighteen-year-olds that was beginning to decimate the student body. But the majority of board members and Whitney opted instead to make two fundamental changes in the college. They first lowered the typical age of admission from eighteen to sixteen or less, so that most students could hope to finish one year of study, and possibly two, before induction. By November 1943, the average age of the student body had dropped to 16.3 years. The second change sprang from the same logic. A two-year, year-round calendar replaced the three-year program that had afforded students summers off. By extending the full program through the summer months, those students who could stay for two calendar years could complete their lower-division studies before leaving the valley. Few were able to do so, however; Bill Allen was the only member of the class of 1942 to finish two full years before being drafted.

Once these policies were implemented, a third unplanned change also emerged. Because students received draft notices on their birthdays, their departures fell randomly throughout each year. Rolling admissions, with a wave of students being admitted every February, June, and September, became the compensatory practice. The college also accelerated its recruitment, more than doubling the number admitted before the war years—up to a peak of twenty-five new admits in 1943. With about the same number of exits for military service each year, the student body did not grow appreciably, but the number of students passing through nearly doubled from 1943 through 1945.

An unexpected financial benefit appeared in 1943 when Telluride closed its Cornell Branch and leased its West Avenue residence to the U.S. Marine Corps for the duration of the war. This arrangement provided significant income while eliminating the expense of providing scholarships and running the house. As a result, the association had the cash and the will to help Deep Springs despite wartime austerities. Following a financial meeting, the *Telluride Newsletter* reported "that it was the sense of the body that the action of the Trustees be approved. . . . Almost everyone felt that Deep Springs has a good possibility of being operated on a satisfactory basis, provided we all give it as much assistance as possible. There were one or two dissents from this conclusion."[14]

Other factors came into play as well. Drought returned in 1943, and hay production dropped to three hundred tons, about half that of good years. This problem prompted the trustees to drill a deep well, aided by Telluride funds. The shaft ultimately descended 777 feet to bedrock. With the water level just 181 feet down, a big electric pump produced a steady flow equal to the average volume of Wyman Canyon.

For its part, Deep Springs operated as frugally as possible, with students slaughtering for food many animals that they would ordinarily send to the glue factory. Johnny Johnson reported on his culinary experience during his annual teaching stint at the college: "For three days [I] have been chomping away at the earthly remains of a rusticated dairy cow with the romantic name of Rosemary—you have doubtless 'pressed her unresisting teat,' as the poet says,—but I have never before nibbled away at a more formidable and resistant set of ligaments and connective tissue. My masseter muscles still ache. . . . Rosemary is indeed durable."[15] On a more serious note, Johnson occupied a unique niche as "the only person at Deep Springs who had actually experienced the personal brutality of combat, if only as a pacifist stretcher-bearer in WWI."[16]

Admissions and academic calendar changes brought concerns far greater than the menu. In reporting to the trustees that autumn, Whitney stated his disappointment that the "younger men are less satisfactory than older." Lost was sufficient "interest in the things we stand for [and a] willingness to read and study independently." They failed to "take responsibility in the outside work and in handling property" and seemed vulnerable to "believing whatever is printed."[17] However, in the students' defense, they may have been responding to the impassioned wartime psychology, not ignoring the requirements of critical thinking.

Complaints about students' sloppiness in dress, speech, table manners, and room tidiness are endemic at Deep Springs, and the war years were no exception. One professor claimed a connection between such laxness and "sloppiness in thought processes." Alice Bergel objected when a student came to dinner shirtless. In late 1944, the *Telluride Newsletter* reported that "too many of the recent Deep Springers do not understand the purpose of DS and perhaps do not care to."[18] Whitney worried that students were not bonding with the college and would not be there to support it later in life. These harsh judgments do not square with the high lifetime achievements of the students of this era, with their especially high regard for the faculty and staff, nor with their extraordinary loyalty to the college in the decades ahead.

That alumni loyalty is largely attributable to the faculty and staff's success in imbuing the students with L.L. Nunn's ethic of leadership through principled service to humanity. "We read the Nunn papers and things of that sort," remembers Ed Wesely who would become chairman of CARE International, "and we were reminded that [with] this total scholarship there would be a return and the return was to be in the form of service."[19] Even so, the students expressed a healthy skepticism about L.L. Nunn's solemn mantra: the Moral Order of the Universe. Bill Allen remembers that "Lindsey Grant was already a photographer, and he created and photographed an image of a middle finger, and underneath the letters M O U."[20] In future years, none would be truer to Nunn's ethic of service than Grant.

Within about six months in 1943–1944, Alice Bergel, Ethel Uhlmeyer, and Eunice Whitney all bore babies; and the homes of several other Deep Springs families were also graced by children and young teens. No one who has lived at the ranch long fails to note the softening effects of infants and children on the tenor of community life. Mealtimes at the Boarding House and the ambiance surrounding public speaking and other community interactions often involve a kind of playfulness and full-life experience that college students rarely encounter elsewhere.

Reporting on the admission of the large new class for the 1943–1944 school year, second-year man Bill Allen told the trustees that the "Student Body, with the cooperation of the Director, assumed for itself a good deal of authority in the management of the institution, specifically the Applications Committee."[21] Neither the students' initiatives nor the results of their work should have surprised the trustees.

Deep Springs had never admitted a Jewish student or an African American, but the rapidly increasing public awareness of Germany's anti-Semitic actions made the time right. If Larry Kimpton had broken the line against Jewish professors, Whitney saw it as his opportunity to invite the first Jewish students. He was well aware that L.L. Nunn had personally upbraided Telluride when its members sought to cancel Hyman Deutsch's housing scholarship at the Cornell Branch, using his race as one of their reasons for this action (see chapter 7). Whitney knew, however, that to succeed with such an initiative would require patience and deft handling.

At the students' behest, the board had been discussing whether "Deep Springs might bring in students of other racial stock than white and other religions than protestant."[22] The student body spoke explicitly about "the immediate question of accepting Jewish and Negro students," although they were not equally direct when engaging the board.[23] The trustees, who may have believed that the admission of foreign students was the aim, "left the matter for the Director to decide."[24] The next month, Student Trustee Ray Munts reported to his peers that Laylin had approved "accepting Jewish students into the Student Body, so long as moderation was observed."[25] Nor did the rest of the board appear to be particularly concerned about changing admissions practices.

The 1943 entering class of which Bill Allen had spoken included Henderson Booth, Barney Childs, Dick Cornelison, Norton Dodge, Lindsey Grant, Bruce Laverty, and Jack Feldman. With these students and others, this class and those that followed over the next several years became some of the notable cohorts in college history. Apparently aware that he would become the first Jewish member of the student body, Feldman had asked Director Whitney at the end of his interview if he would encounter anti-Semitism at Deep Springs. Whitney expressed confidence in both his young prospect and in the community, telegraphing him the news of his acceptance a week or two later. Feldman arrived at Deep Springs in June. Trouble loomed, but not at the ranch. Earlier that spring, Carroll Whitman exposed his bias by telling Whitney that Deep Springs should close because "it is impossible to teach ethics in wartime," especially during a war into which "the Jews had dragged us."[26] That fall, as Whitney was arranging for Project Director Ralph Merritt of the nearby Manzanar War Relocation Center for Japanese Americans to speak at Deep Springs, the student body granted Jack Feldman a two-week leave to go home for Rosh Hashanah and Yom Kippur—in lieu of the Christmas break the other students would take. In Oakland, Feldman talked up Deep Springs to a younger schoolmate, Jules Riskin, who returned to Deep Springs with him to have a look. He subsequently applied for and was accepted into the student body in February 1944.

Alarmed by the admission of a second Jew, Whitman, working behind the scenes before the May 20 board meeting, prevailed upon the other trustees to limit Jewish admissions to a maximum of two at any time.[27] For the student body and Simon Whitney, this action was bitter-sweet. While limiting Jewish enrollment, it also exposed and terminated the long-standing but unstated trustee agreement to block the enrollment of any Jewish student.

Less than a week before the trustees approved this quota on May 20, the director had sent an acceptance telegram to a third Jew, Melvin Kohn of New York City. He

Deep Springs Student Body, 1943. Courtesy of Deep Springs Archives.

responded at once and matriculated at the end of August—bringing Jewish enrollment to three. Riskin, however, turned eighteen the next month and took the customary leave of absence to go home and take his army physical. He expected to be inducted immediately but instead was granted a six-month deferment.

Jules excitedly informed Si Whitney and the student body that he would return immediately. But given Carroll Whitman's mounting rage, Si told Riskin there was no room for him. Unaware of the real reason for his rejection, Jules simply proceeded with his studies elsewhere, did his military service, and still remains a faithful Deep Springs alumnus. He maintains that his seven months on the ranch changed his life for the better. Both Jack Feldman and Mel Kohn continued at the college for two successful years, with Kohn unaware that his presence had blocked Riskin's return. Despite the discrimination endured as a child in New York, Mel remembers nothing but acceptance and complete respect from every member of the faculty, staff, and student body at Deep Springs. The same was true of the trustee who interviewed him and recommended his admission, Parker Monroe.[28]

Kohn relishes memories of sharing a three-man room at Deep Springs with Mark Cannon, a Mormon, and Ed Wesely, a Roman Catholic, all three of whom still delight in strong and positive memories of their rooming arrangement and bonds. They enjoyed late-night conversations and a great deal of camaraderie as "residents of the minority district" at Deep Springs. A loyal supporter of the college over the years, Kohn was back in the valley teaching his favorite sociology methods course in the 2012 summer session.

Whitman, who had been the only trustee to oppose Whitney's appointment as director in 1942, now decided to lead the board in taking him down. But the students, with an eloquent assist from alumni Roy Pierce and Bill Skinner (who would have been among them had he not been drafted the previous year), were quick to challenge the board. Norton Dodge, the student body trustee, informed board members by mail late in October that, after a long discussion about the importance of sticking with *merit* in awarding admission, the students were "unanimously in favor of dropping the quota system applying to Jewish students."[29]

Their earnest effort drew sharp responses from several trustees. Chairman Cadman might have been a moderating force, but by 1944, his declining health severely compromised his leadership. Stepping into the breach, Frank Noon condescendingly asked the student body to define the word "merit." Jack Laylin, normally sympathetic to student views, wrote a long letter claiming that "a fair quota system is not discrimination." He sent a carbon copy to Cadman, with a note explaining that he was "helping the boys to learn how a well-trained mind can and should cope with burning social issues."[30] Carroll Whitman joined the patronizing chorus with a multipage diatribe. He blasted the students for being "lazy, irresponsible, and surly." The student body immediately decided to put other issues aside (smoking, for example) to focus on the race matter at the trustees' meeting in early December.[31]

Cadman, now terminally ill, resigned before that late 1944 meeting. With Waldo still ruling himself out, the trustees elected Frank Noon to succeed Cadman, ignoring L.L. Nunn's warning eighteen years earlier that Noon lacked the vision, strength, and judgment to lead the board. As had been the case since racial issues began to surface, trustee minutes are only minimally useful for understanding what happened at this meeting. But Si Whitney tried desperately to find a reasonable compromise: the quota of two with, in exceptional circumstances, as many as four Jews. He acknowledged the need to avoid the reputation as a "Jewish school."[32]

Dominating the meeting, Carroll Whitman invited Norton Dodge, the student body trustee, to present the students' report, then ensnared them in a long discussion about the admissions process rather than facing the policy issue. The students left the meeting feeling insulted, diminished, and angry. "As soon as the Trustees left," Gatje wrote home, "there was an out-break of chooches (a wild time in which anything goes). Beds were over-turned, door-handles were coated with shoe-polish, pillows were missing, drawers of dressers were found to be upside down as everything fell out upon opening, light switch plates were removed so that in fumbling for it in the dark, the fumbler received quite a shock, and a general good time was had by all."[33]

Parker Monroe, concerned about the students' response, proposed a follow-up trustees meeting to deal with the race issue and regain some credibility with the students. Laylin, who had been unable to attend the December meeting, supported Monroe's initiative, but the meeting never took place.

The three conservative trustees, two of who lived near Los Angeles, Noon and Biersach, plus Carroll Whitman, now moved to consolidate their power. The moderate, Waldo, more comfortable with his contemporaries than with Laylin and Monroe, generally sided with this old guard despite his discomfort with their views and values.

To consolidate his power, Noon engineered the board appointment of Union Oil Company executive Harold Sanders—a man whose social and political views meshed easily with Whitman's and his own. Noon had despised Laylin since Laylin, as Telluride president nearly two decades before, had forced Noon out of the sinecure he had occupied for a dozen years as chancellor of the association. Blocking action by Laylin and Monroe satisfied his latent anger.[34] But the vitriolic Carroll Whitman also bullied and frightened Noon and his western group. These two men could hardly have been more different: Whitman thrived on bombast and conflict while Noon styled himself as an unflappable church-going conciliator.

Director Whitney now became the whipping boy of both board factions. Whitman lambasted the "Director's capacity for creating problems," claiming that Whitney had "dropped in our lap, quite gratuitously, the 'race question.'" Up until that time, he charged, the directors of Deep Springs had shared "our point of view, [and] found no difficulty in explaining it to the boys." Whitman continued: "I wrote some time ago that the race issue, injected into Deep Springs, could do irreparable damage. It is a standard implement of disruption with parlor pinks and their cousins, the communists."[35] Whitman's animosity would nearly wreck the college.

At about this time, Waldo confided in Hugh Davy: "The greatest mistake [I] ever made was in getting Carroll Whitman involved" again after he had boycotted the trustees' meetings for several years. Waldo remembered telling Whitman, "Look, if you don't want to be a trustee, why don't you just resign?" With that, he said, Whitman decided to come back and make life miserable for the other trustees.[36]

Forgetting his Uncle L.L.'s high-mindedness, Whitman claimed that the "history of Deep Springs under Mr. Nunn and succeeding Directors has been pleasingly exempt from such an issue [as race]. Its presence now is directly Whitney's responsibility." In his scholarship and teaching, Whitney questioned the effectiveness of New Deal business regulation and of the labor movement. When a student had complained to him earlier that Kurt Bergel had assigned parts of Karl Marx's *Das Kapital* to his modern European history students, Whitney wrote in his diary that evening: "[The student] tells me that Mr. Bergel is 'half-Marxist.' Maybe next year I will find myself in the position of the 'red-baiting college president'—that is, I may not let him teach it again unless he can prove to me in the meantime that Karl Marx has more on his side than I realize now."[37] No longer progressive in his politics, Simon Whitney remained open-minded, and his understanding of racial justice was clear and unequivocal. In this realm, he was on the leading edge.

The most remarkable aspect of this development was the degree to which students were isolated, and apparently insulated, from the controversy over racism. Whitney's running battle with Noon, Whitman, and other board members rarely penetrated the students' daily routines. This phenomenon is attributable in part to Whitney's ability to continue teaching and leading the community as though nothing else was on his mind. The same is true of the Bergels, who were, of course, anxious about their job security and sobered to see anti-Semitism infecting the college they had come to love. Even though student body minutes record multiple discussions and votes challenging the board's Jewish quota and related matters, few students from these years—including Mel Kohn—remember the issue. Bob Gatje, whose family knew Kohn's parents in New York, wrote home almost every week and roundly denounced the board on more than one occasion, but he did not mention the race issue. The students did, however, almost unanimously view the trustees as stodgy relics of another time.

Norton Dodge, who carried the students' voice into board meetings during the most crucial period, had the keenest recollections and most apt observations. Capturing the disconnect between the old board and the forward-looking culture of the college it governed, as well as the absence of educators among the trustees, he later "wondered why are these guys setting policy in an idealist school that's experimental. . . . A highly principled institution shouldn't be run by a bunch of, you know, mechanics, lawyers, accountants."[38]

Life at the ranch remained as diverse and interesting as ever, although reminders of the war were clear and present. Bombers and fighter planes originating at a secluded Air Force base east of Tonopah, Nevada, frequently flew training missions over the valley, prompting federal officials to post road signs that read: "Warning: Aerial Firing Above." No one knew just how to respond to these notices, but the crackle of machine-gun fire frequently reverberated over the valley, and hikers can still stumble on 50-caliber shell casings in the hills behind the ranch. Deep Springs students and staff were also being trained to fly. The Civilian Pilot Training program graded an airstrip on the desert parallel to the ranch entrance road, erected a windsock, and offered instruction to anyone who wished to sign up. Some grasped this opportunity.

In the spring of 1944, Deep Springs reported that "eleven members of the student body will enter the armed forces in the near future; of these, two will be drafted in May, one is desperately endeavoring to enter a reserve, and the remaining eight are already members of one of the armed forces reserves, subject to call in May, June, July, and November. The majority of the reservists, six in all, are members of the Navy V-12."[39]

The community received word later that year that two Deep Springers had been killed in action. Former student body president Ned Bedell (DS'36) perished in an armored infantry battle in Germany, and Wayne Bannister (DS'39), a staff aide to British General Harold Alexander, died on the Italian front. They would not be Deep Springs' last casualties of war.

Just before the 1944 presidential election, Republican Thomas Dewey defeated President Franklin Roosevelt in a Deep Springs community straw poll 18 to 16. The students paralleled this pattern with a margin of 9 to 7. Socialist Norman Thomas ran a distant third overall. No one was sure about Si Whitney's choice, but Bob Gatje told his parents: "He is a capitalist, and conservative. . . . Being a capitalist myself . . . I usually side with Si; however, of course it is easy to see that frequently his ideas are wrong . . . [but] he wins thru the skill of his quick tongue."[40]

Along with Si Whitney, the most brilliant person at Deep Springs may have been Barney Childs (DS'43). One of his classmates describes him as a polymath, while another wrote just after Childs passed his physical and entered the army: "Barney was an interesting character. Without a father, he seemed to be poorly adjusted to life in general. To a few of us, he sincerely tried to be friendly, to some of the others he just didn't give a darn. He's very smart, and knows it. His judgment in most things is not releiable [*sic*]. . . . At times he was swell, but he always seemed at sea. . . . He thought he'd like to teach math for a living."[41] In fact, Childs won a Rhodes Scholarship within a few years and became an avant-garde poet and composer. He would also serve as dean-director of Deep Springs in the mid-1960s before moving on to the University of Redlands in Southern California.

Students organized a memorial service when President Roosevelt died in mid-April 1945. By early August, everyone hailed the return to peacetime conditions. An end to the rationing and changes in draft policies were especially welcomed. Yet it would be several years before the college resumed its traditional three-year program.

Autumn brought other events. A big sow birthed a litter of seventeen piglets, of which fourteen survived. Madame Fair, the tough-as-nails cook whom no one ever called "Mary" or "Mrs.," remarked after Thanksgiving that "I have never fed so much turkey to so few people," and student Dave Wolgast earned the Turkey Award for totaling the trustees' sedan on Westgard Pass. "We may get a 1946 Ford after all," Bob Gatje wrote his parents. At about the same time, twelve students pooled their resources in a "Stockholders Corporation" to buy a 1931 Model A Ford for exploring the area.[42]

The call to national service precipitated by World War II caught the attention of many students in this era (and before it). Four served as U.S. ambassadors: G. Frederick Reinhardt (DS'24), Edwin Cronk (DS'36), William J. vanden Heuvel (DS'46), and later Vernon D. Penner (DS'57). Prominently involved in other professions on the world stage were CBS foreign correspondent Charles Collingwood (DS'34), leading China scholar Allen S. Whiting (DS'42), Foreign Service officer Cabot Coville (DS'18), and a number of men associated with President Roosevelt's 1941 establishment of the Office of Strategic Services (OSS), forerunner to the Central Intelligence Agency (CIA). William J. Donovan drafted the plan for this intelligence service, assisted by his junior law partner, James R. Withrow Jr. (DS'27), at the prestigious law firm of Donovan, Leisure, Newton, & Irvine in New York. The blossoming new agency enlisted Deep Springers Albert C. Fitch (DS'35), Robert P. Joyce (DS'20), and Withrow himself. Three other 1940s alumni appear to have been involved, but not enough information was released to be certain.[43]

Quakers were well represented in the student body, making pacifism a matter of serious discussion during and after the war. When Greg Votaw was student body president in 1946, his Quaker parents helped him tender an invitation to rising civil rights leader and nonviolent strategist Bayard Rustin, hoping that he could lecture for a week at Deep Springs. But "when the trustees heard about this," Alice Bergel wrote, "they let Si know that no negro [*sic*] was to tread the sacred ground of DS, and Greg was forced to uninvite Bayard Rustin."[44] The black leader responded to Votaw's embarrassment with a remarkably kind letter. In the meantime, Alice had marched into Whitney's office, urging him and the entire faculty to resign in protest. "Si, in his quiet manner, made me sit down . . . and argued that, were we all to resign, this would be just what the trustees would like: they would then hire yes-men in our places. That argument won me over."[45]

More serious consequences of racism were imminent. As Whitman persisted in his effort to oust Whitney, Kurt and Alice Bergel knew they would be next. With Kurt's Ph.D. from Berkeley now in hand, the time seemed right for them to leave on their own terms. After six highly successful years at Deep Springs, they resigned effective June 1947 and moved to Los Angeles to pursue their careers.[46]

During that summer and fall, Whitman and Noon pressed their crusade against Whitney with new vigor. Unfazed by their criticism but observing the agreed-upon limits, Whitney had filled the quota by admitting two new Jewish students, David Werdegar and Morton Weinstein (each of whom would become the students' board representative over the next two years).[47] He had also replaced the Bergels with Marcel and Carmen Weinreich, a Jewish faculty couple with European roots and degrees, drawing additional ire from board reactionaries.

As 1947 wore on, Noon and Whitman pressured Si to resign, but he refused to cooperate in helping them cover their tracks. Noon next assembled the full board for a special Labor Day meeting in Salt Lake City, and Carroll Whitman drafted the key resolution: "Having decided that the terms of agreement under which Dr. Whitney was appointed are no longer practical in application, RESOLVED that the said agreement and Dr. Whitney's appointment as Director is and shall be terminated . . . May 31, 1948." The motion passed five to three. Trustees Jack Laylin, Parker Monroe, and Student Representative Roderick Robertson objected strenuously, but without effect. The student body's support for Whitney had been both unanimous and enthusiastic.

Lonely for his family (Eunice had taken daughter Beth and gone to Chicago for the birth of their second child late that summer) and disgusted with the board, Si Whitney left Deep Springs on business and vacation time, staying away much of the autumn. At its December meeting, the board accepted his written request for a leave of absence for the balance of his contract. Lacking a successor, however, Whitney remained involved until the end of his contract.

The Whitney era at Deep Springs—one of the strongest in student and faculty vitality—ground to a halt. Parting with more than a whimper, Whitney, as the "Retiring Director," wrote a twenty-three-page, single-spaced "Memorandum to the Deep Springs Student Body" on May 31, 1948. It was a detailed advisory on every facet of Deep Springs, a guide for dealing with the trustees, and a summary of the college's guiding principles.[48] Given the circumstances, this document is a monument to reason and fair-mindedness, describing each trustee, summarizing his positions, and recommending respectful persistence in dealing with issues of principle.

Si Whitney had been a brilliant teacher and guide, and his academic leadership ranks among the best, but his external performance as dean-director left something to be desired. Dealing with the race issue, especially once it involved battling with the old trustees, probably siphoned off too much of his energy. Besides, he did not like "selling the college" to high school recruits or to potential alumni contributors. His joint appointment as dean of Telluride Association had also been a distraction.

A scholar at heart, Whitney moved almost immediately to the Economics Department at New York University where he taught and wrote with distinction until 1956 when he became chief economist and director of the Bureau of Economics at the Federal Trade Commission. He eventually returned to the faculty at NYU, retired from there, and then ended his career at Iona College in New Rochelle, New York. Although Si and Eunice's daughter, Beth, was born in Chicago in 1943 while Eunice was visiting her mother there, she spent most of her first five years at Deep Springs. She has distinguished herself as a federal judge and recently served as vice-chair of the trustees of Deep Springs.

At Deep Springs, that second test of L.L. Nunn's principles—his abhorrence of prejudice and ideological indoctrination—teetered precariously and the institution's health waned. The trustees designated Bonham Campbell as acting director. A 1931 alumnus, Telluride veteran, former Procter and Gamble employee, and most recently Si Whitney's administrative assistant, Campbell served under this tentative arrangement from 1948 to 1951. Although many liked him, no one seemed to recognize him as a leader.

Paul Cadman's board seat remained vacant for three years. In 1948, Frank Noon finally engineered the appointment of Haylon R. Roodhouse, a 1923 alumnus and small-pump company owner. Hal attended the same Los Angeles Protestant church as Noon and was his fawning supporter. For a second time, the trustees had failed to replace a retiring educator with someone holding academic credentials. Not one educator remained on the board. It came as no surprise, then, when their final choice for director in early 1951 was sixty-two-year-old Commodore William G. Greenman, the recently retired director of Naval Petroleum Reserves.

Despite this disheartening development, the students persisted with their own rich and perilous experiences. Highly artistic Tom Heitkamp milked the cows as his labor assignment, and the barn's sturdy plank door became a canvas he could not resist. With black paint, a decent brush and bold strokes, he filled

Trustees of Deep Springs, 1950. Top row: Harold Waldo, Frank Noon, Curt Karplus (student). Bottom row: Parker Monroe, Carroll Whitman, Hal Roodhouse, William Biersach. Missing from photo: Jack Laylin, Harold Sanders. Courtesy of Deep Springs Archives.

the top panel with the image of a fanciful cow happily displaying her engorged udder. He painted her, he said solemnly, "as a composite ideal of all those lovely creatures who gave so fully and with udder devotion during my tenure as dairyman."[49] No dairy boy in the last seven decades has gone to work without "Daisy" greeting him at that portal.

Bill vanden Heuvel, who enrolled at Deep Springs in the autumn of 1946, endured a memorable series of events that began when he and several other students slaughtered a hog. This task required building a hot wood fire beneath a large vat filled with water. After shooting the animal, they rolled its carcass into the steaming vat for a brief scalding, a step that facilitates scraping the bristles off the hide. On this day, however, in the midst of the awkward task of removing the hog from the cauldron, vanden Heuvel slipped and his right leg plunged into the boiling water, burning him grievously. The ranch manager rushed him to the Bishop hospital. Assigned to a four-person room for the next two weeks, Bill witnessed the deaths of all three of his roommates. This future U.S. deputy ambassador to the United Nations still regards this experience as a rite of passage.

Deep Springs had enjoyed three stable years under acting director Bonham Campbell. Among his enduring achievements was hiring Merritt Holloway as the professional cowboy in 1948, and admitting Randall Reid as a student the

Dairy barn and silo. Photograph by author.

"Daisy" has adorned the dairy barn door since Thanksgiving 1946. Photograph by author. Courtesy of Deep Springs Archives.

next fall. Randall, Merritt, and Merritt's wife, Nona, would all play prominent roles in the college's life two decades later.

In 1951, Director Greenman found an impressively credentialed dean in Robert D. Howard, a Rhodes Scholar. Howard orchestrated a successful reaccreditation review. But this good start proved short-lived. After students Dave Werdegar and Mort Weinstein graduated in 1949, Bonham Campbell had admitted Stephen Rabin, another Jewish student from the East Coast. His appearance triggered another bitter reaction from the board's western contingent, now reinforced by Hal Roodhouse. Resolved to kill the possibility of any further minority admissions, Noon suggested to Greenman that he scuttle Jewish and black applications before the student body or trustees even knew they had come in. Greenman agreed.

Students suspected Greenman as soon as he issued instructions that all applications be mailed directly to him. They responded vigorously and with much greater awareness than their peers of the previous decade. Humphrey Fisher (DS'50) led the protest. New Zealand–born, British-reared, and educated in Washington, D.C., at the Sidwell Friends School, he had done very well throughout his first year and received an invitation to return for his second. Courageously, he wrote the board:

> At the time I accepted your first invitation . . . , I was able to state truthfully that I respected and would do my best to uphold the principles and traditions governing . . . Deep Springs. However, since I have come to Deep Springs I have been introduced to one of the apparent principles of the institution of which I had no previous knowledge. This principle is the discrimination, practiced in varying degrees, against certain racial groups. With such a principle I cannot agree.[50]

Fisher challenged the trustees' admissions practices as countering "our knowledge of Mr. Nunn's own ideas." He concluded: "In such a case, I feel [that] an objection to the present operating policy is fully justified." Expressing confidence that a good-faith remedy could be worked out, Fisher returned for his second year.

Late that summer, Frank Noon wrote the board, the director, and the dean, omitting the student trustee. He reported that Trustees Roodhouse, Sanders, and he had met with Greenman and Howard to discuss "Dr. Schlesinger, an instructor who has already been hired. . . . He is another orthodox German Jew."[51]

Greenman and Howard had hired him reluctantly, Noon reported, but he was the best they could find. Noon assured the board that, despite Greenman's reluctance, his investigation had "found no evidence of any subversive attitude." Nonetheless, all agreed at this rump meeting that "the Director and the Dean will both watch for any 'un-American' tendencies in his thinking and teaching and eliminate him forthwith if they are detected."[52] These trustees were very much in concert with Senator Joseph McCarthy's frenzy to identify and expose those they considered to be communist enemies within the United States.

A copy of this letter fell into student hands, causing immediate commotion. Humphrey Fisher wrote Whitman: "When I returned to Deep Springs this autumn I found that my hopes for progress had been ridiculously satirized, and that I was being asked to accept policies of discrimination which have been expanded to include [all] the Jewish people."[53] Humphrey had sent copies of his letter to other trustees, so it drew many responses, the first of which came from Harold Waldo. Having been kept in the dark about Greenman's scuttling of selected applications, Waldo wrote: "I can say with all sincerity that I know of no policy of discrimination against Jews."[54] Apparently, he did not see the Schlesinger "watch" as a racial matter.

Other trustees, including Parker Monroe, defended the admissions policy as an example of "practical idealism" that enabled the college to concentrate on educating those most likely to hold leadership in America. Since he arrived just a half-year after the outbreak of the Korean War in June 1950, Greenman had used a similar argument against admitting conscientious objectors, saying that those unwilling to make the ultimate sacrifice for their country could never qualify to lead it. It is perhaps no coincidence that Humphrey Fisher came from a Quaker family. Whitman's sarcastic response to Fisher's letter of protest ran on for seven pages, claiming that there was no racial discrimination in America or among the trustees, but that bad elements were always ready to raise issues that disrupt democracies. To illustrate, he continued: "No doubt you know that co-education has been proposed more than once. I have known some enthusiastic advocates. We do, of course, discriminate against the 'weaker sex.'"[55]

Fisher, with strong student backing, especially from Don Noel and Steve Rabin, respectfully challenged the trustees' arguments. Greenman and Howard refused any personal responsibility, claiming they were simply acting on board policies. One unidentified student trenchantly rejected the attitude of "the Dean and the Commodore" that students "should tend to our studies and work," eschewing policy discussions. "We cannot agree with this; if Deep Springs is all that it is made out to be, founded on ideals that are handed to us, then these policies of the Trustees are not in accord, and we, as beneficial owners . . . have a responsibility to attempt change. If the ideals are only in the telling, . . . then we want no part of them."[56]

This same student detailed developments in the Schlesinger affair. Although this professor remained unaware of his fate until late the following spring, the trustees had already agreed to terminate his contract. Several student leaders, informed in confidence about the decision, wrestled with the grievous ethical dilemma of possessing information that they were honor-bound to keep confidential but which was unfairly victimizing the professor.

When the 1951–1952 academic year drew to a close, the board remained solidly resistant to change and Professor Schlesinger finally learned of his dismissal. Student morale tanked for a variety of reasons, including Dean Howard's forced resignation for having schemed with the student body to get rid of Director Greenman. Although Humphrey Fisher was invited back for a third year, he transferred to Harvard. Two years of battling unsuccessfully with the board had been dispiriting, and the faculty lineup for fall did not inspire him.

Howard's letter of recommendation to support Fisher's application to Harvard glowed with praise for his intelligence and integrity. An even richer reward, however, came from Steve Rabin's parents. The previous autumn, they had written Humphrey: "Stephen has apprised us of the facts of the controversy now going on at Deep Springs. He also enclosed the letter that you had sent to the Trustees. When we received the first letter from Stephen our faith in humankind was shattered, but it was fully restored upon reading your courageous letter. May you never stop being true to your ideals. . . . No matter what the outcome, we hope to welcome you to our home in the near future."[57] Humphrey Fisher's career unfolded at the University of London's School of Oriental and African Studies as an authority on the history of religion in Africa.[58]

The only bright spot on the horizon was the discovery the previous summer, 1953, of the Methuselah Tree, a bristlecone pine in the White Mountains a few miles west of Deep Springs. At nearly five thousand years of age, it was then the oldest known living thing on the planet.

This same year, two granddaughters of George Payson (of Payson Canyon fame), Mary and Clara, visited the cabin at Antelope Springs, which Mary believed she had inherited from her father in 1945. Driving from their homes in Los Angeles, the two cleaned and furnished the little house, then made regular visits with their children. Mary had given notice to the Inyo County tax assessor that she had established residence there and began paying taxes—and did so for the next ten years. Each year the tax assessor sent her money back, informing her that Deep Springs owned the property.

Hal Roodhouse was not pleased with the interlopers and finally, in 1959, petitioned the trustees to let him move the cabin somewhere else on Deep Springs property to discourage their visits. The trustees agreed. Roodhouse gathered up the women's possessions—which included two electric irons (there is no electricity within miles of the site) and a stale loaf of bread—and stored them. Not until 1962 did the sisters, now quite elderly, return to claim their belongings. The college had moved the cabin to the Corral Springs pasture at the lake property, where it burned down a few years later.[59]

Meanwhile, Commodore Greenman hung on for two more years, then joined an oil extraction start-up company in November 1954. By then the college had been on the decline for seven years, suffering from low-quality faculty, few student applications, and sagging morale. Although the school had been fully accredited, passing the periodic reviews could no longer be taken for granted. A national movement was elevating academic standards and assessing various measures of overall institutional health.

One such measure was fiscal stability and Deep Springs' budget was more lopsided than at any earlier point. The mismanaged endowment was now completely inadequate, ranch income was down, operating costs were up, and alumni were discouraged.

Complicating Deep Springs' fiscal situation, Telluride had resumed operations at the Cornell Branch in 1946 and started a new branch in Pasadena in 1947. This branch easily displaced Deep Springs as a funding priority. In 1954, due in part to its discouragement with Deep Springs as a source for new members, Telluride launched its Telluride Association Summer Programs (TASPs) for promising high school students prior to their senior year. Deep Springs soon faded from the association's annual budget allocations.

Bob Aird, Jack Laylin, and other alumni organized a fund-raising campaign, but soliciting gifts for an institution in serious decline was a hard sell. As if to punctuate a death sentence, the college was rocked periodically by early dawn flashes of light followed by earth tremors. The U.S. Government was detonating atomic bombs above ground at the Nevada Nuclear Test site just seventy-five miles to the southeast.

Out of money, out of ideas, and trusting no one in the academic world, the board resolved to run the college itself. Their final rationale may have been that even their trusted Commodore Greenman had allowed Linus Pauling to offer a series of lectures at the college earlier that year. Pauling, who had received his

Nobel Prize in chemistry in 1954, was already highly controversial as an advocate of nuclear arms control. (He would win the Nobel Prize for Peace in 1962.)

As 1955 dawned, Hal Roodhouse gave up his sputtering pump business to assume the directorship, and Carroll Whitman took over as dean in an eerie replay of the 1932 seizing of the reins by P.N. Nunn.[60] Whitman finally had the chance to put things in order his way, although he had no intention of living at Deep Springs. After a couple of organizational months, he headed back to Rochester where he presided over faculty appointments and student admissions, and, along with Frank Noon, worked Roodhouse like a puppet.

Despite being one of the "western trustees," Roodhouse had been popular at Deep Springs because of his interest in the ranch and especially his hands-on involvement in drilling the new well and acquiring the electric pump. Once he was on the ground, however, students found him frustratingly indecisive. Frequently depressed, he medicated himself with whiskey and rum, struggling to deal with the condition of his gravely ill wife.

The entire faculty left that summer of 1955, as did many of the students. Those who stayed behind observed Whitman's effort to pack the student body and faculty with additional white Anglo-Saxon Protestants. Before returning to Rochester, he taught a short course on U.S. history and government. Only five new students matriculated that fall. They joined nine returning members to create the smallest student body since the single class of ten had arrived in 1917. While the college languished, student consciousness of the social justice issues of the 1940s and early 1950s simply disappeared. Students in the late 1950s were oblivious to the institution's immediate past. The Korean War had ended and the fabled "return to normalcy" of the Eisenhower years ushered in an era of social complacency, even at Deep Springs.

Once again, when the summer of 1956 arrived, most of the students left. Some graduated, some fled in despair, others were dismissed for underperformance, and still others made no effort to conceal their smoking. Only three returned that fall, all second-year students. Whitman, better organized, personally admitted ten first-year men. The thirteen came from homes scattered from New York to California and from the deep South to Saskatoon, Saskatchewan. None were Jews, Catholics, or Quakers. Most of them had grown up in small towns. This was Whitman's student body. A safe group, he thought.

CHAPTER 11

AN UNLIKELY AWAKENING, 1956–1960

I hope the Student Body will always accept guidance but that no theorist or creed devotee will have the power to bully it. I hope the Board will always protect the Student Body and that it will not leave the work of protecting it to any who may be appointed by it as instructors, executives, or general representatives of the Board.

—*L.L. Nunn*

One of the ten entering students chosen by Dean Carroll Whitman was Jack Newell of Englewood, Ohio. I had heard about Deep Springs from recent alumnus Brandt Kehoe (DS'51). Our families were close, and Brandt's stories about Deep Springs left me dreaming about little else. I was more adventurous than studious, with the result that a so-so academic record stood in my way. School superintendent O. R. Edgington, who knew every student in his building from kindergarten through twelfth grade, must have written a sterling letter of recommendation for me. I felt extraordinarily lucky that June morning when the rural postman dropped Dean Whitman's letter of acceptance in our mailbox. My first night at Deep Springs that autumn, I lay awake on the upper bunk in Room 7 until dawn, abuzz with anticipation.

The ten members of the new class embraced our responsibilities with great energy. We were keenly aware that the student body was practically starting afresh but oblivious to the political machinations that preceded our coming. A big mahogany table in the Main Room served as the community bulletin board, where notices about meetings, safety warnings, and important news clippings were slipped under the plate-glass top. The first week, a handwritten card appeared: "Let's Make This THE Big Year at Deep Springs!" It remained there until the next summer.

With just three returning students, the culture and traditions of the student body and the college hung in the balance. Two of the three second-year men, bright as they were, displayed little interest in leading us. That left Ed Keonjian with the task of schooling the new recruits. This Russian-born son of a rocket scientist, whose eventful childhood trek across war-torn Europe and subsequent passage to the United States astonished his peers, relished his challenge. He meant business. Ed loved classical music and played 33-rpm records loud and often in the Main Room on our "Hi Fi" sound system with its single chair-sized speaker.

As the primary link between one student generation and another, Keonjian used his bully pulpit as student body president to promote student responsibility, strenuous labor, academic excellence, the "isolation policy," and the glories of opera, especially Verdi's *Rigoletto*. He had strong feelings about everything and his forcefulness often met resistance, even resentment. Heated debates bubbled up over art, culture, politics, class assignments, and whether students should wear white shirts while delivering their public-speaking addresses. Everyone seemed to take strong positions, often in shifting coalitions, as the spotlight moved from one issue to another.

When the rhetoric got too intense, we burned off excess adrenalin and testosterone by racing the student body's horses, competing on the asphalt basketball court beside the Boarding House, or jumping over stacked furniture in the Main Room. Our clashes were sometimes brutal, but we eventually learned to resolve our differences amicably. We were rejuvenating the full and strenuous life of the Nunnian tradition.

Contributing to our engagement and sense of ownership was the absence of effective adult leadership. Dean Whitman remained invisible for the entire year, preferring to transmit encouragement and occasional direction to the student body president or student trustee by telephone or mail. Nor was Director Roodhouse a significant presence. A bland person in the best of times, his wife's death that autumn made this year the worst of times for him. With essentially no director and no dean, we students were pretty much on our own. Our numbers were small and the stakes high.

End of cattle drive, 1958. From left: Rick Coville, Nick Mullins, Ray Randolph, Jack Newell, and Al Bush. Photograph by Ken Pursely, courtesy of Frederick Coville.

Whitman's faculty was as Spartan as the student body that fall, with three newly hired single men, again his personal picks. Albert Glathe taught philosophy, Roland Ball, who came with Telluride credentials, taught composition and literature, and Harold King, a historian and economist, covered those fields. All were in early middle-age. We had no visiting professors to supplement these regulars. Staff members and their families did not eat at the Boarding House, so mealtimes routinely saw just seventeen men dining together. The one exception on the edge of this all-male bastion was Nellie Ferguson. An impish older woman with a halo of white hair, she and her kindly bald husband, Clint, cooked three meals a day seven days a week, Saturday suppers excepted. After serving the chow, typically quite good, the two of them would linger at the kitchen door, listen to the chatter, and smile or shake their heads before retreating to their living quarters in the rear of the building. Their only recreation was an occasional gambling trip to Las Vegas—from which they sometimes returned with a stylish new car.

For many of the students, Louis Azevedo ranked as the strongest and most memorable character at the college that year. The eighteenth and final child of a couple who had immigrated from Portugal, this wiry thirty-year-old cowboy wore a full black beard that accentuated deep-set brown eyes brimming with intelligence. He had served as a horse trainer and mule packer in the U.S.

Spring branding is a common experience for students from all eras. On the ground: Isaac Ericson and Ryan Erickson in 2003. Photograph by author.

Branding. Jeff Griggs, Nathan Leamy, and Tony Sung, 2003. Photograph by author.

Army's last cavalry unit but was court-marshaled for insubordination. He had refused to apologize for falling asleep on guard duty a few days after the Japanese surrender in August 1945. After serving a short stint in military prison in Japan, he earned back an honorable discharge for deftly training an occupying American general's recreational horses. Like Martin Sachse and his family in the early years, Louis, his wife, Lillian, and their young daughters, Kathy and Lucy, made a mark on every part of the community. Not one to suffer fools, Azevedo had clear standards for ranch work, himself, and everything else. "This was a pretty good ranch when I came here," he told the students, "but it's going to be a better one when I leave."

Classes had been meeting for less than a month when Professor King moved our 10:00 a.m. American history class to his living room in the upper faculty cottage. Classes often met in faculty homes, but King had a specific reason. His morning consumption of spiked coffee had increased to the point that walking to the Main Building risked embarrassing him. The Student Body held an earnest discussion and sent a delegation to offer King help in sobering up. Our good intentions brought denials. The problem got worse. King soon became too impaired to lead class discussions. Student body trustee Rich Haynie, a Utah native, called Dean Whitman, seeking advice. The next afternoon, several students watched as Hal Roodhouse, in an unusual display of decisiveness, drove his Ford sedan half-way around the Circle, helped the woozy professor into the car with his baggage, and headed over the pass. Our faculty had been reduced to two.

For spring semester, Samuel W. McCall, brother of Oregon's reformist Republican governor Tom McCall, joined the faculty. Straightforward, clear, and politically progressive, he presented the students with history, political science, and economics courses that were both tough and popular. Professor Ball taught literature, writing, and French, while Dr. Glathe instructed us in philosophy, logic, and geology. The next fall, Dr. Herbert Segall, a recent research fellow in chemistry under Nobel Laureate Linus Pauling at Caltech, arrived with his wife, Miriam, and their new baby. He taught calculus, chemistry, and physics. At the same time, Dr. Alfonse T. Uhle and his wife arrived to replace Professor Ball, who had accepted an offer at the University of Oregon. Uhle taught composition, German, French, and world literature. This was a solid faculty.

Given Carroll Whitman's longstanding aversion to the political left, it is surprising that, once he had the power to select students and faculty, he did so without ideological screening. The eight students he chose for the fall of 1957 again demonstrated this breadth. He could have admitted more first-year men, but all three second-year students returned for a third year and eight of the ten first-year students came back, too. The student body now counted nineteen members. Morale soared, and Whitman seemed to enjoy everyone's respect. In contrast, Hal Roodhouse provided a ready target for parodies and the jokes college students relish poking at the establishment.

Late one evening when water pressure dropped in the dormitory, the students knew immediately that the old redwood water conduit had again burst. The remedy was to send two students in the jeep to drive along the three-mile pipeline until they found water gushing up. They would then drive on to the headworks near Wyman Canyon, turn off the main valve, and return to the breach to make the necessary repair. The routine was well rehearsed and repairs usually took less than an hour, day or night. I was labor commissioner at the time, so I corralled classmate Bill Jensen and the two of us went over to Roodhouse's home to ask for the key to the ranch jeep. It was midnight, but a light still shone through his front window. We tapped on his door. Nothing. We knocked more energetically, and a bit of commotion erupted inside. The door opened a crack, Hal peeked out, and exclaimed, "Oh! Boys!" Quite tipsy and pajama clad, he gestured us inside. We watched wide-eyed as he laid a .45 caliber revolver on a bookcase. We quickly asked to borrow the jeep key, which he was able to find and give us. Bill and I left on our errand, advising our director to "wait about an hour if you want to brush your teeth."

Student body field trips in the fall and spring may have reached their apogee in this era. Twice a year, students shoveled the manure out of the ranch's two-and-a-half-ton Dodge cattle truck, hosed it down, and transformed it into a huge camper. We fitted it with a chest-high deck over the front half, and covered both levels with mattresses. Spanning the back of the open-topped truck, about two feet from the top, we installed a broad plank on which about seven students could sit abreast—making a fine observation deck as we traveled. To minimize the need for frequent stops, a funnel mounted in one corner of the back of the truck bed had a hose attached that dangled a couple of feet out the back. The finishing touch was a large brown tarpaulin that could be drawn over the whole truck bed when it rained, slid partway forward for shade on hot days, or taken all the way off for sleeping under the stars on warm nights. Fifteen or more students could sightsee, read, or sleep in the back. One of several qualified students drove the fifteen-gear manual transmission truck, while a couple of others kept him alert and entertained.

The trustees heartily endorsed these trips, just as L.L. Nunn had done four decades earlier, and no one considered the risk of an accident great enough to put a damper on this grand tradition. During my three years at Deep Springs, this homemade contraption enabled the student body to tour Anza-Borego Desert State Park in Southern California, Kings Canyon and Sequoia National Parks, Big Sur, San Francisco (to attend a performance of *La Traviata* and visit alumni in the Bay Area), Grand Canyon National Park (where we hiked to the bottom and back from the South Rim), Zion National Park, and Death Valley. Sometimes faculty or staff members accompanied us, but we were often on our own. Although the novel vehicle could easily have attracted the attention of law enforcement, we were never stopped, asked for identification, or cited for a traffic violation.

Student interests and energy seemed to explode in every direction. Al Bush built and operated a short-wave radio station for the student body, calling out to the world: "This is K6HKF, The Voice of the Desert, at Deep Springs, California." A Photography Committee hatched a Yearbook Committee. Together, they produced an impressive visual and written record of each year. The student Budget Committee created a comprehensive report for the trustees that not only accounted for income and expenses but included recommendations for improving virtually every element of the college and ranch. A surprising number of these recommendations were implemented over the next decade.[1]

Louis Azevedo initiated a significant step in the development of the labor program. He and his boyhood friend, Dave Scott, who was then manager of the Highway Maintenance Station, delighted in taking a few of the more skilled student riders on excursions into the mountains to capture feral horses, known as mustangs. We saw in Louis and Dave a rare combination of vintage cowboy skills coupled with imaginative strategy and tactics.

Louis also taught interested students to drive cattle, rope steers, shoe horses, brand the new crop of calves, and castrate young bulls. When he and his family decided to move to another job in the middle of my second year, he recommended to Hal Roodhouse that the college could save money by assigning cowboy duties to several students. Over the next two years, Rick Coville, Vern Penner, Dave Hoople, and I shouldered these responsibilities at the ranch and on our summer grazing allotments in the White Mountains under the supervision of ranch managers Gale Murphy and Dave Wallace.

We were living in a rich environment. By almost any measure, student self-governance, the academic and labor programs, and community life had again become positive, robust, and healthy. Elaborate practical jokes kept students and unwitting faculty and staff on their toes, illustrating the playful culture of the era. A story about the Eureka Valley Girls School had surfaced prominently each fall since the 1940s, promulgated by second- and third-year students, and igniting spirited discussions of L.L. Nunn's ideals and the role of the isolation policy. Said to be in an obscure side canyon on the western slopes of Eureka Valley about twenty miles southeast of Deep Springs, this "finishing school for promising young women" became the fantasy escape of first-year students.

Detailed descriptions of the location of the school, the composition of its student body, its labor and academic programs, and its sports teams brought it to life. It was only a small step from there to the possibility of reciprocal visits between these two unusual student bodies. Ed Wesely (DS'45) recalled that he and two buddies mounted horses and "went up over Soldier Pass [and] down into Eureka Valley, looking for the Eureka Valley Girls School which no Deep Springer had ever found."[2] They were not the last to sally forth across the desert, hoping to be the first to succeed.

This fantasy escalated in the autumn of 1957. During a vigorous student body debate, first-year student Vern Penner, who had sneaked away one moonlit night to ride through Eureka Valley in search of the mysterious campus, joined with other members of the new class to ask if they could invite the students of Eureka Valley Girls School to come to Deep Springs for Thanksgiving dinner. After a long debate during which the older students agreed to different sides, the proposal passed by a narrow margin.

One of the second-year students produced the name and address of Jill Walker, allegedly the school's student body president, and the first-year advocates wrote her an enthusiastic invitation. Because Deep Springs managed its own post office, the perpetrators intercepted the missive and talked faculty wife Miriam Segall into writing a warm letter of acceptance from "Jill" on perfumed stationery. The letter was posted in Big Pine; and when it arrived a few days later, one of the second-year students intercepted it at the post office so it could be delivered to Vern Penner during the student body meeting that evening. At the appropriate time, someone plopped the letter in front of Vern. He quickly tore open the letter and read it aloud. After a few lines of pleasantries the letter ended with the statement that the visit could not happen because neither she (Jill) nor the school existed. The first-year students were so angry about being snookered that they vowed never to foist this story on future classes.

They kept their word, but a couple of tattered Eureka Valley Girls School pennants hung in the dormitory hall and a mysterious photograph of twenty young women in 1920s attire graced the Main Room for years thereafter. "Eureka Valley Girls School" T-shirts are still popular and usually available at Deep Springs reunions.

On a cold night in the late fall of 1958, three students preparing for an exam were brightening up with coffee and trading unlikely schemes in the Boarding House. What if no one had socks to wear in his work boots on these freezing days? Just that quickly, they hatched a plan that would gain a life of its own. Stealing the socks would be easy, because we all had lockers in the laundry room into which laundry man Rick Coville deposited our clean clothes.

They decided to take the socks a few at a time late at night. Clint and Nellie lived in an apartment above the laundry room, so the perpetrators asked if they could hide the stolen goods behind their sofa each night. "Are you boys kidding? No!" Clint, however, suggested stuffing the hot property in burlap potato sacks and stashing them behind the unopened sacks in the walk-in cooler downstairs.

For several weeks, the three thieves took turns being the last person awake in the dorm, then slipping down to steal most (but not all) of the socks in each locker. Gradually, the supply dwindled until, by the third week, it had virtually dried up. Then, when we all sat down for lunch on a cold December day, Ed Keonjian, whose bare feet chafed in his work boots, turned to Coville and demanded, "Hey, laundry man, where are my socks?" The dining room erupted with a previously unspoken chorus: "Your socks, hell! Where are *my* socks?"

Rick protested: "I can't wash what you guys don't put in the hopper," which only ignited further uproar and vigorous speculation. Clint and Nellie appeared at the kitchen door, suppressing their amusement with difficulty.

Keonjian, asserting his third-year status, clinked a fork against his glass (the custom before making any announcement) and declared that immediately after dinner he would lead a search for the socks. Continuing to buzz about what could have happened to the socks, the students headed out for their afternoon labor assignments. As labor commissioner and one of the conspirators, I made last-minute changes in the afternoon job assignments of my coconspirators, Rich Haynie and Al Bush.

As soon as students dispersed, we drove the student body truck to the basement door of the Boarding House, loaded it with five bulging burlap sacks, and headed for the dormitory. We raced up the hall with our loot and slipped into Room Five, quickly emptying the contents of Ed Keonjian's dresser, desk drawers, pillowcase, backpack, bathroom cabinet, and closet. We then crammed the empty spaces with socks, pushing them down to be sure they were completely obscured from sight. Satisfied that nothing looked suspicious, we went to our work assignments.

Clint and Nellie agreed to ring the first bell for dinner a bit late (they usually rang it a half hour before dinner) and the second bell as soon as they saw

Keonjian come in from the fields. We hoped he would turn and come straight to dinner. It worked. As we finished dinner, the eager Keonjian took charge. “Follow me,” he said “we will find our socks, no matter where we have to go! We’ll start in the dorm.” We all trailed behind Ed, snaking our way up the dormitory hall room by room. When we reached Room Five, Ed said, “This is my room, no need to look here!” “No way,” someone shouted, shoving him through the door. “We’re looking everywhere!” He snapped, “Be my guest,” as the group surged in behind him. Someone yanked a drawer open and a dozen pairs of socks popped out under pressure.

“Socks! SOCKS!”

Bedlam. Keonjian was screaming, “I didn’t do it, I didn’t do it!” For the next hour, the students heaped their wrath on Ed, Ed blamed Rick, and the whole student body sat down in the hallway to open every pair of socks, read the markings, and lob them to the rightful owner.

The mystery remained unsolved until long after every student present had graduated, taking with him the conviction that Keonjian had engineered the heist, perhaps with the collaboration of Coville. Several years later, I had the opportunity to tell this story on a sailboat with Rick and his girlfriend. Shortly thereafter, at a party for Ed and his new bride, he also heard the full story for the first time. Rick and Ed’s reactions are not printable, though our friendships endure.

Behind this lightheartedness loomed serious developments. Late in the spring of 1958, Trustee Whitman announced on behalf of a nearly unanimous board that Dr. William E. Fort Jr. had agreed to lead Deep Springs, effective that fall. Whitman released a long statement to the Deep Springs and Telluride communities, touting the fifty-three-year-old Fort’s doctorate in philosophy from Duke University and his decade of teaching philosophy, psychology, and business administration at Rollins College in Winter Park, Florida. After digressing into a puzzling rant about the French Revolution and how liberals had taken over American higher education, Whitman stated: “Professor Fort does have his Faith. It is Freedom, freedom of the individual after the fashion of Thomas Jefferson.”[3] He continued, “Now that I have accidentally slipped into freedom propaganda, I am hoping that you of the ‘free world’ will join me” in welcoming this highly qualified academic leader. “Let us do our best not to prescribe a line of thought.” The relief we felt over having a genuine academic professional coming to lead Deep Springs eclipsed the ironic signal sent by Whitman’s rambling introduction.

Fort began working with Whitman to reshape the college before taking office. Faculty recruitment and student admissions were at the top of his list.

Originally announcing Fort as the new "director," the trustees abruptly changed his title to "president," making it clear that his authority included the academic program. This appellation also made him outrank Hal Roodhouse, whose fellow trustees wished him to stay on as business manager, retaining his title as "director." Frank Noon, chairman of the board, believed it best for the western trustees to have one of their own at the ranch.

At Deep Springs, the academic year ended with an air of promise. Eight second-year men—a record—decided to return for their third year. The first-year class reenlisted in equal measure, so that in just two years the number of students returning increased from three to sixteen. On the other hand, Fort's announced aim "to select for character rather than IQ" (not *in addition* to high achievement), eliminated some excellent prospects and resulted in just seven admissions over the summer. The student body numbered twenty-three that fall.

When the students arrived in September, we met our new president, greeted his quietly gracious wife, Gretchen, and took due note of the sparkling 1958 Cadillac Sedan Deville that the trustees had provided. Fort offered to teach "A History of Ancient Philosophy" and a good showing of students signed up.

Less impressive was a new instructor whom Fort had hired, a Mr. Boehr, who taught a variety of humanities courses. This elderly, conservative gentleman was over his head in seminar discussions with frisky Deep Springers and quickly became a target of derision for his frequent appeal: "Gentlemen, let's not go too deeply into this now."

Fort, too, became a curiosity in the classroom. Bill Hoffman remembered:

> Fort was giving his introductory lecture to about eight of us in his philosophy course when he said—in the first few moments, "I want you to know that Plato was *not* a homosexual." Our jaws dropped. This was the 1950s when most of us didn't even know a homosexual (or, perhaps, didn't know we knew one). Dr. Fort's statement was so irrational in implying that either homosexuals are incapable of profound thought or that a great mind could not be gay.[4]

Student interest was piqued the next week when a flatbed truck rolled in and unloaded a creosoted power pole in front of the Forts' cottage. Later that day, Fort asked the labor commissioner to assemble a work crew to erect the pole in his front yard. "What's it for?" the L.C. asked. The president explained that the college's party-line telephone (Deep Springs No. 2) was not secure. He needed a private link with the outside world. Workmen arrived a few days later to install a large parabolic antenna atop the pole. Fort's demand for privacy might not raise eyebrows today, but no one at Deep Springs had objected to the party-line phone before. Speculation became rife.

A few weeks later, the student body decided to ask Fort for $100 to purchase targets and other simple materials to build a rifle range south of the road to the upper reservoir. Target practice with .22 rifles and pistols had become popular recreation, but random shooting at tin cans and an occasional jack rabbit was not safe. Faculty and staff families had minced no words.

I was one of the three members of the student Advisory Committee who visited Fort's home to make the request. He fervently welcomed our inquiry, walked over to the front door, reached behind it, and pulled out a 30-30 carbine. Pumping the live shells out onto the carpet as he talked, he handed the weapon to us to admire. He then explained how important self-defense readiness was in a world filled with enemies of freedom. He invited us into his study to see two loaded revolvers in the knee drawer of his desk. Pulling out the blued one, he explained that it was better for day use because it did not reflect light. He preferred the chromed one for night use. Then, revolvers in hand, he sprang into the living room, ducked behind a chair, popped out and slid behind the sofa, showing us one defensive move after another.[5] If we had been amused by Roodhouse and his midnight method of answering the door, pistol in hand, the previous year, we were now dumbfounded. But we got our $100 and then some.

As the autumn progressed, Fort came under increasing criticism from the older students who were especially offended when he hinted that President Eisenhower was "soft on Communism," objected to the student body's subscriptions to *Foreign Affairs* and the *New Republic*, and issued instructions for us to order *Counterattack*, *Human Events*, and other ultra-right-wing publications. Our subscriptions to the *National Review* and other conservative periodicals were not good enough. Senator Joseph McCarthy, the Red Scare mastermind, may have been censured by his Senate colleagues five years earlier, but the John Birch Society had just been organized nationwide. If Fort was not a member, he was certainly a subscriber to its views.

Fort also began inviting members of the first-year class to meet with him individually, urging them to identify "troublemakers" among the older students. Dismayed, students speculated that Fort was filing reports with the Federal Bureau of Investigation about students and faculty whom he had identified as communists.[6] Ignoring the usual protocol of student and faculty participation, he lined up a series of guest lecturers that included Dr. Harry Elmer Barnes (who had recently sparked international controversy for denying that the Holocaust ever happened), W. Cleon Skousen (anti-Communist activist, author of *The Naked Communist*, and Salt Lake City police chief), and Dr. Howard Kershner (publisher of *Christian Economics*). Fort reported to the trustees that Kershner "gave an inspiring series of talks on the subject of God, our monetary system and government."[7]

After much discussion, the students decided to act. Student body president Ken Pursley and student trustee Bill Hoffman, members of the older two classes of students that Carroll Whitman had admitted, sought his counsel by telephone. Whitman listened patiently and often. Student concerns multiplied.

Twice Fort warned the community that he knew saboteurs were at work among us. He claimed that an arsonist had tried to ignite the generator shed to destroy our back-up power source. But the students who had constructed it discovered immediately that they had nailed the shingles too close to the exhaust pipe. Fortunately, someone spotted smoke from the smoldering tar and dowsed it before real damage was done. Later, Fort asserted that his Cadillac's brakes faltered mysteriously as he descended Westgard Pass on his way to Bishop. Our mechanic, Norm Myers, found no tampering, and concluded that Fort had ridden his brakes down the pass until they overheated, as many newcomers to the area do.

Throughout that autumn the students exercised remarkable restraint in responding to the president's paranoia and his efforts to engineer their thinking. Motions to confront him or react with hostility were voted down decisively in student body meetings as calmer voices called for reasoning with the man. Meanwhile, Whitman slowly but clearly revealed his own concerns about Fort. Trustee Jack Laylin, too, became a listening post for the students. Both counseled forbearance but went to work behind the scenes without the students' knowledge.

The student body organization at this time culminated in the Advisory Committee made up of the student body president and two other students. In the winter and spring of the 1958–1959 school year, the president was Kenneth Pursley; Mike Putney and I were the committee members. Those elected to this leadership group met regularly as a body with the adult authorities at the college and took turns chairing student body meetings. In mid-January 1959, "Mike Putney reported for the Ad Committee that they had had a long, serious talk with Dr. Fort about his policies for the school. The faculty, Dr. Fort's politics, and the lack of intellectual stimulation were the main topics." The conversation had been open, Mike reported, but "no real conclusions had been reached."[8]

As was the custom, students voted that week to retain or release each of their three faculty members, pursuant to advising the president about their wishes. Professor McCall received unanimous support for retention, but the students resoundingly rejected his two colleagues. Not a single student voted to retain Boehr and only two supported Uhle. When given the results, Dr. Fort refused comment.

Early in February, Mike Putney surprised and disappointed his peers by resigning from the student body and leaving Deep Springs. In a long, thoughtful letter, he listed four reasons for his decision. One was his extreme dislike for Uhle, both in class and in the community. More importantly, he believed that "Dr. Fort's personal fight against the Communist Conspiracy and against subversion in this country should not have the importance at Deep Springs . . . which he thinks it should have. I have read the Gray Book and I have seen nothing in it . . . to warrant any stress being placed upon any cause except that of 'making leaders of America,' and 'total men.'"[9]

By spring, first- and second-year students worried that Fort would deny them reinvitation to continue at Deep Springs. Further, Fort's obvious dislike for Sam McCall, by far the most respected professor, placed the renewal of his contract in jeopardy. The younger students became cautious, or more passive aggressive; but third-year men, with little to lose, tended to lead out. Clearly, however, the entire student body felt the burden of Nunn's "beneficial ownership." We were not going to let Fort seize our college for his purposes. We viewed with increasing disbelief his repeated claim to the trustees and students that he was "leading by L.L. Nunn's principles as contained in the Gray Book as closely as humanly possible!"[10]

At precisely this point, Carroll Whitman parted ways with Fort. He read and reread his Uncle Lu's letters, apparently dwelling on one of Nunn's last missives to the board chair, Harold Waldo, which read in part: "I hope the Student Body will always accept guidance but that no theorist or creed devotee will have the power to bully it. I hope the Board will always protect the Student Body and that it will not leave the work of protecting it to any who may be appointed by it as instructors, executives or general representatives of the Board."[11]

To counter the left-leaning predisposition of academics across the nation, Carroll Whitman had handed the college reins to a far-right idealogue. Apparently recognizing how he had endangered the college (for which he had long styled himself its special guardian), he reversed his position on William Fort, strongly encouraging the student body to resist mind-control at every turn.

Herbert and Miriam Segall had been very popular with students the previous year, but when the couple asked to come back for a spring visit Fort blocked their request with procedural obstructions. Then, when the students pushed him, he flatly refused to invite the Segalls. Similarly, he tried to prevent Trustee Jack Laylin from visiting the college by giving him impossible calendar options. In March, the students drew up a list of grievances for the Advisory Committee to discuss with the president. We gave Fort the list "and suggested that he give a public speech" to explain his position on each. Fort was not hospitable, stating that he "would not meet with the entire SB and he would absolutely not give a speech." Our report continued: "Dr. Fort announced that he was going to give temperament tests to those of the SB who wished to take them."[12] There were no takers. Fort now refused to recognize the student body as a governing entity.

Whitman expressed his approval of the student body's intransigence, writing his fellow trustees in mid-March: "According to multiple testimonials, coming from all directions, including members of the Deep Springs Board, the present student body is of superior quality and has never been surpassed, if equaled." Responding to those who criticized the students, he continued, "No group of boys, at any educational level, are pliable captives. In fact, no boy worthwhile for our purposes will be either pliable or captive. Some of them may even be as intractable as you were at their age!"[13] Whitman later explained to Trustee Harold Sanders: "Mr. Nunn decided that enlightened morality was the most that could be done [in education], leaving intelligent, well-informed thinkers to find their way out. Deep Springs was his Method, I'm all for it."[14]

For a few of the trustees, remembering their own youthful years may have been a challenge. When L.L. Nunn organized the trustees of Deep Springs in 1923, the average age of the eight members was forty-one. With half of the charter members still in office nearly four decades later, the average was now nearing seventy. Biersach was eighty-five, Noon seventy-six, Waldo seventy-one, and Whitman sixty-nine. Only Waldo and Noon enjoyed good health.

Student trustee Bill Hoffman had grown up near San Francisco in a family that actively supported human rights. He had had much more exposure to McCarthyism and its consequences than the rest of us. When he questioned Fort about stonewalling Laylin's visit, the president "exploded and ordered [me] out of his house." Bill stood his ground. When Fort's temper cooled, he "announced that the Grey Book was the truth, the good, virtue, right, etc. and that he followed the greybook, so his actions and policies toward DS were not wrong and the fault . . . lay with the Student Body."[15] A week later, Chairman Noon arrived for a visit and listened to the students' concerns about "next year's faculty, reinvitations and relations with Dr. Fort." Students appreciated his careful listening but were impatient with his reminder "that Dr. Fort was a new man, picked after much investigation, and that we must be sure and do our share towards smoothing over the rough spots."[16]

Four days later, Fort delivered a surprise address to the students. According to Rick Coville's minutes, the president "made a few vague announcements about academics next year . . . and the purpose of Deep Springs and the students' place here," concluding that "there was little place at DS for someone who did not believe in a God."[17] The next week, Bill Hoffman read a letter "from Judge Whitman which hinted that it was not too late to take corrective action about the feared coming collapse and that he [Whitman] will be out here soon."[18]

Hal Roodhouse now informed the students that alumnus Robert B. Aird of the San Francisco Medical Center had succeeded Parker Monroe, who had left the board the previous year. This news seemed to be a positive sign. Some of the students had met and liked Aird. At the same time, however, Sam McCall told the students that Fort had terminated his faculty appointment effective in June. Student anger deepened. Uhle's contract had been extended despite their recommendation to terminate. Fort's steely silence about student reinvitations, which he claimed were solely his decision, heightened the furor.

A week before the board gathered for its spring meeting, the student body voted sixteen to one to inform the trustees that "Dr. Fort is not 'the man for Deep Springs.'"[19] With reinvitations hanging in the balance for a majority of the students, it was a courageous stand, even if they had opted for this oblique wording over a rival motion requesting Fort's dismissal.

On the eve of the trustees meeting, Fort announced the appointment of two professors for the following year, but he refused "according to policy" to release the names of the students admitted to the fall's entering class. At the same time, Hoffman also received (apparently by accident) a letter from board chair Frank Noon addressed to his fellow trustees that accused the students of "harboring a subversive Communistic element."[20]

The board meeting got underway without Whitman who instead sent a letter to the trustees and the student body. By now, he knew that Fort had barred six students from returning, had fired McCall, and had rehired Uhle. In handwritten scrawl, Whitman wrote: "I ask to have my vote counted in favor of each and every one of first and second year students. I believe reinvitation is vital to the tradition prescribed by Mr. Nunn."[21] Except for this general missive, he confined himself to spirited communications with student trustee Bill Hoffman.

Over the two-day meeting, the board expressed support for Fort. Surprisingly, however, they reversed two of Fort's six ousters: second-year student Nick Mullins and first-year student Jim Dean. They also voted to reassert the board's authority to make final decisions on reinvitation, wresting control back from the president. Perhaps their boldest decision was dismissing Professor Uhle.

These actions constituted a "no confidence" vote on Fort, yet the board persisted in defending him against student criticism. Meanwhile, Fort announced that "ten new 'Christians,' at least nine Protestant, would be brought into the Student Body next year." The student body also learned that the "Trustees decided that the acceptance of [student] Mac Burnham, who professes no belief in God, for two years here, was a mistake and recommended a more careful selection regardless of merit."[22] The board thus disregarded the Advisory Committee's strong recommendation: "Though he calls himself an avowed atheist, Mac is a considerate and well-mannered individual; surpassing most of his fellow students in these respects. Tops in the school academically last year, he shows in other respects as well that he is one of our finest citizens."[23] Sam McCall had rendered an equally compelling assessment of Burnham's character and intellect. But Mac and three other students—Bo Gehring, Reed Cundiff, and John Henderson—remained on Fort's expulsion list.

Burnham went on to become a distinguished professor of sociology at McGill University in Montreal, Gehring would later serve as a trustee of the college, and Cundiff and Henderson have succeeded in their own rights. Of those invited to return, Nick Mullins went on to become a professor of sociology at Indiana University and Jim Dean served as a Foreign Service officer in the Middle East. Turned off by the succession of events, second-year students Ken Pursley (the student body president) and Lex Larson joined Mike Putney in leaving Deep Springs.

In the final weeks of the academic year, two students caught Hal Roodhouse rifling through the filing cabinet containing student body minutes. Roodhouse knew these records were off-limits to nonstudents. Outraged, the student body installed homemade locks on the large cabinet. Fort took six weeks off to lecture at Brigham Young University. Behind closed doors, the trustees began to plan for presidential succession.

Erratic as the old curmudgeon Carroll Whitman had always been, without his early 1959 epiphany regarding Nunn's most hallowed educational principle and lacking his encouragement and counsel, the Deep Springs Student Body could not have held the trustees' attention. The hope inspired by Fort's appointment the previous spring, which resulted in a record number of students returning that autumn, had utterly dissipated before my class said our farewells that June. Sadly, ten first- and second-year students were saying good-bye with us.

Astute politically and always determined, Trustee Robert Aird joined the board thanks to Harold Waldo's persistence. He had lobbied for Aird's appointment for years, gradually gaining ground. Laylin and Aird had been competitors since their student days at both Deep Springs and Telluride, and their relationship could be described as one of approach-avoidance.

As a university professor, Aird was regarded as too liberal by most of the other trustees. One alumnus remembered that Carroll Whitman had previously regarded Aird as being "a little socialistic." Troubles over Fort prompted Whitman to reconsider, however, creating the majority that elected Aird. Having been active in supporting the college for two decades, Dr. Aird considered Fort as a recent symptom rather than the underlying disorder at Deep Springs. The disease was an ancient and reactionary board.

As Aird began to formulate plans to energize college leadership during the summer and fall 1959, Deep Springs continued to sink. Fort had assembled a faculty supportive of his extreme political views, but his paranoia flourished unchecked. The student body became more fractious than ever. All ten members of the first-year class had been screened and picked by Fort. "He was trying to set up a little spy ring," Roger Seiler (DS'59) reflected, "to tell him everything that was going on." It seemed to be working because most of Seiler's classmates "had no exposure whatsoever to anything except ultra right wing political philosophies."[24] Only the ranch flourished, due to timely rainfall and the practical wisdom of another memorable Deep Springs cowboy-cattleman, Fogger Dunagan.

With a chasm between most of the older students and the new class, consensus on even the most basic issues proved impossible. The isolation policy became a joke. Students slipped away alone or in small groups to party in Big Pine or Bishop and, according to one report, visit the Nevada brothel on Montgomery Pass. When Vern Penner and Jim Dean discovered Lisa, a sixteen-year-old delinquent, hitchhiking along Route 168, they slipped her up to Olin's cabin by night and set her up with food, water, bedding, and a Bible.[25] In less than a week, the cook got curious about two students who left the Boarding House after each meal with a plate of food. He reported the mystery to Roodhouse, who quietly investigated and then called the state police.

Roodhouse increasingly enjoyed the company of college secretary Mary Austin, a widow in her late fifties. He began to attend mass with her in Bishop, and they frequently enjoyed dinner at a roadside bar and grill on the south side of town. A student driver who returned from Big Pine late one night with a load of chicken feed saw them parked at the Toll House Spring, locked in a fond embrace. A joke about Austin's bra dangling from the rear-view mirror entertained students and faculty for weeks.

There was actually nothing inappropriate about this relationship between two single middle-aged people, but the entire community, and certainly Trustee Aird, regarded it as scandalous. Aird insisted on calling Mary "Mrs. Austin," with emphasis on the *Mrs.* A real problem did develop, however, when Austin refused to do secretarial work for anyone but Roodhouse. The faculty became irate. Then she demanded time off due to fatigue, and Roodhouse granted her request.

The autumn trustees meeting was a debacle, with a circus atmosphere captured best by the letter Whitman sent to explain his absence. It opened: "I have never liked funerals. For that reason, I do not plan to attend next week's meeting. The ten 'fine young men' not now in the student body, callously purged at your meeting last May, for declining to become subservient thinkers have been on my mind. The remnant of five who have been allowed to return on an obviously 'mind your cue' basis, is a token reminder of last year's vandalism. I do not believe any first grade scholar will accept 'education' by dictation."[26] Scrawled across the top in Whitman's unmistakable longhand was "Original to President of S.B." Fort would describe Whitman after this meeting as "mentally unbalanced but still politically sound."[27]

Bob Aird arrived a few days before the meeting to get the pulse of the community. Fort found him "much influenced by the other side." Roodhouse confided to Fort that "some of the older boys complained to the Trustees that they believed [you] had some spies watching everything they do and named two of the boys they thought were acting as spies. . . . The Trustees were not happy with the news."[28]

In a letter dated October 18, 1959, addressed simply to "Dear Sir," Fort reported the details of the trustees' meeting.[29] General business and housekeeping items took the morning of the first day; but that afternoon Aird brought up the spy issue, saying that "some of the older students are operating under a real sense of fear."

Fort side-stepped: "That's very interesting, because the report that got to me was that some of the older boys have been reading the mail of some of the younger boys." He continued: "Since I am supposed to keep in contact with what goes on here, I hear many things. . . . Nothing happens here without you knowing about it sooner or later. . . . Over five of the new boys have come to me quite shocked and distressed by the attitudes of the older students who tried to smear the whole administration by their lies."

Aird asked Fort if he had been sending reports to the FBI. Fort replied, "I will neither confirm or deny what I have been doing."

"You must realize," Noon interjected, "that you are making statements that would permit us to draw our own conclusions."

"While I will make no statements concerning what I am now doing," Fort answered, "I have many times in the past done what President Eisenhower has asked all good American Citizens to do, namely, that when they run across any signs of subversion to report it to the FBI. . . . The FBI is not in this and has nothing to do with what I do as a private citizen."

Aird said, "I urge you to stop sending any reports [because] if you are doing so [it] would probably make the older students suspicious."

"If I were doing such a thing, there is no possible way that the older students could know what I am doing."

"The students around here find everything out," Aird retorted.

"I am certain that what I do or would not do along such lines would not be an issue," Fort said with confidence, before launching into a lengthy stream of doubletalk. "I do not mail anything through the local post office and all incoming letters are met by a member of the family. . . . The reason I am here now is because I believe in the principles that Mr. Nunn established: Loyalty to God, to moral principles and to our country; and any action that I would take as a private citizen in reporting any subversion that I would see any place is my own private business and has nothing whatsoever to do with the college as such." He added, "The FBI has nothing whatsoever to do with it and that whatever information I . . . send to them, I do as a private citizen as I hope that you yourselves would do if you came across . . . such a thing."

Another board member interjected, "Send the reports to us and we will decide whether it would be a good thing to ship it to the FBI or not or whether to call in an FBI investigator."

Fort replied, "Mr. Noon urged my discontinuing my reports on such things last spring so I have not continued writing up reports on what has been going on here. . . . I didn't think they were interested in receiving them. . . . However, that is a matter of conscience with me and dedication to God and moral principles of my country and I will continue wherever I see occasions of subversion to report them to the proper authorities."

Waldo observed that he had gone over the material Fort had mailed to Noon: "I could see nothing in the report that indicated any subversion here."

"I am sorry," Fort said dismissively, "but you simply do not understand what constitutes subversion and I have made a study of such subject for many years, and [in] my opinion, the college was in a very serious condition last year and still has some extreme left-wing influence here."

Aird spoke up and "gave an example of how some people could like Communists and not be Communists."

"You have been accused of keeping the facts about Communists from the students," Waldo said, obviously referring to Fort's accusations toward some students and faculty, but Fort misunderstood and reacted indignantly.

"This is perfectly ridiculous. . . . I have tried my best to educate the students about the real facts of Communism as well as the other isms. . . . I have taught courses in the isms for many years, both at Rollins College and to graduate students at Brigham Young University."

Waldo voiced another concern about possible FBI reports. "Since you are being so secretive as to whether or not you sent reports into the FBI, how do we know that you have not sent in a lot of secret reports about Trustees?"

"Of course, none of us Trustees are Communists," Aird offered.

Fort replied, "I feel sure that none of you gentlemen here are Communists."

Not satisfied, Waldo kept asking questions and pushing Fort for more information. It unnerved Fort enough to speculate afterward in his letter to his confidant: "[It] made me wonder what is really on his mind or whether some leak could have occurred somewhere either locally or in the mails, I will try to find out if Mr. Roodhouse can throw any light on the matter." The mention of a possible leak—together with his double-speak—left little doubt that Fort had, in fact, been sending reports to the FBI on the trustees, as well as on the students and faculty.

Aird suggested that the board form three supervisory committees. One committee would oversee and have the final say on admissions, another on reinvitation, and the third on academics. Fort objected that they "might tie my hands pretty closely in my choice of both students and faculty." The trustees ordered Fort to hand over his files in those three areas. The Academic Committee was to include educators from the board as well as outsiders "to keep an eye on the scholastic side of the college and to advise concerning faculty members." Fort believed: "A lot would depend upon just who constituted this committee."

In his letter to this unidentified correspondent, Fort offered his evaluation of the board:

> I don't think . . . any of these men are Communists or left-wingers. In fact, I believe they are right-wingers but they certainly are blind to the facts of life concerning Communism and the way it operates. Many of them are old and simply cannot take it in. This job is one tough

> assignment and I doubt if much more progress can be made here. After the end of this year or next, I hope to about finish the clean-up . . . and the rest from then on will be the process of building.

After the meeting Fort reflected on "Cleon Skousen's suggestion that something be done to give the president . . . enough power to do something so that some of these things can be ironed out." During a recent visit to Deep Springs, Skousen had told Fort to "take definite positive action instead of having to stand around with your hands tied behind your back by the Constitution and Deed of Trust." When Fort had made a proposal to the trustees about this issue, he was disconcerted to be told "that nothing can be done along those lines." "Frankly," he continued, "the situation here is set up for trouble by the very Deed of Trust that established it. I think I can work things out with the right type of young men as students but one or two bad men can cause a lot of trouble."[30]

Fort was apparently more open with the students he admitted in 1959 than he had been before; and one of them, Roger Seiler, remembers Fort identifying his contact as "FBI Agent Wall."[31] Then, at Fort's behest, Seiler and a classmate traveled to Los Angeles that autumn to attend a meeting with Wall or another agent. Fort warned them that "the communists had a list of the people that they would assassinate if they took over the United States and he [Fort] was number two or three on the list." Seiler later reflected wryly, "I assumed that the President was number one [but] where does the Vice-President fit in there? Anyhow, he [the agent] was very interested in knowing what the activities were of the classmen."[32]

As winter approached, the Forts isolated themselves further. Fort rarely emerged from his home except to meet his philosophy class or confer with Roodhouse. On December 19, he submitted his resignation effective June 30, 1960, and offered to leave at the end of the semester (February 2) if the board continued paying his salary for the balance of the academic year.

Roodhouse reported to his board colleagues, however, that the Forts left abruptly just before Christmas "without disclosing to anyone their destination." According to mechanic Norm Myers, Roodhouse continued, the trustees had made a big mistake "in monkeying with a Government man." Roodhouse then tried to distance himself from Fort, explaining that he had spoken with an FBI agent again the previous Monday and "it was very clear that they share our opinion that there is something radically wrong with the man."[33]

Fort had apparently bragged that he had "enough information [on Deep Springs] to blow the situation wide open," but Roodhouse assured his fellow trustees that the FBI was "afraid he is dragging them into the middle of a situation which might embarrass the Bureau. They also asked if, . . . when they have occasion to make security checks on former students (which, incidentally, is frequently done), they can bypass Dr. Fort and come to me directly. This is somewhat of a routine matter but certainly indicates their opinion of Fort."[34] In any event, the Forts did not return. Frank Noon called an emergency meeting of the trustees for January 23, 1960, and Waldo negotiated the legal details.

Because these events had occurred during winter break, the students were startled when a moving van rolled up to the Forts' cottage and a crew loaded up their belongings and many boxes of college records that turned out to contain official records that Fort had carried down from the Main Building. When this heist was discovered, Waldo negotiated vigorously for the return of the college records but only partially succeeded.

Fort went on to direct Walter Knott's ultraconservative Freedom Center at Knott's Berry Farm near Los Angeles. He and Gretchen converted to the Mormon Church there, after which he taught in the Religion Department at Brigham Young University until he retired in 1972.[35]

Early in 1960, two more leading students withdrew from the student body: Bill Maughan and Milton "Mitty" Musser. They had been serving respectively as student body president and student trustee. Having had their fill of politics and rancor, they saw little reason for hope. Only three experienced students remained: third-years Vern Penner and Dick Neville, and second-year Jim Dean. From the low point of the previous spring, Deep Springs had bumped down another notch.

Looking back at Deep Springs' bout with McCarthyism, Edward Keonjian, a conservative Republican as a student (1955–1958) as well as today, commented recently on the balance between liberal/Democrat versus conservative/Republican students during his final year at Deep Springs. That was in 1957–1958 when the trustees were hiring Fort. Ed concluded that "it was about fifty-fifty; we were as split down the middle over politics as we could have been."[36] He went on to classify Rich Haynie and me as among those, like himself, who had come from stoutly Republican homes. The importance of Keonjian's observation can hardly be exaggerated when one considers how quickly and thoroughly the student body united in opposition to William E. Fort's political philosophy and educational methods. L.L. Nunn's liberality of spirit and generosity of heart would prevail again at Deep Springs, but the old board retained its grip on the institution. If the fleeting renaissance of 1956 to 1958 were to rekindle, it would depend on the sparks provided by Bob Aird.

CHAPTER 12

THE REFORMATION, 1960–1976

Deep Springs was not meant to be Utopia. The Utopian dream [is] of a world already perfect, a world in which truth, idealism, and brotherhood are as free and unpolluted as the desert air. In such a world wisdom is piped in like water from the inexhaustible fountains of great minds, and one need only drink deep to acquire it. Many students come to Deep Springs expecting to find such a perfect pipeline of wisdom. They soon discover, however, that at Deep Springs nothing is automatic—even the ordinary water supply, and there is no guaranteed flow of wisdom at all.

—Dean Randall Reid

If anyone questioned Deep Springs' precarious condition as the new decade dawned in January 1960, events at the ranch over the next several months removed all doubt. In the larger world, however, there were few harbingers of the challenges and traumas the new decade would soon release upon the nation. President Dwight Eisenhower cruised confidently into the final year of his second term, the civil war in Vietnam involved only a limited number of American military advisors, and the civil rights movement was still gathering steam. Somehow, Deep Springs was able to rebound from its slump in time to deal reasonably well with reverberations from these larger social forces, thanks to the herculean efforts of Bob Aird and a phalanx of other able alumni from the early years.

When Aird became a trustee back in the fall of 1959, he was fifty-five years of age. With a compact body and stout mind, he was at the height of his career as founding chair of the Department of Neurology at the University of California Medical Center in San Francisco. Aird had known L.L. Nunn as a child in Provo, Utah, as his parents' friend. He had excelled at Deep Springs in the early 1920s, and for two decades he had lent the college his moral and financial support.

When William E. Fort vacated the presidency at the end of December 1959, the board did something it had become accustomed to doing in times of crisis. It turned to one of its own. Unscarred by previous trustee politics and a generation younger than the old guard, Bob Aird agreed to serve as director-from-afar, if given authority to do things his way with reasonable advice and consent from the other trustees.

Deep Springs' new leader rolled out the "Aird Doctrine." This multifaceted plan started with administrative reorganization. He appointed a chief academic administrator-in-residence, or dean, and a chief business manager-in-residence. They reported to him independently by telephone or mail. Seeking a measure of stability, he chose to work with one of William Fort's two faculty appointees as his dean. His first choice was revisionist historian James J. Martin, a prominent protégé of Harry Elmer Barnes, but his demands proved excessive and the new director soon sidelined him.[1] Harold E. Kirkby, who had earned his Ph.D. at Stanford University in chemistry five years earlier, got the job. His frequent demands for a loftier title and increased compensation tested Aird's patience.

The business manager position was a trickier matter since incumbent and fellow trustee Hal Roodhouse already held the title of director. Aird knew that Roodhouse had been Fort's devoted ally, largely sharing the deposed president's ideological bent. Further, he would not be happy with a less-exalted title. Trusting neither man, Aird made clear to both that every significant decision must be cleared with him in advance.

Aird was also aware that Roodhouse used his trustee status to lord it over people at Deep Springs and communicate directly with the board chair, Frank Noon. Aird negotiated Roodhouse's continued status and title as dependent on signing an "administrative charter" specifying that Roodhouse could neither invoke his trusteeship at Deep Springs nor communicate directly with Frank Noon. Roodhouse or Kirkby must channel all communications through the new director.

Within weeks, Aird discovered that Roodhouse had been secretly exploring with George Benson, president of Claremont McKenna College, the transfer of Deep Springs to its control and possible ownership.[2] Aird demanded an explanation from Noon. Noon immediately called an informal meeting of the western trustees to deny the plan and tried to keep Laylin and Whitman in the dark by urging Aird to keep their secret. Aird equivocated, then partially accommodated the chair by toning down the report he wrote for the two eastern trustees. He risked alienating Noon to preserve his credibility with Whitman and Laylin.

Meanwhile, Roodhouse's romance with college secretary Mary Austin became a substantive issue. Aird had been dismayed by Roodhouse's injudicious agreement to limit Austin's job description to serve him alone, leaving faculty without assistance, but now he learned that Roodhouse had also raised her salary and benefits. He went to Noon with this information, only to realize that Noon already knew about the changes and had at least tacitly approved them. It also became clear that Noon knew Roodhouse had recently transferred the title of the trustees' Ford sedan into his own name. Aird cried "Embezzlement!"[3]

Aird charged Roodhouse with multiple violations of his charter agreement to report exclusively to Aird himself, ordered him to fire Austin, and directed him to return the Ford to college ownership. Roodhouse had to comply, but with Noon's continuing support he retained his position for two more years.

Emma Rachel ("Pat") Schrock succeeded Austin in an expanded position that included managing the office, serving as college registrar, and coordinating fund-raising. This tall, sovereign, single woman with long straight hair had energy and intelligence aplenty, and she unleashed them for the benefit of Deep Springs. Still in her early thirties, over the next decade and a half her common sense, magnanimity, and institutional memory made her an anchor for the community and alumni.

After these explosive first months, Aird announced his comprehensive agenda. As a new trustee, he had already proposed forming a Faculty Advisory Committee of prominent academic leaders with close ties or loyalties to Deep Springs. His first appointments were Robley Williams Sr. (Telluride Association, 1929), chair of the University of California's Faculty Advisory Committee, and Konrad Krauskopf, chair of the Earth Sciences Department at Stanford. The former president of the University of California, Robert Gordon Sproul (not to be confused with alumnus Robert Lamb Sproull), and the former University of Chicago president and Deep Springs director, Larry Kimpton, soon joined them. These four visited Deep Springs, generated ideas for Aird and those at the college, and added credibility to his reform efforts. Their eminence helped recruit better-qualified faculty and more promising students.

Aird's academic reform package also included: (1) renewing the accreditation of the college; (2) returning to the two-year program of the 1940s that used summers to push the full program of study into twenty-seven months instead of three academic years (while leaving the option of a third year in exceptional cases); (3) restoring a higher level of student participation in college governance; and (4) expanding the student body to as many as twenty-eight.

By enlarging the student body and completing the full program in two years, Aird significantly increased the number of students educated at Deep Springs. The case for foundation support would be strengthened and, ultimately, more alumni would be available to sustain the institution. With the exception of increasing the size of the student body, all of these changes transpired within several years.

The new director proposed three other reforms that proved more challenging and took years, even decades, to achieve. The first and most manageable required changing the trustees from "a board of for-life members to one with rotating memberships [with] fixed terms." The second sought "to establish an active fund-raising program that would also build continuing relationships between the school and its alumni." The third and most difficult aimed to restore a positive working relationship with Telluride Association.[4]

A year earlier, Laylin and Whitman had sought to recast the board, but they could not muster the necessary coalition among long-warring parties. One complication was the voluntary resignation of lifetime appointees, a status they all enjoyed; a second required designing a new governing compact.

A series of "I'll step off only if *he* goes too" negotiations ensued, motivated by fears of power shifts. Carroll Whitman refused to leave under any circumstances; but in 1963, Jack Laylin resigned in an agreement that also removed Hal Roodhouse, William Biersach, and Harold Sanders. Frank Noon was finally isolated, stripped of his "western" allies, but he agreed to the exchange since it removed his old nemesis Laylin. Harold Waldo could again become the moderate that he was at heart. He remained on the board until 1969 as a fine listener and respected presence.

By the autumn of 1963, the way opened for the appointment of four distinguished, vigorous alumni as trustees: Jim Withrow (DS'27), Charles Gilbert (DS'27), Hugh Davy (DS'28), and Ralph Kleps (DS'32). With Waldo now a firm reform supporter, Aird could proceed with a dependable majority that included the student member.

The new compact limited trustee appointments to four years, renewable once for a total of eight years. All trustees who retired in this process were granted emeritus status and invited to attend trustee meetings for the rest of their lives. Rivals since their student days, Aird and Withrow availed themselves of this privilege for many years—partly to keep an eye on each other.

Aird's new coalition also fashioned and won legal approval for the Deep Springs Corporation. This supplemental governing entity, according to Legal Counsel Christopher Campbell (DS'73), originally did little more than facilitate tax-deductible fund-raising. Thirty years would pass before the corporation became the primary vehicle for governance, enabling an increase in the number of trustees and streamlining succession paperwork.

Students, the administration, and the board were now slowly fostering closer ties with alumni and friends. The first *Deep Springs Newsletter* did not appear until 1966, and the first alumni reunion, a fiftieth anniversary celebration, occurred a year late in June 1968. The board also extended an invitation to Telluride Association to hold its annual convention at Deep Springs that summer. The association accepted the invitation, convening a few days after the reunion ended. Together, these events drew nearly two hundred Nunnian alumni to Deep Springs Valley.

By this time, Telluride had taken steps to integrate women into its programs. Its first female member joined in 1962; and two years later, Telluride authorized the admission of undergraduate women in their final year to live at Cornell Branch. These moves eventually turned into a morally charged older sibling–younger sibling argument over coeducation between Telluride and Deep Springs.

An important link between the two institutions for several decades was the Telluride Association Summer Program (TASP) that the association had initiated in 1954. Designed as a liberal arts counterpart to the National Science Foundation's summer science programs for gifted high school seniors, the courses normally ran about six weeks. These intense college-like courses were offered first at the Telluride House at Cornell, then on other campuses. Deep Springs had hosted its first TASP in 1957. At that time, the college was not in session during the summer months, so there were no conflicts with its own schedule. A skeleton crew of Deep Springers, however, worked at the ranch each summer. At the outset, they also provided transportation, led weekend field trips, and directed labor assignments for TASP students.

Two issues complicated hosting TASPs at Deep Springs. By 1963, the college had switched back to a year-round calendar and, therefore, had a summer curriculum of its own that required the same facilities. One solution was to combine the TASP with the summer course for first-year students. When Telluride opened its summer programs to young women, however, the question arose as to whether its Deep Springs TASP would remain all male. Or, might Deep Springs integrate Telluride's women into its student body during the summer?

After considering different options, none of which proved satisfactory, Telluride Association and Deep Springs agreed in 1972 to suspend their four-year run of combined summer programs.

Telluride had invented TASPs partly as a source of future Telluride Associates. But the benefits ran the other direction when TASPs, especially those held at the college, produced a stream of successful applicants for Deep Springs. In the 1960s, many bright high school students also heard about Deep Springs and applied, prompted by the description and accompanying photograph of the valley on the final page of the TASP brochure. Similarly, a group of outstanding professors taught the combined seminar for these summer courses. Jack Schaar, noted University of California, Berkeley (and later Santa Cruz) political theorist, his colleague and wife, Hanna Pitkin, and his protégé, Jeff Lustig at California State University, Sacramento, became perennial favorites at Deep Springs with rigorous and germane summer courses titled "Community and Authority," and "The Individual and the Common Good." One of their summer understudies was Deep Springs' current president David Neidorf.

The financial and intellectual returns that TASPs provided Deep Springs had been significant enough to rekindle a relationship that generated a new run of summer programs at the college from 1978 to 1990. Coeducational Telluride groups participated at the college the latter three summers. Cooperative projects, including limited student exchanges and strategic financial cooperation, continued into the twenty-first century.

When Harold Kirkby and Hal Roodhouse relinquished their academic and business posts at Deep Springs, Aird granted their successors greater independence. Alumni Ed Loomis (DS'42), Randall Reid (DS'49), and Barney Childs (DS'43) rotated through academic leadership, bringing new energy, ideas, and perspectives to the Nunnian tradition. Aird remained the titular head, but Loomis as dean felt almost solely in charge.

In 1963, Loomis hired Dick Strong as ranch manager. The son of the chancellor at U.C. Berkeley, Strong was no stranger to agriculture, but neither was he an old hand. Students believed his appointment had more to do with his father's friendship with Aird than an objective assessment of his qualifications. Strong, a handsome, lanky man with a broad grin, welcomed the challenge, as did his energetic wife, Helen (who had some training in veterinary medicine), and their two young sons.

By 1965 the faculty consisted of Joseph Balachowski, a highly disciplined former Polish artillery officer and German prisoner of war who taught European languages; young and intense Roger Dell, who taught calculus and physics

Faculty in 1966. Back row: Dean Barney Childs, Roger Dell, John Mawby, Jack Newell, Joseph Balachowski. Front row: Mary Childs (Margaret), Marilyn Dell (Nicole), Office Manager Pat Schrock, Linda Newell (Chris), Jean Balachowski. Courtesy of Deep Springs Archives.

Heroes of Labor on Mother's Day, 1966: Marilyn Dell with Nicole, Linda Newell with Christine, Cece Holdaway with Tina. Photograph by author.

"with a cigarette in one hand and a coffee cup in the other"; austere paleontologist and geologist John Mawby (DS'53), who knew earth sciences inside out; and Jackson Newell (DS'56), who taught history and economics. Young and highly motivated, all four professors brought families with them. All, too, would serve the college in multiple positions over many years.

Barney Childs (DS'43) presided as dean and quasidirector under Dr. Aird. Hunch-backed from childhood polio, this pipe-smoking, avant-garde composer and poet also taught a composition course required of all first-year students. A Rhodes Scholar who could switch from charming to caustic in an instant, Childs loved to entertain his faculty and staff colleagues with extended weekend poker games. His wife, Mary, and preschool daughter, Margaret, added a lively air to Boarding House meals.

Marilyn Dell, Linda Newell, and Cece Holdaway (wife of staff cowboy Darrell Holdaway) all gave birth to daughters in February 1966. For Mother's Day, the students made "Hero of Labor" medallions for these women to wear, celebrating their success in increasing the number of females in the community.

The same month, the inaugural issue of the *Deep Springs Alumni Newsletter* ran a solemn notice of something else that could only happen at Deep Springs. Framed in a black box it read simply: "In Memoriam WHITE COW November 5, 1964."[5] For the better part of two decades, this patient creature had been the dairy boys' revered companion and most prolific producer, giving as much as nine gallons a day.

The Free Speech Movement at Berkeley in 1964–1965 spawned the idea of the "free university," or education liberated from bureaucratic overlays with the aim of becoming more relevant to students' needs. At Deep Springs students had been involved in admissions in varying degrees since the late 1920s, and in faculty selection and review occasionally since the 1940s—again in a rhythmic pattern. The Admissions Committee became increasingly active with Aird's permission and Childs's encouragement (followed later by Randall Reid). By 1964 students were participating directly in admissions decisions (dropping the question about religious affiliation the next year) and were gaining a voice in faculty hiring and academic policy.

Reinvitations, however, remained almost entirely a trustee prerogative, a formal arrangement that the board and Childs took for granted. The student body accepted the status quo, too, until Steve Oliver (DS'63) asked why, if the student body could weigh in on admissions decisions, it should not have a comparable role in reinvitations.[6] When the trustees refused to renew the scholarships of several students without warning or explanation in 1964, the student body cried foul.

Childs sympathized with the students and agreed to let them decide on reinvitations in 1965. Some recall that he signed a letter to the student body confirming this understanding.[7] When the trustees learned what was going on, they refused to endorse the arrangement, citing the Deed of Trust. Childs backed down formally but finessed the issue by letting the students know that he wanted their counsel on reinvitations. Even the board conceded that greater student participation would be healthy. Those who were aware of Fort's purges in 1959 were particularly pleased with these developments.

Satisfied with his record as director, Aird resigned in 1966. First, however, he secured Frank Noon's long-overdue resignation as board chair, while agreeing to let him remain on the board for life. (He died in 1973.) Aird welcomed his own election as chair, then announced Barney Childs's assumption of overall executive authority for the college, thus completing the leadership transition.

Improving student recruitment and upgrading admissions standards had been among Aird's objectives, and he had engaged alumni in finding good applicants and interviewing finalists. He also contacted officials at leading high schools. Recent entering classes had included truly exceptional students. Childs disdained recruiting, however, resulting in much smaller applicant pools.

One of Aird's successes, David Mossner, whose father was an eminent philosopher at the University of Texas, had arrived in 1963. By his third year, David had excelled in his scholarship, devoted himself to every labor assignment, and served with distinction in several student body offices. He had even won the annual steer-riding contest by staying astride the longest of any student. David began his farewell speech in 1966 by saying: "After three years at Deep Springs, I think I would make a pretty good first-year man."[8] Randall Reid, who had taught him during his first and second years, admired Mossner's "fine subversive wit, [which] showed you there was more than niceness to the person."[9]

Joining the student body over the next two years were other men who went on to earn distinction in their professions, among them Stephen Noll (DS'64), Michael Stryker (DS'64), and Eric Swanson (DS'65).[10] Regardless of gift or status, all students in this era felt the turbulence of the larger culture. The civil rights movement had heightened sensitivities to injustice and placed a premium on action, advocacy, and protest. By the middle of the decade, President Lyndon Johnson, responding to the demands of civil right leaders, pressured Congress to pass the Civil Rights Act (1964) and the Voting Rights Act (1965). Years of activism, popular music, and personal sacrifice had borne fruit.

Youthful idealists who had come to see the federal government as a force for good, however, became disillusioned with the escalation of the Vietnam War.

David Mossner posing as L.L. Nunn, 1966. Courtesy of Ron Alexander.

Faced with military conscription, millions of young men struggled with the moral dilemma of the war's rationale and the use of incendiary agent napalm against enemy targets. The draft drove tens of thousands of these young men into college—or kept them there—to obtain deferments. Many were keenly aware that their asylum meant that others would serve and perhaps die in their places. This moral burden also fell upon conscientious objectors. In an environment like Deep Springs, where ethical issues are often the center of conversation, the pain of awareness became acute—whether students chose to serve or refused the call.

On many college campuses, rage over Vietnam burst out in forceful demonstrations, with some reaching into the chambers of administration buildings. By the end of the decade, protests at Kent State and Jackson State had spun into tragedies.[11] At Deep Springs, the students lived in the administration building (the Main Building); and even there, no unreasoning bureaucrat lurked down the hall. But in response to the U.S. invasion of Cambodia that had sparked the lethal demonstrations at Kent State and Jackson State, Denis Clark (DS'69) remembered that "some DS students, in Betsy Ross tradition, hand-stitched a flag that said 'We Won't Go' and replaced the American flag on the Circle flagpole with it."[12]

Perhaps for this reason, student malaise turned inward. Less mature or less popular students became targets for bullying and endured humiliation. Witnessing only the effects of this harassment, the staff and faculty became deeply concerned. A wider but even less public manifestation of student rage was the flight from reality offered by psychedelic drugs, which may have had special allure at Deep Springs. Being physically removed from the movement engulfing their generation, many students saw these popular new drugs as a way to join in. Also resonating with some Deep Springers was the theory that using marijuana, LSD, and other consciousness-altering substances might open new possibilities for human harmony or personal achievement.

One group of students began smoking marijuana while hiking the historic Hance Trail in the Grand Canyon during the autumn break in 1966. They continued to experiment privately when they returned to Deep Springs. Availability broadened when a student returned from the winter holiday with a generous supply of cannabis.[13] Then, four students, who spent the February 1967 break in San Francisco, returned with LSD from the Haight-Ashbury district. They had been visiting at Telluride's Berkeley Branch.

By spring, the student body had divided into three groups: the users (a large majority of the student body), those who knew the users and kept their secret while personally abstaining, and two or three who had no idea what was going on. Dean Childs, the faculty, and the staff remained oblivious to the situation. The fact that the dean and a number of faculty and staff members routinely consumed alcohol to the point of embarrassing themselves in public was not lost on the students who also knew that at least one short-term professor had been using drugs at Deep Springs.

Dave Mossner and other alumni who were now living at Cornell Branch soon learned about the students' frequent use of drugs. Alarmed by the loss of student self-governance, Mossner expressed his and others' concern to his friends within the student body. They suddenly realized that their chances of going on to Telluride were in jeopardy. The student body debated various strategies for dealing with this threat.

When two influential third-year students—both nonusers—were absent for a few days, the student body called a special meeting on May 30, 1967. Those present quickly passed a new ground rule prohibiting the use of nonmedicinal drugs by students. The motion passed with a wink, because everyone apparently agreed in advance that conformity would be left entirely to the discretion of each member. The body sent the resolution to Childs and Telluride Association leaders. When the two absent students, Dan Ihara and Ron Alexander,

Student body, 1969. Courtesy of Denis Clark.

returned and got wind of the sham, they were doubly incensed. They had been deceived by their peers, and their peers had betrayed Childs's trust.

Alexander's conscience drove him to tell Childs that he had been misled. The dean immediately called a meeting with student leaders Joel Coble, Glen Kaufman, and Eric Swanson to express his indignation over the student body's dishonesty. The person who tipped off the dean, according to a visiting student from the Berkeley Branch, "spoiled it for the rest of us."[14]

Once drug use was forced into the open, some continued the practice secretly, and a few dared their peers to stop them. With users and their friends in the majority, some of the most frequent consumers gained peer support for reinvitation, while the issue became a factor in others being forced out. Wounds from these events cut many students so deeply that emotions still ran high when they gathered for a reunion forty years later—even as forgiveness was readily granted by all.[15]

In December 1967, student body president Bill Pezick (DS'65) and student trustee Eric Swanson launched an effort to restore confidence in the student body. They reached out to improve ties with Childs and Telluride officials, while urging self-control by their peers. Drug use apparently waned for the balance of that calendar year; but by the end of the 1968 spring term, the student body again seemed to have given up any pretense of enforcing the ground rules.

During spring vacation that year, Rick Hansen (DS'66), one of the students who stayed to milk the cows and maintain the ranch, drove to Bishop on college business. Having accomplished his errands, he went to visit a woman with whom he had become acquainted when she visited staff friends at Deep Springs. When he knocked on her door, a police officer in plain clothes opened it and pulled him inside. Rick had inadvertently walked into a drug raid and he spent the next several hours under interrogation. The authorities released him with instructions to stick to college business the next time he came to town.

The following week, Ralph Kleps (DS'32), a Deep Spring trustee and director of the Administrative Office for the Courts in California, did a routine review of police bulletins and noticed a Deep Springs College address. Dean Childs's phone rang moments later. He stormed outside, found Hansen, and demanded an explanation. Rick had already confided in "Mother Pezick," his nickname for the always-caring Bill Pezick, the student body officer he trusted most. Now he told the full story to a disbelieving Childs. Still shaken, Childs addressed the students as a body that evening, appealing to them once again to accept responsibility for the conduct of their own members.[16] They took the matter under advisement without clear results. Meanwhile, with the exception of Kleps, the trustees remained largely oblivious to the turmoil at Deep Springs.

At the same time, the board commissioned a master plan for physical plant expansion, renovation, and maintenance—acutely needed given the growing regular number of visiting faculty. Frantz Albert of HCD Collaborative Architects and Planning won the contract with Robert Gay (DS'60) as architect.[17] The first three fruits of this initiative were a new guest cottage named for Jim Withrow, a new faculty residence nearly joined to it named for Robert Aird, and a major expansion of the Boarding House dining room.

The Withrow Cottage project received a surprising and significant boost when student trustee Doug Von Qualen (DS'64) worked up a plan for the student body to offer $1,000 toward its construction, contingent on ten trustees or alumni matching the students' commitment. When the students presented their challenge at the board meeting in April 1967, Trustee Withrow boomed, "Consider your money gone!" By the first week of October that year, Trustee Hugh Davy (DS'28) reported that he and nine other alumni had pledged at least one thousand dollars each.

The juxtaposition of these two buildings is symbolic because Aird and Withrow's rivalry was legendary. They had competed with one another for supremacy in influencing Deep Springs from Withrow's joining the board in 1963 until his exit in the spring of 1980. Aird had joined the board in 1959 and left in 1971, but the two continued to duel throughout the 1970s as leading donors and dominant players in alumni politics. Their legacy buildings nearly touch, yet they are positioned blindly to one another.[18]

Meanwhile, conflict simmered between students and staff. Ranch Manager Dick Strong became a lightning rod for discontented students and faculty, many of whom challenged his managerial competence and criticized his free-wheeling style. He spent much unexplained time away from the college. Labor Commissioner Eric Swanson recalls: "In Spring of 1967, I was required by Student Body resolution to keep a calendar of the days on which Strong was away from the valley."[19] The students moved gradually from emotional appeals for board action to a rational statement of their concerns.

Bill Pezick was the student body trustee at the spring 1968 board meeting. With the unanimous consent of his peers, he submitted a concise, critical evaluation of Strong's performance. A few months later, Strong resigned after the board rejected his request for a salary increase. George Conley succeeded him in January 1969, but he left the next fall because the trustees opted not to invest in ranch improvements.

Into this pressure cooker walked two leaders, both ardent westerners and restless wanderers, yet an unlikely pair. Neither Randall Reid nor Merritt Holloway was a stranger to Deep Springs or to one another. Merritt had been Deep Springs' professional cowboy in 1948–1949, earning an estimable reputation. He was also known for having taken an interest in two dilapidated one-room cabins that the U.S. Forest Service had built at nearly 10,000 feet on upper Crooked Creek in 1912, the first ranger station in the White Mountains. Located near the center of the college's grazing allotment, Merritt received permission to fix these cabins up. Known as Deep Springs Cow Camp, they still serve that purpose.

Merritt returned late in 1969 as ranch and operations manager. His wife, Nona, and their daughter, Nonie, joined him at the end of the school year. Their three sons were now grown and on their own. A tall, angular pipe-smoker, he was plain spoken, bighearted, hard working, and honest to the core. Nona, too, exuded integrity and possessed a literary gift that produced three books about their family's saga of love, labor, and western adventure.[20]

Randall, Earline, and their son, Eric, had arrived a few months earlier when Randall became dean and director. They enrolled daughter Katharine in a boarding school in Marin County, "a solution to the daughter-at-Deep Springs problem that had [earlier] stood in the way of the Reids' taking the job."[21]

Born in Paso Robles, California, Randall had entered Deep Springs as a student in 1949 when Holloway served as cowboy. He left after less than a year because of an appendicitis attack during a student trip to Death Valley.

Merritt Holloway astride Kuskey works cattle with student cowboys Jeff Boyd (DS'69) and Phil Shaw (DS'71), center, Spring 1972. Courtesy of Denis Clark.

Paying for emergency surgery in Bishop dictated that Reid take a job rather than return to Deep Springs. When the Korean War draft loomed, he enlisted in the U.S. Navy and became a personnel officer, eventually stationed in Hawaii. He and Earline were married with two children when he mustered out in Honolulu. Returning to California, he enrolled as a freshman at San Francisco State, then joined Wallace Stegner's writing program at Stanford University (along with classmates Larry McMurtry, Ken Kesey, and Robert Pinsky) where he earned his master's and doctoral degrees.[22] "This was something that placed him near the source of 1960's culture," recalled his son-in-law, Denis Clark, and "Earline once described themselves as 'Beatniks' in those years."[23] Leaving the

Cabins at Cow Camp at nearly 10,000 feet elevation, Summer 1971. Courtesy of Denis Clark.

San Francisco Bay area, the Reids moved east when Randall joined the University of Chicago faculty and its Committee on New Social Thought.

Aird had been badgering Reid to lead Deep Springs and "repeatedly tried to get him to come with increasing inducements."[24] Reid had taught twice at Deep Springs while pursing his doctorate, earning respect. On the second stint, he also served as interim dean. His arrival as director and dean seemed a logical and promising next step to everyone concerned. A literary critic and fiction writer, Randall smoked unfiltered cigarettes and carried not a single extra pound. One of his students would later reflect that Reid possessed "all the insights of us young cynics but [remained] positive despite lacking illusions."[25] For Earline, this move to Deep Springs required sacrifices, one of which was being uprooted from her engaging life in Chicago.

Randy and Merritt, the Reids and the Holloways, together provided stability at the top for the troubled decade ahead. Their devotion to the college, to its ideal of service, and to the students shone through. Their integrity rubbed off, and Deep Springs' leadership seemed to renew the Nunnian contract with students: In return for receiving a full scholarship to an institution that grants you the highest level of engagement in directing your own education, you agree to devote yourself wholeheartedly to its success, setting aside your self-interest for the duration of your stay and living for the benefit of the community.

It is impossible to say how cultures change, because so many factors are involved; but within two or three years, the student body had regained its

Earline and Randall Reid in 1975. Courtesy of Earline Reid.

balance and its members were again taking their duties to the college seriously. Student bodies over the years have rarely if ever observed the ground rules perfectly, but by 1971 wanton disregard for the basic contract between students and the institution had subsided. Reid reflected later that the drug problem had "progressively [gotten] better and was essentially cleaned up to the point that there was . . . no more Student Body collusion in ignoring the ground rules."[26] While greater self-discipline and student self-governance certainly had developed by 1971, it appears that Reid was either uncharacteristically naive or consciously reconstructing the past in an effort to shape institutional culture.

Reid credited the students of this era with rediscovering L.L. Nunn as a venerable figure. For years, the founder had been interpreted as just another turn-of-the-century robber baron. As the Vietnam War dragged on, the liberal establishment under President Lyndon Johnson appeared as immoral to young idealists as the Republican old guard. Reading Nunn afresh revealed a far more nuanced character—the gatecrasher who made it big, mingled with the rich and influential, but never lost his focus on justice. His leadership and business philosophies, too, were personal not bureaucratic.

Reid later wrote: "Like so many of L.L. Nunn's phrases, 'abundance of heart' may carry enough late Victorian echoes to invite parody. But something like 'abundance of heart' is surely necessary to sustain any serious vision of life. Its absence condemns one to the superficial or exploitative or irresponsible or cynical attitudes so depressingly common in every human vocation, and it rarely develops without a variety of direct experience."[27]

Students found Nunn an unusual elitist as they rediscovered his aim of preparing promising young men "to free the rich from the bondage of their riches and the poor from the bondage of their poverty."[28] The founder was back in style at Deep Springs. Randy Reid himself had begun laying the groundwork when he taught there in the mid-sixties.

To Nunn's broad ethic of service, Reid also added contemporary urgency. Speaking at the traditional "Sunday Service" one spring morning on "How to Be Intelligent Even If You Are Bright," he concluded:

> The burden of intelligence is so difficult and so necessary that we cannot afford to waste our energies in dodging problems and acquiring meaningless merit badges. We must try to accomplish something, and we must be tough enough to risk failure and to live through it when it comes. . . . The revelation that you aren't worth very much has among other possible morals . . . that nonetheless you have to go on living, living with other people, and probably you ought to have a little charity towards them, and even charity, though not indulgence, toward yourself.[29]

By the early 1970s, according to Denis Clark, the decisions the trustees made about admissions, faculty hiring and retention, and academic policy almost always followed Reid's recommendations but he, in turn, respected "Student Body leanings," or at least did not ignore their "strong opinions." The students felt that their voices were heard and "the Trustees probably felt there was a stopper against rampant student opinion."[30] Importantly, Clark continued, "I remember that Reid asserted himself more in student opinions of faculty—he pointed out that there were contractual and professional issues, and you could not evict or hire anyone on a tide of opinion." These themes would play out repeatedly in subsequent decades.

No governance decisions at Deep Springs generate more conflict, emotion, and outright pain than the spring round of Reinvitations Committee (R-Com) hearings. When the process is politicized it can be both brutal and unjust, as was the case in the Fort era at the end of the 1950s and in the late 1960s when drugs demolished trust within the student body. But when it works well, though it is never easy, students learn volumes about the difficulty of judging the heart and mind of another human being. R-Com can be Deep Springs education at its best.

The winter of 1968–1969 was one of the harshest and snowiest on record. Spring runoff down Wyman Canyon and Crooked Creek was extraordinary, and the ranch had all the irrigation water it could use that summer. Then, on July 30, a violent thunderstorm burst directly over the headwaters of Wyman Creek. With the ground already saturated from the late melting snow, there was nowhere for the torrent to go but down the canyon.

To service its power lines, Southern California Edison had recently cleared much of the willow and wild rose undergrowth in the canyon and dynamited the narrows (replacing a long by-pass) to open a jeep trail. The wall of water, therefore, met little resistence and overwhelmed everything in its path. The entire horse pasture at Roberts Ranch washed away. The old cabin just above it survived.

The surging waters reamed the canyon to bedrock in many places. Barely a trace remained of the Wyman Canyon jeep road to Cow Camp or the power and telephone lines that served the college. Many thousands of tons of debris flushed out of the mouth of Wyman and spread the width of Deep Springs Valley, wiping out the irrigation headworks and sections of the highway and engulfing Deep Springs' corrals and haystacks.[31] Those at the college compared the flood's noise to a freight train. Classmates Denis Clark and Jan Vleck (DS'69) and a staff member, returning from a driver's trip, became trapped and spent the night in the cab of the big GMC truck. A California Transportation Department (Caltrans) crew with heavy equipment found them the next morning and towed them to safety through the receding flood waters and debris.[32]

Everyone at Deep Springs gets frequent lessons in the power of nature, but this "five hundred year" flash flood also became a watershed for the ranch operation.[33] The old redwood water pipe had been replaced by a domestic well two years earlier, so drinking water was available, but the water lines and irrigation ditches were filled with sand and silt. The trustees had neglected physical plant maintenance for nearly twenty years, choosing to spend the funds on the new cottages. Now the infrastructure could wait no longer.

The first priority was to repair or replace the damaged water lines. The trustees hired Wally Rooney, carpenter and jack-of-all-trades, while his wife, Jo, became the relief cook. Their skills earned them high respect and they remained on staff for many years. After retiring from Yale, Herbert Reich (DS'17) began spending his winters teaching physics at Deep Springs and working on maintenance. He had helped install the electrical system in the Main Building as a student and now upgraded it.

Irrigating the alfalfa fields had used a flooding technique of placing movable canvas dams in open ditches. Now Merritt Holloway proposed converting to rolling, pressurized aluminum water pipes with multiple sprinklers. This change came slowly because of the expense. It also inspired a renewed debate about the purpose and philosophy of the labor program. Should Deep Spring adopt efficient new technologies if they reduced the challenges and rigors of manual labor? What skills remained important and why? Why did the dairy boys milk the cows by hand (still do) but draft horses had given way to tractors to plow, plant, and harvest the fields? The conversion to sprinklers occurred gradually over a decade, but the conversation about technology and labor endures.

Neither in the architectural master plan nor with any warning came a new need in January 1975. The original stone and concrete block mechanic shop burned to an empty shell, the apparent result of an electrical short coupled with a gas leak. Scores of alumni rallied with the funds to replace it.

Nona and Merritt Holloway's deep, practical knowledge of high desert fauna and flora, cattle and horse cultures, and natural cycles entranced many students and aided not a few scholars. A house-sized block of granite known as the Druid sits atop the ridge just east of the ranch. An unmistakable landmark, it has always been a popular destination for student hikers and a challenge for climbers. On his forays to the Druid, second-year student Jan Vleck noticed unshod hoof prints and fresh horse dung. Having heard stories about feral horses along that ridge, Merritt Holloway urged Vleck to organize a field project for his zoology course to study these mustangs. Over three months in the spring of 1971, Vleck identified nine horses and four or five burros that frequented the high hills east of the college.[34] He named one "White," another "Knot" for a tangle in its mane, and so on. He also determined where the animals watered and how they managed to live such a stealthy existence within a mile or two of the Deep Springs community and ranch.[35]

In the 1970s, too, and with John Mawby's assistance, Deep Springs students and field biologists from afar became increasingly interested in the unique toads that live in and around the springs in the south end of Deep Springs Valley. Identified as *Bufo exsul*, they had evolved in the isolation of Deep Springs Valley for so many thousands of years that they are a species in their own right. In 1975, with Deep Springs' support, a campaign to secure their protection succeeded; and the National Park Service designated the Deep Springs Marsh, *Bufo exsul*'s habitat, a Registered Natural Landmark "for its exceptional value as an illustration of the nation's natural heritage."

The Druid, Deep Springs' most prominent landmark and hiking destination. Photograph by author.

Mawby also worked successfully with the U.S. Geological Survey (USGS) office to change the name of local landmarks to the terms that local residents commonly used. Deep Springs Valley's most prominent feature, Chocolate Mountain, for example, officially replaced Piper Mountain on USGS maps.[36] In a related effort, Mawby successfully petitioned the USGS to name a previously unnamed peak east of Deep Springs Lake "Nunn Mountain." Students have since made this high but relatively nondescript promontory a popular destination for weekend climbing.

Since the 1920s, a favorite release from the perpetual responsibility of life at Deep Springs has been student trips to the remote Eureka Valley sand dune. Rarely does a spring or autumn full moon approach without someone suggesting a late night drive to the 700-plus-foot-high dune in the south end of this huge, unpopulated valley in the northwest corner of Death Valley National Park. Invariably having it all to themselves after traveling seventy-five miles over rough roads, largely unpaved and unimproved except for graveling, the students toss their sleeping bags near the base of the dune, strip, and climb to its highest point. After howling at the moon, they leap off, either feet first or head first, and slide down the steepest surfaces. With the added weight of the students, the layers of sand, already poised at their angle of repose, slide over one another in huge sheets, emitting an eerie low hum. "During the naked full-moon

Students from all eras have visited the Eureka Valley Sand Dune. Courtesy of Deep Springs Archives. Photograph by author.

summer dune visits of my era," Brad Edmondson (DS'76) remembers, "these noises were attributed to the sandworms in Frank Herbert's *Dune* novels. . . . These dunes have always been one of my favorite places on earth."[37]

Academic high points also came from visiting faculty. Poet, environmental philosopher, and activist Gary Snyder delivered a series of lectures at the college in 1974. His belief in the wisdom produced by hard physical labor and his celebration of life as a journey generated a mutual kinship with students and faculty. Conservationist and Sierra Club leader David Brower also visited Deep Springs and found similar resonance within the community.

Snyder and Brower did not offer regular classes; but by the mid-1970s, the curriculum had evolved significantly away from traditional survey courses that spanned broad areas of knowledge. By then most students had taken Advanced Placement (AP) or International Baccalaureate (IB) courses in high school that covered broad content. Students now requested specialized science courses, created in response to their interest in studying local phenomena like wild horses and isolated toads. In the humanities, Deep Springers, like their student counterparts elsewhere, also pushed for courses that concentrated on one author or a contemporary theme rather than courses that swept broadly across Western or non-Western cultures. Young professors, having come out of increasingly narrow doctoral programs, were only too eager to support this movement.

Randall Reid received a fellowship from the National Endowment for the Humanities for 1972–1973, and the trustees granted him a leave. But the year's absence and changed focus weakened his influence at Deep Springs, and he was unable to regain the magic of his earlier leadership when he returned. With Reid's influence diminished, conflicts within the student body and faculty boiled up again. By the mid-1970s, Paul Starrs (DS'75) described relationships among first-, second-, and third-year students as "class warfare," with the older students striving to force newcomers into their image of strenuous and devoted Deep Springers. "It didn't work," he reflected, "and the result was great alienation, conflict, and disillusionment at the end of the Reid era."[38] From the previous class, Miguel Dozier (DS'74) described it as "an era of disaffection," but added, "Even in the worst of times, Deep Springs works for those students who stay with it."[39] One factor in the persistence of many students during this stressful period was the home of Wally and Jo Rooney. Their common decency and down-to-earth intelligence made their living room at the lower ranch a haven for students who needed perspective and a little gentle humor.

Battling fatigue and depression, Randall Reid knew that his continued directorship was neither in his best interest nor the college's. Five years seemed an appropriate term, so he and Earline packed their bags and bade farewell to the college in June 1975. Including his interim deanship in the late 1960s, he had led the college longer than anyone since L.L. Nunn.

After Reid's departure, veteran professor John Mawby stepped up as acting dean-director. He had earned respect for his decade of teaching earth sciences. Inherently shy, Mawby found himself in a position he neither sought nor enjoyed. His artistic wife, Dian, continued to grace Deep Springs publications with her drawings of native flora.

Mawby was not responsible for selecting the entering class that commenced with his leadership, but the 1975–1976 student body turned out to be especially fractious. Reid's uncertain final year and abrupt departure had destabilized the community—a situation now complicated by the ambiguity of an interim leader.

A particularly painful blow occurred in May 1976 when the community mourned the death by cancer of Pat Schrock. She had been an integral part of Deep Springs' life and the primary alumni contact at Deep Springs for sixteen years. That autumn Merritt and Nona Holloway announced their plans to retire. He was pushing sixty, and his arduous work and a family history of heart disease were catching up with him. The couple reconsidered, however, and remained another three years. Even so, these five distinctive people—the

Holloways, the Reids, and Pat Schrock—had given greatly to Deep Springs and fortified it in many ways. Their absences would be felt.

One event early in their service, however, captures more poignantly than any other the hopes and struggles, as well as the moral promise and pathos, of this whole period. When David Mossner left Deep Springs in 1966, he enrolled at Cornell, lived at Telluride House, and joined the association. His draft deferment expired when he graduated in 1969, presenting him with a moral dilemma. He had written his senior thesis on Thoreau's theory and practice of civil disobedience and had quite consciously committed his life to advancing peace and justice. Conscientious objector status was not an option because Dave could not claim such a heritage in good faith, nor could he put another man in harm's way by refusing to serve. Still, Dave equivocated. Conspiring to defer his induction, he enlisted fellow Deep Springer Jim Partridge (DS'66) to break his arm by slamming the heavy door of an old refrigerator on it.[40] After several excruciating attempts that produced only severe bruises, they abandoned the effort.

A short time later, Dave privately burned his draft card and stuffed its charred remains between the pages of a borrowed biography of Henry David Thoreau. He then walked downtown and enlisted in the U.S. Army. With this act and the Vietnam experience sure to follow, he hoped to earn a lifetime of credibility as a champion of peace. He received training as a staff sergeant. On June 1, 1970, only weeks after he joined a combat unit in Vietnam, David Mossner stepped on a land mine. Death came instantly.

For Mossner's Deep Springs and Telluride classmates and friends, for Earline and Randall Reid, Linda and me, and many others who had taught and enjoyed David's rich company, the tragedy of Vietnam became an agonizing reality.[41] The college dedicated a new library extension to him, Paiute sculptor Ray Stone carved a peacemaker figurine in his memory for the entrance, and we all learned something indelible from a short life well lived.

CHAPTER 13

SPIRALING, 1976–1994

The most important thing . . . is that the director be someone with a vision of Deep Springs that he or she is willing to articulate. In the absence of such a vision, community life can degenerate into a contest of wills. Of course, the wrong vision is not so desirable either.

—Sharon Schuman, Professor, 1982

Leadership transitions always pose challenges, but Deep Springs' tiny scale, democratic nature, and high-spirited populace almost assure tumult. For the next two decades, nine individuals would serve at the crux between a purposely empowered student body and a legally and fiscally answerable board of trustees. These dean-directors or presidents, as they were variously titled, ranged in age from their forties to their seventies, from conservative to radical, and from inexperienced academics to retired attorneys and civil servants. For most of these years, another unusual ranch manager would provide needed continuity.

To understand Deep Springs from 1976 to 1994 requires an awareness of the cleavages in American culture and the state of the U.S. economy. The shortage of money magnified every other issue for the college. For many of these years, a smoldering yet unfocused discontent outweighed the potentially uniting effects of hard times. The dependence of the college on one dominant benefactor was a mixed blessing. Trustee Jim Withrow continued to write checks each spring to close the gap between the minimalist budget and available revenue, but the magnitude of his generosity corresponded with his control. Resentment, especially among students, rivaled appreciation. "Withrow is a small country lawyer," they joked, "Bolivia, Ecuador . . . "

In the midst of this period, Allan Bloom of the University of Chicago wrote *The Closing of the American Mind.*[1] This 1987 best-seller attacked college and university humanities faculties for fostering a Nietzschean moral relativism that "impoverished the souls of today's students" and undermined democracy. By denigrating the wisdom in classical texts, he charged, academic culture had left students unprepared to render ethical judgments and made them smugly intolerant of those who lived by Judeo-Christian or other moral codes. Bloom's charge that liberal culture had stripped the rising generation of its capacity to make rational value judgments played well in right-wing circles, but he seemed curiously blind to the rising conservative political culture that celebrated self-interest as the foundation of a good society.

America's cultural and political shift toward conservatism began with Richard Nixon's election in 1968. In response, a counterculture movement struck back, protesting the Reagan era's materialism and egocentrism. On college campuses, the children of 1960s activists carried their parents' more liberal child-rearing practices into their own adulthood. The battle between resurgent conservatism and lingering radicalism was waged on many fronts.

Deep Springs' rapid succession of leaders oscillated between these cultural poles, pummelling students, faculty, and staff. Yet Deep Springs continued to attract superior students, challenging them to reach deeper to become more responsible citizens and leaders. What appears to be an enigma has a surprisingly rational explanation.

L.L. Nunn's educational formula that gives so much responsibility to students can and often does intensify their sense of duty when the college is in trouble or adult leadership falters. Brad Edmondson (DS'76) believes that the elusive fourth pillar of Deep Springs education, the "Voice of the Desert," becomes increasingly important when events spiral out of control.

Finding an effective leader for Deep Springs has never been easy, and identifying one who will come cheap added to the challenge. Leading this college is not a reliable step to another presidency. Its physical isolation and small size mean that it cannot become a long-term home for any professional who requires regular interaction with colleagues doing related work. Staying longer than three years at Deep Springs jeopardizes professional growth and credibility as a scholar. Further, the central engagement of students in every decision, and living in a community of common meals and concerns, can discourage all but the most unusual candidates. It is not always possible to find the right fit. Two presidents lasted less than six months.

Many of these issues also bear on Deep Springs' ability to recruit and retain faculty and staff. Especially daunting is the reality that academic policies and professorial performance reviews are largely in the hands of students. Student empowerment at Deep Springs cuts into traditional faculty rights and responsibilities, creating frequent conflicts and resentments. The saving grace is that, when the match is right for presidents, professors, and staff, Deep Springs can be an exhilarating place to live and work for them and their families.

Appointed president in January 1976, Edwin Cronk (DS'36) and his wife, Dorothy, jounced across the cattle guard unannounced early that spring "in their lemon yellow Ford Mustang, sunny and optimistic." The trustees had neglected to tell the student body of Cronk's appointment and Chris Campbell (DS'73), "distinctly recall[s] it being a shock to us."[2] After nearly a year without significant direction, the student body had become accustomed to near autonomy. The rumor that Withrow had singlehandedly arranged Cronk's appointment accentuated student forebodings as the new leader settled in.

With a full head of white hair, erect bearing, and kindly manner, Cronk and his similarly bright and pleasant wife came to Deep Springs fresh from his final diplomatic assignment as U.S. ambassador to Singapore. Nearing sixty, Ed had been a student during the Kimpton years, knew Deep Springs well, and enjoyed strong support from the board and alumni. His would be the longest tenure of this era—at nearly four and a half years. His diplomatic skills served him well, but his lack of professional experience with higher education was crippling. Most Deep Springs directors or presidents have tended to be either too dominant or too *laissez faire.* Cronk began decisively, making difficult budget and personnel decisions during a series of strategic visits before taking residence in June.

His faculty included veterans John Mawby and Joseph Balachowski, who had taught earth sciences and European languages respectively for over a decade, but also three able young couples who overlapped with each other: Jacqueline and Alan Paskow (literature and philosophy, respectively), Peter Lehman (chemistry) and Carolyn Polese (art), and Sharon and David Schuman (both English). Until Cronk's final year, Merritt and Nona Holloway also continued to stabilize the community.

To supplement the regular faculty, Cronk and the trustees appealed to retired academic alumni to volunteer as short-term professors. Herb Reich (DS'17), distinguished professor emeritus from Yale, responded again, dividing his time between physics and critical maintenance issues. Harvey C. Mansfield Sr. (DS'21), professor emeritus of law and government at Columbia University, taught political philosophy several times and entertained students with the story of his first ascent of Mount Winchell (elev. 13,768 feet) and other Sierra peaks during his student years.

The renewed board of trustees that Bob Aird had mobilized faced a seriously depleted endowment. As an emeritus trustee, Aird volunteered as chief fundraiser. He went beyond standard appeals to an imaginative "graduated income gift plan" by which alumni were asked to pledge from 1 to 3 percent of their annual income. Everything helped, but nothing sufficed.

Another innovative idea from Ed Cronk and Merritt Holloway urged alumni and trustees: "Adopt an Un-Wed Mother!" They put up "44 beautiful heifers" on sale for $220 each.[3] These yearlings remained on the ranch, but buyers received a formal certificate and the satisfaction of owning a stake in the herd. Cronk remembered with a huge grin that the dubious Holloway bet him that the alumni would not embrace their offer. The wager was a $100 cowboy hat. The result was something of a standoff. "We did sell all of them but one," Cronk reported, "and I bought the last one. So I won, but he said I cheated. He bought me the hat anyway and . . . to make it even I bought him one of the same."[4]

Dorothy Cronk planted and nurtured three bounteous flowerbeds in the community's central spaces. It was "her personal protest against the deteriorating condition of the place," alumnus Brad Edmondson remembered, "and we could not help but notice and respect what she did."[5]

Meanwhile, the students lived in squalor in the dilapidated dormitory wing. Fuel and heating costs had spiked dramatically in 1973, due to the Arab oil embargo. After an autumn board meeting a year or two later, Chris Campbell rallied the student body to endure new austerities. Turning down thermostats was already common practice, but now they shut down the Main Building's oil-burning furnace completely and dragged heavy-duty sleeping bags into the Main Room where the wood-burning fireplace made it warm enough to study and sleep. Faculty and staff complained about frigid offices and students struggled with their academic work. Still, savings mounted impressively for several years. But on an especially cold night one February, water pipes froze in the bathrooms and burst over the library. No one objected when the furnace was turned back on and set at 50 degrees.

In 1977, students asked chemistry professor Peter Lehman to teach a course on solar energy. Together, they constructed a solar water heater on the roof of the dairy barn. It was a simple, flat glass-covered box with coiled black pipes inside that absorbed the sun's radiation as water flowed into the building. It worked. Savings may have been modest, but this foray into energy production heightened interest and the students soon persuaded physics professor Douglas Martin to offer a course on sustainable energy.

Student Kurt Gilson (DS'80) developed a keen interest in the budget during his first year and successfully lobbied the trustees to create an Alternative Energy Committee that outlined a multistage plan. Phase 1 monitored energy consumption of all kinds—electricity, gasoline, heating oil, and propane—and assessed the most promising options for conserving and producing energy.

Next, the trustees consulted Bruce Laverty (DS'43), a civil engineer with Southern California Edison, and asked him to explore alternative energy sources. With thirty-five years' experience designing and building hydro, fossil fuel, and nuclear-generating facilities for his company, he tackled the Deep Springs challenge with relish in 1981. He was joined by Kurt Gilson, then the student labor commissioner, and Dr. James Moyer, head of Southern California Edison's Research and Development division. Wind, solar, and geothermal power proved impractical given extant technologies. More promising was hydroelectricity, based on stream flow studies conducted by students and faculty at the mouth of Wyman Canyon. The case for hydro strengthened when Herb Reich found and shared this passage in his student journal six decades earlier: "Mr. Nunn is considering the feasibility of a power plant powered by Wyman Creek."[6] If the college existed because of L.L. Nunn's pioneering work with hydroelectricity, then what could be more irresistible than to use the same technology to meet this crisis? Might this become the pitch that alumni could not resist?

Paul Swatek (DS'33), a civil engineer who specialized in the design and construction of cellular cofferdams all over the world, heard about Deep Springs' new project and flew out to see if he could help. Before he left, he had prepared a preliminary design layout for the entire job. The Deep Springs hydro project was a tiny fraction of those that Swatek and Laverty routinely managed, yet they developed remarkable esprit in this endeavor. Both of them had much more to offer as well and were pleased to accept invitations to serve as trustees.

Swatek procured penstock pipe and a pair of 100-kilowatt turbine-generators, in the process meeting Gene Newman, an industrial equipment company representative, whose no-nonsense manner resonated with his own. A decorated World War II veteran who had served with the U.S. Army's 10th Mountain Division in northern Italy, Newman delivered exactly what Swatek needed. He also pitched in as a consultant—a role he continued pro bono for more than twenty years. Jeff Johnson (DS'55) added organizational skills and valuable ties to his employer, the Bechtel Group's hydro division. Bechtel became a major player, doing the formal engineering and providing other essential services without charge.

One hundred fifty-six alumni and friends responded to the fund drive. Grants from the James Irvine Foundation and the Fletcher Jones Foundation, together with the value of Bechtel's support, more than matched the sum of individual gifts for a grand total of over $450,000. This campaign met all project expenses, and the construction team worked through one construction hitch after another until the plant opened in November 1988.

Even as the hydro project united the extended Deep Springs family, another issue was driving a spike into its heartwood. Coeducation. Students had supported the admission of women for years and young alumni had repeatedly urged the board to consider the change. By the spring of 1977, the trustees knew it was time to pay attention and responded favorably when the student body proposed appointing a Co-Education Committee. It consisted of two members each from the board (one of them being its only female trustee, Beatrice Renfield of New York), the student body, and the alumni. One well-respected faculty member, Sharon Schuman, and Director Cronk (who was succeeded by Dean Mawby) rounded out the group. Professor Schuman and trustee Paul Todd served as cochairs.

The committee worked hard for two years. Its members were split, sometimes passionately, over the issue. Thanks to the personal respect both Schuman and Todd commanded, however, committee deliberations remained civil—a spirit that carried forward into board deliberations.

The budget emergency weighed heavily on every trustee. Senior alumni were Deep Springs' most generous financial backers and most (but not all) of them fumed over the prospect of admitting women. They expressed fears of rampant sexuality within a small, isolated student group and argued that L.L. Nunn had prescribed an all-male student body in the Deed of Trust precisely to prevent such "social distractions." Alumni who favored coeducation believed that it was unethical for Deep Springs to deny young women access to the same privilege that Nunn had granted to "promising young men." Concerns about sexual expression were old-fashioned, they argued—an inappropriate defense of single-sex admissions. Women increasingly held leadership positions in government, business, and the professions, and Nunn's college needed to select and prepare the most promising future trustees for the nation, regardless of gender.

The committee delivered its report at the spring 1979 board meeting, offering two recommendations: "Resolved, that Deep Springs continue its present educational policies, including its status as an all-male institution, but that these policies be reviewed in five years in order to assure the board that the primary educational objectives of the Founder can be achieved, in view of changes which may occur in social conditions and attitudes in the meantime."[7] Although most board members had strong, and mostly negative, views on coeducation, the motion passed easily.

Judging by accounts written at the time, the deliberations were conducted more rationally than they would be remembered even a short time later. The *Telluride Newsletter* devoted a single column inch to reporting the trustees' decision.[8] Advocates of the change recognized the complexity of the budget issues and knew that altering the Deed of Trust could be challenged in court.

As time passed, students and faculty who had invested heavily in producing a responsible report felt increasingly that the board had too easily dismissed their views. By saying no so quickly to coeducation, had board members kowtowed to wealthy alumni or, worse, hidden behind fund-raising concerns to camouflage their own misogyny? To pro-coeducation people the board's decision left scars that stiffened with time.

In 1978, prior to the coeducation decision, I had gained trustee support to conduct the first comprehensive study of alumni. The board's chief interest was to learn more about the alumni for fund-raising purposes, but I wanted to explore the long-term effects of a Deep Springs education on students' personal and professional lives.[9] Withrow endorsed my survey but admonished me to avoid questions about coeducation. I believed the credibility of my research would be compromised if it did not encompass all the important issues facing the college, nor was I willing to abandon my scholar's duty to investigate freely. Therefore, I crafted the questionnaire with an uneasy compromise, concluding with an invitation to comment on any issue that alumni wished to air. One-fifth of all respondents offered their views on coeducation, some at great length. I analyzed these responses along with all other data. When I reported my findings at the trustees meeting on November 8, 1980, Jim Withrow was not pleased. He urged the board to reject the survey and refuse, even, to thank me for it. Undeterred by his colleague's temper, Trustee Bob Sproull presented a resolution of acceptance and appreciation on which, eventually, even Withrow voted positively. The resolution included an admonition to omit my academic policy recommendations (which included pathways for converting to coeducation) from the final bound edition for Deep Springs Archives and other libraries. I printed these recommendations as a separate document and tucked it inside the back cover of each book.

Christopher and Jane Breiseth when he served as a trustee in the 1990s. Photograph by author.

Unlike the trustees' cloistered appointment of Ed Cronk, his successor was chosen after an open search. Highly verbal and exuding energy, forty-five-year-old Christopher N. Breiseth took a three-year leave of absence from his professorship in American history at Sangamon State University in Illinois to accept the dean-director's baton in June 1980. He had been a doctoral student at Cornell, had lived at Telluride House, and had received the association's exchange fellowship to Lincoln College, Oxford. As a member of Telluride Association, he had quickly taken leading roles there and had served as its president in 1965–1967. No stranger to Deep Springs, Breiseth had taught a summer session there in 1969 and helped found the Association of Deep Springs and Telluride Alumni (ADSTA). The *Telluride Newsletter* commented that Breiseth's appointment promised "a bright future for Deep Springs."[10] His stately wife, Jane, and three daughters, ages eleven, ten, and less than three months, added to a sense of new vitality.

Breiseth was comfortable with academic repartee and supremely patient by nature. He sought consensus by instinct and was willing to talk with any student, professor, or alumnus at any time and at any length. He did not like to set boundaries so long as any opening remained for negotiation. These qualities worked both for and against him at Deep Springs. From the day he took office, a particularly assertive group of students saw his lack of administrative experience as their opening. Student body president Lars Wulff cornered Breiseth his first afternoon on the job, reported what he had heard about his plans to make staff changes, and challenged his judgment. Wulff's information had been inaccurate, but the confrontation set Breiseth back on his heels.

Of the challenges he faced, none proved more vexing than an admissions issue. An applicant who had attended a TASP at Deep Springs the previous summer and had done well made the short list of Deep Springs applicants under consideration the next spring. His materials, however, featured his active participation in the North American Man/Boy Love Association. He praised sexual relations between adult males and underage boys. Some students took up the applicant's cause as a civil rights issue. Faculty and staff immediately expressed alarm about the safety of children in the community.

Withrow called Breiseth, spelled out the legal perils concerning child sexual abuse that could threaten the college's endowment, and strongly advised Breiseth to slam the door. Opting instead to treat the issue as an educational opportunity, Breiseth committed himself to reason with the Applications Committee until its members agreed to drop the case on their own. Weeks of indecision ended at 3:00 a.m. the day the matter had to be resolved when one student switched sides and gave the candidates' opponents a majority. The residue of anger over the prolonged process and, for some, about the decision itself, cost Breiseth dearly during his final year. Accentuating the problem, he reflected later, was the absence of a "mediating bureaucracy" at Deep Springs.[11] Nowhere else in academe is the president routinely and directly engaged in negotiations such as these.

In 1981, Breiseth appointed English professors Barbara and George Newtown. Devoted to each other, dressage-style horsemanship, and traditional academic values, the Newtowns' classes were among the best of the era. One alumnus described them as "valiant figures, trying to keep up culture, especially music and drama." Throughout their five-year tenure, they often stood apart from other faculty and staff, while remaining on good terms with almost everyone.

A natural networker, Breiseth built closer ties within the national higher education community, gathered fresh ideas for the curriculum, learned to better navigate the accreditation process, and recruited professors at professional meetings.[12] These initiatives benefited the college, and his commitment to improve faculty quality and morale earned respect. The students he recruited, taught, and led have remained unusually engaged with Deep Springs as alumni. Six have already become trustees, while others have served as faculty or alumni leaders.

One of Breiseth's satisfactions was arranging the gift of Grace Mansfield's Steinway grand piano. Her husband, Harvey Sr. (DS'21), gave it to Deep Springs shortly after she died in 1982. Chris asked Owens Valley musician Dick Dawson to tune this 1906 instrument, but he advised a complete rebuild. The task took him nearly a year, but the piano responded beautifully and became a treasured community asset. Thirty years later, Dawson continues to care for the piano and teach students on it.

The best decision he made as president, Breiseth remembers, was hiring Geoff Pope as ranch manager. From Roderick MacKenzie to Merritt Holloway, this key position had usually been held by seasoned cattlemen whom the students held in high regard. The previous three years under Tom Payne, however, had been rocky. Highly educated and broadly experienced, Payne knew his business but did not like to work with students. He also had a penchant for strong drink. Relationships broke down completely when, under cover of darkness, two students savaged his collection of coyote and bobcat pelts to protest his trapping hobby—and simply to anger him.[13] He threatened violence against the perpetrators but never identified them. He left the college early in 1982.

Geoff Pope, his wife, Sue, and their three young daughters arrived in June of that year. Reared on a Montana cattle ranch but educated at Occidental College in Southern California with a degree in Russian literature and art, Geoff was still an old-school cattleman. A bushy mustache accentuated his serious temperament, and it was clear he meant business, whether on a horse with a lariat or discussing a college policy over dinner. Looking back later, one alumnus who enrolled in 1985 recalled his relief over Geoff's presence at Deep Springs: "Finally, a sane adult had arrived." While Pope, then in his early thirties, would become important as an adult model, he was not easily approached for personal advice.[14]

Sue became Deep Springs' development officer. A year and a half later, she was struck with a rapidly advancing respiratory illness. Geoff rushed her to Northern Inyo Hospital in Bishop where she died the same night. She was a heavy smoker, but this did not explain her rapid death. A decade later, Dr. Robert Schechter (DS'80) reflected on Sue's unexplained illness and asked Geoff to have her lung tissue that had been preserved at the hospital sent to the Centers for Disease Control and Prevention in Atlanta. Laboratory tests identified hantavirus as the cause of death, making Sue among the earliest confirmed cases of the hantavirus pulmonary syndrome (HPS).[15]

Reeling from his loss, Geoff faced rearing three daughters alone—ages nine, seven, and three. With the help of students, other community volunteers who tutored and tended the children, and a German nanny, he pulled his family together and continued as ranch manager. In 1987, he married Iris Kouns, an intensive care nurse at Northern Inyo Hospital who had, by coincidence, been on duty the night Sue died.

Iris and Geoff would both serve Deep Springs for over twenty years—she as office manager, bookkeeper, emergency nurse, and "on-site veterinarian" and he, ultimately, as vice president for operations as well as ranch manager. Their unflappable personalities and unquestioned commitment to the college and its students provided a rudder that helped guide the community through successive storms. Iris would become a touchstone for countless students who benefited from her lively conversational style and no-nonsense advice. When Darren Olson (DS'97) was asked after his graduation who had taught him the most, he said simply, "Iris Pope!" As in the past, students continued to find some of their most inspiring mentors and teachers among the college and ranch staff.

Breiseth commenced the final year of his three-year term in autumn 1982. With their two older daughters becoming teenagers, Jane and Chris resolved to leave. To recognize his achievements and increase his chances of securing a comparable position, the board advanced his title from dean-director to president. While tumultuous in many ways, Breiseth's tenure brought tangible improvements in academic quality, management practices, fund-raising, and staffing.[16]

Fifty-year-old Brandt Kehoe (DS'51) assumed the presidency in July 1983. On a three-year leave from his professorship in physics and following his service as dean of the School of Natural Sciences at California State University, Fresno, this tall, angular man sported a shock of graying hair and a quick smile. He and Breiseth had served back-to-back as presidents of the Telluride Association. Unlike Breiseth, Kehoe thrived on confrontation. As a way of commanding students' attention, he might initiate a conversation by saying: "The students of this college have no right to [this or that]," recalls Charles Abbott (DS'84).[17] Kehoe urged the Applications Committee (ApCom) to admit headstrong applicants and enjoyed watching students challenge each other—and him. Brandt's wife, Sandra, had devoted much of her energy to the National Organization for Women (NOW) since its founding in 1966. She anticipated their move to Deep Springs with mixed emotions but soon found satisfaction teaching studio art courses.

Although it had been in the works for much of the decade, Kehoe orchestrated the final phases of installing the hydroelectric plant. His ease in dealing with industrial pipes or Pelton Wheels matched his comfort in the physics lab, serving him and the college well. Whether lecturing in a classroom or helping students fix a leaky roof on the dairy barn, Kehoe was a natural teacher and an inexhaustible force. But other qualities of his leadership were problematic. As career academics, both he and Breiseth were keenly aware of the upturned power relationship between students and faculty at Deep Springs.

To a significant degree, the powers L.L. Nunn accorded the student body in the 1923 Deed of Trust came at the expense of traditional professorial authority. Deep Springs faculty are highly vulnerable to student judgments and opinions. Faculty feelings about this situation ranged from tacit acceptance to bitter resentment, depending on their own temperaments, those of student leaders, and the particular issue. Wise presidents have tried to buffer these inherent conflicts while others, inadvertently, have contributed to them. At worst, the adults revert to adolescent behavior.

Sexuality and sexual issues mounted during this era at Deep Springs, as on most American campuses. Professional standards had not kept pace with changing social behaviors since the 1960s. Academic leaders found it difficult to set standards of professional behavior for faculty and staff when they strayed across ill-defined frontiers.

At Deep Springs, the early 1980s were a time of thinly veiled—even open—sexual liaisons among faculty, staff, and students. Some alumni trace the phenomenon back to the latter Cronk years, when his leadership had become distinctly laissez faire, but incidents multipied during Breiseth's tenure and took new twists during Kehoe's administration. When faculty and staff became romantically involved with students, the level ranged from poor judgment or effrontery to serious breaches of professional ethics.[18] The fact that students initiated some of these liaisons did not reduce the adults' responsibility for them. A unique element of this problem at Deep Springs was the direct involvement in meals, recreation, and work of the spouses, partners, and children of faculty and staff.

Sexual relations between students and members of the administration, faculty, and staff and their families had occurred before, but never to this degree or with such destructiveness. One student from the Kehoe years later explained the rationale given by participants: If open marriages are being explored by the avant-garde in American culture, then why not an open community? This explanation ignored the reality of unequal power relationships between faculty and students. The specter of exploitation is always present, enabled by the adults' control over grades and grading, mentoring opportunities, and the gatekeeping function of letters of recommendation. Even so, one alumnus from this period opined that "a bigger problem was guilt and shame, secrecy, sneaking around, plus the fact that not everyone can have a sexual relationship at Deep Springs, which probably bred jealousy."[19]

All American colleges and universities struggled to establish clearer standards of professional ethics to govern the challenge of greater sexual openness in American society. At Deep Springs, a decade would pass before the faculty, staff, and president hammered out and gained trustee approval for a comprehensive faculty personnel policy that included this passage on professional ethics: "Sexual interaction or sexual harassment involving any member of the faculty (or his or her family members) with any student will be regarded as unethical and improper conduct . . . and constitute grounds for dismissal."[20]

Homosexual and bisexual students at Deep Springs in this era generally handled their relationships privately. There were, however, exceptions, and new forms of abuse emerged. As elsewhere, the new openness also left possibilities for unwelcome and intimidating dormitory encounters. A notoriously misguided episode occurred late one night when a female faculty member entered a gay student's dorm room, stripped, and slipped into his bed, whispering something he remembered as: "I have come to straighten you out."

He shouted, "Get out!"—his words reverberating through the dormitory. His would-be seductress promptly complied; but students and others were appalled as news spread through the community, and their shock from this and a few other incidents remained long after they left Deep Springs.[21]

Looking back, the students from the 1980s and early 1990s (some of whom are rearing teenage children today) often describe aspects of their experiences at Deep Springs as toxic. A few reflect that it was at least interesting to have lived the "culture of that era in American history," while others simply express relief that they got through that time and moved on. The most serious damage appears to have been to the underlying mission of Deep Springs: "What happens to your conception of higher things—like service to humanity—when one of the adult women in the community comes and crawls in bed with you in the middle of the night?"[22]

When adults act like children, one alumnus opined, then students can either wallow with them or choose to assume adult roles. Some maintained their personal standards, while others wrought new codes of personal ethics. Many found the task difficult or impossible. One student carved notches on a yardstick hung near his desk. He apparently scored often but also received stinging criticism from his peers.

On a positive note, Misha Hoekstra (DS'82) recently reflected that "the antipathy between the students and non-students (including trustees) was something . . . that helped the Student Body define itself and made us quite fierce in our sense of ownership."[23] These conditions "inspired the feeling that we could do it. The frequent incompetence of faculty and staff fueled [the] feeling that we could figure it out. That we could decide. All those student-run independent studies that never earned any credit. All that unsupervised labor. All the student-led trips." This is the bright side of Deep Springs in crisis. As Hoekstra readily conceded, however, it described reality for only a portion of the student body.

For many others, disengagement became their primary coping strategy. As manifestations of lost student body cohesion and community spirit, many students abandoned their dormitory rooms, flung their sleeping bags on the desert sand each night (a practice also long cherished for the sheer joy of retiring under the resplendent stars), or slept in a dairy barn silo or on a cot in one of the sheds. As another significant indicator, nearly half dropped out before completing the full two-year program.

The use of mind-altering drugs within the student body again became widespread.[24] Faculty and staff matched them in heavy drinking, a fact not lost on students because the general labor crew collected the weekly trash from each house. Booze for the old folks, marijuana for us, became a cynical student response. Perhaps the most lasting physical reminder of the era is the long-abandoned power company lineman's cabin at Roberts's Ranch in Wyman Canyon. Sometime in 1983, one alumnus remembered, "some angel-dusted schizoid [students] spewed all kinds of paranoid vitriol in magic marker on every available wall."[25] Thirty years later, the hulk of this old lodge still bears testimony to an era gone sour.

Brandt Kehoe's hands-on style and theoretical knowledge were both put to good use in overseeing the installation of the hydro plant. But when he hired Rick Cummings as construction engineer, the already frayed community unraveled further. Described as an aging "hippie with long gray hair held up with a leather strap," he astonished the students with his welding and mechanical skills. But he also entertained them with colorful stories reportedly magnified by marijuana and perhaps more powerful hallucinogens. Some claim that he and another staff member began to supply interested students with pot and other drugs. Those who crossed Rick could find him threatening. "He packed a pistol in a leg holster and loved to show it off," recalled Ranch Manager Geoff Pope.[26] The situation became so tense that Iris Pope and farmer Dave Slayton began carrying handguns to meals in the Boarding House for self-defense. Christof Bove (DS'86) remembers that year as one of "dramatic lunacy." No one seemed to be in control.

As the hydro headworks were being excavated, a student found a petroglyph on a boulder about fifty feet from the construction site. This discovery surprised no one, since petroglyphs adorn other boulders in the canyon, but its proximity to the work site was disturbing. All work ceased immediately, and the Bureau of Land Management (BLM) brought in an anthropologist to examine the relic. He determined that the scarring was fresh and the tool used to chip the rock had probably been a geologist's pick. Construction resumed the following day. The snaky figure still wriggles across the top of a large granite rock near the site. Though never proven, the mystery artisan was thought to be a disenchanted student hoping to stop construction.

The hydroplant draws from a catchment area of fifty-three square miles in the White Mountains. Waters from Wyman Creek and Crooked Creek are captured at the mouth of Wyman Canyon and carried two and a half miles across the valley in a fourteen-inch diameter steel pipe or penstock laid in the stone ditch that had carried water to the ranch for over a century. A drop in elevation of 433 feet produced sufficient pressure to drive the 100-kilowatt generator after which the water flowed, as before, into the reservoir to irrigate the fields. Electrical output, of course, depended on the volume of creek flow, hour by hour and year to year.[27]

Optimistic forecasts had predicted that the generating plant could meet all of Deep Springs' electrical power needs in an average year. In 1989, the first full year of operation, it supplied 54 percent of the electricity used at Deep Springs, but that number fluctuated from a rare high of 83 percent in 1993 to a low of 8 percent three years later. Stream flow measurements, it turned out, had been taken during an unusual wet cycle. Under drought conditions, not only did output drop dramatically, but the ranch needed to run its heavy-duty deep well pump in the northwest corner of field no. 1 to supplement creek water for irrigating the fields. When output flagged, unfortunately, demand spiked.

The 1984–1985 academic year represented the five-year anniversary of the board's coeducation decision. Students geared up for the reassessment by publishing five articles and a letter on the topic in the fall 1985 issue of the *Deep Springs Newsletter*. Views ranged from pro to con and included the announcement that the student body had established a Coeducation Trust Fund. The college trustees did not challenge the student's right to air their views in the *Newsletter.* Nor did the board try to stop the students' establishment of the independent trust fund.

Rhetoric and emotions soon escalated, however, and the board tried to slam the door on further debate—citing fund-raising as the chief consideration. Some older alumni threatened to cut off support if the board decided to admit women, but Norton Dodge (DS'43) countered by refusing to give *unless* the

Class of 1985 portrait at the metal dump. Courtesy of Deep Springs Archives.

college embraced coeducation. Many younger alumni joined him.

The student body urged contributions to the Coeducation Trust Fund instead of giving to the college. The fund was "dedicated to allaying the cost of the eventual conversion of Deep Springs to a coeducational institution, and to studying and promoting non-discriminatory admissions."[28] The funds were to be held until the trustees of Deep Springs made a positive decision to admit women, after which the money would be turned over to the board. It was a move designed to show the number and strength of pro-coeducation supporters. Student Ted Shelton's father provided legal assistance, and members of the student body who were at least eighteen became the fund's trustees.

After a few years, small contributions had brought the fund to about $8,000. Shortly after Alvan Bradford Judd, M.D. (DS'46) died on September 9, 1989, the student body was surprised to learn that he had made the Coeducation Trust Fund the beneficiary of a $70,000 life insurance policy. Orchestrating the fund now became a significant worry. It did not qualify for tax-exempt status, and if Deep Springs did not admit female students by 1998, all gifts to the fund were to be returned to the donors.

The rising gay rights movement played into events at this point. The past had not been pretty, even at Deep Springs. In spring 1961, one student came out as a homosexual and marijuana user. His peers reported this information to the academic dean, Harold Kirkby, who informed the trustees and arranged for Dr. Robert Denton in Bishop to conduct a psychological evaluation of the student.[29] Former director Robert Aird, M.D., then arranged to move the student to San Francisco to live with an alumnus's family where he received long-term counseling and continued his education in the city.

Given professional estimates of the number of homosexuals in a typical male population, the Deep Springs student body has probably included gay students since the beginning.[30] Before the 1960s, however, their sexual orientation or gender identity was only occasionally known to other students or community members. Those who came out privately were generally accepted by their peers, making the 1961 case unusual as well as unfortunate. Later in that decade, as homosexuality became more socially accepted on most campuses, attitudes shifted at Deep Springs, too. With his edgy wit, David Mossner had written lyrics to be sung to the tune of Petula Clark's new release, "Downtown," at a community songfest in which he alluded humorously to L.L. Nunn's homosexuality.[31]

By the mid-1970s, the student body included openly gay students. None had acknowledged their sexual preference as applicants, but other students accepted their self-disclosures without alarm. The trustees and some adults remained in the dark or in denial. The first openly gay applicant, Random Turner-Jones, was admitted in 1985. High school student Tom Hudgens was encouraged when he heard about this acceptance from a mutual friend in San Francisco. Neither obscuring nor featuring his own homosexuality, Hudgens applied and was admitted in 1988.

Prominent alumni both, Random and Tom opened the way for others to follow. Random is a psychiatric nurse who practiced in Los Angeles for many years before moving his home and office to Springfield, Illinois. Tom, who had honed his cooking skills as a Deep Springs student, apprenticed at the celebrated Berkeley restaurant Chez Panisse under chef David Tanis (DS'71) and launched his career as a chef. He returned to Deep Springs as chef from 1998 to 2001, and has written a popular cookbook of five hundred recipes that he developed primarily during those years.[32]

For the extended Deep Springs community, especially more senior alumni, adjusting to the reality of gay students sometimes involved replaying the kinds of arguments common among anti-Semitic trustees in the 1940s. Some feared that by opening admission freely to this group, Deep Springs would soon be overwhelmed with homosexuals and become known as "a gay college." This did not happen.

Changes in student body demographics came slowly in other ways. Recruiting black, Latino, and American Indian students—even Asians in the early years—proved difficult. The premium placed on highly groomed verbal and mathematical skills prior to admission disadvantaged those without the benefits of intense enrichment programs and elite college-preparatory schooling. Some students acquire high levels of literacy and intellectual sophistication primarily through a passion for reading and reasoning, but these appetites are often a function of family acculturation as well. Standardized tests were often culturally biased, too, giving the edge to mainstream, middle-class applicants.[33]

In a community as small as Deep Springs, the likelihood of minorities enjoying camaraderie with and support from others with the same racial or ethnic background remained minute. Finally, in a time when parents hover increasingly over their college-going children's decisions, many of them advise "safer" Ivy League opportunities as stepping stones to a premium career.

While these factors may have discouraged many students of color from applying, neither Deep Springs' Application Committee nor its presidents and trustees always made consistent or wholehearted recruiting efforts. After the 1960s, recruiting competition for high-achieving minority students became so intense that Deep Springs was just one among many full-ride scholarship options available at prestigious institutions—and its scholarships ran only two years. This dilemma is one with which Deep Springs still grapples because premium scholarships are rarely available to transfer students.

Deep Springs enrolled its first black student, Sterling Lacey, in 1969. Its first American Indian, Miguel Dozier, arrived from the Santa Clara Pueblo in New Mexico in 1974. Michael Gelobter became the second African American to enroll in 1978, followed by Hugh McGuire in 1981. They did not establish a trend, and it would be decades before nonwhite admissions became common. Similarly, it had taken many years after trustee discrimination in the 1940s and 1950s to interest Jewish students again; but by the early 1970s, they began to apply in significant numbers. Since the mid-1990s, American students of Asian descent have found Deep Springs an attractive choice. Many students from Africa, Asia, Europe, and the Middle East have matriculated. Still, American minorities remain underrepresented. With foreign admissions, however, the blending of cultures has become a major educative force at the college.

While students ventured across new social thresholds in this era, many also reacted strongly against modernizing ranch equipment and communications. The shift to sprinkler irrigation with its dependence on pumps and pipes rather than gravity and ditches remained contentious over the half-dozen years it took to achieve the conversion. Geoff Pope aptly noted that students were responsible as never before for irrigating because they could roll the pipes and manage the new system themselves. The old flood irrigation technique had depended on the constant attention of a skilled hired hand.

With more efficient water distribution came the reopening of the twenty-acre north field, which had lain fallow for many decades. Expanded alfalfa harvests resulted in purchasing a larger baling machine that produced bales heavier than the students could easily load on a flatbed trailer. This change then required a mechanical loader that replaced student labor to buck the bales onto the trailer for hauling to the stack yard. Students lamented the end of a strenuous but valued work detail.

When an aphid infestation hit the new alfalfa in the north field, the USDA Extension Service prescribed aerial crop dusting, an issue that divided the community. Fortunately, these insects did not persist. But gophers persistently riddled the fields. Poisoning them takes a toll on their predators—hawks and vultures that eat carrion—so the search for effective and safe alternatives for controlling these rodents remains a challenge to this day.

As new trucks and cars depended increasingly on computers rather than rotors, contact points, and other mechanical parts that could be replaced or repaired by students and staff, everyone at the college liked the idea of maintaining and buying old equipment that could be repaired on site. A case in point is the beloved 1946 Marine Corps dump truck. Acquired for a pittance as a military surplus vehicle in 1953, this rugged but battered truck remains in service over sixty years later.

The hand-cranked, party-line telephone that had served the college since its founding came under increasing criticism from faculty and staff. Breiseth found it a serious impediment to official communications, fund-raising, and management. Students resisted, but by the mid-1980s black dial phones finally superseded the old oak wall-mounted boxes. In 1992, when the telephone company refused to upgrade the copper line that bought service over the White Mountains from Bishop, the parents of Gene Fang (DS'90) provided a gift that funded the components for a microwave radio relay phone system. Science professor Joseph Szewczak engineered and installed the complicated system with student assistance. It continues to serve the college, supplemented in recent years with satellite internet service.

The possibility of personal computers provided the most telling example of technology's strains as well as convenience. After David Hitz (DS'80) arrived, he inquired about having a computer shipped to him, igniting a controversy

Military surplus dump truck still in service after six decades. Photograph by author.

that echoed the 1934 student body debate about allowing students to have radios in the dormitory. After a heated argument in the Boarding House that lasted until 2:00 a.m., Hitz gained his peers' approval. He would go on to cofound and help grow NetApp, now a Fortune 500 company. The college purchased its first office computer in 1983, but another decade passed before internet and email came into regular use at Deep Springs.

One reform that everyone seemed to applaud was Geoff Pope's introduction of new grazing practices on the valley floor and on the summer range in the White Mountains. Inspired by the ideas of Allan Savory, a Zimbabwean farmer and ecologist, he founded and chaired the Deep Springs Resource Management Team (RMT) in 1992.[34] Capitalizing on a new provision in Forest Service regulations designed to encourage innovation, Pope assembled representatives from all government agencies and many private interests that had a stake in Deep Springs' grazing lands and won approval for this team to manage them as one piece. The Forest Service, Bureau of Land Management, Soil Conservation Service (now the Natural Resources Conservation Service), and California Department of Fish and Game all designated representatives, as did the California Native Plant Society, the Sierra Club, and, of course, the Deep Springs student body. Forging cooperative relationships took at least five years of regular meetings and occasional team field trips to study the quarter-million-acre area, but Pope succeeded in generating trust among the disparate parties. His incentive, and that of other participants, was that every agency involved could waive its traditional rules to allow any new grazing, range management, or water quality innovation that members of the RMT could agree upon. Some of the team's decisions did not sit well with Pope or the students; but the fresh thinking that came with each specialist being required to focus on *all* facets of the land—the soil, water, range, wildlife, landscape aesthetics, herd's health, and economic interests of the college—eventually produced cooperation, thoughtful experimentation, and encouraging results. An ethic of sustainable practices and land stewardship has emerged, although changes in representatives from government agencies and Deep Springs personnel have continued to challenge the team's effectiveness. Still, RMT objectives fit well into the larger objective of environmental stewardship at Deep Springs.

The educative value of direct engagement with the Resource Management Team, as well as Deep Springs' organic agricultural practices and renewable energy projects, have proven their worth. Deep Springs students benefit from rare opportunities to understand the complexity of issues that must be solved to achieve sustainability in agriculture and energy. Some have pursued careers in public policy where they are able to use their special experience in finding solutions to environmental, scientific, and economic problems.

Among those students who benefited most from Pope's range management and problem-solving efforts were and are the Deep Springs student cowboys. The employment of especially interested and able students as summer cowboys began modestly with Louis Azevedo's suggestion in the 1950s. Merritt Holloway and Tom Payne built on this precedent in the 1970s. Geoff Pope institutionalized the practice. Like his predecessors, he appointed one second-year man each autumn for the cowboy labor position—the only student job not assigned by the elected labor commissioner. One of the bitterest disappointments some Deep Springers report is failing to win this coveted assignment.

The cowboy works with the ranch manager to care for the cattle throughout the rest of the academic year, assisting with herding, calving, and caring for sick or injured cattle. He also takes the lead at the spring roundup when all students participate in branding, castrating, earmarking, and inoculating over two hundred new calves.

In June, when this student graduates, he becomes a paid member of the staff as junior cowboy, joined by his counterpart from the previous summer (now the senior cowboy). The two of them drive the herd to the Crooked

Creek grazing allotment high in the White Mountains. Living on their own at 10,000-feet elevation in the century-old Forest Service cabins reclaimed by Merritt Holloway, the cowboys are responsible for the health of the cattle, the welfare of the land, and observance of all regulations and rules set by the Range Management Team. They shoe their own horses, cook their meals on a cast-iron, wood-burning stove, collect water from a spring, and heat it over an open fire to wash their dishes and clothes. They must cope with injuries, fatigue, their own mistakes, and sharp differences that sometimes arise in working and living together for long periods. These simple, lonely, and taxing experiences produce some of the most remarkable lessons students gain from Deep Springs.

In late summer, the senior cowboy departs to resume his studies at the university to which he has transferred. His junior colleague works until October after the cattle have returned to the valley and the calf crop—the yearling steers and heifers—is shipped to market. He will return the next summer as senior cowboy, and the cycle repeats itself. Past cowboys have carried what they learned on the mountain into professions as diverse as agriculture, education, engineering, law, medicine, and the ministry.

Generous and irascible Jim Withrow died suddenly on April 23, 1987, leaving more than one million dollars to Deep Springs.[35] His will, however, specified that "should Deep Springs College cease to be an educational institution 'for the education of promising young men' as provided in . . . the Deed of Trust . . . or should the Ground Rules . . . be so changed by action or inaction of the Student Body or the board of trustees as to permit the use of intoxicating liquor or of illegal drugs . . . , all of the funds . . . shall revert to the Telluride Association . . . or the Visiting Nurse Service of New York."[36]

Seven months after he signed this will, Withrow wrote student trustee Philip Kennicott (DS'83) who had asked Withrow about his position on a proposed coeducational TASP at Deep Springs and, further, his opinion about the regular admission of women to the student body. "I am all too aware," Withrow responded, "that the responsibility of making the major decisions about Deep Springs rests with the board of trustees. . . . The alumni and friends of Deep Springs, its President and Faculty (past and present) can express their views but are hardly under the same moral and ethical obligations under which the trustees and Students ought to operate. . . . Having said that," Withrow concluded, "it is clear that the trustees and Students must vote their conscience and not mine."[37] His words and strategy echoed L.L. Nunn's own passionate appeals to the student body and trustees to do what he wanted, while also urging them to think for themselves and granting them the right make their own decisions.

Some believed that Withrow, a savvy attorney, deliberately left the door to coeducation ajar because the board could probably gain legal approval to amend the Deed of Trust. He wanted to make coeducation difficult but not impossible, they argued, assuring a deliberate process that would build strong trustee support over time.

By the time the last assets were distributed over a decade later, the total bequest was nearly $1.5 million. At Withrow's request, this money was used to establish a visiting professorship in the social sciences, a distinguished visiting chair in government, and a general fund—all in his name. His aims were not only to bolster the college, but to benefit Deep Springs with the real experience of successful leaders as a counterweight to academic theorizing. Within a decade, Jim Withrow's bequests would become the difference between Deep Springs' death and survival. The issue he left on the table regarding coeducation and the ultimate power to govern the college, however, would remain controversial for many decades.

Meanwhile, Withrow's presence continues to mark time at Deep Springs. His ashes lie behind a modest stone monument-sundial on the northeast arc of the circle in front of the Main Building.[38]

The pace of presidential successions picked up again when Brandt Kehoe left in June 1987. At the trustees' request, he had remained a fourth year. John Ure ("Buzz") Anderson (DS'39), a recently retired attorney from Pittsburg, agreed to lead Deep Springs for the next three years. An avuncular figure, slightly stooped and looking every bit his sixty-six years, he and his wife, Betty (aptly described in the *Deep Springs Alumni Newsletter* as "a burst of sunshine"), relished their interactions with students and got along well with everyone.[39] Anderson did not know academic culture, however, and left the direction of daily affairs to Dean Tim Hunt or whoever else seized the initiative. Hunt, a gifted humanities teacher and rising Robinson Jeffers scholar, served throughout Anderson's presidency. He strengthened the science curriculum, built up the library, and bolstered the academic program overall.

Anderson's passivity and lack of academic experience prompted an increasingly vigorous group of trustees to engage a wide range of policy questions with new resolve. For several years, only one member of the board had had roots in the academic world, Robert Sproull (DS'35, University of Rochester president). In rapid succession, however, three other professors joined the ranks: Charles Christenson (TA, Harvard), Frederick Balderston (DS'40, University of California, Berkeley), and Jackson Newell (DS'56, University of Utah). Their elections recognized the need for greater academic oversight and clearer direction for the college. A moribund Long Range Planning Committee was revitalized to spearhead the effort.

In Anderson's final year, the trustees launched a search for a dynamic new academic leader. Educational vision became the quality the trustees sought most in presidential candidates. Forty-one-year-old Saul H. Benjamin, director of the Honors Program at Montana State University, got the nod. Having earned his undergraduate degree at Kenyon College in Ohio, he proceeded to Oxford University in England where he claimed many distinctions. Small in stature with a bushy head of hair, he radiated charm, energy, and ideas.

Although his appointment was effective July 1, 1990, Benjamin did not establish his residence at Deep Springs until August 20. On several brief visits during those first seven and a half weeks, he announced the imminent arrival of four well-qualified faculty members whom he had hired without consulting anyone: ethicist Elizabeth Kiss, political scientist Jeff Holzgrefe, and natural scientists Joe and Susan Szewczak. He also spoke of sweeping plans for changing the college, including a disconcerting plan for constructing a high wall around the ranch to protect it against dust storms. If the trustees could not afford his ideas, he said, he would pay to implement them himself. Although impressed with Benjamin's energy, students and staff already had the uneasy feeling that he had no interest in their ideas.

Four highly respected perennial visiting professors, including former dean-director Randall Reid and U.C. Berkeley political theorist Jack Schaar, taught the Deep Springs summer course that year. They sensed trouble immediately, as did professors David and Sharon Schuman. Early in the second week of August, these four and two other faculty wrote a joint letter to board chair Bruce Laverty. They noted Benjamin's continuing residence elsewhere, then asserted: "More alarming than his absence has been his presence."[40] These professors offered specifics and then asserted that "the community appears to us to have inferred that Dr. Benjamin lacks appreciation for Deep Springs' commitment to reasoned discussion, debate, and consultation, carried out in an atmosphere of mutual trust and respect." The new president, they reported, "now faces a student body united in its distrust." They counseled the board that "irreparable damage" would be done unless it intervened immediately.

The trustees quickly assembled a Presidential Evaluation Committee chaired by board member Charles Christenson, a senior professor at the Harvard School of Business. It monitored the situation and, at the autumn board meeting, confidentially reported further deterioration. As if on cue, Benjamin rolled out his unilateral plan for the trustees, leaving no element of the college unchanged. The same day, the student leadership offered a critique of the president's performance and called for the restoration of Deep Springs' deliberative method. The board discussed the situation in depth but made no record of its conversation. In the following weeks, the Evaluation Committee continued to monitor events, finding little evidence of improvement.

Early in December, one of the faculty members whom Benjamin had hired called me at my University of Utah office. I had chaired the presidential search committee, and the professor asked if we could speak in confidence. I offered quick assurance and then received an extraordinary report bearing on the crisis at Deep Springs. Not wishing to prolong the conversation, this individual thanked me for listening and respectfully ended the call.

I rang board chair Bruce Laverty immediately and recounted the new information I had acquired. The two of us agreed to assemble the board's executive committee for an emergency session the next week at the San Francisco Airport Hilton. Meanwhile, we investigated the new issues surrounding the president. Laverty asked me to summon Benjamin to attend the scheduled meeting. Although he protested vigorously, he arrived at the appointed hour. Before sunset, the Deep Springs presidency had been vacated by mutual agreement.[41]

The spotlight now swung to Edward Hoenicke (DS'46), who had just retired from his post as senior vice president and general counsel for United Airlines. Trustee Donald H. Read (DS'59) ascertained Hoenicke's willingness to step into the breach at Deep Springs. The executive committee negotiated an eighteen-month contract with Hoenicke that commenced on January 1, 1991. He and his wife, Johnny, served without remuneration.

Democratic decision-making with empowered teenagers could hardly have been further from Hoenicke's professional acculturation, but he assured the trustees that he remembered his student years at Deep Springs and could adapt to the demands of leadership there now. Adjusting to Deep Springs' culture, however, proved more difficult for him than anyone anticipated. When the student trustee and the student body president challenged one of Hoenicke's decisions in a board meeting that autumn 1991, the new president shuddered visibly with disgust. After the session, another trustee asked him how he felt about the students' resistance. Hoenicke snapped, "I'll get even with those sons of bitches!"[42]

Ed and Johnny served their year and a half loyally but with little joy. Even Ed's good business sense proved difficult to apply because his authoritarian style toward students and staff generated more resistance than cooperation. The adage that "no good deed goes unpunished" proved valid in the Hoenickes' case. They had sacrificed much to serve Deep Springs, but the chasm between the cultures of United Airlines and Deep Springs College proved unbridgeable. They left feeling unappreciated, and their bonds with the college would not be fully restored for years.[43]

The same presidential search committee that had recommended Benjamin went back to work and came up with a winner: Sherwin W. Howard (Ph.D., University of Wisconsin, MFA, Yale), an academic dean and theater professor at Weber State University in Ogden, Utah, and former Utah Poet of the Year. Lanky, upbeat, and imaginative, Howard secured a three-year leave of absence (1992–1995). Students and faculty liked him immediately. His effectiveness rested as much on his sprightly intellect and essential decency as on his administrative abilities. His wife, Annette, visited occasionally but kept her residence in Utah to maintain her own career as an educator. Sherwin took his duties as a fund-raiser seriously, initiated important contacts with foundations that would play key roles in Deep Springs' future, energized the faculty, and inspired the student body.[44]

Coeducation again rose as a sizzling issue in the early 1990s for many young alumni, the majority of students and faculty, and academic dean Susan Szewczak. At the same time, trustee and Harvard Business School professor Charles Christenson was analyzing Deep Springs' endowment in light of new guidelines for not-for-profit organizations promulgated by the Financial Accounting Standards Board (FASB). In a January 1994 report, "Doomsday Is Closer Than You Think," he identified errors in recent audits that had led to unjustifiably rosy forecasts.[45] A grim chart, "Projected Degradation of Quasi-Endowment Funds," illustrated recent patterns of revenue gathering and operating expenses and projected Deep Springs' bankruptcy in seven years. L.L. Nunn's educational experiment was on the brink of disaster, and it would edge even closer.

The Long-Range Planning Committee, for which Christenson had prepared his report, assessed the options. On the revenue side, the board would have to raise money on a scale never before imagined. Trustee Don Read (DS'60) had led a successful campaign to celebrate Deep Springs' seventy-fifth anniversary in 1992 by raising over $750,000. That drive cleared its own target by a good margin and eclipsed the earlier mark of nearly a half-million dollars that went to the hydro plant.

But these figures paled beside the needs Christensen had uncovered. Major new resources were needed (1) to underwrite annual operating expenses which were running 25 percent above available revenue, (2) to quadruple the quasi-endowment from its nadir below $1.3 million, and (3) to completely rebuild the deteriorating Main Building, including the dormitory, and much of the rest of

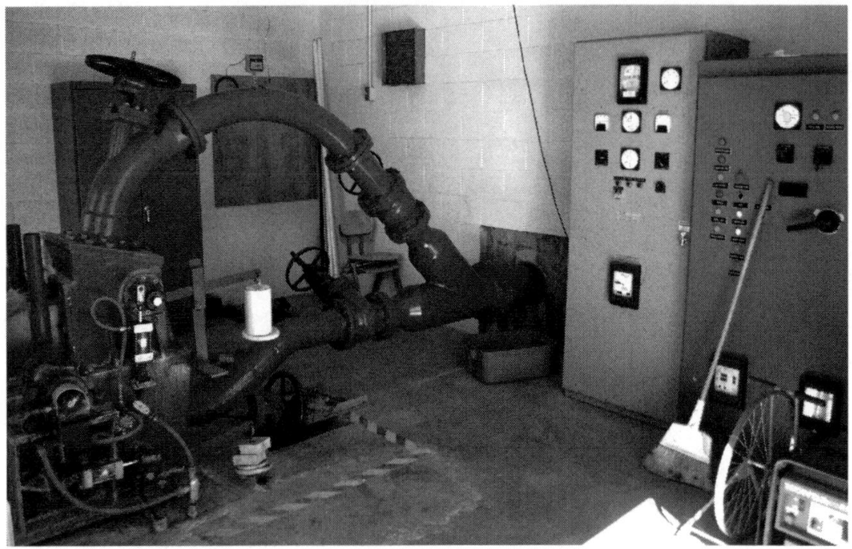

Hydroelectric plant. Photograph by author.

the physical plant. Many of the buildings, it was clear, could not pass muster with Inyo County building inspectors if they ventured out for a look.[46] None of these demands could wait.

With the future of L.L. Nunn's grand experiment on the line, the trustees stepped up. Summoning the spirit of the founder, they commissioned an independent study to determine the potential of Deep Springs' alumni to support a capital campaign at least ten times the magnitude of any previous drive. They also resolved to face the coeducation question forthrightly. With Sherwin Howard entering his final round and not wishing to continue, the trustees also launched a search for the fifth president to serve within seven years.

CHAPTER 14

RECKONING, 1994–1995

If a President were committed to stay for ten years, he could be charged with developing plans that he might live to see carried out, but that has not been a practicable solution lately, if ever.

—Harvey Mansfield (DS'21)

From 1994 to 2004, I served either as chair of the Board of Trustees (for the initial year) or as president of the college (for the next nine years). From here forward, therefore, the narrative combines a leading participant's view with a scholar's detachment. My hope is that my direct engagement in key events through this period will illuminate the pulse of life at Deep Springs in ways typically inaccessible to a historian. It imposes upon me the signal task of meriting the reader's confidence. Striving to do this, I anchor the story on archival documents, interviews with other players, and personal records.

Historians are justly wary about writing recent history, so I contemplated ending the book in 1994. Such an option, however, would have ended the narrative on an uncertain note, visited an injustice on the healthy institution Deep Springs is today, and undercut the promise of its future. I wrote on, therefore, leaving to future historians the task of crafting a scholarly account of my stewardship and subsequent events in the history of Deep Springs.

The coeducation controversy was coming to a head when the board chair, Charles Christenson, handed me the gavel on January 23, 1994. We had consulted extensively with scholars who study student development and leaders who had guided other colleges through transitions from single-sex to coeducation. The students, faculty, staff, alumni, and outside experts who served on the Coeducation Commission (formally the Impact Commission on Size and Gender) were diligent in their analysis and in projecting potential pathways to coeducation should the trustees choose to make that decision.

As the decision drew near, almost everyone associated with the college had chosen sides. Most of the players had changed, but opposing arguments mirrored those voices fifteen years before. Dean Susan Szewczak led the pro-coeducation group that included the entire long-term faculty and most of the students. Iris and Geoff Pope spoke forcefully against the change, backed by most of the staff and a few students. These partisan camps neither liked nor respected one another, adding an extra burden to the task.

Some board members who were initially inclined toward coeducation in principle began to pull back when they realized the magnitude of the college's deficits and the simple fact that its most generous contributors were opposed—often bitterly opposed—to coeducation. Others noted that Nunn had warned students since Olmsted and Claremont that social distractions could undermine their devotion to the project.[1] Heard more often now, however, was an argument that a single-sex student body was an important element in Deep Springs' distinctiveness: physically remote, academically elite, student self-governance, labor program, small scale, and all male.

On the other side, many younger alumni, students, and faculty seemed to believe more passionately than in 1980 that it was unethical to deny women an equal chance to be educated at Deep Springs, that same-sex education perpetuated archaic sexual stereotypes, and that if Nunn's overarching purpose was to educate trustees of the nation then the board would be irresponsible if it did not double the pool of promising candidates. They believed that alumni, friends, and foundations would arise and give generously to make the change possible.

Supporters of coeducation, particularly those at Deep Springs, also pointed out that not admitting women students had hardly eliminated sexual tensions with their attendant social distractions. On the contrary, they had just been expressed in different ways, certainly in homosexuality but also involving faculty and other adult women in the community. These liaisons reflected social changes that L.L. Nunn could never have imagined. With or without coeducation, sexuality had become a major complicating factor in life at Deep Springs.

These arguments aside, proponents argued, Nunn's highest purpose could not be fulfilled without making the change.

Some alumni proposed compromises. Why not alternate between an all-male and an all-female student body every decade or two? Or, after a century of serving men, should the college dedicate its second century to the education of women? A second campus dedicated exclusively to the education of women captured more serious attention. For a time, Telluride Association considered joining or leading such a project. None of these options generated momentum.

As the core issue escalated, positions hardened, justifying dubious tactics such as commandeering the college mailing list and using it without authorization to disseminate partisan material. Charges of bad faith shot back and forth across the chasm, and rational voices became harder to hear through the din.

Hoping to settle the matter at its spring meeting, the board delayed the date until June 24, 1994, giving its members more time to prepare their positions. The Main Room was electric with energy and rife with distrust as the community gathered for the final debate. As chair, I opened the first session with an appeal to everyone "to express themselves freely and candidly."[2] They did. When trustee Ernest Tucker (DS'50), a proponent of coeducation, expressed a troubling reservation, a student shouted: "Don't be an asshole, Ernie!" Tucker persevered and cooler heads prevailed, but civility had taken a severe blow. After an extended and fractious debate, the board decided to defer action on coeducation until its autumn meeting. Despite the waves of ill will, the board moved steadily through the rest of its packed agenda on long-range planning and fund-raising.

A month later, I received a long, handwritten letter from our newest trustee, Margaret ("Peggy") Sibert Miller.[3] Only six months into her first term, her tie with Deep Springs was through the James Irvine Foundation, which had supported many projects at Deep Springs. Peggy had been stunned by the ferocity of the board's and community's wrangling over coeducation. Aware that hers might be the deciding vote, and conscious of her brief association with Nunnian education, she concluded that it would be inappropriate for her to play a key role in the outcome. She resigned, therefore, expressing heartfelt respect for the college and warm wishes for its future.

Between August 29 and October 26, the board engaged in copious correspondence and held five long meetings by telephone. We had to settle the coeducation question, face another budget deficit, plan a capital campaign, and organize the search for Sherwin Howard's successor. All of the other issues turned on the coeducation decision.

In August, we agreed that each member would draft and circulate a succinct statement of his or her position on coeducation, providing reasons. In carrying out this exercise, several trustees changed their positions, generally moving from pro to con. Anthropologist Clare Selgin Wolfowitz, a Telluride veteran with two young daughters and a son, became convinced that, given the vicious divisions that existed within and among the student body, faculty, and staff, the social dynamic would be poisonous for female students entering the community at the time. Then Richard Cornelison began using the term "shacking up" to capture his fears about student behavior if coeducation were adopted.

I remained on the side of coeducation, writing to my board colleagues on September 1:

> I don't like to lobby or be lobbied, you have no doubt noticed, but I'm going to make my pitch now. . . . If Einstein was right that "everything has changed but the way we think," then the education we offer at Deep Springs must help students to think differently about one another, and to work differently with one another. . . . Everyone we educate, male and female, must learn to work naturally and effectively in an environment comparable to the ones they will inhabit throughout their lives and careers.[4]

With Chuck Christenson's fiscal doomsday looming closer, I also noted: "Deep Springs does not exist to raise money, though raise it we must; our mission is the education of gifted students for societal leadership. Let's take fundraising advice from our able and experienced fund-raisers, but make educational policies based on our experts in that arena. . . . Those alumni and friends who are currently leading and teaching in institutions of higher learning are overwhelmingly in favor of coeducation."

Bearing down on all of us as we searched for ways to resolve the impasse was our awareness of the mounting frustrations of Deep Springs' primary benefactors. On the initiative of Chris Breiseth, now a trustee, the board agreed in advance that a super majority (a two-to-one margin) would be required to trigger any change, reasoning that a clear mandate would be necessary to secure confidence in a smooth transition.

In late September, we tentatively approved a three-year experiment with coeducation to begin the following year—meaning that the first women admittees would be chosen in the spring of 1995. We invited the student body and all community members to weigh in. The extra time proved crucial. When we reconvened a couple of weeks later, we scuttled the plan as unworkable.[5] On the eve of our regular board meeting at Deep Springs at the end of October, we voted on a motion framed by Ernest Tucker: "The trustees of Deep Springs approve the concept of developing a program of co-education at DS. A comprehensive, detailed proposal for such a program [is] to be developed by a committee appointed by the Chairman." The eight remaining trustees, including the student member, split evenly, four for coeducation and four against. "Deep Springs will remain a single sex, all male college," Chris Breiseth's minutes concluded dryly.

Peggy Miller's July withdrawal from the board did not change the outcome, but her absence denied either side the consolation of a moral victory. The immediate reaction of all partisans seemed surprisingly muted, although part of the restraint may have been exhaustion. Below the surface a maelstrom began to spin.

The trustees addressed other issues before adjourning. The Long Range Planning Committee reported its preliminary recommendations for fund-raising and infrastructure renewal. The board authorized a baseline study and hiring a professional fund-raising consultant to interview key alumni for a capital campaign feasibility study. We already knew that rebuilding the physical plant and supplementing the endowment would require many millions of dollars.

The meeting ended my second and final term as a trustee. Vice-chair/chair-elect Richard Cornelison and I both worried about how to unite the board and reach out to the deeply polarized Deep Springs community and alumni. The afternoon before the final session at which I would pass the gavel to Cornelison, the two of us took a long hike on Bitterbrush Flat across the valley from the ranch. Dick and I had developed strong rapport despite our differences over coeducation. As we strode past the remote outcropping where the Cinderella Mine murders had occurred over a century before, we forged what we called our "clamshell" strategy to unite the college for the coming campaign.

In my farewell speech, we agreed, I would appeal especially to the trustees and community members who favored coeducation to rally with the single-sex advocates to concentrate on fund-raising. Our argument was simple: if the college did not survive fiscally, then whether it died being coeducational or single-sex meant nothing. I would then pass the gavel to Dick, who would respond in kind, addressing the single-sex half of the board and community and asking them to surmount the bitterness of their counterparts to pursue an epic drive. We followed our plan that evening, each stressing that the viciousness of the fight over coeducation had demonstrated at least one common value: we all held L.L. Nunn's visionary experiment in highest regard. It therefore merited great sacrifices to preserve. Now was the time to lay aside monumental resentments to ensure that the college would *have* a future. Coeducation could and would be argued later, but only if the college continued to exist.

When the meeting ended, Cornelison had not only succeeded me as chair, but Jim Olin, one of the strongest alumni voices against coeducation, had moved into the seat I vacated. Despite his unquestioned devotion to the college, Dick and I both expected that Olin would perpetuate the harsh politicization fraying the board.

The next morning Linda and I started home over Gilbert Pass, reminiscing about the two years we had lived at Deep Springs when our first child, Christine, was born, and the eight years of my trusteeship that had brought us to the ranch at least twice a year through the heart of our four children's growing-up years. Deep Springs was in our family's blood, and we felt pangs of separation.

The fact that I had just turned down the chance to continue my association with the college accentuated my feelings. Before we left the valley that morning, Dick Cornelison and Chris Breiseth (who chaired the presidential search committee) invited me to become a candidate.[6] It was clearly an honor and a mark of their esteem, but I had refused their request for two reasons. First, having given up my deanship at the University of Utah only five years earlier, I loved being a full-time professor and wanted to spend the rest of my career in that role. Second, as a former trustee, I had argued repeatedly against the pattern of short-term presidents. I agreed with Harvey Mansfield who had summed up Deep Springs' dilemma. "If a President were committed to stay for ten years, he could be charged with developing plans that he might live to see carried out, but that has not been a practicable solution lately, if ever."[7] I was determined to work toward that goal.

Less than a week after we got home, Breiseth called to say that the student body had nominated me for president. I fully realized the dimensions of that honor, but I again answered no. The telephone rang again the next evening. "Hi, Jack," Iris Pope said, "I've got news for you! The faculty and staff have finally found something we agree on: You!" Faculty, staff, students, and trustees—the temptation to reconsider was strong, even though Linda and I had carefully weighed our decision to remain in Utah. I told Iris that I was touched by the unexpected unity at Deep Springs and the confidence shown in me. Linda, who had heard my side of the conversation, asked, "You're *not* going to say yes, are you?" "How can I not?" was all I could muster. That evening, we talked for hours.

Chris Breiseth called the following day, clearly pleased by the news from Deep Springs. I reported Linda's and my conversation, and our agreement that I would become a candidate. I assured Breiseth, however, that if I were selected we would stay only three years. "It would be better," I said, "to find someone who might stay significantly longer."

I talked with Sherwin Howard the next day and we came up with an idea that might work for us both if I were chosen. He would return to Weber State that summer but remain on staff part time to direct fund-raising, while I dealt with the duties of the president-dean. This arrangement would even enable me to continue to teach winter quarters at the University of Utah, commuting to Deep Springs three days each week.

In February I was chosen as one of six finalists to interview at the college. By then, however, Howard's commitments at Weber had grown and his possible role had faded to consulting. Linda and I took the wintry drive to Deep Springs for my interview as the last of the six finalists. I was encouraged by the reception given my ideas for further uniting the community, restoring the college's service-to-humanity mission, and generating financial support. Breiseth notified me a few days later that the Search Committee was recommending me for the job. He invited Linda and me to a trustees meeting the first week of March in St. Louis.

At that meeting the board wished to negotiate a contract with me and confront a set of interrelated issues. The budget deficit yawned even wider because rancor over coeducation had hit the annual giving drive; the continuing feud between faculty and staff loomed ever larger; the bitterness many students felt toward the trustees was playing out in dysfunctional ways; and, finally, the architectural assessment had revealed greater entropy in the physical plant than anyone knew.

Linda and I flew to St. Louis and our Deep Springs–born daughter, Chris, came down from Chicago to spend the weekend with us. After reviewing the state of the college as the meeting began, Cornelison reminded me that Deep Springs' most successful fund-raising campaign had netted just over $750,000, and we now needed to raise ten to fifteen times that amount.

With that preface, he laid out the board's proposal: "We want you to spend 80 percent of your time meeting with alumni, foundations, and prospective donors around the country," he said, glancing at the board's assertive new fund-raising advisor, Chuck Thompson, for approval. My head spun. "Personally," I responded, "I would hate the job as you envision it, and I would fail miserably." He and the other trustees could not hide their disappointment, then one asked: "Then what would you do?"

I explained my theory about why the college had received only one gift or bequest of a million dollars since the founder's death in 1923.[8] "Deep Springs has rarely lived up to the promise L.L. Nunn or any of us as alumni have had for it," I stressed. "Who believes that it's living up to its educational potential now? Why would you or I, if we had the means, give our life's savings to something that has so often fallen short of our expectations? Why build a safe new dormitory for a college that may not survive beyond the end of this decade? The case for what is happening at Deep Springs—the health and vitality of this educational project—must be so compelling that alumni and others will rally to save it."

Reversing the board's formula, I proposed to spend at least 80 percent of my time at the ranch. My platform included striving to attract the highest quality student body, faculty, and staff, boosting morale, giving students a stronger sense of ownership by involving them more fully in college governance at the board level, and, above all, trying to restore L.L. Nunn's ethic of service as the spirit of the program. I also proposed to engage directly in the educational process by teaching every year. If I could succeed in these ways, then when I went on the road to meet with alumni, friends, and foundations, our reputation would have preceded me; and people would feel a new eagerness to support the college.

Chuck Thompson, the newly hired fund-raising consultant, challenged this plan, stubbornly insisting that the president's foremost duty was to bring in the money. He was correct that fund-raising had steadily inched up the priority list for most college presidents, but that was not a bandwagon I would climb on. I told him that as a life-long educator, I would love to tackle the job as I had just described it, and I was confident that I could become an effective fund-raiser under those conditions. But if the board thought otherwise and could not enthusiastically support my vision of the president's role, then I was not the person they needed to lead the college.

After a long discussion, the trustees accepted my strategy. We agreed on a three-year contract. Some trustees tried to talk me into a longer commitment, but I refused. The University of Utah would not award me a leave longer than three years without surrendering my tenure. Jim Olin, whose distrust of me was rooted in the coeducation controversy, strongly agreed with the three-year limitation. He wanted to keep me on a short leash.

I had long admired L.L. Nunn's 1923 statement titled "The Man Required for Deep Springs." It offered an inspiring archetype, but one passage now resonated especially: the leader "should not live constantly at Deep Springs but be a visitor of universities."[9] Keeping one foot in the larger realms of national, global, and academic life by maintaining my professorship at the University of

Utah could be an important asset. In addition, maintaining my tenured professorship would provide Linda and me with a measure of security should the college collapse beneath us. Another advantage to maintaining my partial teaching schedule at the University of Utah was that the trustees saved one-fourth of my compensation—no trivial matter.

The business meeting took a sharp turn when President Sherwin Howard introduced student body officers Josh Breitbart and Jamie Twiss along with Dean Susan Szewczak. The three of them described the imminent arrival at Deep Springs of four sophomores from Hobart and William Smith Colleges in New York, the first step in a proposed student leadership exchange between the institutions. The trustees were so eager to extend an olive branch to the student body that they approved this project without asking if women would be part of the visiting delegation. As the discussion unfolded, Linda scribbled a note to Sherwin Howard, who was sitting next to her: "Does the board know some of the visitors will be women?" His reply: "Don't ask, don't tell!" In fact, three of the four were women.

As the meeting closed, Szewczak invited the students and me to her room to celebrate the trustees' inadvertent approval of a coeducation experiment. When I returned to our room, I told Linda and Chris, "I'm going to be the one who deals with the consequences of this sleight of hand." A few days later, when the trustees discovered their naivete, the last vestige of trust between the board and the students vanished.

The ranch became a pawn in this standoff, something we learned on one of our preparatory visits to Deep Springs in May. While I attended a meeting with students, Linda was reading in the Withrow Guest Cottage, our quarters for the visit. Surprised by a knock, she looked up and saw Susan Szewczak at the door. "I've always gotten along well with older women," Linda recalls her saying as they began a long chat about the college. As we drove home that weekend, we pieced together fragments of disquieting information from Susan's meeting with Linda and informal conversations with faculty and students.

Whether the resulting scenario was a scheme or just entertaining fiction was not clear, but it ran something like this: Because the Popes were the most forceful opponents of coeducation at Deep Springs and because most other staff members reported to Geoff, the faculty envisioned ways to eliminate the hay and cattle operation—and thereby Geoff's job. Even more sweepingly, they may have concluded that bankruptcy could be a good thing, resulting in everyone's termination. Coeducation proponents could then reopen the college with a new deed of trust and different trustees—and rehire chosen faculty members. The ranch staff, however, would not be rehired because the labor program would switch to carrot farming, a crop that was gaining popularity among farmers in Fish Lake Valley. This convoluted plan for achieving coeducation was baffling. How an institution in bankruptcy could suddenly find money to reopen, or how control would pass to a different board with a new charter defied reason. Linda and I were cautious about where to draw the line between political hardball and fantasy. Still, we knew we had received an early warning of a storm about to break.

CHAPTER 15

RENAISSANCE, 1995–1998

The few have always had an abundance of heart and out of that abundance they have spoken. The developing influences of Deep Springs should make the student conscious of that abundance of heart, should make that abundance coherent, and should bring it to expression.

—L.L. Nunn

L.L. Nunn's "abundance of heart" has been evident throughout this history, but the number of people who came to the college's aid in the late 1990s and early 2000s, and the wisdom and force of their personalities, topped anything I had previously witnessed or seen in organizational literature.

I have long entertained a theory that truly difficult problems are rarely solved except with the serendipitous convergence of a small circle of unusual people whose skills are complementary and whose common aims join them in uncommon solidarity. When I assumed responsibility as president of Deep Springs College in 1995, I began to experience an exquisite decade-long instance of this phenomenon. What became a team of seven consisted of some of the most strong-willed people I have known. All had excelled in their chosen fields. Two were new to Deep Springs circles: retired fund-raising guru Chuck Thompson and architect Peter O'Connor. Four were alumni from the glowing Kimpton-Whitney years of the late 1930s and early 1940s: Dick Cornelison,

Bob Gatje, Bruce Laverty, and Jim Olin. These four remembered the college at its best. Now with ample means, good health, and time to volunteer, they saw an opportunity to restore something of great value to them and, they believed, to society. I rounded out the team. As a student from 1956 to 1959, I had seen a strong but brief revival squelched by some of the most notorious leadership debacles in the college's history. I had known one of the worst chapters in our history; the other four alumni had known one of the best. The combination proved to be a good mix.

How and why we five alumni came to see Deep Springs' renewal as a mission we might help accomplish is not clear. Nor can one explain easily the high degree of commitment that O'Connor and Thompson brought to the project. We may find clues along the way, but I must begin with the observation that any college or university would envy the talent and energy that rallied to Deep Springs' aid at this crucial time.

As compelling as the talents, commitments, and good will of this group may have been, from the outset the student body was also centrally involved in rebuilding Deep Springs. Following a series of *laissez-faire* presidents and chaotic times, when students pretty much had things their own way, those conditions vanished overnight. The students resisted almost every change initially, but their responses across the years of the Campaign for Deep Springs and the Building Program (1995–2001) oscillated between hostility and cooperation.

The constant intrusion of campaign advisors and volunteers, donors and potential donors, architects, contractors, and other well-meaning visitors disrupted the flow of community life. We welcomed the many visitors with ranch tours, the Boarding House experience, and a deluge of conversations sandwiched between the lengthy policy meetings in which many of them were engaged. Through it all, our demanding academic schedule and labor program continued unbroken, but the isolation and solitude so central to L.L. Nunn's purpose and methods suffered serious compromises.

To orchestrate the renewal of Deep Springs' commitment to its historic service ethic, I also knew that I risked encroaching on the student body's Nunnian autonomy. While opportunities to learn about institutional life were unusually rich for students during this era, the changes were marked by ferocious conflicts.

Perhaps the biggest challenge I faced as the new president was that the college, adrift in many ways, had suddenly become the object of many people's interest. The arena filled rapidly with would-be captains, each one intensely focused on what he or she felt was the key to overall success. We had eight trustees at the time, and there was not a weak opinion among them. Not only was the board tempted to micromanage the college and the student body; but our fund-raising counselor, the building committee chair, several individual trustees, and even a former trustee or two were similarly inclined. I had to repel advances by each of these parties, sometimes repeatedly, to protect the integrity of the student body, the community, and what I believed to be the larger interests of the college. I did my best to draw upon my long experience with Deep Springs to parry well-meaning intrusions. But the fact remained that I had to say "No" and even "Hell, no" an uncomfortable number of times.

However prickly these showdowns became, they provided valuable opportunities to define and protect the essential elements of Deep Springs' culture. I was determined that in rebuilding the college we would not cause it to end up acting and feeling like any other American college. Trustee Edwin Wesely (DS'45) became my strongest ally. Before every board meeting he read L.L. Nunn's letters in the Gray Book, and the Deed of Trust, and admonished his peers to join him in making such immersion in the founder's ideas a regular practice.

The coeducation issue continued to fuel student and faculty cynicism. A frustrated contingent of trustees and some alumni wanted very much to "trim the students' sails," an unfortunate attitude that inevitably generated conflict. With this background, and as a guide to the complex story just ahead, I will introduce more fully the seven individuals who came together in 1994–1995 to snatch Deep Springs from the brink of collapse.

Board chair, Dick Cornelison (DS'43), was tall and slightly stooped from his seventy years. A good listener and kind to the core, he was a successful engineer with twenty-two patents to his credit. In the 1970s, he had negotiated the turbulent waters of venture capitalism by working out the engineering barriers to mass-producing catalytic converters for automobiles. He seemed to command everyone's respect. "There is no limit to what we can do, so long as no one cares who gets the credit," he loved to say.

The major gifts coordinator, Jim Olin (DS'38), retired as a vice president at General Electric at age sixty-two and ran successfully for Congress as a Democrat from Roanoke, Virginia. He served with distinction, but retired at seventy-two to devote his next decade to fund-raise for Deep Springs. For Jim, repelling coeducation was both a personal conviction and a practical matter of keeping the trust of the college's most loyal and generous alumni.

Fund-raising consultant Chuck Thompson was introduced to the board by his brother-in-law, Will Cowan (DS'43). Chuck had served in World War

Jim Olin, trustee, and Dick Cornelison, board chair, in 1995. Photograph by Linda K. Newell.

II, attended Harvard on the GI Bill, and played football there. He looked the part, even as he pushed seventy. He shaved and polished his balding pate every morning. A bulldog, Chuck was forceful, relentless, and shamelessly self-promoting. But he knew fund-raising principles and provided invaluable advice and support throughout my presidency. My challenge was to keep him in bounds and off others' backs—including my own.

Chairing the Building Committee was Bob Gatje (DS'44), a former trustee and internationally known architect. He had been a major player in Deep Springs and Telluride affairs all his adult life. Tall but not physically imposing, urbane Bob lives on New York's Fifth Avenue. He matched Chuck Thompson's tenacity measure for measure. The two of them frequently disagreed, but Gatje's chief antagonism was with the student body—over issues of orderliness and cleanliness. Gatje's attempt to impose standards through architectural details challenged what the students prized as their nonmaterialistic values.

Construction advisor Bruce Laverty (DS'43) had recently served as board chair and was retired from supervising the construction of power plants for Southern California Edison, including the San Onofre Nuclear Generating Station near San Clemente. Trim and erect, Bruce typically granted others most of the airtime, but he always did his homework. He could change the direction of a conversation with a few words. A lifelong bachelor, Bruce lived alone in Pasadena, California, from which he made frequent trips to inspect each step of construction.

Chief architect Peter O'Connor practiced on Bainbridge Island near Seattle, Washington, and was recommended to us by alumnus and architect Robert

Bob Gatje, Building Committee chair. Courtesy of Sue Witter.

Gay (DS'60), who had done all our preliminary planning but was not licensed to practice in California. Peter adapted quickly to Deep Springs' culture, recognized the students as major players, and tailored his work to their needs and those of other community members. He worked beautifully with us. His near undoing, however, was designing heating and ventilation systems for desert conditions that were vastly different from the cool, humid Puget Sound climate he knew.

I was the final member of the team. Anchored at the hub, junior to all but O'Connor, and the lone academic, I enjoyed the complete trust and confidence of Dick Cornelison. In his five years of chairing the board, through a blinding array of issues and several crises, he backed me on every judgment I needed to make and invariably rallied the support of trustees and alumni to help turn decisions into actions.

When events seemed to spiral out of control, especially with the students, the board's unflappable legal counsel Chris Campbell (DS'73) was my off-site confidante. Chris practices water law in Fresno, California. Two other men provided especially apt counsel when I needed it most. Bill Allen (DS'42) had chaired the board in the midst of my trusteeship and remained a most candid and sympathetic friend throughout my presidency. Former Deep Springs president Christopher Breiseth served as president of Wilkes University in Pennsylvania throughout my leadership, but remained a trustee of Deep Springs through 1999. In addition to cannily maneuvering me to repeatedly consider—and finally take—the job at Deep Springs, he continued as a wise and enthusiastic supporter.

It would be hard not to succeed with this capable team, as long as we remained in harness together. Fortunately, the stout wills of most members were accompanied by a generous sense of humor. My most important job was to keep our hopes and energy high and to be sure that whatever we did merited genuine satisfaction because of its quality and timeliness.

A second circle of gifted and key people worked with me every day at Deep Springs for all or part of the next nine years. They included ranch manager Geoff Pope and his wife, Iris, our office manager, both of whom were unfailingly competent professionals and constant sources of encouragement and (importantly) good humor for Linda and me. Historian Ross Peterson was a frequent visiting professor and, with his wife, Kay, played similarly vital roles for us and the community.

Linda served as coordinator of special projects, a role that included everything from restoring priceless antiques (and preserving a signed Gustav Stickley sofa) to overseeing the interior decorating of the new or rebuilt buildings as they came on line. She also prepared for and welcomed myriad official guests of the college, worked with the student orderlies, and chaired the Community Needs Committee that worked with Peter O'Connor. This remarkable team provided a cast of over a dozen characters that assured intelligent and literate consideration of every issue we faced. Deep Springs Valley, the ranch, and the college provided taxing challenges, quick-paced drama, and even danger.

Pulling a heavy U-Haul trailer across Nevada, Linda and I reported for duty at Deep Springs on July 1. When we walked into the Aird Cottage, the residence reserved for presidents, a recent alumnus worked at a large drafting table in the study. He was helping Robert Gay (DS'60) develop the architectural baseline study. After greeting us matter-of-factly, he resumed his work. When I suggested a half hour later that I was unloading our trailer and needed to shelve my books in that room, he shrugged and took his time packing up. In the meantime, Linda came into the living room looking puzzled: "Where is the queen-sized bed that was in our bedroom when we visited last month?"

Iris and Geoff Pope, office manager and ranch manager/vice president, 2005. Courtesy of the subjects.

Chris Campbell, legal counsel. Photograph by author.

As he exited my study, the interloper commented over his shoulder, "Oh, some students moved it into their dorm room last night." Students were taking L.L. Nunn's gift of beneficial ownership to a new level of entitlement.

Having so recently served on the board and interviewed at the college, I was well aware that most students and faculty had become almost reflexively hostile toward authority of any kind. They also knew that I had been upset over their presentation of the Hobart and William Smith project. Nor was I, given the other commitments I had made, lining up as an automatic partisan in the continuing pro-versus-con guerrilla fight over coeducation. The students may have participated in drafting me as president, but I was now categorically suspect.

There were pleasant exceptions to this polarity. Linda and I established especially warm and trusting camaraderie with second-year students Matt Kwatinetz and John Dewis, and first-years Mihir Kshirsagar and Aron Fischer—among others. Confident and adept at almost anything they undertook, these men also cultivated friendships throughout the faculty and staff that provided a measure of equilibrium during the most strident periods of our first year.

A few days after we arrived at Deep Springs, I got an early-morning intercom phone call from Iris: "Jack," she shouted, "we've got a mess up at the shop! Joe Wessely crashed the fire truck into the student body truck, and then the momentum rammed it into Chuck Teel's new pickup! They're both in a rage. Geoff is off on a cattle drive. Hey, this one's all yours. Welcome aboard!"

Over the next half hour, I had equally frenzied conversations with Chuck (the college mechanic), Joe, and, by phone, Joe's mother in Texas. It turned out that, as part of their graduation festivities the previous week, students had ignited fireworks on the desert, exercising admirable caution by bringing the fire truck (a flatbed truck with a big water tank and pump mounted on it) to the site in advance. Joe, one of the student firemen, returned the truck to its place near the Green Shed, but he parked it aiming up the hill instead of parallel to it—a safety precaution everyone who drove the vehicle observed.

Chuck, the responsible staff member, had already asked Joe twice to rectify the situation. That morning, he minced no words. Temper flaring, Joe stalked up the hill and swung his heavy boot into the block of wood he had placed behind the rear wheels. The truck lurched backwards and began to roll toward the shop. Joe jumped on the running board and tried to crawl through the window, getting about halfway into the cab before the truck slammed into the other vehicles. I was left to negotiate a reasonable settlement of Joe's responsibility to the college and to Chuck Teel. Concerned about getting sucked into micro-management, I took some comfort in knowing that, if the student body had been in session, they would have taken the lead in resolving the issues.

Before my first week ended, I was also hit with explosively critical blasts from faculty members about Geoff and Iris Pope and other staff members. From the other side came complaints about faculty arrogance and irresponsibility. Students lobbied me from both sides. The polarization was so intense that many members of the opposing groups avoided eye contact with one another and would not sit at the same tables at meals. A few students refused to set foot on the lower ranch.

Cornelison and I, with our team of seven, launched the Campaign for Deep Springs that fall. Chuck Thompson had reported his feasibility study of alumni giving potential at a summer trustees meeting. With a concerted effort, he believed, we could raise $5 million, but $10 million was on the outside edge of possibility. The trustees deliberated long and hard, then concluded that anything less than the larger figure would fall short of saving the institution. It was all or nothing; we chose the audacious goal.

At a critical moment in that trustees meeting, Jim Olin rose slowly to address the board and community. "Phyllis and I are prepared to commit $500,000 to this campaign tonight, but we do so with one condition." We braced ourselves for a no-coeducation ultimatum. But Jim surprised us. "This board must first commit itself to the principle that it will not accept a single dollar from any donor who wishes to dictate to the board what its policy should be on coeducation or any other issue for which it bears responsibility. Even if they wished to do so," he continued, "no board has the power to make such a pledge because it has no authority to control what future trustees may decide is in the best interest of Deep Springs." Silence reigned for a moment, then the room burst into applause. The board agreed immediately to Olin's principle. He had set a high note for the campaign.

"October in the Valley," the initiating event of the Campaign for Deep Springs, was a gathering like none other in the college's history. We sent formal invitations to this gala kickoff to every alumnus and friend whom Chuck Thompson had identified through his interviews as a potentially significant supporter. Pulling out all stops for that autumn 1995 weekend, volunteer coordinator Jeff Johnson (DS'55) ordered a huge white circus tent that the students erected on the site of the earthen tennis court west of the Circle. Leaving nothing to chance, he also rented chairs, tables, tablecloths, china, and flatware.

Rather than catering the event, Chef Jack Aldworth and his student cooks arranged menus and cooked all the meals, including the banquet. Jack's brother, a professional maître d'hôtel, volunteered to drive up from Los Angeles to teach students the art of banquet serving. To supplement guest housing at the ranch, we reserved rooms at motels in Big Pine and Bishop. Alumni got caught up in the excitement and responded in large numbers.

Linda and others were preparing food and drink for a welcoming reception at our home the first afternoon while I attended the trustees meeting. When I finished making a pitch for a special budget allocation to upgrade the septic system, Jim Olin chided me: "Oh, come on, we've always had problems with it, but it always seems to do the job!" Just then, I glanced outside and saw Chuck Teel driving the large backhoe toward our home. A moment later, Linda burst into the meeting: "Jack! The toilets and bathtubs in our house and the Withrow Cottage are gushing up and flooding the buildings!" I raced off with her to find Chuck digging a trench to divert the main sewer line into the adjacent alfalfa field. The overload on the Boarding House dishwashing operation had plugged the line with grease. Fortunately, the discharge into our house was mostly dishwater. Chuck's wife, Elaine, took command of the cleanup with an impressive volunteer crew of students and staff while Linda and others continued to prepare for the reception. Within two hours we were entertaining, almost as though nothing had happened.

Under the big top the next day, Dick Cornelison presided. I reported on the state of the college and its finances. Bob Gatje followed, unveiling the board's ambitious five-phase plan for rebuilding the entire physical plant. Jim Olin then described our decision to pay for construction costs as we went—making his pitch for the major gifts and pledges necessary for the plan to work. Finally, Dick announced the trustees' make-it-or-break-it Campaign for Deep Springs goal: $10 million in five years to fund construction and recharge the endowment. At that propitious moment, I announced that Ambassador William J. vanden Heuvel (DS'46) had called earlier in the day to say that he and Melinda were matching Jim and Phyllis Olin by pledging $500,000 to the campaign. We were on our way with our first million.

Underpinning this initial success were quietly effective Bishop friends of the college, John and Bea Berger. One of the directors of the H. N. and Frances C. Berger Foundation, John knew we were critically short of operating funds until the campaign could supplement the endowment. Seeing a unique way to help, he arranged for the Berger Foundation to write a check for $120,000 to $150,000 each year throughout the campaign so that I could balance the budget without further depleting the investments we were striving to build up. These infusions comprised over 10 percent of our annual revenue during this period.

As our plan unfolded, I felt like the ringmaster of a three-ring circus, with all three vying for the center spotlight. The campaign, of course, could not wait, and the building program began almost immediately. Over the next five years, these priorities persistently rivaled my commitment to refocus the educational mission of the college—the pivot upon which the whole show turned.

By November, it was becoming clear to me that Geoff Pope was the most competent, even-handed, and even-tempered member of my staff. With very different but complementary qualities, Iris Pope was a lightning rod. She played no games, spoke her mind emphatically, and, though tenacious, listened to others with uncommon attention. Together, the Popes were becoming high-spirited partners with Linda and me. Without Geoff, I could never have distributed so much of my time and attention to the campaign or building program. Without Iris, I would have been without the brutally honest sounding board every decent leader must keep close. The lurking presence of a good laugh got us all through many rough days.

I continued to struggle, however, with a variety of faculty issues. The trustees had approved a policy in 1984 that limited professors' tenure to five years to counter the drop in teaching effectiveness and community engagement that so often happened beyond that point. With student support, however, Joe and Susan Szewczak had convinced President Howard and the board the previous year to change the limit to six years. Now they petitioned for nine years. Howard had endorsed the extension on his way out, pending board approval. Warily, the trustees awaited my recommendation.

Knowing how deep and complicated the schisms had become at Deep Springs, I took time to size up the situation. Withholding an immediate decision, however, further politicized the situation. I felt duty-bound to honor the agreement Dick Cornelison and I had sealed to postpone the coeducation decision, a decision the board had subsequently sanctioned until Deep Springs' future was secure. But many students and faculty argued that I was copping out on the question. This issue got dragged into the Szewczaks' nine-year proposal.

Throughout the autumn of 1995 I dealt daily with highly charged community issues. The board had approved a second visiting program for students from Telluride House at Cornell. Three of them would be women, and living arrangements became a new point of contention between the students and the board. The students argued that their self-governance gave them authority over it, quoting Nunn's Deed of Trust: "Therefore, it shall be the duty of said trustees . . . to accord the student body the full right, power and authority of . . . the control of the conduct of its members and of the buildings used as student dormitories."[1] The trustees, on the other hand, felt strongly that women should not be assigned rooms in the dormitory, especially not with male roommates. They proposed the Main Building guest rooms instead. Refereeing this battle and the ongoing strife between faculty and staff taxed my diplomatic powers.

Relationships between faculty and staff at Deep Springs have varied greatly over time. Highly educated professors, often young and with little life experience, work alongside and are dependent upon skilled staff every day. Staff members often have a great deal of life experience but little advanced education. Professors and staffers who are secure and comfortable with their lives usually handle their differences well and savor relationships across the community. Those who are less sure of themselves tend to struggle with one another.

"Hitting the wall," Deep Springs' term for coming face to face with our own frailties and foibles, is a revelatory jolt that spares few faculty, staff, or students. One of my moments of truth as president came with the realization that, despite my initial optimism, my power to pull the community together in a spirit of cooperation had met its supreme challenge. The dysfunctional climate within the college had not lifted. With the capital campaign now rolling and the building program about to begin, I knew that time was running out for creating an educational environment worthy of high respect. If the two groups refused to work together, I reluctantly concluded, either the four long-term professors or most of the staff would have to go.

Before taking that radical step, however, I tried once more to understand the impasse and listen as carefully as I could to each of the warring parties. The faculty members were the least tractable party engaged in the coeducation dispute, and they had a substantial student majority behind them. Staff attitudes were more varied, and at least one, chef Jack Aldworth, favored coeducation.

Returning from a late-night walk around the snowy ranch on December 7, I had a moonlight-and-conflict-inspired epiphany. "It simply seemed clear what I should do," I wrote in my journal:

> Write the trustees confidentially with this message: Coeducation has been tearing this community apart for decades and it isn't going to get any better until we admit women. What we should be doing here as educators is being warped by the conflict, and so are a lot of students, faculty, and staff. . . . In the meantime, the conflict could conceivably erupt into lawsuits, illegal actions (admitting women under false authority), or destructive behavior toward the college—all of which teaches or encourages all the

> wrong learnings in our students. And any one of which could do irreparable harm to the college and to the campaign to re-endow and rebuild Deep Springs.[2]

Could I convince the trustees of the deadly peril I sensed, and get them to embrace coeducation quickly and decisively?

I called Dick Cornelison the next morning and tried out my idea on him, stressing the importance of getting beyond this issue and back to our educational responsibilities. He received the proposal nervously but rationally, and suggested we have a private conversation with Chuck Thompson.[3] Chuck liked the idea but strongly counseled delay for fear of alienating several alumni who, we all three knew, were considering very substantial gifts. Dick had gotten the reinforcement he was looking for, and I knew they were both right. Solving the internal problem at this time, as I proposed, would kill the campaign to save the college. Further, I knew I could not convince the board at this time. My willingness to entertain this fantasy revealed how desperate I was to resolve the issues blocking the restoration of the community's health. Reluctantly, I shelved the proposal.

The problem could hardly have been made clearer than when Jim Olin called me a few days later with "some truly curious news." A neighbor in Roanoke, Virginia, knowing that Jim was a trustee, had come over to ask if he might assist their daughter, Emily, with her application to Deep Springs. Jim replied bluntly: "We don't admit women. She'll be wasting her time." The neighbor retorted, "Oh no, she has a letter from the admissions committee *inviting* her and seven other women to apply this year!"[4] Jim screamed at me: "What the hell is going on out there, Jack?" Rocked back on my heels, I assured him that I would investigate. Before I could find ApCom's chair, Frank Zaromb (DS'94), however, Dick Cornelison called and demanded more information about what he called "the insubordination at Deep Springs." He was as angry as Jim, and he threatened to "fly out and lecture the students real good." At that point, I suggested a conference call that included Jim. After much talk, their fury dissipated, they accepted my assurance that I had not been involved, and agreed, though with misgivings, that I would handle the situation. Without waiting for me to investigate, however, they pegged Susan Szewczak as the source of the invitations. Jim threatened to call the board into an emergency teleconference to fire her if I didn't do so first. Somehow, I convinced them to keep the matter among the three of us until I learned more.

I buttonholed Frank at lunch and told him what had just happened. The two of us shared a hearty laugh about the utter improbability of Jim's experience in

Roanoke, then I began firing questions at him. He candidly explained that the students acted alone, and their purpose was not to secretly admit women but to demonstrate that fully qualified women awaited the chance to attend Deep Springs. He produced the letter that ApCom had sent to the eight women. It authenticated his story, making clear to the women that they could not be admitted and spelling out the role their applications could play in highlighting the viability of coeducation. I quickly passed this information on to Jim and Dick, partially easing their concerns.

Student body trustees and trustees-elect Keith Hiestand (DS'94), Abe Lentner (DS'95), and Mihir Kshirsagar (DS'95) came to see me that evening, seeking advice on the best strategy to restore the trustees' faith in their integrity. I advised them to call Cornelison and Olin, and follow up with letters and pertinent attachments. They acted immediately and maturely, restoring relationships with surprising speed.

Deep Springs had never developed a clear and professional review process for faculty and staff, but the need was evident. I developed one modeled on best practices at other colleges. It included faculty self-evaluations of teaching and scholarship, and their plans for sustained growth. Students were asked to evaluate each professor's teaching and community engagement, and, finally, faculty needed to assess each other's progress. All of this information was to be assembled confidentially in a single portfolio on each faculty member for the president to consider in making salary and retention decisions. For professors at the third- and fifth-year levels, a dossier containing all of the above material was to be sent to two outside professors in the faculty member's own academic specialty for evaluation.

The purpose of this multilayered process in colleges and universities is to help junior faculty monitor their progress and provide their peers (including administrators) with information upon which to judge their progress toward achieving academic tenure and promotion in rank. As president, I was keenly aware of how much I needed this information.

Not surprisingly, the four long-term professors reacted with immediate resistance, finding the process unfair and hostile—even though it was a standard review protocol. They accused me of imposing scholarly expectations without warning. I could see their point, but responded that unless they got constructive feedback through this process they would be unprepared for the careers they hoped would unfold at other institutions of higher learning.

I also worked with the faculty to create a mini-sabbatical policy. Those who passed their third-year review would be awarded a semester free of teaching to be used for developing their scholarly credentials as recommended by their peers at other institutions. These new policies and procedures laid the groundwork for future faculty, but time was running out for this group.

I was being pulled in many directions; but after much soul searching, it was clear to me that my experience equipped me better to develop a new professorial corps than to build a new ranch, farm, and service staff. I decided to move all four regular faculty members out as soon as possible and hire a new teaching staff, by the fall of 1996 if possible. Painfully aware that I was violating L.L. Nunn's democratic principles as well as my own, I acted alone, simply informing the student body of my decision. Its members were rightly furious. They pressured me to reverse the dismissals and expressed deep cynicism about my pledge to work closely with them through CurCom to conduct job searches and appoint new faculty.

I met separately with professors Andreas Kriefall and Patrick O'Connor well before the March American Association of University Professors deadline for notifying untenured faculty that their contracts would not be renewed. I explained that I had decided to let them go because internal relationships at the college appeared irreparable. I also hastened to say that I could and would support each of them in his search for another position, trusting that his competence as a scholar and teacher would be better expressed in a less politicized environment.

A member of Telluride Association, Patrick O'Connor had received his doctorate at Yale the previous year in comparative literature, and Andreas Kriefall had recently earned his doctorate at Cornell in philosophy and religion. Both were understandably incensed, and they appealed for an additional year or two to prove they could make things work at Deep Springs. Most of the students jumped into the fray as well, championing their aggrieved professors. I stood my ground over the next few weeks, while endorsing the right of Kriefall and O'Connor to appeal my decision before the board. They did not take this option, knowing their chances of success were near zero, and immediately started searching for teaching posts elsewhere. I assisted them with letters of recommendation. O'Connor joined the Hispanic Studies faculty at the University of Chicago and Kriefall went to teach literature at Union College.[5]

The Szewczaks' case was more complex because they had been on the faculty longer, and President Howard had already extended their contracts through the controversial sixth year. Joe was the strongest teacher and most productive scholar on the faculty, a widely recognized authority on bats who taught courses in physiology, biology, calculus, and even physics. Susan held a doctorate from Brown University in biophysics but had recently developed an interest in organizational communications. She taught life science courses. Fortunately, the Szewczaks both had ties with the University of California's White Mountain Research Station in Bishop. Our relationship disintegrated almost completely, but we did negotiate an arrangement whereby they would move to Bishop that summer and travel to Deep Springs once a week throughout the following year, teaching all of their courses on a single day each week.[6]

The impending loss of Joe's special skills essential to Deep Springs' operations, particularly communications, added a serious complicating factor, so characteristic of this tiny, interdependent community. He had installed and maintained the microwave radio equipment and remote relays on which our telephone and internet service depended. His departure would mean that we no longer had the expertise to maintain and repair these links with the outside world until Geoff Pope and several students picked up the challenge.

In the meantime, an abrupt failure of our recently established internet link occurred early in 1996, while the Szewczaks were still living at Deep Springs. Joe had arranged for the college to piggyback on the IP address of the Owens Valley Radio Observatory (OVRO) while he worked to establish our own internet domain. Our signals came from OVRO via our radiotelephone lines. OVRO's data link originated at the California Institute of Technology (Caltech). One morning, Joe received a fretful phone call from Steve Scott, OVRO's computer specialist. A hacker, he reported, had noodled his way into Caltech's computer system and OVRO's director, Nick Scoville, had traced the assault back to Deep Springs. Scott, who had put the college on OVRO's account as a courtesy, was now blamed not only for the breach in security but also for his unauthorized decision to help the college. After his conversation with Scott, Joe rushed over to my office and demanded that I find and dismiss the person responsible for the breach.

Everyone knew something strange had happened because our internet service was down and the phones were still working. By a process of elimination, within a half-hour Joe and I narrowed our list of suspects to one student. I called him to my office after lunch, told him that Caltech's computer system had been violated, and that a number of facts in the case pointed to him. I asked him pointblank: "Did you do this?" He looked away for a few seconds, then denied any knowledge of the incident. I told him that, as our most computer-savvy resident, he could probably help solve the mystery by going back to the dormitory and thinking through how this could have occurred at Deep Springs, or how OVRO might have concluded in error that someone at the college was responsible.

Working in my study near midnight, I was surprised by a knock on our front door. When I opened it, the same student stood there, trembling. Before stepping across the threshold, he confessed responsibility for the breach. Once inside, he assured me that it was not a malicious act. He had simply been bored and got curious about how far he could follow the links that connected us to the cyber world. He offered to do anything within his power to make amends. By the next morning, everyone knew who was at fault. He had chosen to break the news himself. Reflecting back, I recalled that he had given a talk on computer hacking for a public speaking assignment back in November.

Officials at Caltech and OVRO had magnanimously assured me that, once we had identified and punished the perpetrator, they would restore our internet connection. The faculty demanded that I dismiss the student and restore e-communications immediately. I was pondering how best to proceed when Nat Birdsall (DS'95), the student chair of the Review and Reinvitations Committee (R-Com), came to see me. R-Com, like our other standing committees, was not only chaired by a student but had a large majority of student members.

Nat asked if, rather than me handling the situation, R-Com could take the case and decide on an appropriate action. That is the Deep Springs way, and I agreed. Before he left, the two of us reviewed Caltech's conditions for hooking us up again, the larger matters of the college's credibility, and the student's rights.

Over the next five days, R-Com held hearings with the student and all parties affected by the hacking incident, keeping confidential transcripts of the conversations. They assembled facts, weighed motives, assessed damages, and prescribed penalties in a multifaceted protocol. To make things right, the student would have to (1) pay all costs and damages incurred at Caltech, OVRO, and Deep Springs for reestablishing security barriers and compensating for losses incurred when service was down, (2) apologize in writing to everyone who suffered inconvenience or embarrassment due to lost service, (3) lead a public seminar at Deep Springs on internet ethics, and (4) abstain from using the internet for the rest of the year. Before reporting back to me, Nat and his committee called the student in and presented him with their conclusions. He thanked them, said they had been more than fair with him. He promised to comply fully and speedily.

Nat then came to me to summarize R-Com's work and give me their list of steps required for the offender to make things right. I thanked him and the other members of R-Com and pledged my support in seeing that their prescribed penalties were followed.

I called the director of Computer Services at Caltech to describe what R-Com had done and the offending student's response, adding my endorsement of the process and outcome. He sounded pleased and pledged to restore our service. Then he asked if I would send the list of sanctions to him that I had just read, saying, "This is the most thorough and constructive response to a hacking case that I have seen. I would like to circulate it as a model for others to consider at Caltech." He continued, "I've heard about your remarkable college but how in the world do you get students to handle responsibility so professionally?"

The student responded in good faith to every point R-Com set forth, with the exception of the public lecture. He could not bring himself to do this presentation that spring, and he chose to move on from Deep Springs after that year. He made a special trip from the East Coast the next fall, however, to fulfill this public responsibility—which he did with a flourish. He went on to earn his degree at a prestigious university and has become a highly successful computer engineer.

The student body had alternated that winter and spring between confronting me and offering unexpected cooperation. We needed to work together, and did, in the process of hiring two new long-term professors, employing several visiting professors, and selecting the new class for admission the next year. The latter was not easy.

Over the previous few years, the student body had come to assume that the Applications Committee's (ApCom's) decisions were final and that the president was a rubber-stamp. Its members were offended, therefore, when I said that I expected to review and approve their judgments before candidates could be informed about their admission. The trustees had insisted that I assume this task; but even if they had not, I deemed it important as a means of exerting some influence on the culture.

Complicating matters in working out our differences was the provision in my contract that I would also teach at the University of Utah winter quarter (early January through mid-March). I set up an alternative Deep Springs office at the university and spent half of every week there, commuting across Nevada in my Ford with a high-gain cell phone antenna on the roof so I could work as I traveled. I happened to be in Salt Lake City when the ApCom matter came to a head. I wrote in my journal the morning after a long phone meeting with the committee:

> Last night's telephone conference with the Applications Committee (ApCom) was a real test of wills. They have grown accustomed to the benign neglect of the Howard years and now roundly

> challenge my playing any role in the admissions process for next year's class. There have been a number of surprises upon my arrival at Deep Springs, and the discovery that the students believe they are in *total* control of admissions (along with the curriculum and faculty hiring and firing) is simply astonishing. It is unacceptable to me because I can have no effect over the nature or quality of the college, and it is unacceptable to the trustees who have grown increasingly restless.[7]

If changing the culture required starting afresh with new faculty chosen with a high level of student participation, my challenge was even more difficult with the student body. Most of the first-year class would return in leadership roles the next year.

When I assumed my advise-and-consent role in the admissions process back in November, I met with ApCom's members and asked them to consider the importance of diverse religious, political, and intellectual predispositions within the student body. Living by democratic principles within a group that thinks alike about basic things, I argued, is not preparation for leadership in society at large. At Deep Springs, I urged, we must avoid the temptation to replicate ourselves as we select the incoming class. Before leaving the meeting, I explained that although I did not wish to participate in the committee's regular meetings or applicant interviews, I would be doing something that my recent predecessors had not done: meeting with each applicant myself.

The thirty-five finalists from the applicant pool came for their interviews in groups of three or four in February and March. Popcorn with Jack and Linda the evening before each applicant left became part of the interview protocol. We very much enjoyed these conversations and had a chance to talk about the service-to-humanity ethic of the college, and offered to talk by phone with any skeptical parents. In March, with applicant visits concluded, I participated in a marathon session in which ApCom ranked the candidates and chose the top thirteen to recommend for admission. Because I held a potential veto later in the process, I explained, I would participate in the discussions but not vote on candidates. Out of this joint effort came a slate of new students that I was able to endorse with confidence.

A number of highly experienced visiting, one-term faculty, together with their partners and children, lent special stability to the community throughout this turbulent year. Among them, as previously noted, were Ross Peterson, a senior historian at Utah State University, and his wife, Kay. They became especially capable community members as well as warm personal friends. Geologist Peter Guth (DS'69), on sabbatical leave from the U.S. Naval Academy, his wife, Mary, and their children brought infectious curiosity and unfailingly good spirits. John Drabble, a historian trained at U.C. Berkeley, proved consistently thoughtful and upbeat; and photographer Michael Smith and his wife, Paula Chamlee, also a professional photographer, brought both energy and a variety of nonconformist ideas into the community.[8] Finally, Misha Hoekstra (DS'82) taught literature and took such a deep interest in the entire operation that I hired him to return as academic dean for 1996–1997.

That year began on a positive note. A new long-term faculty couple, David S. Peritz and Angelia K. Means, assumed responsibility for humanities instruction, while another group of able visiting professors pitched in enthusiastically. Among them, Dick Carter taught anthropology, Adnan Husain (DS'87) and Katy Fleming covered Middle Eastern history, and Margaret Hayden taught ceramic arts. They proved eager to begin and excited by the opportunities Deep Springs offered.

A year later, by the autumn of 1997, the entire student body and faculty had been admitted since the difficult transition year. The new norms for working together seemed to have borne fruit by the end of my third year in office. I entertained few illusions that conflicts were over, but the tone of community life had changed. Still, the student body's evaluation of my performance at the end of my second year in office came as a humbling reminder of my inadequacies, especially my need to improve relationships with students and faculty.

With the faculty and new class in place, we were gearing up for the gigantic effort that the building program represented; but simultaneously, Bob Aird offered a distraction. The trustees assigned me to serve as editor of Aird's memoir about L.L. Nunn and Deep Springs. He was in his early nineties and harbored strong personal views about every aspect of Deep Springs, especially during his years of intense involvement.[9]

The initial conversations were discouraging. Bob took the novel position that I could not change anything in his writing except typographical errors. The work, however, contained many misleading claims and unsupported criticisms of people with whom he had differed over issues. Some of these claims could seriously damage the reputations of others and incur libel suits for him and for the college as the publisher. Another issue was Aird's claim, repeated several places in the text, that Deep Springs was not a college at all until he made it into one as director in the early 1960s. Since this would be the first published history of Deep Springs, I felt strongly that it should be reasonably accurate.

Aird's close friend Jack deBeers (DS'32) became his confidant and defender. The copy editor I hired to prepare the work for printing, Lavina Fielding Anderson, soon found herself dealing not simply with the manuscript with my corrections, but also with a flurry of demands from Aird, deBeers, and Aird's son John—each of whom claimed that he was in charge. When Aird and deBeers each called my administrative assistant and admonished her to ignore me and print the book as written, I had reached my limit.

In exasperation, I wrote Dick Cornelison, describing the immediate problem with the book and the larger issue that some alumni felt entitled to continue managing the college after having served their stints in leadership or trusteeship. "Dick, this book matter has escalated to the point I should resign over it immediately. . . . If . . . Bob Aird can call the shots on a project funded by the college, issue orders to employees or contractors hired by the president, and attempt to undermine the credibility of the president with his own employees—and do this all with impunity . . . then the trustees need a sycophant for my job and the college is ungovernable."[10] If the trustees let this situation continue, I argued, then they would be as indulgent of bad behavior among alumni as they sometimes accused me of being with regard to the student body.

Dick heard me and sent a letter to Lavina Anderson, with copies to Aird and deBeers, confirming that the college was the publisher, that I was the editor, and that Anderson was answerable only to me on this project. Aird and deBeers backed off, and we printed the book within a few months. I ached from having hurt Bob and agonized over whether my own ego had gotten out of control.

I had recently fended off a similar intrusion by Jim Olin, who had skirted both Cornelison and me in issuing an order to the Building Committee. More trying was Chuck Thompson, whose insensitivity to ordinary institutional and social boundaries astonished even his closest allies—of which I was one. When Linda and I slipped away for an afternoon of relaxation after a trustees meeting, Chuck, who had not yet left the valley, went to my office and asserted that, while I was away, he was in charge. He then told one trustee who was still at the ranch that he (the trustee) would be appointed vice-chair at the next board meeting (not true), said that another trustee would be kicked off the board if she failed to make a campaign pledge within two months, gave the student office manager a list of computer equipment that I would buy, ordered my assistant to write a loyal donor and demand immediate payment of his pledge (which would have offended him grievously), and announced that I was going to appoint him vice president and he would soon be moving to Deep Springs (a complete fabrication).[11]

Linda and I returned from our calm afternoon to a college in uproar. I dealt systematically with those affected by each claim, then met with Chuck. I was sufficiently clear that nothing like this happened again. I had previously set limits on internal politicking and insisted that students, faculty, and staff exercise reasonable decorum. I believed that the same standards must apply to those serving Deep Springs in its extended family.

The building program lingered behind the curtains while the Campaign for Deep Springs generated enough money to bring it on. The time was not wasted, however, as Peter O'Connor went to work on the creative planning done by Robert Gay. Robert's scheme called for repurposing the Main Building for purely academic, library, and public use, moving the student body into a cluster of new straw bale–constructed residences rather than one large dormitory, building a new administrative center on the site of the tennis court—all to be encircled by a new ring road outside the existing one and the new buildings. Gay completed this plan just as I took office. The students featured it as the centerfold in the spring 1995 alumni newsletter.

The trustees hired Peter O'Connor as architect when the building program began because Gay was not licensed in California. He assessed Gay's plan and invited students, faculty, staff, and trustees to share their reactions to it. Peter also advised us to form a broadly representative Community Needs Committee. Linda chaired the group and encouraged the free flow of thoughts about what changes or additions to the physical plant might enhance daily life and promote good interaction.

From this process came everything from a playground for the children of staff and faculty to a completely different kind of dormitory, and from a music practice room to the planting of scores of trees to replace the aging cottonwoods and Chinese elms. Some of the ideas were adopted immediately. For example, the students enthusiastically designed and built the playground using parts from old farm implements. Iris Pope had already planted dozens of cottonwood saplings around the ranch, but we initiated a new effort to plant additional trees at the end of each phase of rebuilding.

By this time, everyone seemed to agree that the first step would be to construct a new dormitory so that the student body could move out of the very cramped Main Building. Once the old dorm wing was empty, the Main Building could be completely reconfigured to accommodate its other functions.

When O'Connor presented his draft plans for a new student residence, however, a student blurted out: "That one's a Motel Six!" Peeved, O'Connor asked and received a host of specific criticisms and suggestions. When he went back to his drawing board in Seattle, he also had a packet of ideas from the Community Needs Committee. For example, when issues arise at Deep Springs, members of the community seem unable to see beyond the circle or look beyond the immediate crisis. The committee therefore suggested that dorm rooms face out toward the fields and the desert beyond. The student body also strongly recommended a mix of two- and three-person rooms, each one uniquely configured.

Peter O'Connor responded creatively and produced an imaginative dormitory plan. His stubby check-mark design fit the site perfectly, allowed him to vary room sizes and shapes throughout, and gave almost every room a view of the ranch and valley. Topping it off was a penthouse study room with extraordinary natural light and views. The students, community, and Building Committee, including its chair, Bob Gatje, all embraced the new plan.

The hottest issue was Gatje's insistence that the design include a spacious "mud room" where students who had completed their daily outdoor labors could shed their work clothes and shower before proceeding to their rooms. Students scoffed at this attempt to prescribe good habits, but Gatje prevailed. When the building was completed the students hijacked the mud room, installed a pool table and weight-lifting machines, and used the lockers for storage.

By the time O'Connor had completed the drawings, we had secured the money to underwrite construction. With Jim Olin's special encouragement, Robert (DS'35) and Mary Sproull tendered a $1.5 million pledge, specifying that they did not wish to set a precedent by having the new residence named for them. The Sproulls did wish to establish a different precedent, however, by setting aside a portion of their gift as a permanent endowment for the building's maintenance.

Venerable alumni Herb Reich, who had helped complete construction of the Main Building as a student in 1917, and Bob Aird, who arrived shortly thereafter, wielded shovels to break ground for the new student residence at the eightieth anniversary alumni reunion in September 1997. Rudolph Construction of Mammoth, California, commenced operations within days; and Lee Powell, the superintendent of construction, rapidly became a fixture in the community, as did lead carpenter Kelly Williams. These men loved their work, and their genius for innovative problem solving and flair for finishing touches earned them laurels again and again.[12]

Powell, for example, salvaged an old telephone pole of rare and priceless bristlecone pine from a legal source. He and Williams cut and milled it to make the mantle for the fireplace in the living room of the new student residence.[13] The

Bob Aird and Herb Reich at groundbreaking for the new student residence, October 1997. Photograph by author.

New student residence, 1998. Photograph by author.

student body gathered and hauled twenty-five tons of granite rock from near Deep Springs Lake for the exterior and conducted site cleanup chores every evening. Finally, Bruce Laverty contributed his wealth of construction supervision experience—through countless phone calls and occasional visits—to assist me in overseeing the work.

As the building neared completion, students expressed increasingly negative attitudes toward the high-class dormitory, fearing the loss of traditions associated with their eclectic old dorm rooms and resisting gentrification. The architectural design called for the then-standard installation of conduits for internet wiring. The student body objected, noting that, consistent with its definition of the isolation policy, it had long-since resolved to keep email and telephone access out of dorm rooms. Internet use was confined to the library, offices, and homes. The Building Committee insisted that future student bodies might choose otherwise and decided to go ahead. The students won an agreement, however, not to install wires or fiber optic cables in the conduits. More significantly, the students succeeded in getting a large solar water-heating facility built into the roof design, an important addition that would prove its value many times over.

Another showdown came over plans to install standard institutional furnishings in all rooms. Students surprised the Building Committee when they protested the sterility of uniform dormitory desks, chairs, and beds. When O'Connor and the Building Committee pushed back, the student body parried with a proposal that we entrust them with the money set aside for furniture and let them purchase what they wanted. After some negotiating (bunk beds and wardrobes would be standard issue), the deal was sealed. With Casey Sanchez (DS'96) leading, a student body committee took the cattle truck and spent spring vacation visiting used furniture stores from Portland, Oregon, to Los Angeles, purchasing a lively assortment of couches, easy chairs, desks, bookcases, and lamps.

Meanwhile, the Campaign Committee, the Building Committee, Peter O'Connor, and I moved on to the next major step, the complete renovation of the Main Building. We had hardly begun planning when the urgency of our task became unmistakably clear. On the evening of Friday, November 14, 1997, the faculty and staff were enjoying a party at the home of biology professor Jack Murphy (DS'78) and his wife, Caroline, in the east duplex. Suddenly, the floor began to heave and sway. Jack shouted, "Earthquake! Everyone out!" Caroline grabbed baby Annajane from her crib as we all ran out onto the lawn.[14] The students, who had just finished their student body meeting in the Main Room, poured out onto the front porch with its wide-span roof. Had the quake been more severe, they would have been crushed. After an hour of frenzied chatter on the Circle, most went home to assess the damage. Then a significant aftershock bumped the ranch.

When I called 911 to report the quake, the woman said she had just received an emergency seismic bulletin: "It was a 5.3 quake with its epicenter eight miles south of Deep Springs, wherever that is!" Then our phones and email went down and stayed out for the next two days. The quake emanated from a point at the base of the Lake Mountains adjacent to Deep Springs Lake. The aftershock had registered 3.9 on the Richter Scale.

Interior damage at the ranch was limited to a stack of barrister bookcases from the original library that crashed and splintered in a student's room. Small items had toppled off almost everyone's bookcases and countertops, many of them breakable. Significantly, a large crack opened in the forty-foot-wide support span of the Main Porch—causing a noticeable break at the center. To forestall a possible calamity, mechanic Chuck Teel built a steel brace the next morning and inserted it under the crack to stabilize the heavy roof.

I took photographs of the sagging beam with its corrective brace and mailed copies to the trustees and members of the Building and Campaign Committees. Plans for the Main Building renovation proceeded apace, and the standard seismic provisions took on greater importance. The existing building would be gutted to the stone walls. Then a completely new structure built inside it would meet contemporary needs. Once the new roof, windows, and doors were installed, the iconic exterior would appear almost unchanged while the interior would be state of the art—with an estimated tab of $1.8 million. Could we raise the money in time to keep Rudolph Construction engaged seamlessly when they completed the student residence?

Carol Owen and Denis Clark (DS'69) were in transition in and out of the presidency of Telluride Association at the time. Its coffers bulged with funds resulting from a newly conservative reinvestment policy coupled with the unprecedented stock market boom. Because Telluride was a qualifying nonprofit organization, some of its members believed that the association needed to disperse additional resources from its endowment, then approaching $50 million. Sympathetic to Deep Springs and supported by prominent members of the association who were also Deep Springs alumni, especially Jahan Sharifi (DS'80), Brad Edmondson (DS'76), Lars Wulff (DS'79), Bill Pezick (DS'65), and Jay Pulliam (DS'78), Owen spearheaded a proposal for the June 1998 Telluride Convention scheduled for its sabbatical occurrence at Deep Springs. Carol hoped to convince the membership to support the total cost of rebuilding the Main Building as a grand renewal of the historic ties between L.L. Nunn's two educational legacies.[15] There was nothing timid about her. The fact that she was not a Deep Springer made Owen's advocacy particularly persuasive, but time would tell.

My three-year academic leave from the University of Utah was expiring at the end of the 1997–1998 academic year. Dick Cornelison and the board leaned heavily on me to make a long-term commitment to Deep Springs instead of leaving in the middle of our huge project to return to my tenured professorship. Linda and I recognized that our center of gravity had shifted over the last two and a half years. The challenges and excitement that motivated us, we both agreed, were now overwhelmingly at Deep Springs. I applied for early retirement at the university, received emeritus status, and then signed a five-year contract to remain at Deep Springs.

Not long after making this decision, we were braced by a letter from anthropologist and trustee Clare Wolfowitz, who had visited the college regularly for eight years. After the trustees' meeting in spring 1998, Clare wrote Linda and me:

> The difference the two of you have made in the atmosphere at Deep Springs is so dramatic that I would have liked to discuss it with you from an anthropological point of view. A change in culture doesn't happen without some effort. I am not the only visitor to notice the change. What impresses me most is the quality of the current student body, which seems to me to be as stellar in character as in academic ability. There is a rare quality of openness that is extremely refreshing.[16]

Nothing could have been more soul satisfying. Responding to this kind sentiment by return mail, I summarized the issues we had faced:

> The road from the starting gate to the shared vision—and beyond—is built on the gut issues that present themselves along the way: defining the admissions decision-making process with the students, settling the six-year limit battle with faculty, refusing to let the fund-raising tail wag the educational dog, helping make our Range Management Team effective . . . [and] hammering out a salary-benefits policy with faculty and staff who began as skeptics. . . . We define

Linda and Jack Newell, 1998. Photograph by Eric J. Newell.

> our ethics and reveal our commitments (to being vigorous, just and humane) by the way we handle these conflicts. Falter and we produce contentious cynics. Discipline ourselves and we create citizens with ethics and initiative of their own.[17]

This strategy, of course, was not as smooth or easy as I made it sound, nor would it get any easier.

CHAPTER 16

REALITY, 1999–2004

And if someone will say, "But what have you done?", there will be no pointing with the material finger to a fortune achieved. . . . There will be the witness of the fruits of the Spirit, for as out of the abundance of the heart the mouth speaketh, so out of the knowledge of life the soul beareth fruit.

—L.L. Nunn

Neither the revival of Deep Springs' educational mission nor the ongoing renewal of its physical plant could ensure smooth sailing or sustained progress. Even before the renaissance project reached its crest, the college encountered new challenges and suffered the most devastating loss in its history. Yet new supporters emerged to provide fresh energy, add critically needed resources, and bring understanding that helped carry the institution forward despite its trials.

In early June 1998, Telluride associates gathered at Deep Springs for their annual convention. Rudolph Construction had just finished the stunning new student residence, on time and on budget, and the women in the community added a finishing touch by sewing curtains for all the rooms. The student body moved its impressive furniture collection into the structure. They elected to remain in the old dorm wing of the Main Building for an extra week, however, so that Telluride members attending the convention could enjoy the new quarters. (To put the sumptuousness of their new residence in perspective, the students then camped on the desert beside the community's dumpster for several nights before moving in.)

As convention guests settled in, steely eyes revealed a sharp feud within the association over a proposed $1.8 million gift to Deep Springs. A majority opposed the initiative. While some regarded it simply as too generous, other powerful Telluride figures believed that such a gift would be patently immoral because of Deep Springs' single-sex policy. As they railed against the proposition, emotions overflowed, some wept, and one even spoke of the presence of evil at the college. Deep Springs students, many favoring coeducation, listened in disbelief to what they regarded as sophomoric fury. When the aggrieved Telluriders assuaged their anger with beer and bourbon (after the student body had asked them not to imbibe publicly because Deep Springs was in session), student bewilderment turned to derision. The contrasting cultures of the two institutions were magnified out of proportion on both sides. Telluriders stereotyped Deep Springers as unpolished male roughnecks, whereas Deep Springs students viewed Telluriders as ineffectual intellectual snobs.

When the gift appeared doomed, Telluride President Carol Owen huddled with her most sympathetic colleagues—all veterans of the association as well as the college—and came back with a different idea. They suggested making Telluride's support into a business transaction in the form of a long-term, low-interest loan to the Trustees of Deep Springs. On the convention floor, however, securing the proposed loan became an issue.

This matter was eventually resolved by establishing the L.L. Nunn Limited Liability Company (LLC). Deep Springs became the majority partner by securing the $1.8 million loan with property of greater value at the college—chiefly the land on which the college buildings stand. Carol Owen and Chris Campbell would spend most of a year negotiating the details of this legal agreement. With interest pegged at the Consumer Price Index (CPI) each year, the association's membership approved the partnership but later reserved the right to require repayment of the principal and interest if, after twenty years (that is, by 2019), the college had not converted to coeducation. Confident that they would be in a position to repay the loan when it came due (which they now are), the Trustees of Deep Springs and Telluride Association launched the L.L. Nunn, LLC, in 1999.

In connection with establishing the L.L. Nunn, LLC, for the Main Building, we launched a $1.8 million matching campaign to create the Simon and Eunice Whitney Endowment to honor the late dean-director (and his still lively wife) who had inspired so many students in the 1940s. Alumni from that era, as well as professors Kurt and Alice Bergel who taught at that time, stepped up in large numbers to make this drive successful. The aging Bergels announced their $100,000 gift publicly at an alumni gathering at the ranch, then remarked to me privately: "Jack, you didn't think a couple of old professors could give so much, did you?" The Whitney Endowment fund is now held at a separate brokerage and pledged to the Telluride Association should it demand payment. The college has never wished to let anyone or any other party dictate its policies—one reason it has continued to eschew federal aid.

With our funding nearly secured, Richard Stack of the Hugh and Hazel Darling Foundation gave an additional $250,000 grant to establish a pleasant reading room and an archive in the new library wing of the building. Before work on the Main Building could begin, however, Labor Commissioner Aaron Jacobson (DS'97) directed the student body in extracting every moveable item from the building, including eighty years of abandoned student property from the huge attic—an archeologist's delight. They also moved the entire library to a rented triple-wide trailer.

When the Main Building finally stood empty and deconstruction began (a term that inspired countless puns in this literary community), Lee Powell's keen eye caught a few fixed items for salvage. One was the old fire bell in the dormitory that students had used to call student body meetings and public speaking sessions since the earliest years. The buzzer would find a new home on the expansive front porch and continue its function when the building was returned to service.

The huge watercolor painting of the Ontario Power Works and Niagara Falls that the Nunn brothers had commissioned in 1904 to commemorate their achievement had been rescued from eighty years of storage in the Green Shed by Octavian Drulea (DS'95) while serving as orderly. It was too large and heavy to hang, but Powell devised a way to countersink its frame in the Main Room wall, then invited all community members to sign their names in the back of the recess before a student crew lifted the heavy painting into place.

Reconstruction took about a year, during which faculty taught classes in their living rooms, and the college offices were moved to the Upper Faculty Cottage. This game of musical chairs, played repeatedly over the next several years, enabled the college to function fully while all the other structures were similarly renovated. During the rebuilding of the Boarding House two winters later, all food preparation moved to a U.S. Forest Service mobile field kitchen parked next to the Museum. Except on stormy days, almost everyone ate outside in the cold.

The Main Building during reconstruction, 1999. Photograph by Elaine Teel.

Main Building after reconstruction. Photograph by author.

While the Main Building was being gutted and rebuilt, Linda Newell arranged with Jerry Fendon at Fendon's Furniture in Bishop to restore and reupholster the historic couches, desks, chairs, and tables, a significant portion of which had belonged to L.L. Nunn. Studying old photographs, she also obtained Asian carpets akin to those that had once graced the Main Room. In architecture as well as interior appointments, the spirit of the Building Program was to preserve the culture and feel of the community in its renewed state.

By the end of the summer of 1998, the Campaign for Deep Springs had met its $10 million goal—two years ahead of schedule. At the same time, we knew it would cost much more than we had anticipated to complete the renovation of the entire physical plant. It also became clear that the endowment was nowhere near a sufficient level because of escalating operating costs. Fearing donor fatigue, the Campaign Steering Committee and trustees engaged in earnest discussions about whether to declare victory and end the campaign or to continue the drive. They decided to raise the overall target to $15 million within the prescribed five years. We were greeted with cheers from the very people who had sacrificed most in getting us where we were, many of whom proffered new commitments.

Support for Deep Springs began to flow from fresh sources as well. Younger alumni began to rival the generosity of those from the late 1930s and 1940s, especially trustees David Hitz (DS'80), cofounder of Network Appliance Corporation (now NetApp), and Kurt Gilson (DS'80), then chief executive of the Kinetics Group. Gilson also provided strategic leadership for budget planning and managing board resources.

David Goldfarb (DS'84) initiated an important development during this period. Between 1981 and 1992, six Deep Springers had received Truman Scholarships, including Will Masters (DS'79), Adam Condron (DS'90), and Goldfarb himself. He now urged me to renew contact with the Truman Foundation and nominate one of our students the following year. The criteria for Truman Scholarships mesh beautifully with the mission of Deep Springs: "to find and recognize college juniors with exceptional leadership potential who are committed to careers . . . in the public service, and to provide them with financial support for graduate study [and] leadership training."[1] The foundation had made an exception to its stipulation of junior standing so that Deep Springs could nominate students.

I contacted the Truman Foundation's executive director, Louis Blair, who responded enthusiastically to the prospect of Deep Springs' nominating students again. Early in his second year, Tim Ruttan (DS'97) showed strong

Truman Scholars Nick Gossen, Sam Houshower, and Christian Stayner, at their induction in Independence, Missouri, in 2002. Photograph by author.

interest. Dean Ross Lewin made an enormous effort to prepare our institutional nomination papers and groom Tim for making his case. Tim excelled in the selection process and won a Truman Scholarship in 1999. It paid for the balance of his undergraduate education at Harvard University and provided substantial support for his study of medicine at Baylor. First, however, he worked on community health issues in Mexico and participated as a Teach for America volunteer in Brownsville, Texas. A remarkable element of this story is that Tim had helped lead a student effort to release Ross Lewin from his faculty contract earlier that academic year because of disputes over grading. Lewin, fully aware of this fact, went to bat for Ruttan as a Truman nominee.

Over the next five years, Deep Springs nominated five other students. Dean Gary Gossen and Professor David Arndt (DS'84) teamed up with other faculty to support these nominees. All five succeeded in winning Truman Scholarships, some right after they transferred to other universities. Nicholas Gossen (DS'98), Samuel Houshower (DS'99), and Christian Stayner (DS'00) were inducted together in 2002 at the annual ceremony in the Truman Library in Independence, Missouri. At that meeting, Louis Blair gave Deep Springs a special commendation, and a foundation representative traveled to Deep Springs later that year with a plaque recognizing the college for its outstanding success in preparing public servants. Truman Scholar Andrew Kim (DS'00) went on to win a Rhodes Scholarship.[2]

Medievalist and lawyer Madeleine Pelner Cosman had joined the board with something of a flair in 1995. She announced that she had lofty standards for giving to nonprofit organizations and hoped that Deep Springs might be the first institution to merit her support. After several years and a brief romance with widower Dick Cornelison, Cosman determined that Deep Springs had also failed her charitable giving test and asked to be excused from service.

She returned to the board in 2003 at the behest of Jeff Johnson, Cornelison's successor as board chair. When she noticed a display of historic Soviet labor posters in the library, a gift from Soviet dissident art collector and alumnus Norton Dodge (DS'43), Cosman protested vigorously. Finding no sympathy among board members, she resigned again, explaining that the college was too liberal for her.

Ulric Haynes Jr., U.S. ambassador to Algeria for President Jimmy Carter, succeeded to the board vacancy in 2001.[3] He had recently spent a week at Deep Springs as the holder of the James Withrow Chair in Government, earning high praise for his lectures and discussions on foreign affairs.[4] As a result, the student body had nominated him for election to the board. Denied the opportunity to attend Deep Springs in 1948 because he is black, Haynes told me that he considered it a most distinct honor to serve as a trustee a half century later. He leaned helpfully on the student body, ApCom, the other trustees, and me to become more active in recruiting and admitting students and faculty from American minority groups. We had long languished in our efforts to make Deep Springs more representative of the larger culture, and he admonished us to make a spirited new effort.

Since the mid-1990s, the student body has typically included members from Asia, Europe, the Middle East, and sometimes Africa. Everyone recognized the positive effects of this development in enriching conversations and classroom discussions at Deep Springs. Still, Haynes ultimately became discouraged by what he considered less than wholehearted student, trustee, and administrative support for diversity initiatives and, following an unfortunate gaffe by board chair Jeff Johnson, resigned as a trustee. Rick continued to offer his services to ApCom and the president, however, and gained some satisfaction from progress that came in his wake.

Deep Springs has always placed highly in annual college rankings, particularly in the *Princeton Review*'s "The Best 377 Colleges" (the number changes from year to year, but Deep Springs has typically been near the top) and *Peterson's Guide*. In 2013, *The 50 Best Colleges in the United States* ranked Deep Springs number one.[5]

Former trustee (1976–1984) and Telluride member Paul Todd had always been elated by the physical beauty and solitude of Deep Springs Valley. When he heard that the decommissioned highway maintenance station one and a half miles north of the ranch was to be auctioned off by the State of California, he called and urged me to secure the property for the college: "We can't risk having other parties with possible commercial aims corrupting the isolation that is so important to Deep Springs. Go to the auction with my promise to provide as many dollars as you need to prevail." I did, and when I called Paul to tell him of our success, he simply said, "Good, now why don't you name that the 'Henderson Station.'" The late Bob Henderson (DS'35) had been Todd's friend and a fellow trustee. Deep Springs was in critical need of additional housing, and the three homes on the property were put to immediate use.

When Paul Todd came west for the dedication of the Henderson Station, he pressed me for further action. "I know there are many parcels of privately held land in the valley that may also threaten our isolation. As they become available I hope you will go after them. Hell, go after them even if they're *not* on the market." As before, he assured me of his financial backing.

I called Connie Johnson, for several decades the proprietor of the Big Pine General Store, to whom I had sold Deep Springs' eggs and garden produce as a student. Now retired, he owned a forty-acre parcel that straddled the dirt road to Deep Springs' lake pastures. He and his son Tim had established a simple farmstead, fenced it, put in a well, and experimented with garlic seed production. He told me he had been thinking about selling the property and that a "hippie couple" was pestering him about buying it. If this happened, Geoff Pope reminded me, we could have right-of-way issues getting to the lake pastures.

Johnson quickly agreed to terms that included his mediation of environmental and aesthetic issues at the site. Upon receiving the news, Todd exclaimed, "Oh, good, having returned it to nature, why don't you name it the Cronk Pasture" (for former president Ed Cronk)? This partnership with Todd continued throughout my tenure with the purchase of several comparable tracts of land in Deep Springs Valley. The board was more than happy to endorse each of the schemes that Todd and I cooked up. The biggest prize, however, was garnered across Gilbert Pass to the east.

Just when drought conditions were causing restrictions to our grazing allotment on Crooked Creek in the White Mountains, Geoff Pope learned that the Lida Ranch in Nevada would consider an offer on its 160-acre home ranch in the south end of Fish Lake Valley.[6] It had a good well and two associated Bureau of Land Management (BLM) grazing permits, the South Oasis allotment with much white sage (excellent forage), and the ephemeral Eureka allotment (available for use only in especially wet years). We purchased the home ranch in 2003, and Geoff applied for the BLM allotments (with 477 animal units, or close to two months' grazing for our herd each year). Without these timely developments, Deep Springs' cattle operation would have been in jeopardy. With them, however, and the college's recent acquisition of the Dead Horse Meadow grazing allotment on lower Crooked Creek, Pope was able to shift much of the burden of summer grazing away from our two highest and most vulnerable White Mountain meadows, Big Prospector and Campito. This addition also opened another summer cowboy job for graduating students.

The final achievement of this remarkable partnership with Paul Todd materialized during Ross Peterson's presidency in 2006. With Todd's lead gift and a generous boost from Alice Dodge Wallace (sister of Norton Dodge), to acquire a 470-acre parcel that bordered the ranch to the north and Highway 168 to the west. For fifty years, Deep Springs had sought to buy this land from a family of real estate speculators in southern California. Paul Todd lived to enjoy the satisfaction of seeing the transaction completed. The trustees dedicated this crucial parcel as the Todd Tract, a fitting tribute to the man who took such pleasure in applying the names of those he admired to the acquisitions his previous generosities had made possible.[7]

One of the rites of passage for students is the slaughter of farm animals for consumption at the Boarding House. Carried out with solemn respect, students take pride in conducting the process on their own. Working in teams of four or five, they have passed the skills down from one class to the next. The only element of the slaughter that students rarely perform themselves is shooting the animal. It is important that it dies instantly, so that task usually falls to an experienced staff member. Students witness the process as an essential element in understanding what is involved when humans eat meat or use animal products. Vegetarian students sometimes observe or even participate in slaughters for the same reason. A few vegetarians have opted to eat meat while at Deep Springs because the animals range freely on the land and mature naturally without nutritional antibiotics and other drugs.

Similarly, the garden and orchard have been an important part of the labor program and self-sustaining philosophy. Under the successive guiding hands of staff gardeners Heather Jennings, Karen Mitchell, and, more recently, Shelby MacLeish, two decades of students have known the calluses and pleasures of working the soil. They expanded the garden's acreage and increased its efficiency, planting and cultivating potatoes (growing twenty-seven varieties one summer) and garlic sufficient for Boarding House use all year. The garden and orchard now supply roughly half the vegetables and fruits annually consumed by the community. Students have also gained satisfaction from winning prizes for their best fruits and vegetables at the Tri-County Fair in Bishop—year after year—and in sending boxes of exotic spuds or braided garlic each holiday season to alumni and friends who have been especially important to the college.

Few students derived greater pleasure from their farm and garden labors than Michael Pihos (DS'98). Reared in the upscale Chicago suburb of Glen Ellyn, Illinois, he reveled in strenuous physical exertion and embraced asceticism. The summer between his first and second years, he labored largely on the alfalfa operation, driving the big Case tractor daily to mow, rake, bale, and haul hay.

Two ferocious thunderstorms complicated life at the college and threatened the harvest that summer, one in July and the other in August, each dropping an inch of water on the desert in an hour or two. Profuse lightning during the first storm knocked out our radiotelephone system so completely that it took

Michael Pihos. Photograph by author.

almost two months to fully restore phone and internet communications with the outside world. (In addition, flash floods obliterated sections of Route 168 over both Westgard and Gilbert Passes, stranding many motorists overnight.) I spent several hours on my cell phone every day for six weeks coordinating fund-raising, construction, and faculty and student recruiting from a promontory high on Gilbert Pass. Sitting in my truck, I enjoyed a stunning view of the valley in what I dubbed the "most beautiful phone booth in the world." This locale, however, would soon have dark undertones for the community and me.

By mid-September, Geoff Pope and the students had restored phone service, and the new class settled into the routines of academics and labor. A few days into fall term, Michael Pihos, who had just started building a grape arbor south of the dormitory, welcomed a visit from his older brother, Peter. Farm manager Andy Jennings (DS'89) and his wife, Heather, had put a "For Sale" sign in the back window of their Audi station wagon. The Pihos brothers wanted to buy it for a road trip the next spring. They asked if they could take the car for a test drive, drove to the top of Gilbert Pass, and started back down.

Wanting to test the Audi's all-wheel-drive feature on a rough power-line road, they turned off the highway and descended a perilously steep pitch. Safely at the bottom, they found that the road did not continue across the ravine. Turning around, they discovered that the car lacked the power and traction to crawl back out. Distraught, Michael and Peter hiked back to the road and caught a ride down to the ranch. Michael told another student he had done the stupidest thing in his life, then secured Jennings's permission to borrow the Case tractor. The two brothers rode it up to the site. When he maneuvered the heavy machine to the cusp of the gorge, Michael asked Peter to jump off the fender on which he had been riding. He then spun the tractor around and began backing down the steep grade. He had gone only a few yards when the tractor suddenly lurched to one side and tumbled helter-skelter down the mountainside. Michael died instantly. Aghast, grief-stricken Peter made his way back to the ranch with the help of a passing motorist.

In the agonizing hours that followed, the state police and other emergency personnel made their way to the inaccessible scene. An unseasonably hot mid-September day gradually turned dark as storm clouds gathered over the White Mountains. Later, as the van bearing Michael's body to the mortuary passed the ranch, someone tolled the Boarding House bell—the traditional parting salute to those who graduate or leave the valley for the last time. The bell tolled for fifteen minutes.

As it did, the third ferocious thunderstorm of the season descended over the ranch. Exhausted and numb from shock, community members sprinted out into the darkening tempest to sling sandbags and wield shovels to protect the entrances of buildings from another surge of coffee-colored flood waters coming down the slope above the Circle. When the lightning, wind, and rain abated, I drove Michael's brother to Las Vegas International Airport to meet his inconsolable father and bring him back to the ranch.[8]

Our counseling psychologist, Dr. Mel Lewin, who typically visited the college once a month, hurried up from his home in Pacific Palisades, arriving by noon the next day. His insights about grieving individually and as a community proved to be invaluable. That evening a community-wide Quaker-style meeting convened around a campfire next to Michael's half-built grape arbor. There we talked, reflected, and consoled one another for many hours.

The next day, student Michael Brownstein called an official at one of the major airlines who offered to qualify the student body as an athletic team and the faculty and staff as coaches—affording us a significant reduction in ticket prices. The trustees then offered to pay the fare of anyone who wished to go to Illinois for Michael's funeral. Almost every student and some staff members joined Linda and me in making the trip.

During these agonizing days, a few members of the community, like Michael Brownstein, chef Tom Hudgens (DS'88), professor David Lopez and his wife, Cecilia, and Linda exhibited extraordinary presence and resilience. Most others managed to function adequately. A few were truly incapacitated by their grief.

Michael Pihos's Deep Springs classmates served as pallbearers and the Greek Orthodox funeral drew over a thousand family, friends, and Glen Ellyn townspeople. Dick Cornelison came to represent the trustees. The next day, Michael's parents, Sandra and William Pihos, insisted that the entire Deep Springs delegation join them to decompress at their lakefront cottage in Wisconsin. Their strength, and that of Peter and their two daughters, Deanna and Andria, was immense.

In the aftermath of this tragedy, Bill Pihos returned to Deep Springs to complete the grape arbor his son had begun to build. The Pihos family and friends provided funds to build a greenhouse by the garden to honor Michael's memory. They also asked us to redouble our commitment to safety training and emergency preparedness at the ranch. Recognizing the inherent risks of educating students at Deep Springs, however, they requested that we not compromise the raw and robust experience at the core of the college's method—on which Michael had thrived. The accident had not occurred on college business or ranch property, but safety consciousness and emergency preparedness became and remain paramount at Deep Springs.

At about this time, Deep Springs' friend and future trustee Alan Farnham of New York met international agriculturalist Bill Weaver on a railroad trip to Montreal. In the course of their conversation, Farnham recalls, "He told me about his Nevada ranches and I realized one of them was the old Cord Ranch in Fish Lake Valley. I asked him if he knew he had a wonderful neighbor—Deep Springs." Weaver had never heard of the college, so Farnham explained: "It is where the ablest and smartest young men read Plato in the morning and ride the range in the afternoon."[9] Weaver was sold on the spot but expressed concern about Farnham's description of Michael's fatal accident and the need for more modern farm implements.

By the time they reached the Canadian border, Weaver had planned a trip to Deep Springs and committed $100,000 to upgrade the ranch with better and safer heavy equipment. His implement supplier, Bill Botello of Sparks, Nevada, procured as much good used equipment as that money could buy and delivered the goods on a huge tractor-trailer. He was so impressed by what he discovered

Shin Yamaguchi (DS'96) prepares to rake hay. Photograph by author.

at Deep Springs that he and his wife, Jackie, supplemented Weaver's gift with additional machinery. Not to be outdone, Weaver upped the ante with a second gift of his own.

The catastrophic loss of Michael Pihos reverberated in the community, especially among the students whose overwhelmed emotions spilled out both creatively and destructively. Mark Dunn (DS'99) masterminded a giant image of Michael Pihos's face and organized his peers to paint it on the expanse of the new outdoor basketball court. Using surplus construction materials from the Main Building and receiving much-needed advice from Lee Powell, Michael Thoms (DS'98) built a cabin to honor Pihos on the mountainside above the dairy barn.

Mysteriously, however, a large screen television set for watching videos in the loft of the student residence disappeared one winter night—only to be found on the desert a week later with a rock through its screen. At about the same time, someone in the community (judging by boot prints found and photographed at the site) used an ax to cut the buried cable that powered our radiotelephones. After Geoff Pope's repair, it happened again at a different place along the cable. Same footprints. This Luddite prank left the community with no emergency communication, so I announced at dinner that if such a thing happened again, I would call the sheriff to investigate. There were no other occurrences.

One Friday evening the following year, the student body decided to honor Michael by marking the new dormitory unmistakably as its territory. They resolved to paint murals on the hallway spaces adjacent to their doorways. Some of the art had real merit but as the night wore on many spaces were slathered recklessly with crude images and obscenities. Having gotten wind of the mess, I met with several faculty, Geoff Pope, and Linda and asked them to say nothing to the students about what had happened. Nor did I put the issue on the agenda for our Monday Coordinating Committee meeting with student, staff, and faculty leaders.

The two students braced for a reprimand or more serious reaction, but none of us mentioned the painting spree. Just before the meeting concluded, student body president Ben Turner looked at me uneasily and asked: "You do know about the dorm, don't you?" I nodded without comment. "Well," he said, "the student body was preoccupied with it all weekend. We are embarrassed. Mortified." He promised that anything that did not pass as genuine art would be covered with a coat of the original paint the next weekend. The students were as good as his word.

The student body's definition and enforcement of the ground rules slipped badly during this frightful period. Alcohol and drugs presented a persistent no-win dilemma for the trustees, the student body, and me. Federal law holds college officials liable if they know about underage drinking or illegal drug use on campus and do nothing to prevent it. At any other college, officials can plead ignorance; but when the president and dean live fifty yards from the students' residence and eat three meals a day with them, this claim is not defensible. Nor are students at other colleges handling heavy equipment or making key decisions for the institution.

The student body is keenly aware that L.L. Nunn granted it the power to govern the conduct of its own members. Yet the trustees insist on strict enforcement of the law for the reasons just noted. Formally, students have no choice but to ban the use of alcohol and illegal drugs and enforce that policy. It galls them, however, to have been granted the right of self-governance while the trustees, and therefore the president, are duty-bound to trump their judgment.

This conundrum can breed student body contempt for authority, especially if a faculty or staff member has an obvious problem with alcohol. As a result, student and nonstudent deceit almost always abounds over this issue. Whenever student malaise or anger welled up over any issue from coeducation or gentrification to an intrusive trustee or Michael Pihos's irreversible tragedy, I found myself dealing with the student body over ground-rule issues—either directly or as a mediator between the board and the students. Nothing was more irksome among my duties.

I did not face these issues alone. Geoff Pope and whoever was serving as dean also bore responsibility to reason with the students and keep the issue within rational bounds. On one occasion, the student body voted to abandon the ground rules entirely. When Andy Jennings learned of this action, he assembled the seven students on his farm team. "I understand you guys have dropped the ground rules," he said, "and I have something to say about that. If you choose to drink or do drugs, please ask the labor commissioner to transfer you to another job immediately. Given the heavy equipment we use every day, I refuse to work around anyone who is not totally clear-headed." Within a week the students formally reinstated the ground rules.

Despite the presence of remarkably able and committed students, after Pihos's death normal patterns of community life did not resume until the graduation of all the students who had been at Deep Springs when Michael was killed. His passing not only cut his life brutally short but it also exacted a heavy toll on his peers—and on the life of the college—not to mention inflicting a blow from which the Pihos family would always carry deep bruises. Before this tragic event occurred, Deep Springs had functioned for eighty-two years without the death of a student. With vigilance, we can hope that such a calamity will never strike the college again.

Adding to the pressures on the Deep Springs community at this time was the continuation of the Building Program. We proceeded with Phase Three renovations of the Boarding House and the Museum (Deep Springs' term for the building that houses the science laboratory, scientific collections, and a large meeting room). This work followed immediately upon completion of the Main Building.

I proposed to Richard Stack at the Hugh and Hazel Darling Foundation that he underwrite the full cost of this project. He had generously provided funds for the reading room in the Main Building and other projects before that, but those grants were not on this scale. Rick said he would consider my proposal, but only if we named the renewed structure the Darling Museum. The public buildings at Deep Springs had always had functional names, a precedent we did not wish to change. Explaining how the Sproulls had recently reinforced this tradition, I offered a compromise—not renaming the building but posting a brass plaque in the entrance acknowledging the Darling Foundation's proposed role.

As the trustees' meeting at which a go or no-go decision on the renovation drew near, Rick and I had a series of cordial conversations in person and by phone. On the eve of the meeting, I called him and asked if the foundation was prepared to grant the needed funds. "What about the name?" he inquired. I explained that I had not changed my mind and that a plaque recognizing the Darling Foundation's generosity was as far as I could go. After a long pause, Stack said: "I must admit, I admire your principles. Tell the trustees I will fund the Museum project."

The timing was perfect. Lee Powell commenced work on the Museum the day after he finished the Main Building. But he came to me before noon, saying, "We've got trouble. Come see." We walked over to the northwest corner of the Museum, and he pointed to a hole he had chipped through the stucco with his claw hammer. "There's really nothing left inside that wall!" he said. "I can't build on something that isn't there!" At ground level, the original framing had rotted beyond repair.

We reassigned Rudolph Construction to an infrastructure project scheduled for later, while Peter O'Connor designed a completely new Museum. He proposed a superior layout that included a music practice room. We were soon back on schedule.

When Rick Stack came to Deep Springs in June 2000 for the dedication of the new Museum, he remarked as he handed me the generous check: "It is such a pleasure to work with Deep Springs. You people can build buildings faster than I can write checks."

We had an irrigation problem the following year that required an expensive new agricultural pump. I went to see Rick Stack with a proposal for the Darling Foundation to fund the purchase. "This is truly a naming opportunity," I promised him. After commenting that this was the most unusual proposal he had received from a college, he granted the funds with a handshake and a smile. For the dedication of that equipment, students welded a rugged steel plate bearing the words "DARLING PUMP."

Once the Museum and Boarding House projects were complete, the final phases of reconstruction included rebuilding and seismically refitting every dwelling at Deep Springs—around the Circle, at the Lower Ranch, and at the Henderson Station. Staff and faculty moved as though on a chessboard, with some of them living for a time in temporary trailers.

Running parallel to all the building construction was the replacement of Deep Springs' infrastructure. We drilled a new well for drinking water, replaced all buried utilities, installed a new sewage system, replaced electrical services, including many power poles, and brought the radiotelephone system up to date.

One big issue remained as we anticipated a celebratory reunion in 2001. From the beginning, Bob Gatje had advocated paving the sandy road around the Circle and installing curbs to stabilize the edges. He believed this step was necessary to protect the buildings, inside and out, from the corrosive effects of blowing dust and tracked-in dirt. The student body vigorously opposed the idea, citing the risk of falling on the hard, paved surface during their Frisbee games and soccer matches on the Circle. Often going barefoot, they also argued for the pleasure of walking directly on the earth in this natural place, rather than on asphalt or concrete.

While negotiating for student support of other elements of the Building Program, I promised the student body that the Circle road would not be paved under my watch. Understandably, Gatje saw this project as the finishing piece of the five-year building program. The board, somewhat daunted by projected costs, left the decision to me. But Dick Cornelison, who was nearing his final meeting as chair, felt intense pressure from Gatje. He ducked the issue, instructing Bob and me to resolve the matter on our own.

Bob flew to Las Vegas and drove up to the ranch for our meeting. We took a long walk, a fiery one as it turned out, during which he reminded me that the board had empowered him as chair of the Building Committee to do what was necessary to secure the physical plant. He intended to complete the project as he deemed appropriate. I said, "Bob, I made a promise to the student body, and it happens to reflect my personal view of the kind of community this is. I'm the one who writes checks on the trustees' bank accounts. As long as I am president, the Circle will remain as it is." He sighed, looked me in the eye, and said quietly, "Okay." The bond of our long friendship survived this confrontation, a testament to Bob's character.

Every year members of ApCom divvied up the responsibility and pleasure of notifying the successful applicants for admission, after which I would follow up with an official letter of acceptance and welcome. The evening ApCom members telephoned the newly selected students in March of 2000, our phone rang. "Is this President Newell?" a well-modulated voice intoned from the other end. When I answered in the affirmative, he continued: "This is Peter Jennings in New York. I want you to know that my son, Chris, is the happiest man in America tonight." Then, the noted ABC Evening News anchor added: "You should know, too, that I am the second happiest man in the country. There could be no better place for Chris than Deep Springs College."

Peter did find the college almost irresistible, visiting three times over the next two years. He joined me in carving seven large turkeys for our Thanksgiving feast one year and pitched in to sweep the Boarding House floors or do any task that needed doing.

One of the leavening traditions of the community across the whole history of Deep Springs has been evenings of music, theater, and skits. Known for many years as "Chinamans," for reasons no one remembers, these gatherings more recently became known as DSPACs (pronounced "dis-pacs") organized by the Deep Springs Performing Arts Committee. The wealth of musical and theatrical talent within the student body, faculty, and staff means it takes little planning to mobilize such a public performance.

A catalyst for DSPACs for two decades has been Dick Dawson, the eccentric Owens Valley piano tuner with a passion for long-distance horse racing. After rebuilding Grace Mansfield's Steinway grand in the early 1980s, he began teaching piano performance and music composition at the college. Dick often performed at DSPACs, but his delight in accompanying other artists was most infectious. Now in his eighties, Dawson still drives over Westgard Pass to teach music.

Another boon to Deep Springs' cultural life at this time was the periodic teaching of short-term professor Louis Fantasia. In addition to playing the double bass in community concerts, he directed a number of plays, including a memorable, wide-ranging performance of Shakespeare's *Julius Caesar*. An experienced director and screenwriter, Louis brought a wealth of energy and insight.

By late 2000, we were putting the finishing touches on the physical renewal of the college and ranch, and summing up the Campaign for Deep Springs. At the five-year mark, gifts and pledges totalled $18.2 million, nearly $15 million of which had already been paid. With the pay-as-we-build philosophy, we had invested almost $9 million in the physical plant. After covering the expense of running the campaign and managing the building program (less than $1 million), the college's once meager endowment grew to nearly $10 million. While this sum fell below our highest hopes, largely because the Building Program exceeded original estimates, it was still far greater than anyone projected when we launched the campaign. The stock market jitters that began early in 2000 before it plunged in 2002, however, took a toll on that $10 million benchmark. This was strangely ironic, because our highly successful campaign had been made possible in part by the unprecedented rise of stock prices during the years that we were appealing for gifts and bequests.[10]

With new board chair Jeff Johnson taking the lead, we staged a gala Renaissance Reunion at Deep Springs over Labor Day Weekend 2001 to honor the many people who had joined in rescuing Deep Springs. We all knew enough about the college's history to dispel any illusion of institutional deliverance, but we did share an unspoken pride in having earned our spurs as Nunnians. No one captured the feeling better than Dick Rudolph, however, when he spoke at the victory celebration about his company's five-year construction experience with Deep Springs: "On the eve of my retirement," he said, "I can truly say that our participation in the restoration of Deep Springs has been the high point of my career. We take pride in having been part of something done so well."

No alumnus had worked harder or sacrificed more for the renaissance project than Bruce Laverty. The last visitor to leave the ranch when the reunion ended, he spoke what so many of us felt on that day. With a tear in his eye as he got into his car, he said: "Jack, this has just been fun from the beginning. I hate to see our grand project come to an end."

The "abundance of heart," so important to L.L. Nunn, has expressed itself in the lives of alumni across many decades. Their camaraderie buoyed them and their college through a narrow and turbulent passage. The survival of Deep Springs will ensure that this spirit is passed to new generations of students.

Our phone rang just after dawn on September 11, 2001. Our daughter, Chris, broke the news of the terrorist attacks on the World Trade Center. At breakfast, Geoff and Iris Pope, who had the only satellite television at the ranch, announced that their home would be open throughout the day to anyone who wished to watch the crisis unfold. Community members drifted in and out as Peter Jennings at ABC News led the nation through the tragic events of that day. On the initiative of student Andrew Kim, we all gathered in the Main Room that evening to process the catastrophe.

Peter Jennings returned, along with his wife, Kayce Freed, and other family members, to witness his son Chris's graduation. Deep Springs' commencements are planned and orchestrated entirely by members of the first-year class to honor and roast their departing elders. Always staged out of doors but never alike otherwise, the salute to Chris's class took place at the end of a rough dirt road on a lonely knoll overlooking Deep Springs Valley from Westgard Pass. The senior Jennings gleefully drove his rented Ford Expedition, loaded with other graduates' family members, to and from the site. Thanks to Chris, we also benefited earlier that year from a pair of discussions led by his mother, author Kati Marton, and his stepfather, diplomat Richard Holbrooke.

Linda and I accepted an extension on my second contract and remained at Deep Springs until July 2004. Over our last several years, we tied up loose ends from the campaign and building program and relished at least the partial return of Deep Springs' prized desert solitude. The successful revival of the college, however, brought many requests for visits from journalists and documentary filmmakers, each of which the student body weighed carefully, granting permission only to a few. They knew that onlookers inevitably alter behavior.

Two feature articles appeared in our last year, one on the front page of the *Los Angeles Times* and the other in *Vanity Fair*.[11] In addition, while serving briefly as a visiting scholar in 2001, Frank H. Wu wrote the epilogue for his book *Yellow: Race in America beyond Black and White* (New York: Basic Books, 2002), suggesting Deep Springs as a community worthy of study and emulation.

For some time, interest had been rising among students, alumni, trustees, and even in Telluride Association for designing a second Deep Springs that would be either for women or coeducational. Several students and I initiated a seminar on the history of higher education, basing it on the task of founding an ideal learning environment for the twenty-first century. Naming our brainchild Hidden Springs or Deep Springs II, students Nick Gossen (DS'98), Jacob Hundt (DS'98), Bryden Sweeney-Taylor (DS'98), and Japhet Weeks (DS'99) joined professor Jack Murphy (DS'78), visiting scholar Andrew Gossen, and me in exploring every academic, financial, governance, and practical consideration for creating an ideal institution of higher learning today, be it coeducational or for women. We distributed our working conclusions to the trustees and Telluride leaders to see what interest might arise.[12] Beyond the valley, an all-women's version of Deep Springs drew the most attention, but we were keenly aware that the last thing the world needed was a women's college designed by men. Stimulating and instructive as our readings and conversations had been, we knew we were in no position to act on our recommendations. Two decades later, however, Hundt and Sweeney-Taylor both founded progressive colleges.

A most rewarding facet of my final two years as president was a humanities seminar I offered in the autumn of 2002 with first-year students Tony Sung, Nick Tsang, and Jeff Griggs. The reading list for "Personal Values and Social Ethics" included *The Autobiography of Henry Adams*, Albert Camus's *The Plague*, and Fyodor Dostoyevsky's *The Brothers Karamazov*. We met weekly for three hours around the table in our living room. When our searching conversations ended in December, the students asked if we might continue throughout the winter and spring terms, choosing the books together. I agreed, and several other students joined us in January. We resumed with Michael Sandel's *Democracy's Discontent: America in Search of a Public Philosophy*. When we neared the end of the academic year, several students asked if we could continue the next fall with a new set of books. This three-semester course buoyed me into the next phase of my

Student Will McGinty and guests at public speaking event, 2004. Photograph by author.

Johan Ugander and Noah Beyeler prune an apple tree. Photograph by author.

Deep Springs community, 2003, with students, faculty, and staff behind portrait of L.L. Nunn. Courtesy of Edwin P. (Phil) Pister, LJN Papers.

career, teaching in the University of Utah's Honors College and in the Venture Course in the Humanities for low-income adults in Salt Lake City.

Things were coming together for me. With a sense of satisfaction at the end of the second semester of this class, I wrote in my journal: "I acted on all of the serious problems that were bugging me [this week], and I made headway against the backlog of work facing me. At the heart of this, however, was the remarkable conclusion of my ethics class Thursday morning with Tony, Nick, and Jeff. In one of those rare moments, everything converged like lightning in me, and I saw what matters most so clearly, and I saw my life as a whole. . . . After such a peak, I feel a deep spiritual peace—with a quiet sense of purpose, confidence, and courage."

Our ninth and final year at Deep Springs brought additional rewards, but Linda and I were ready to move on. The exertions of nearly a decade left us yearning for a different pace—one that would include time with and proximity to our grandchildren. Our final months remain a blur, but the farewell party thrown by students, staff, and faculty will always remain among our most cherished memories. On behalf of the community, Geoff Pope made a beautifully tooled saddle for me, and a team of volunteers made a tapestry featuring incidents from our nine years for Linda. A few days later, we made another last drive over Gilbert Pass, our hearts and minds filled with gratitude. We were later asked if we regretted spending so many years of our lives and careers at Deep Springs. The question stunned us. We had experienced a great adventure—and the rewards far surpassed everything we invested in the college and its students, past and future.

EPILOGUE

Results, 2004–2014

Healthy institutions bring out the best in people, sick institutions bring out the worst. Leaders are responsible for the health of their organizations.

—Justice Richard Goldstone

Over a decade after the renaissance project, Deep Springs is stronger and healthier in almost every respect than it was when we left. On July 1, 2004, F. Ross Peterson commenced his presidential duties. His extensive experience as a visiting professor, and more recently as a trustee, propelled him to the front of a national search. Ross and his wife, Kay, moved into their new roles with confidence and served valiantly for three years.

Ross established remarkable rapport with students, working more fruitfully with them than I had been able to do. His soft touch with alumni and foundations also enabled him to lead an ambitious new fund-raising campaign while maintaining the bulwark already in place. Kay's warmth and enthusiasm were infectious, and her interest in the attractiveness of the buildings and grounds made living or visiting Deep Springs especially pleasant. So successful were the Petersons that Utah State University lured Ross back to its campus as Vice President for Development. Their departure in 2007 left everyone sad.

Geoff Pope continued as vice president and ranch manager through Peterson's first year, then retired after a record twenty-three years of service. Twenty-two

Kay and Ross Peterson. Photograph by author.

of the twenty-three student cowboys he had trained returned to the ranch for his farewell. This loyalty communicated not only their respect for Geoff but also the bonds of their unusual experiences. Iris Pope continued as the college bookkeeper, spending one day a week at Deep Springs. She retired in June 2013, having spent twenty-six years on staff—besting Geoff's record. The Popes moved to Bishop where he founded the Black Mountain Air Service, flying charter routes over the Eastern Sierra region.

Today Deep Springs' college and ranch are both thriving. Descending Gilbert Pass, you can see a solar array nestled next to the North Field, the result of an initiative prompted by short-term science professor Robley Williams and his students, an expiring California solar energy subsidy, and Peterson's leadership. It generates more than three-quarters of the electricity consumed at Deep Springs, netting significant savings. Coupled with the hydro plant, the college is nearly energy independent in wet years. The combined system of solar and hydro remains the only dual green energy operation in California. If you scrutinize the ridge above the dairy barn, you can make out an anemometer that recently tested (with disappointing results) the feasibility of adding wind turbines to the mix.

Crossing the cattle guard and entering the ranch brings you to luxuriant alfalfa fields that recently produced a thousand tons of hay in one season, more than four times the yield in their run-down condition six years earlier. Artist Mark Dunn (DS'98) returned to Deep Springs as the farmer in 2006, determined to restore the productivity of the depleted fields. He researched the problem, called in soil scientists and extension agents, developed an action plan, and achieved extraordinary results with a combination of improved fertilization and irrigation, crop rotation, and hard work. Then, to protect the bounteous harvests so the hay could be sold at peak market prices, Mark and the students built a large shelter in the stack yard, using surplus pipe from the hydro penstock installation two decades earlier. Instead of having to buy hay to supplement its own production, Deep Springs has become a supplier. The Darling Foundation stepped forward again to enable the college to afford these fundamental improvements.

The road between the ranch gate and circle is lined with maturing cottonwood trees. Iris Pope planted them as saplings twenty years before. A closer look reveals a new ranch house under a grove of aging cottonwoods along the spur road leading to the garden and corrals. Ranch manager Janice Hunter lives there with her working border collies. The ranch and herd suffered entropy in the years following Geoff Pope's departure; but solidly backed by the president and trustees, Janice is restoring the vitality of the cattle operation in the same spirit that Mark Dunn had revived the alfalfa fields. She also brought the moribund Range Management Team back to life to assure Deep Springs' best stewardship of land and water resources.

In the process, an old question demanded new answers: How can the ranch be made a more environmentally sustainable, state-of-the-art operation while continuing to provide vital hands-on experiences for students? They, of course, are helping to answer this complex question. For starters, Deep Springs now has a small herd of sheep that graze on grasses and unsightly weeds inside the perimeter of the fenced alfalfa fields. These animals are sheared for wool and consumed for meat.

Other new efficiencies are being considered. Would adding a new computer-controlled, pivot-irrigation system in the dry field southwest of the stack yard begin to deplete the valley's aquifer or, of equal concern, diminish the educational purposes of the ranch by almost completely automating irrigation? Would electric minitrucks like those seen on golf courses bring significant fuel savings,

Entrance to Deep Springs with alfalfa fields and the new student residence in background. Photograph by author.

Deep Springs from the air. College buildings around circle on the left, lower ranch buildings at top right. Courtesy of Geoff Pope, pilot, photograph by author.

especially when Deep Springs generates its own power, at the expense of challenging students' resourcefulness in coaxing another year's work out of the ranch's battered old trucks?

A decade without the dislocations and disruptions of building construction or a major calamity has helped bring tranquility to this desert enclave. Talking with a group of students who are double-digging a garden patch, or the team that is slaughtering a steer, you would notice that the long-sought racial and ethnic diversity within the student body is on the rise.

Much of the credit for this stability is attributable to the presidency of David Neidorf (2008–present). A gifted humanities teacher, he possesses a genius for understanding students' motivations and intentions—as well as those of alumni and friends of the college. Neidorf began as Peterson's vice president and then, after the brief presidency of Louis Fantasia in 2007, earned the job in his own right. Neidorf, in turn, benefited from the long and loyal service of Academic Dean Justin Kim and Vice President David Welle (DS'80).

When you sit down for dinner at one of the big round tables in the Boarding House, your conversation with faculty and staff brings more evidence of institutional health. Again, the spirit is upbeat; but more importantly, the academic program is better rounded than before. For two decades, the college struggled to secure and retain highly qualified, long-term faculty in the physical and life sciences. Failing that, it relied on excellent short-term scientists who taught on sabbatical leaves or during retirement.

Increasingly, women hold key leadership and staff positions. President Neidorf hired multitalented Jill Lawrence, a British native and former head of Outward Bound Denver, as director of operations (Deep Springs' equivalent of business vice president). She joined widely experienced ranch manager Janice Hunter. Brother Kenneth Cardwell, a member of a Roman Catholic lay order devoted to education, served as academic dean until 2013, when Amity Wilczek agreed to assume that responsibility.

Amity Wilczek, who earned her doctorate in evolutionary ecology at Harvard and holds Deep Springs' Herbert Reich professorship in science, anchors a strong science curriculum that holds its own against always strong student interest in literature and philosophy. The faculty is also politically diverse with the presence, among others, of repeat visiting political scientist and conservative policy analyst Ronald Mortensen.

Since the college's earliest days, alumni have returned to teach or serve as trustees. Half the board is typically drawn from alumni, while others represent land stewardship, nonprofit finance, and more.

Ranch manager Janice Hunter roped calf at spring branding, 2014. Photograph by author.

President David Neidorf offers commencement remarks, 2009. College and ranch oasis below Chocolate Mountain in the background. Courtesy of David Welle.

Now students from the late 1990s are coming back to serve in staff positions to start their careers. In addition to Mark Dunn's notable service, Padraic MacLeish (DS'99) returned in January 2010 as maintenance manager after studying auto mechanics and serving as a beekeeper and farm manager at New York's Stone Barns Center for Food and Agriculture. Shelby, his wife, is also a veteran of Stone Barns. She oversees the garden. Adam Nyborg (DS'97), a Yale graduate in evolutionary biology, succeeded Dunn as farm manager in 2011.[1] Wellesley-educated Jill Brewer, Adam's spouse, is the college registrar and development officer. Both couples have young children, adding a dimension that enriches Deep Springs' community life.

Since 2009, Dave Hitz (DS'80) has served as board chair. He helped quicken the pace of modernization by bringing younger and expertise-diverse men and women onto the board of trustees. He has also used his personal resources imaginatively to stimulate broader and deeper giving by other alumni. With Hitz's generosity and the determined sequential leadership of Presidents Peterson and Neidorf, the endowment exceeded $20 million in July 2014.

With full-ride scholarships for all students and no government support, the college could not survive a single year without the considerable generosity of its alumni and friends. Even with the significantly increased endowment, almost half of each year's operating expense, or nearly $700,000, is provided by the annual giving drive.

As important as financial assistance may be, it does not exceed in value the moral support of former students. Alumni provide critically needed help in recruiting students, faculty, and staff, finding distinguished nominees for the annual Withrow Chair in Government, identifying able men and women to serve as trustees, and volunteering in supporting roles from the annual funds drive to academic advisory committees. Further, the alumni are a stimulating and important source of ideas and contacts.

Always a work in progress, Deep Springs will never be without its serious issues. Such is the nature of the place, given the bright, energetic people who are attracted to come as students, staff, and faculty. No doubt, the college would lose part of its educational muscle if it ever became satisfied with itself or too assured of its own future. As matters stand—and long may they persist—a shared awareness of their uncommon experiences and a mutual respect for Nunnian ideals of service and leadership has created at Deep Springs a tighter relationship between students and alumni, both young and old, than at other institutions.

An involved alumni body, of course, supplies plenty of criticism as well as support. Their questions are both urgent and persistent: Is isolation too confining in today's instantly interconnected world? Or does it provide students with a valuable respite from commercial and social pressures so that they can center their lives and prepare to serve more wisely? Does Deep Springs continue to benefit from the absence of cellular telephone service in the valley? Is it still wise to eschew satellite access to television? Is the curriculum too light on technology? Is the college too focused on educating highly literate, academically elite students, or should it broaden its conception of high-potential future leaders?

Could a contemporary nonconformist like L.L. Nunn be admitted if he were to apply today? Should labor, academics, and self-governance be more consciously or explicitly linked at Deep Springs? What is the measure of the college's success? Finally, of course, there remains the issue of whether the college would serve its highest purposes better if it admitted women as well as men.

As one element of a five-faceted, long-range planning effort initiated in 2009, the trustees revisited the work accomplished at a board retreat led by then-chair Jeff Johnson in 2003. They concluded that the time was right to reconsider the question of coeducation, noting the importance of keeping faith with those who had agreed in 1994–1995, not without pain, to table the argument until the future of Deep Springs had been secured beyond reasonable doubt.

To refresh the institution's mission and test the educational merits of coeducation in principle, board chair Dave Hitz pledged his own resources to make a possible transition to coeducation cost-neutral. He did not wish the issue to be argued on economic grounds, a critical element in each earlier consideration. First, he advised, decide what is best educationally in pursuing the service-leadership mission of Deep Springs. Then, if coeducation is judged to be superior, ask if implementation is feasible and how the change can be made.

For about a year, the students and alumni joined the trustees in the calmest weighing of coeducation's pros and cons that had occurred in the controversy's long history. When polled, the five long-serving ex-presidents, going all the way back to Ed Cronk (1976–1981), were unanimous in their support for admitting women. Similarly, many alumni from the 1940s who had opposed coeducation in the past agreed in 2011 that the reform was in the best interest of the college and its mission in the twenty-first century.

When the board met at Deep Springs on September 19, 2011, its members voted on this motion: "The Trustees have carefully considered the purpose of Deep Springs, how best to achieve the purpose, and changes in society since the college was founded. Therefore, the Trustees determine that it is appropriate to plan and implement a transition to a coeducational student body, subject to ongoing board review." The tally was ten in favor, two opposed, no abstentions. Both student trustees supported the motion.

As word of the resolution spread, most alumni breathed a sigh of relief, welcoming the end of the bitter dispute that had first erupted in the late 1970s. The board instructed President David Neidorf to create a Transition Committee and work with everyone at Deep Springs to prepare for the admission and full integration of female students in 2013. Neidorf hired Laura Marcus, who had developed a keen interest in L.L. Nunn's philosophy of education while studying intellectual history at Yale, to help recruit the initial coeducational class.

In addition, to assure alumni and friends that they were not taking an action that was legally prohibited, the trustees filed a petition on February 6, 2012, requesting that the Superior Court of California, Inyo County, interpret L.L. Nunn's 1923 Deed of Trust as providing the board with sufficient discretion to adopt coeducation or, as an alternative, for the court to modify the trust to permit the admission of women as well as men.

Trustees Kinch Hoekstra (DS'82), a political philosopher at the University of California, Berkeley, and Edward Keonjian (DS'55), a retired attorney who had spent his career with the U.S. Postal Service, were the two who voted against modifying the trust to grant the trustees discretion to admit women. Rather than accept the will of the large majority, they filed a response with Judge Dean T. Stout in the Superior Court in March 2012, arguing that L.L. Nunn's 1923 Deed of Trust could not be interpreted or altered to allow the enrollment of women. They sought an injunction to stop the work of the Transition Committee. On January 8, 2013, Judge Stout issued a partial ruling that the trustees of Deep Springs could not admit women without modification of the Trust. He constrained the board from further developing their plan to admit women pending resolution of the litigation.

In the meantime, the Applications Committee for the 2013–2014 academic year had received submissions from 260 highly qualified applicants, over 100 of whom were women. The latter number was significant because all female applicants had been warned in advance that their admission would be denied if the court ruled against the change. When these women were notified that their candidacies must be terminated, many responded magnanimously while acknowledging bitter disappointment.

The future of Deep Springs hung on the resolution of the coeducation issue. The default position of remaining single-sex had long trumped change as the safer course for institutional stability, but the polarity had now reversed. After four decades of intense conflict, turning back, in my judgment, would perpetuate dysfunction and place the college in grave danger of losing its edge for leadership. Retreat would also risk squandering the verve of the vast majority of the alumni and friends on whom its future rests.

The legal battle went on for three years, but on November 19, 2014, Judge Stout released his decision. In a tightly reasoned fifty-one page ruling, the Superior Court rendered a strong endorsement of the arguments advanced by the Trustees of Deep Springs. The Conclusion read simply:

> The Court hereby decrees that the L.L. Nunn Trust should be modified by substituting the word "people" for "men" in the phrase "for the education of promising young men" in paragraph 1 of the instrument. Counsel for Petitioner [Trustees of Deep Springs, David Hitz, chairperson] shall prepare the Order.[2]

Upon hearing the decision of the court, Ambassador Vernon Penner (DS'57), a long-time skeptic regarding the merits of coeducation, summarized an almost universal feeling when he wrote his closest alumni friends: "As they say in Portuguese, Basta das Palavras, or Enough of Talking. . . Let's get on with the job!"[3] Yet the opponents of coeducation appealed Judge Stout's decision on January 25, 2015. The Trustees of Deep Springs still hoped to admit the first coeducational class for the 2017–18 centennial year. The legal wrangling was to continue, however, and the college lost more time.

I concluded *Maverick Colleges* with the observation that successful progressive and experimental colleges have found ways to survive, and thrive, by adapting imaginatively to the evolving societies they were created to serve. No one denies that the United States is mired in a leadership crisis at all levels and in every dimension. The question before the students and trustees of Deep Springs now and in the future will be whether they can continue to tap the reformist energy that propelled Lucien L. Nunn to create the college a century ago. The institution's long history suggests a positive response.

Two distinctive outcomes of a Deep Springs education shine through and they offer hope. The first is the instinct to act decisively when problems arise. The second is a penchant to reflect critically on one's own behavior and experience. Jumping in to solve a problem—any problem—comes naturally. Whether a vehicle refuses to start on a cold morning or a committee has fallen into dysfunction, Deep Springers seem to carry throughout their lives a proclivity to lift the hood or suggest a fresh perspective to get things going again. This

Evening milking time. Photograph by author.

characteristic is cultivated by having borne responsibility for a community that exists beyond the reach of ordinary municipal services or the instant availability of experts. When things fall apart, a Deep Springer's first response becomes "What can I do?" rather than "Whom should we call?" or "Oh well, it's not my problem."

Living in a community that requires and rewards these attitudes prompts a heightened consciousness of what we can do, who we are, and what we might do better. "The one thing in common I see among former Deep Springers," Barbara Poetter recently told her husband, Michael Stryker (DS'64), "is that they are among a very small group of people whom you could absolutely count on if you called on them when you truly needed help."[4]

Deep Springs' purpose is to prepare students to become genuinely free individuals who have the knowledge, skills, and predisposition to serve the common good. In pursuit of this ideal, the college practices democracy in learning, accepts risks, and endures inefficiencies no other college would tolerate, precisely to offer its students the possibility of extraordinary growth in attitude, character, and capability.

Looking back, it is clear that L.L. Nunn aspired to give his students the same mettle-testing, life-changing experiences he himself had endured in Leadville, Durango, and Telluride from 1879 to 1882. A century and a third later, the formula is still being tested at Deep Springs. What is the value of a sojourn in the wilderness? How important is it for young men and women to test their limits physically, mentally, and ethically? What happens when young people in the earliest stages of adulthood face, with very real consequences, the timeless struggles between liberty and equality, justice and mercy, self-absorption and service to humanity?

It is fitting, I believe, to end this volume with the reflections of a recent student on his experiences at Deep Springs and after. Utah native Andrew McCreary (DS'06), after graduating from the college and Yale University, and after serving as a White House intern, wrote: "Deep Springs brought me up against unexpected and sometimes downright embarrassing limits of what I know and can do. Problems that were supposed to be simple to solve, like fixing a fence or hiring a short-term professor, proved pretty difficult. No amount of pretending would get the job done; and no amount of pretending the job had been done well would keep the cows where they should be or make a slow seminar stimulating."[5] He continued:

> The results were always clear, and the results mattered. I had to admit my ignorance and inability early, to think through and tinker and invent, to ask questions of others, and to suck it up and go back to the shed for the right tools or to the group to reconsider the right principles to bring the best result. Deep Springs drove me to expect untold complexity in the social and environmental problems I sought to work on in the world at large. These experiences inspired integrity in thinking and acting. When thought through and done well, a good fence stands for itself.

Deep Springs' worthiness to exist rests on its capacity to inspire and, more importantly, to equip a few particularly able students each year to apply their talents to improve a precarious society and protect our endangered planet. In a society fraught with alienation and cynicism, Deep Springs' goal is to foster an educational and community experience so vigorous, so just, and so humane that our students will hold it up as an achievable standard toward which they can strive wherever they may later serve. Creating and maintaining such a community will be the supreme challenge as long as the college exists.

APPENDIX

Presidents/Directors and Trustees of Deep Springs

Presidents/Directors

The person holding executive responsibility at Deep Springs was originally known as the Director. Starting in 1958, the title of President was introduced but not used consistently until 1983. Where two names appear with overlapping or matching years, authority was shared by two individuals with different titles.

Director/President	Dates of Service	Affiliation[1]
L.L. Nunn	1917–25	Founder
Otto B. Suhr	1925–32	Charter Trustee
Paul N. Nunn	1932–33	Charter Trustee
Walter Crawford (acting)	1934–36	Mission Schools
Lawrence A. Kimpton	1937–41	Cornell University
Armand W. Kelley	1941–42	DS 1930
Simon N. Whitney	1942–48	DS 1919
Bonham Spence Campbell	1948–51	DS 1931
William G. Greenman	1951–54	U.S. Navy (Ret.)
Haylon R. Roodhouse	1955–58	DS 1923
Carroll N. Whitman	1955–58	Charter Trustee
William E. Fort Jr.	1958–59	Rollins College
Robert B. Aird	1960–66	DS 1921
Barney Childs	1966–69	DS 1943
Randall C. Reid	1969–75	DS 1949

John Mawby	1975–76	DS 1953
Edwin M. Cronk	1976–80	DS 1936
Christopher N. Breiseth	1980–83	TA
Brandt Kehoe	1983–87	DS 1951
John U. Anderson	1987–90	DS 1939
Saul H. Benjamin	1990	Montana State U.
Edward H. Hoenicke	1991–92	DS 1946
Sherwin Howard	1992–95	Weber State U.
L. Jackson Newell	1995–2004	DS 1956
F. Ross Peterson	2004–07	Utah State U.
Louis Fantasia	2007	Los Angeles, Theater
David Neidorf	2008–20	Middlebury College
Susan Darlington	2020-23	Hampshire College
Andrew Zink	2023-26	San Francisco State

Trustees of Deep Springs

Charter trustees were appointed for life or until they chose to resign, as were their successors until 1960. Since that time, with important exceptions, appointees have served once-renewable four-year terms. In 1995, the trustees voted to expand board membership from nine members (with one held by a student) to as many as thirteen members (with two reserved for students). Because their numbers are much larger, student members are not listed here. An asterisk (*) designates those who served as board chairs.

Trustee	**Dates of Service**	**Affiliation**
William L. Biersach	1923–63	Charter Member
Paul F. Cadman*	1923–45	Charter Member
Francis C. Noon*	1923–73	Charter Member
Paul N. Nunn	1923–39	Charter Member
Otto B. Suhr	1923–38	Charter Member
Ernest A. Thornhill	1923–41	Charter Member
Harold R. Waldo*	1923–69	Charter Member
Carroll N. Whitman	1923–72	Charter Member
John G. Laylin	1939–63	DS 1920
Parker Monroe	1941–58	TA
Harold Sanders	1945–63	Friend
Haylon R. Roodhouse	1948–63	DS 1923
Robert B. Aird*	1959–71	DS 1921
Hugh W. Davy	1963–70	DS 1928
Charles M. Gilbert	1963–67	DS 1927
Ralph N. Kleps	1963–69	DS 1932

James R. Withrow*	1963–80	DS 1927
Robert L. Sproull	1967–75	DS 1935
Frederic S. Laise	1969–77	DS 1931
Robley Williams Sr.*	1969–77	TA
Francis Tetreault	1970–78	DS 1937
David A. Hodges	1972–76	TA
Robert Henderson*	1972–81	DS 1935
Robert F. Gatje	1973–81	DS 1944
Beatrice Renfield	1975–81	Friend
Paul H. Todd Jr.*	1976–84	TA
David Werdegar	1976–83	DS 1947
Dale R. Corson	1977–84	Cornell Pres.
Thomas E. Fairchild	1979–82	DS 1929
Kenneth A. Odell	1979–87	DS 1961
Robert M. Gorrell	1981–84	Friend
Eric M. Pell*	1981–89	DS 1941
Edwin M. Cronk	1982–88	DS 1936
Robert L. Sproull	1983–87	DS 1935
E. Paul Swatek	1983–85	DS 1933
Bruce R. Laverty*	1984–91	DS 1943
William F. Scandling	1984–91	Friend
William H. Allen*	1985–93	DS 1942
Charles Christenson*	1986–94	TA
Frederick E. Balderston	1987–91	DS 1940
L. Jackson Newell*	1987–94	DS 1956
Donald H. Read	1989–93	DS 1959
Clare Selgin Wolfowitz	1989–00	TA
Christopher N. Breiseth	1991–99	TA
Edwin J. Wesely	1991–99	DS 1945
Richard C. Cornelison*	1992–2000	DS 1943
John S. deBeers	1993–97	DS 1932
Ernest S. Tucker	1993–98	DS 1950
Henry Fang	1994–98	Parent
Abraham Markosian	1994–97	Friend
Margaret Sibert Miller	1994	Friend
Madeleine Pelner Cosman	1995–1998	Friend
Raymond F. Jeanloz	1995–2003	DS 1970
James R. Olin	1995–2000	DS 1938
Karen I. Spear	1998–99	Ft. Lewis Col.
Louis Gehring	1998–2001	DS 1958
Jeff Johnson*	1998–2006	DS 1955
Lea Carol Owen	1998–2007	TA

Kurt Gilson	1999–2007	DS 1980
Alan Farnham	2000–08	Friend
Michael P. Stryker*	2001–09	DS 1964
Ulric Haynes Jr.	2001–04	Friend
Paul Foster	2002–04	TA
William C. Hoffman	2002–10	DS 1956
William Masters	2002–11	DS 1979
F. Ross Peterson	2002–04	Utah State
Madeleine Pelner Cosman	2003–04	Friend
Eunice (Beth) Whitney Thomas	2004–12	Friend
Edward J. Keonjian	2004–12	DS 1955
Dave Hitz*	2004–19	DS 1980
Jessica Catelino	2004–06	TA
Rebecca Carter	2006–08	TA
James Bartolome	2007–14	Friend
Erik Mueggler	2007–15	DS 1980
Kinch Hoekstra	2008–14	DS 1982
Sharon Tregaskis	2008–10	TA
Tom Hudnut	2010–18	Friend
Sally Carlson	2010–18	Friend
Frank Wu	2010–17	Friend
Jamie May	2010–11	TA
Michael Kearney	2012–20	DS 1969
F. Ross Peterson	2012–17	Former Pres.
Alan Kaufman	2012–14	DS 1967
David J. Welle	2014–21	DS 1980
Marina Hsieh*	2014–22	Friend
Eric V. Swanson	2015–23	DS 1965
Katie Peterson	2016-23	Friend
Jacob Giessman	2016-24	DS 1994
Aron Fischer	2018-	DS 1995
Felicia Wong	2018-22	Friend
Dan Fulwiler*	2019-	DS 1985
Jefferson Cowie	2019-	Friend
Mark Taylor	2020-	DS 1972
Brighde Mullins	2020-23	Friend
Marcella David	2021-	Friend
Jonathan DeWeese	2021-	DS 2007
Adnan Husain	2023-	DS 1987
Lynn Huntsinger	2023-	Friend
Rebecca Carter	2024-	TA
Theresa Tensuan	2024-	Friend
Noah Rosenblum	2025-	DS 2003

ACKNOWLEDGMENTS

My gratitude abounds for those who helped make this project possible. Richard Stack of the Hugh and Hazel Darling Foundation embraced my proposal immediately and underwrote much of the research. Greg Thompson, Associate Dean for Special Collections at the University of Utah's Marriott Library, proffered encouragement and archival support throughout the project. Dean Sylvia Torti in the Honors College where I teach granted me writing space and professional development resources, and, earlier, Dean Frank Brown and Matt Basso let me use offices in the College of Mines and at our American West Center.

Linda King Newell, my wife, joined me in ferreting out the documentary evidence on which this story depends. We made multiple trips to Cornell University's Carl A. Kroch Library, where Director Elaine Engst and her staff in the Division of Rare and Manuscript Collections provided important assistance. At Telluride Association's home office adjacent to the Cornell campus, we found Director Ellen Baer and Cynthia Estes-Smith not only helpful on site, but they responded unfailingly to my many requests for follow-up information.

In the West, we visited archives and courthouses in Telluride, Durango, and Delta, Colorado; at Olmsted, Utah; and in Bishop, Independence, Laws, Lone Pine, and Orange, California. The richest repository proved to be the archival holdings at Deep Springs College, to which we returned over a dozen times.

I remember the days when the minutes of student body and trustee meetings and other vital documents were thrown haphazardly into cardboard boxes and stashed under tables in the old library—or in the musty, windowless storage building known as the Block House. A year-long project conducted by student Keith Sweet (DS'97) with the periodic assistance of Madeline Brunson, retired archivist from Independence, Missouri, saw the priceless contents of those dusty boxes organized, logged, and processed. Keith and other students of his era also copied over eighty years of student body and trustee minutes so that these documents are permanently preserved and available at the Kroch Library as well as in Deep Springs Archives.

My personal papers, including thousands of documents about Deep Springs and L.L. Nunn, are being accessioned by Special Collections at the University of Utah's Marriott Library. Jennifer Sessions organized and indexed the first wave of these papers, and Roger Paxton continues the work.[1]

Striving to understand L.L. Nunn's achievements in hydroelectric generation and long-distance transmission, I received counsel from physicists Robert L. Sproull and Orest Symko about the early history and development of DC and AC electricity. Bruce Laverty and Stan Lloyd tutored me regarding the early application of these technologies in the Eastern Sierra region and at Deep Springs. Wayne Barnes, who has managed the Olmsted Power Station in Provo Canyon, Utah, for nearly four decades, offered extraordinary support during several visits to this still-functioning generating facility. Greg Solverg showed us around Nunn's Beaver River Power Station in southern Utah.

Misha Hoekstra, who shares Linda's and my keen interest in the history of Deep Springs Valley, offered bounteous information and insights about its human history. Michael G. Delacorte's exhaustive research and writing about the archeology of Deep Springs Valley and the White Mountains proved invaluable. Jack Holt rounded out my study of the geology of the area. Linda Williams of Dyer, Nevada, extended my grasp of historical relationships between Deep Springs ranch and the ranches in Fish Lake Valley. Illuminating Deep Springs' history of activities in Fish Lake Valley were Link Stanley, Jim and Verna Wallace, and Leland Wallace of Dyer, Nevada. Roberta Hanlan and John Klusmire at the Eastern California Museum in Independence provided photographs and documents on the early history of the Deep Springs area. David Wright of Big Pine, California, scoured local newspaper archives for news from Deep Springs Valley over the last century. My understanding of the history of Telluride Association and its relationship to Deep Springs was enhanced by many friends in the association, especially Denis Clark, Brian Kennedy, and Carol Owen.

The watershed in my research came in the autumn of 2009 when Linda Lu Nunn contacted me from her home near Seattle, Washington, asking for information about her great-uncle Lucien L. Nunn and the college he founded. This granddaughter of Nunn's younger brother Josiah (or J.J.), had become curious after discovering another surviving grandniece, Helen M. Heckman of Apple Valley, California. Helen is the granddaughter of L.L.'s older sister Miriam. The three of us struck up a rich correspondence.

Helen, then in her ninetieth year, invited Linda and me to visit her. She led us to a large bedroom that she had long-since converted to serve as the Nunn family archive. She threw open scores of cabinets and file drawers and directed our attention to thousands of letters, photographs, press clippings, and other documents that illuminate the life of her beloved "Uncle Lu" and other members of the extended Nunn family. Over the next year, this trove would greatly magnify my understanding of L.L. Nunn's family heritage, upbringing, and early adult years. I mailed chapters to Helen as I drafted them, receiving helpful suggestions in return. Her gentle spirit, liberal mind, and enthusiastic support added immeasurably to this volume.

Essential to understanding L.L. Nunn's later years, and Deep Springs' early years, was the oral history project conducted by former president Chris Breiseth and alumnus Brad Edmondson in the early 1980s. They recorded and transcribed conversations with at least twenty-seven alumni whose memories reached back to Nunn and the founding of the college in 1917. Over the last decade, I added to this collection by recording conversations with more recent Deep Springs alumni and some former members of the faculty and staff.

My access to photographic collections supporting this project received an enormous boost from alumnus Denis Clark, who recently assembled a large collection of images documenting the history of the Telluride Power Company and, to a lesser extent, Deep Springs and Telluride Association. Ron Alexander (who is amassing a sizable video record of recent years), Bob Gatje, Helen Heckman, Robert Reich, Elaine Teel, and Sue Witter all added to the photographic history, supplementing the growing collection in the Deep Springs Archives. Peter O'Connor and Brandon Hogg provided excellent maps of the college and ranch, and Gerald Hughes crafted the three large maps. Keith McKeown offered both artistic and technical support in preparing the photographs and maps for print.

Most college and university leaders exercise tight control over their histories for fear of offending the sensitivities of key donors and alumni. I have witnessed these concerns at both public and private universities and have seen proposals for the scholarly examination of their histories scuttled by presidents and boards. At Deep Springs, the environment could not have been more different.

I experienced nothing but encouragement for my research and writing from president David Neidorf, board chair Dave Hitz, the trustees, and the student body, all of whom threw their historical records open to me without reservation. That Deep Springs has a checkered history is a secret to no one, nor are the controversies surrounding L.L. Nunn. Defensiveness, however, was entirely absent, replaced by curiosity and a genuine desire to understand how the college has functioned over time, and how it has survived its many crises.

It would be hard to imagine a more exacting but eager audience for this book than the alumni of Deep Springs and Telluride Association. To six knowledgeable alumni and an ex-president, I owe a special debt of gratitude for reading the entire manuscript with notable care and responding with candor: William H. Allen, Christopher N. Breiseth, Christopher L. Campbell, Denis E. Clark, Bradley Edmondson, and Robert Gatje. Helpfully critiquing multiple chapters were Katherine Chaddock, Joyce Chesnut, Nicholas W. Hillman, Misha Hoekstra, David Neidorf, Ross and Kay Peterson, Geoffrey and Iris Pope, Michael P. Stryker, David Welle, and Lenette Wilde.

Offering especially valuable counsel on one or more specific chapters or issues were Ron Alexander, Charles Abbott, Christian Anderson, Janet Barnhill, John Beischel, Christof Bove, Chandler Cook, Rick Coville, William Cowan, Michael Delacorte, Jacob Dickinson, Aaron Dulles-Coelho, Betsy Frank, Gareth Fisher, Rick Hansen, Rich Haynie, Bill Hoffman, Tom Holloway, Jack Holt, Claudia Horn, Angela Jayko, Jeff Johnson, Renelle Keesler, Ed Keonjian, Melvin Kohn, Bruce Laverty, Nancy Marsh, Nancy Masters, Will Masters, Scott McDermott, Matt Mandelkern, Jon Michaelson, Andy Moore, Heide Sachse Moore, Tony Morgan, Barbara Moss, Ted Packard, Dirk Paloutzian, Bobbie Paranick, Vern Penner, Bill Pezick, Phil Pister, Hannah Rhadigan (Artists Rights Society), Paul Starrs, Christian Stayner, Marsha Stout, Eric Swanson, Eunice (Beth) Whitney Thomas, Random Turner-Jones, Jonathan West, Sherry Wilkinson, Graeme Wood, and others whose names will occur to me too late.

I thank Peter Delafosse for his early counsel and encouragement at the University of Utah Press, and Editor-in-Chief John Alley for guiding this project toward conclusion. Just when I needed a boost to finish this work, my long-time colleague and friend Lavina Fielding Anderson read and provided early editing for each chapter and built the bibliography. She also indexed the book. I am also indebted to Virginia Hoffman for her careful copyediting and patience with my last-minute changes in the manuscript.

My heartfelt gratitude goes to Bill Vollmann for writing the foreword, to Denis Clark for critiquing the entire manuscript at two stages, and to David Hitz and the Trustees of Deep Springs for their special support of publication expenses. My greatest debt is to my wife, Linda. An ace in any archive, her eye for finding important documents sometimes left me speechless. She was my full partner in researching this book; and although I wrote virtually every word of the text, she was my best and most fearless critic, chapter by chapter.[2] Few historians have the privilege I enjoy of working and living with a distinguished biographer.[3]

The able and good-hearted assistance of the scores of people who have helped me along this journey is appreciated beyond words. The faults that remain rest entirely on my shoulders.

NOTES

Introduction

1. Park Honan, August 11, 1964, Alumni Essays, Subgroup 23, Box 2, fd. 3, Deep Springs Archives (hereafter DSA).
2. "L. L. Nunn's letters copied from addenda to biography, Jurisdiction," 5 (not published), Subgroup 15, Box 1, fd. 8, DSA.
3. L. Jackson Newell, Katherine C. Reynolds, and Scott Marsh, eds., *Fourteen Notable Experiments in American Undergraduate Education,* 2d ed. rev. and expanded (Salt Lake City: Educational Policy Center, University of Utah, 1996). In 2009, MIT's OpenCourseWare Program published this entire book online for its Learning Seminar, Experiments in Education (SP.291/ESG.SP291).
4. Burton R. Clark, *The Distinctive College* (New Brunswick, NJ: Transaction Publishers, 1992 edition). Thelin's comment was made in personal conversation with the author.
5. Gerald Grant and David Riesman, *The Perpetual Dream: Reform and Experiment in the American College* (Chicago: University of Chicago Press, 1978).
6. Ibid., 17.
7. Stephen A. Bailey, *L. L. Nunn: A Memoir* (Ithaca, NY: Cayuga Press for Telluride Association, 1933; rpt., Ithaca, NY: Cayuga Press for Telluride Association, 1993).

8. Orville Sweeting, "The Education Experiment of L. L. Nunn" (Unfinished typescript, 1976, Lucien L. Nunn Papers, # 37-4-1770. Division of Rare and Manuscript Collections, Cornell University Library, Ithaca, New York).
9. Robert B. Aird, *Deep Springs: Its Founder, History, and Philosophy with Personal Reflections* (Deep Springs, CA: Deep Springs College, 1997).
10. Denis E. Clark, *Telluride Power: A Brief Illustrated History of the Early Days* (Ithaca, NY: Telluride Association History Committee, June 2001).
11. Michael A. Smith, *The Students of Deep Springs College*, with accompanying essays by L. Jackson Newell and William T. Vollmann (Revere, PA: Lodima Press, 2000).

Chapter 1. The Diminutive Dynamo, 1853–1890

1. Associated Press, "Nunn's Special Train: Racing over Union Pacific," *Los Angeles Times*, July 4, 1905; "Special Is Too Slow: L. L. Nunn Makes Vain Effort to Catch Union Pacific Flyer," *Salt Lake Herald*, July 4, 1905; "Nunn Has a Race with Death: Son Is at Point of Death in Niagara Falls," *Ogden Standard*, July 4, 1905; "Death Is Racing with Him: Telluride Man's Mad Flight to Reach Dying Wife Reached Here This Morning and Immediately Hired a Rio Grande Special to Take Him to His Home," *Denver Post*, July 4, 1905, L. Jackson Newell Papers (hereinafter LJN Papers) (Accn 2342), Special Collections Dept., J. Willard Marriott Library, University of Utah, Salt Lake City.
2. "L. L. Nunn's Thrilling Ride," *Telluride Daily Journal*, July 7, 1905, LJN Papers.
3. Nunn had received a telegram on July 2, 1905: "Tonight . . . diagnosed with considerable certainty as rapid form of Lander's disease [now Gullian-Barre syndrome], . . . probably fatal within a week." Quoted in Orville Sweeting, "Education Experiment," 337. Sweeting spent years in the 1960s and 1970s compiling this 1,759-page typescript. It remained unfinished at the time of his death in November 1976, the date I have assigned to it. Sweeting copied verbatim hundreds of Nunn's letters and other critically important documents but seldom identified the location of the original documents and often omitted dates. In the intervening years, many appear to have been lost. Where the originals can be found and matched against Sweeting's manually copied versions, the integrity of his scholarship has been confirmed. Sweeting considered his first-draft manuscript "the mother lode for two or three books." Several iterations of his manuscript are housed in the Lucien L. Nunn Papers, # 37-4-1770. Division of Rare and Manuscript Collections, Cornell University Library, Ithaca, New York (hereinafter Nunn Papers).
4. Bailey, *L. L. Nunn*, 17. All quotations in this volume are from the 1993 reprint. The family disembarked from the *Margaret Evans* in New York on June 16, 1851.
5. Jennie D. (Mrs. Josiah J.) Nunn, Letter and attachment to F. C. Noon, November

23, 1938, Box 4, fd. 5. LJN Papers. Grandmother Mary endearingly inscribed an 1846 King James edition of the Bible to Lucien before she died. He kept the treasure but seldom read it, judging by its excellent condition. Nunn Papers.

6. Bailey, *L.L. Nunn*, 21.
7. L.L. Nunn's paternal grandfather was a farmer. His own father's profession was listed at different times as a baker, cobbler, and farmer. Misha Hoekstra, email to Denis Clark, Jackson Newell, et al., January 3, 2010. Nunn's maternal grandfather was a wheelwright, according to Louise Nunn McGilvra, "Notes Concerning Nunn Family," quoting Paul N. Nunn, circa 1900, copy in LJN Papers, courtesy of Helen Heckman.
8. L.L Nunn to Frank Whitman, 1909, in Sweeting, "Education Experiment," 20–26. Linda Guilford first founded the Cleveland Female Seminary and then, in 1866, the coeducational Cleveland Academy, both of which she managed for several decades. Her demanding four-year curriculum was based on Greek, Latin, and modern European studies, science, and mathematics. My thanks to the Cleveland Public Library, Kuen Yu, and Deep Springs alumnus William W. Cowan.
9. Sweeting, "Education Experiment," 8.
10. Bailey, *L.L. Nunn*, 39. Guilford's sentiment was probably inspired by the Greek tragic dramatist, Aeschylus (525–456 B.C.), who wrote of a Greek hero: "His resolve is not to seem, but to be, the best." *Seven against Thebes*, I.592.
11. Bailey, *L.L. Nunn*, 39.
12. Miriam Eliza Nunn was an alumna of the college.
13. Correspondence from "Avis," in the *American Bee Journal* 10, no. 7 (July 1874): 1.
14. Sweeting, "Education Experiment," 24. Quoted from a letter to nephew Frank Whitman, posted June 16, 1909, from Provo, Utah. The letterhead read: "Telluride Institute, L.L. Nunn and P.N. Nunn, Directors."
15. The Nunns' habit of using nicknames for each other, including middle names, presents a puzzle for historians. The second daughter, Ellen Miriam, was usually called Ellen or Nellie, while the fourth daughter, Eliza Miriam, went by Miriam.
16. Sweeting, "Education Experiment," 23–24. Lucien and Fred apparently parted at the end of September. L.L. returned to New York on January 15, 1874, but Fred stayed on in Europe until May 4. In Italy he acquired dozens of excellent queen bees. Ship manifest data from Misha Hoekstra, LJN Papers.
17. Sweeting, "Education Experiment," 24. The Colony Collapse Syndrome decimated apiaries early in the first decade of the twenty-first century. At first judged to be a new disorder, CCS has been identified as a recurrence of an earlier disease, possibly the one that had destroyed the Nunns' business.
18. Ibid., 24–25.

19. Ibid., 25.
20. Herder (1744–1803) is known best for his masterwork *Outlines of a Philosophy of Man*. His philosophy influenced Goethe and German Romanticism.
21. Nunn, quoted in Bailey, *L.L. Nunn*, 41–42. Bailey attributed these words to a translation of Herder's *The Spirit of Hebrew Poetry* (1833). I have been unable to find a near-quotation in James Marsh's translation (Burlington, VT: E. Smith, 1833). Even so, Nunn kept *The Spirit* close at hand throughout his life. The quotation may allude to Psalms 51:6: "Behold, thou desirest truth in the inward parts: and in the hidden part thou shalt make me to know wisdom."
22. Sweeting, "Education Experiment," 25.
23. Noon's account of this exchange was written about forty years after the conversation reportedly occurred. Frank Noon, circa 1960, Subgroup #23, Series 2, Box 2, fd. 4, DSA.
24. Ibid., 26.
25. Lesley Schoenfeld to William W. Cowan, quoted in letter from Cowan to Newell, n.d., [circa April 23, 2008], LJN Papers.
26. Sweeting, "Education Experiment," 26. According to David Anderson, the Colorado Bar Association's legal historian, such supervised readings, an apprenticeship, and sometimes attending lectures at a recognized college of law was a typical legal education. Telephone interview.
27. Bailey, *L.L. Nunn*, 78.
28. Sweeting, "Education Experiment," 27.
29. L.L. Nunn, "The Moral Sense," *Mansfield Herald*, March 22, 1880, Nunn Collection, copy in LJN Papers. Bailey, *L.L. Nunn*, 118–32, renders a similar version of the text of "The Moral Sense."
30. Nunn's conclusions aligned with the rising intellectual tenor of his era, captured expertly by Mark Warren Bailey in *Guardians of the Moral Order: The Legal Philosophy of the Supreme Court, 1860–1910* (DeKalb: Northern Illinois University Press, 2004).
31. Robert B. Aird, M.D., was a leading neurologist who knew Nunn in Provo when he was a child and who was later a student at Deep Springs. He retrospectively identified this eye malfunction as "a slight left-sided strabismus" or misalignment of his eyes. See Aird, *Deep Springs*, 5. None of the many photographs of Nunn, however, suggest such a misalignment.
32. Bailey, *L.L. Nunn*, 33. He hung a print of Jacques-Louis David's 1912 portrait of Napoleon in his home. Aird, *Deep Springs*, 5.
33. Sweeting, "Education Experiment," 27.
34. M[alachi] Kinney, "A Sketch of the Pioneer Life of Lucien L. Nunn from June

1880 to November 1887," November 20, 1927, with a "P.S." dated November 27, 1927, Subgroup 8, Box 2, fd. 11, DSA. (Hereafter, "Pioneer Life of Nunn.")

35. Ibid.; see also Sweeting, "Education Experiment," 37; Bailey, *L.L. Nunn,* 47–48; Utah Power and Light, *Utah Power and Light: History of Origin and Development. Prepared in Connection with Federal Power Commission Request* (Salt Lake City, Utah: January 28, 1941), order dated May 11, 1937, Appendix Statement "A", 90, photocopy in Box 7, fd. 4, LJN Papers. Hereafter, Utah Power, *History.*
36. Lucien Nunn to Emily Nunn, February 10, 1881. Holographs of all correspondence to and from L.L. Nunn cited in this chapter are in the Nunn Papers.
37. Emily Nunn to Frederick Nunn, February 25, 1881. She addressed him as "Judge," since he had just graduated from the University of Michigan's law school.
38. Emily Nunn to Frederick Nunn, March 12, 1881.
39. Ibid.
40. Emily quotes Lucien's letter in ibid.
41. Kinney, "Pioneer Life of Nunn," 3; Bailey, *L.L. Nunn*, 49. Harge Eskridge, James Garret, and Oscar Pruitt (whose name Kinney could not recall) were a wing of the infamous Ike Stockton Gang.
42. Kinney, "Pioneer Life of Nunn."
43. Sweeting, "Education Experiment," 2, 3.
44. L.L. Nunn (Telluride, CO) to Ellen Nunn, February 3, 1882.
45. Miriam Kendall Nunn to Frederick Nunn, postmarked November 28, 1881. Fred's own poor health prevented him from doing as she asked.
46. Sweeting, "Education Experiment," 40.
47. Kinney, "Pioneer Life of Nunn."
48. L.L. Nunn to My Dear Brother [Fred], January 23, 1882.
49. Ibid.
50. Ibid. Lucien's mother died in October 1885.
51. Urban, though L.L.'s occasional business partner, was never able to manage his own affairs.
52. The practice of law was rather loosely governed in frontier towns at that time, well before the Colorado Bar Association was organized. It was not until 1885 that Nunn assembled the necessary letters of good character and a judge's recommendation to forward to the Colorado Supreme Court seeking a license to practice. His request was granted without delay. David Anderson, JD, Colorado Bar Association historian, provided this information by telephone in September 2006.
53. Helen Heckman, comp., "Snippets from Alice Bird's Diaries," Nunn Papers.
54. Kinney, "Pioneer Life of Nunn," 8.
55. Ibid., 6.

56. Ibid., 1; Sweeting, "Education Experiment," 42.
57. Kinney, "Pioneer Life of Nunn," P.S. dated November 27, 1927, and Bailey, *L.L. Nunn*, 50.
58. Bailey, *L.L. Nunn*, 60–66.
59. Sweeting, "Education Experiment," 227; Utah Power, *History*, 8–9.
60. Bailey, *L.L. Nunn*, 62. In 1892, Nunn built an impressive stone building on a prominent corner lot for his bank, later named the First National Bank of Telluride.
61. This robbery has generated many colorful accounts. My version is based on the points of agreement among the most creditable sources. Bailey, *L.L. Nunn*, 62; Richard Lowenberg, "Lighting up the Nineties," 1–3, InfoZone, n.d., http://infozone.telluride.co.us/store/acpower.com, Box 11, fd. 8, LJN Papers.
62. Sweeting, "Education Experiment," 142.
63. Bailey, *L.L. Nunn*, 51.
64. Ibid., 66. James Campbell was the wealthiest individual in St. Louis and a major player in East Coast financial circles. His stake in Telluride businesses was minor in his investment empire, but it grew after he established ties with Nunn.
65. Thomas Kirwan, *Boston Herald*, November 30, 1890, clipping in Nunn Papers, Acc. #7, Box 3, fd. 3.
66. If the gold weighed thirty pounds, at the 1890 value of $21 a troy ounce it would have been worth $10,000 at the time. In 2010 dollars, that would be $250,000.
67. John S. McCormick, *The Power to Make Good Things Happen* (Salt Lake City: Utah Power and Light Company, 1990), 9.
68. Sweeting, "Education Experiment," 58; Bailey, *L.L. Nunn*, 67–68. Paul had no middle name, but from his youth added "N," which he explained stood for "nothing." L.L. claimed he persuaded Paul to use the "N" for "Napoleon." "P.N." was his preferred family and business name for the rest of his life.
69. Engineers would later discover that, at very high voltages, direct current can efficiently carry electricity up to one thousand miles.
70. By 1886, Westinghouse had teamed with entrepreneurs in Massachusetts to provide alternating current for street lighting, but it was generated at low voltages and was not applied to industry or across significant distances. "Milestones: Alternating Current Electrification, 1886," IEEE Xplore Digital Library, IEEE Berkshire Section, Dedication: 2 October 2004.

Chapter 2. Rising with Power, 1891–1912

1. Sweeting, "Education Experiment," 897.
2. Ibid., 97.
3. Utah Power, *History*, 101, and McCormick, *The Power to Make Good Things*

Happen, 39–50.

4. Succinct accounts of Nunn's first power installation are found in Obed C. Haycock, "Electric Power Comes to Utah," *Utah Historical Quarterly* 45, no. 2 (Spring 1977): 173–87, and M. L. Cummins, "An Industry and an Institution of Higher Learning Are Born at Ames, Colorado—1891," *Pioneers of the San Juan Country* (Libby, MT: Sarah Platt Decker Chapter D.A.R., Big Mountain Publishing, 1961), 4:130–34.
5. Sweeting, "Education Experiment," 254.
6. Major G. T. Fishry to Mr. L.L. Nunn, October 24, 1891, photocopy in LJN Papers.
7. James Cain also teamed up with Westinghouse on similar power projects for the mines around Bodie, California. His power plants came on line more than two years after Nunn's Ames plant, but some still credit Bodie as the seat of the electric power revolution. See, for example, Barbara Moore, "Bodie Electrifies the World," *The Album* [Bishop, California], July 1988, Box 7, fd. 4, LJN Papers, 29–33.
8. Robert L. Sproull to L. Jackson Newell, March 26, 2010, LJN Papers.
9. Ibid.
10. The Telluride Power Company incorporated on February 19, 1900. Utah Power and Light Company, *Utah Power and Light*, 8–9.
11. Quoted in Bailey, *L.L. Nunn*, 136.
12. *Telluride Journal*, January 5, 1905.
13. Bailey, *L.L. Nunn*, 79.
14. Cornell University initiated its major in electrical engineering in 1883. As late as 1890, its curriculum "Register" listed no courses on alternating current.
15. I am indebted to physicists Robert L. Sproull of the University of Rochester and Orest Symko of the University of Utah for coaching me on electrical technology through this pioneering era.
16. Scott McDermott, "Prologue," in Bailey, *L.L. Nunn*, vi.
17. The Cornell House was restored in the 1990s. The owners gave Linda and me a tour of the house on two occasions.
18. *Telluride Journal*, April 10, 1902.
19. *Telluride Journal*, February 2, 1905.
20. Sweeting, "Education Experiment," 273–75, Bailey, *L.L. Nunn*, 70–72.
21. *Rio Grande W. Ry. Co. v. Telluride Power Transmission Co.,* Utah 22, Vol. 63, p. 995 (1900). See also Sweeting, "Education Experiment," 278.
22. These heavy-haul trucks were probably steam powered.
23. Sweeting, "Education Experiment," 299; "Trucks Are Gone: Dispute over Hauling Machinery: Company Tries Its Hand: Power Plant People Say Watson Bros. Violated Their Contract," *Provo Daily Inquirer*, November 13, 1897; "Conflict at

Provo: Power Company and Watson Bros. at Outs," *Salt Lake Tribune*, November 14, 1897. All Salt Lake newspaper citations are on microfilm, Utah State Historical Society Library.

24. Haycock, "Electric Power Comes to Utah," 180.
25. Sweeting, "Education Experiment," 308–11.
26. Ibid., 309.
27. Smith became president of the LDS Church in October 1901 and served until he died in the 1918 flu epidemic.
28. Reed Smoot was elected to the U.S. Senate as a Republican in 1902, but his right to his seat was challenged on the grounds that he was a polygamist (he wasn't) and that he was a Mormon apostle (true) and therefore had a higher loyalty than his oath of office. After four years of hearings and a negative committee recommendation, his membership was confirmed by an all-Senate vote in 1907.
29. *Telluride Journal*, February 3, 1899; and *Telluride Journal*, April 3, 1902.
30. *Telluride Journal*, April 10, 1902.
31. Sweeting, "Education Experiment," 304–5.
32. Ibid., 306.
33. Bailey, *L.L. Nunn*, 29.
34. One of the many railroad passes in Nunn's wallet when he died was for the Las Vegas and Tonopah Railroad.
35. My thanks to Wayne Barnes, Olmsted Area Foreman for Pacific Corp Energy; personal conversation on March 23, 2012.
36. Letter from John Olmsted to Brad Edmondson, February 4, 1984; photocopy in my possession courtesy of Edmondson, LJN Papers; original in Edmondson's private collection. John is Fred Olmsted's son. See also "Legends of Deep Springs," Subgroup 23, Box 2, fd. 2, DSA.
37. Telluride Power Company headquarters were located at 48 N. Academy Avenue, and Nunn's residence was at 382 S. Academy Avenue, with the Utah County Courthouse between them. Academy Avenue was renamed University Avenue in 1904.
38. *Telluride Journal*, August 13, 1903.
39. Richard L. Fetter and Suzanne Fetter, *Telluride: From Pick to Powder* (Caldwell, ID: Claxton Press, 1979), 102.
40. For a sober examination of the ferocious labor-management conflicts across the West in this era, see J. Anthony Lukas, *Big Trouble: A Murder in a Small Western Town Sets Off a Struggle for the Soul* (New York: Simon and Schuster/Touchstone, 1998), 227.
41. MaryJoy Martin, *The Corpse on Boomerang Road: Telluride's War on Labor,*

1899–1908 (Lake City, CO: Western Reflections Publishing, 2004). Wells had succeeded Arthur Collins at the Smuggler-Union Mine and was apparently using Wrench to secure special favors from the bank.

42. The Institute Building no longer stands, but the Quarters Building is still in use, as is the generating facility next to it. Clark, *Telluride Power*, 20–25.
43. Sweeting, "Education Experiment," 392–94. As the program developed, Thornhill and the two Nunns experimented with the mix of labor and study during the first two years.
44. Ibid., 413.
45. Ibid., 658–59. Thornhill led Nunn's Telluride Institute program until he became Dean of Telluride Association and Dean of Deep Springs College, a dual post he held until 1930. He also served as a trustee of Deep Springs College from 1923 until 1941. He died in 1943.
46. Bailey, *L.L. Nunn*, 27–28. Nunn was fifty-two when he met the slightly older Walcott (1850–1927).
47. *Telluride Journal*, December 14, 1905.
48. *Telluride Journal*, October 8, 1908.
49. A photograph of the well-dressed young men, posed in front of a large wall map of the development in the summer of 1915, is currently located at Telluride House at Cornell University. Thanks to Denis Clark, it will soon be lodged in the Nunn collection at the Kroch Library. Electronic copy in LJN Papers.
50. "The Telluride Power Company, Provo Office: Balance," December 31, 1906.
51. Nunn was compulsive about filing copies of his full correspondence and making lists of people he assisted. Evidence of this habit is plentiful throughout the Sweeting manuscript. In this way and others, he seemed determined to shape his own historical legacy.
52. Helen Heckman, interviewed by Jack Newell, Apple Valley, CA, November 23, 2009.
53. For an excellent analysis of changing attitudes toward homosexuality and LGBT history, see Milt Ford, Grand Valley State College, "A Brief History of Homosexuality in America," http.//www.gvsc.edu//allies/a-brief-history-of-homosexuality-in-america-30htm. Also see the American Psychological Association's report, "Sexual Orientation and homosexuality," http.//www.apa.org/print-this-aspx.
54. Scott McDermott, "Prologue," in Bailey, *L.L. Nunn* (1993 ed.), xvii, is a masterful treatment of this Ashworth episode. McDermott is quoting Ashworth, Autobiography, 1956.
55. McDermott, "Prologue," vii.

56. Ibid., viii–ix.
57. This wedding cake was among Nunn's personal effects in his collection at the Kroch Library. Archivists eventually discarded it for fear that it would attract pests.
58. When Wrench died at about age forty-seven in Salt Lake City, the *Telluride Daily Journal*'s eulogy noted that when Addison, Minnie, and their two sons moved to Utah in 1905 they "effected a distinct loss both to the social and business life of this city." *Telluride Daily Journal*, May 8, 1915.
59. L.L. Nunn to Ray Fruit, December 9, 1915, Nunn Papers, Kroch Library; photocopy in LJN Papers, and transcribed in Sweeting, "Education Experiment," 1702–3.
60. See McDermott's insightful discussion, "Prologue," xviii.
61. Ibid.
62. Aird, *Deep Springs*, 22–23.
63. Frank Noon's second-hand information that Nunn chased German women in Leipzig in the 1870s is the only known reference to heterosexual activity by Nunn. Frank Noon, Chair, Trustees of Deep Springs, ca. 1960, typeset but apparently unpublished, LJN Papers.
64. The Alta Club was founded in 1883 by a group of wealthy non-Mormon miners. Women were invited to join in 1987. It remains the state's most prestigious social club, occupying a historic building in the heart of Salt Lake City.
65. See Oral History Interviews, ADSTA Project, September 1987.
66. Sweeting, "Education Experiment," 44–46.
67. This ugly showdown was documented exhaustively by Sweeting, with more than two hundred pages of evidence. Ibid., 448–657.
68. Ibid., 645.
69. Ibid., 481.
70. Ibid., 490.
71. Ibid., 507.
72. Ibid., 526.
73. Bailey, *L.L. Nunn*, 98.
74. Andrew White, Diary, July 14, 1909, quoted in Sweeting, "Education Experiment," 488–89.
75. See Thorstein Veblen's acerbic *The Higher Learning in America: The Conduct of American Universities by Business Men* (1904; rpt., New York: B. W. Huebsch, 1935). Abraham Flexner, Robert Maynard Hutchins, and Alfred North Whitehead were among the leading voices who challenged Veblen's recommendation that universities abandon liberal education for undergraduates.

76. Sweeting, "Education Experiment," 488, reports: "The negotiations with President Schurman, former President Andrew D. White, and the Board of Trustees consumed many months. With the way cleared, L.L. took personal charge of selecting a site and getting construction under way."
77. *Telluride Journal*, January 13, 1910.
78. Ibid.
79. Sweeting, "Education Experiment," 416.
80. Ibid., 365.
81. Bailey, *L.L. Nunn*, 96.
82. Ibid., 95–96.
83. Sweeting, "Education Experiment," 1149.
84. Bailey, *L.L. Nunn*, 86.
85. "Marshal Did Not Serve L.L. Nunn," *Telluride Journal*, June 29, 1911.
86. *Telluride Journal*, June 29, 1911.
87. Sweeting, "Education Experiment," 432.
88. Ibid., 438.
89. *Salt Lake Tribune*, May 31, 1911, and subsequent articles over the next fourteen months. See also Sweeting, "Education Experiment," 640–44.
90. Dedicatory marble tablet at the entrance to the Rockefeller Memorial Chapel, dated December 13, 1910, University of Chicago.
91. Bailey, *L.L. Nunn*, 99; Sweeting, "Education Experiment," 602. See chapter 8 in this volume for the disposition of Nunn's estate.
92. Sweeting, "Education Experiment," 656.
93. Bailey, *L.L. Nunn*, 90.
94. Ibid.
95. L.L. Nunn saved the Telluride Power Company name and continued to use it as the umbrella for some, but not all, of the power stations he held outside the original company. For a very professional history of the Utah Power and Light Company, see John McCormick's *The Power to Make Good Things Happen*.
96. William Biersach to Elmer M. Johnson, February 13, 1932, LJN Papers.
97. Nunn had developed a friendship with Rudolph Diesel and arranged for him to be one of the first guests at Telluride House. Diesel was lost at sea in the English Channel in 1913.
98. L.L. Nunn (aboard Rock Island Train) to Lionel G. Nightingale, quoted without a date, in Sweeting, "Education Experiment," 676. Nunn's holograph was liberally interlined as he refined the language.
99. Henry Adams, *The Education of Henry Adams* (1918; rpt., New York: American Heritage Library, 1961). Matthew Arnold voiced this idea originally in his 1865

poem, "The Grande Chartreuse": "Wandering between two worlds, one dead / The other powerless to be born, / With nowhere yet to rest my head, / Like these, on earth I wait forlorn. / Their faith, my tears, the world deride— / I come to shed them at their side."

Chapter 3. In the Spirit of the Time

1. "Extracts from Letters Concerning the Educational Work at Deep Springs," DSA, Subgroup 15: Unpublished Letters, Box 1, fd. 8, 2.
2. The TB vaccine was introduced in the 1920s but was not widely administered until the 1940s. The disease passed from one person to the next only with sustained personal contact, so the fact that Nunn had few and fleeting intimate relationships probably spared those closest to him.
3. L.L. Nunn to C. D. Walcott, April 5, 1915.
4. A useful source of information about Nunn's library holdings is the shipping manifest listing the books sent from Telluride to Olmsted in May 1909. It was clearly just part of his library because the books known to be dearest to Nunn were already with him in Utah. Sweeting, "Education Experiment," 1053.
5. Kenneth A. Hovey, professor of English at the University of Texas, Austin, "The Intellectual Origins of L.L. Nunn," 5–9.
6. Ibid., 6.
7. Ibid., 7–8.
8. Ibid., 6.
9. John Dewey, *Democracy and Education* (New York: Macmillan, 1916), 239.
10. Abraham Flexner, "A Modern School," *American Review of Reviews* 53 (1916): 465–74.
11. Howard Crosby Warren, "Academic Freedom," *Atlantic Monthly* (November 1914): 689–99. Jurist Lord Adam Gifford's will established the lectures at the four Scottish universities in the late 1880s.
12. He wrote this letter to young associates at Cornell's Telluride House about 1909, quoted in Sweeting, "Education Experiment," 676.
13. John Erskine, *The Moral Obligation to Be Intelligent and Other Essays* (New York: Duffield & Company, 1915).
14. Andrew Dickson White, *A History of the Warfare of Science with Theology in Christendom*, 2 vols. (1896; rpt. in the Great Minds Paperback Series, New York: Prometheus Press, 1993).
15. "Senate Page for Cornell," *New York Times*, December 20, 1914, clipping in LJN Papers. The *New York Times* archive cites the article as "published December 21, 1914." The young man's surname was actually Bailey, not Barley. He was inducted

into the Telluride Association three years later as a junior at Cornell and remained actively involved for many years.

16. Alexander Meiklejohn, "The Freedom of the College," *Atlantic Monthly* (January 1918): 83–89. Meiklejohn became a leading exponent of First Amendment rights nationally.
17. See L. Jackson Newell and Padraic Macleish, "Alexander Meiklejohn (1872–1964)," in *Encyclopedia of Education*, 2d ed., ed. James L. Guthrie (New York: Macmillan Reference, 2003).
18. This sentence has been spoken at every Antioch commencement since Horace Mann said it for the first time.
19. Robert I. Rotberg, *The Founder: Cecil Rhodes and the Pursuit of Power* (New York: Oxford University Press, 1988). Like Nunn, Rhodes never married. Without wives or families, both men drove themselves almost single-mindedly to achieve their dreams, but each suffered grievously when a young protégé left his company and married a young woman. John Olmsted, son of Fred Olmsted for whom Nunn's Provo Canyon facility was named, became a Rhodes Scholar and charter professor at the University of California, Irvine.
20. The best accounts of this operation are provided by Arthur ("Cy") Ross, a young laborer on the Bliss power plant in 1912 who became a pinhead member of Telluride Association (1916) and Nunn's trusted agent and friend until the latter's death. Arthur ("Cy") Ross, Oral History, interviewed by Christopher N. Breiseth, August 1982.
21. I am indebted to Denis Clark for finding the Eoff-Brady-Hon House, as it is now called, and uncovering much of its history. Doug Stan Wiens at the Boise Architectural Project is the primary source of knowledge about this property.
22. A March 1913 photograph taken on the front lawn of the Brady House shows L.L. Nunn standing behind a group of about twenty young men. LJN Papers. One account tells of bedazzled students who witnessed Nunn command the governor's attention while displaying equal interest in the ideas and plans of the students in attendance. Ross, Oral History.
23. Copies of *The Harlequin* are in the Nunn Papers, LJN Papers, and DSA. I do not know if subsequent volumes were produced, but the short life of this branch makes it doubtful.
24. Telluride Association to L.L. Nunn, July 2, 1913, LJN Papers.
25. "Charge Trespass on Forest Lands," *Deseret News*, February 14, 1914, quoted in Sweeting, "Education Experiment," 818–19.
26. I am indebted to attorney Aaron Dulles-Coelho (DS'01) for his legal and contextual analysis of this controversy.

27. "The Congress shall have Power to dispose of and make all needful Rules and Regulations respecting the Territory or other Property belonging to the United States." U.S. Constitution, Art. IV, sect. 3.
28. William H. Allen (DS'42), email to L. Jackson Newell, February 24, 2010. His legal assistance was crucial in understanding the implications of this case. He commented: It "has been cited within recent memory for the proposition that the government is not bound when someone takes action in reliance on a government official's assurance if that assurance is not within the governing law."
29. Sweeting, "Education Experiment," 335–37.
30. Ibid., 1029.
31. J. B. Bailey to L.L. Nunn, February 11, 1916, quoted in Sweeting, "Education Experiment," 1634–36. Nunn held onto the property until his college had a permanent home.
32. L.L. Nunn to J. B. Bailey, February 21, 1916, LJN Papers.
33. L.L. Nunn to Charles D. Walcott, February 26, 1916. I photographed this document at the Kroch Library on November 23, 2005.
34. Charles D. Walcott, "The Post-Pleistocene Elevation of the Inyo Range and the Lake Beds of Waucobi Embayment, Inyo County, California," *The Journal of Geology* 5, no. 4 (May–June 1897): 340–48. Coville and Walcott became such close friends that, when Coville developed four hybrid varieties of blueberries, he named three of them for his children and the fourth one "Walcott." Frederick V. Coville, M.D., email to L. Jackson Newell, April 7, 2011.
35. Sid Walcott to Robert Aird, April 20, 1977. The aging Sid Walcott remembered the year as 1909, but the evidence suggests 1912.
36. Nunn first heard descriptions of this property along the California-Nevada border from Charles Walcott in 1914.
37. Gilbert Miller and Sidney Walcott, "Report on Virginia as a Home for the Central Branch of Telluride Association," 14, circa summer 1916, Subgroup 8, Box 1, fd. 4, DSA; copy in Nunn Papers.
38. Nunn's Chicago physician, a Dr. Oxner, first suggested this unrecovered burnt-over district from the Civil War as an investment opportunity. See "Transcript of Remarks by Mr. Waldo," November 10, 1973. Ross, Oral History, 1, knew of the link with Poe's foster family.
39. Frank Noon advised Nunn on December 6, 1916, that he had acquired six hundred acres to date and had good prospects of buying more. "Telluride Association Establishes Another Branch," December 6, 1916, *Telluride Newsletter*, Subgroup 8, Box 1, fd. 4, DSA.
40. Ibid. Nunn's right-hand man, Frank Noon, arrived with this party as well.

41. Nunn to "Gentlemen" (student body at Claremont), January 27, 1917, notes that he had left about December 1.
42. L.L. Nunn to Ray W. Fruit, December 26, 1916. In the same letter, Nunn expressed satisfaction that his students at Cornell had recently hosted Rabindranath Tagore for two days of conversation about his renowned school in India. Tagore's philosophy and educational plan was another model Nunn studied and admired during this period. It is likely that he set up the visit.
43. "Chet Dunn, dictation at request of Mike Cravey, 1974," Subgroup 23, Box 2, fd. 5, DSA.
44. Sweeting, "Education Experiment," 1686.
45. Reed Smoot, telegram to Nunn, September 24, 1916, Nunn Papers. I photographed the documents cited here on September 29, 2003.
46. Ernest Thornhill to Committee on Scholastic Standing, January 17, 1917.
47. Nunn to "Gentlemen," January 27, 1917.
48. L.L. Nunn to C. O. Jandl, February 3, 1917.
49. L.L. Nunn to Members of the Telluride Institute of Virginia, February 4, 1917.
50. L.L. Nunn to Gentlemen, February 8, 1917.
51. L.L. Nunn to Gentlemen, February 20, 1917.
52. Ibid.
53. Quoted in Sweeting, "Education Experiment," 937.
54. L.L. Nunn to Oliver Clark, March 7, 1917, quoted in Sweeting, "Education Experiment," 939.
55. In their multiple oral history interviews in the 1970s and 1980s, Cy Ross and Chet Dunn, both of whom had been students at Beaver before Claremont and continued their education at Deep Springs thereafter, spoke about liaisons between "the town girls" and the students. Nunn generally proscribed behaviors he deemed unworthy of serious leaders. In his "Grant of Authority to the Olmsted Student Body" in 1909, he had written: "No member shall partake of intoxicating liquors, smoke cigarettes, gamble or play any games of cards." Early students also recall Nunn intervening in similar cases where Olmsted students became involved with young women in Provo.
56. J. E. Meehan, president of the Student Body at Claremont, to L.L. Nunn, May 8, 1917.
57. Nunn to Walcott, December 9, 1916.
58. *Inyo Register*, March 1, 1917; rpt. from the *Big Pine Citizen*, LJN Papers.
59. Harold Waldo, Dictated recollections, untitled typescript, Subgroup 23, Box 2, fd. 21, DSA, November 10, 1973, 10.
60. *Inyo Register*, March 1, 1917, LJN Papers.

61. For over a decade, William Bird continued to orchestrate the acquisition of water rights around the valley, and Harold Waldo picked up additional acreage for the college and for himself. For the price Nunn paid for these properties and his other expenses in launching Deep Springs College, see chapter 5.
62. *Inyo Register*, June 21, 1917, 1, LJN Papers.
63. Anticipating a community of two hundred may not have been an error introduced by the *Inyo Register*, inasmuch as Nunn had mentioned that number when contemplating purchase of a parcel of the King Ranch in Texas. Regarding the acreage, the 160 acres under cultivation in 1917 has remained rather constant over the last century.
64. Chet Dunn, who turned twenty that summer, remarked that Nunn trusted him completely with liquidating property worth $50,000. Chester Starr Dunn, "An Interview with Chester Starr Dunn," by Wm. L. Mills, February 13, 1975, Subgroup 23, Box 2, fd. 5, DSA.
65. L.L. Nunn to Chet Dunn, May 15, 1917.
66. Sweeting, "Education Experiment," 1031.

Chapter 4. A Fortuitous Place: Deep Springs Valley

1. In his *The Sage Brush Ocean: A Natural History of the Great Basin* (Reno: University of Nevada Press, 1989), 3–8, Stephen Trimble describes four ways to define this region.
2. John A. McPhee, *Basin and Range* (New York: Farrar, Straus and Giroux, 1980).
3. A playa is a dry lakebed, whereas a salina typically retains a vestigial lake. Deep Springs Lake is a salina.
4. S. N. Bacon et al., "Last Glacial Maximum and Holocene Lake Levels of Owens Lake, Eastern California, USA," *Quaternary Science Review* 25, nos. 11–12 (2006): 1264–82.
5. William J. Miller, "Geology of Deep Springs Valley, California," *The Journal of Geology* (1928): 510–25. See also Michael Gibson Delacorte, "The Prehistory of Deep Springs Valley, Eastern California: Adaptive Variation in the Western Great Basin," PhD diss., University of California, Davis, 1990; Jeffery Lee, Charles M. Rubin, and Andrew Calvert, "Quaternary Faulting History along the Deep Springs Fault, California," *GSA Bulletin* 113, no. 7 (July 2001): 855–69.
6. Delacorte, "Prehistory of Deep Springs Valley," 16–19. The National Weather Service reports annual weather patterns and events at Deep Springs.
7. Mary Austin, *Land of Little Rain* (New York: Dover Publications, 1903), 4.
8. For a description of the bristlecone pine's importance in carbon dating, see Xiahong Feng and Samuel Epstein, "Climatic Implications of an 8000-Year Hydrogen

Isotope Time Series from Bristlecone Pine Trees," *Science* 265 (August 19, 1994): 1079–81. This study concluded: "The climate of the White Mountains has been cooling since 6800 yrs B.P." Even so, the drop has probably not exceeded 5.5 degrees F. over this period. For temperatures, see Lisa Graumlich, "A 1000-Year Record of Temperature and Precipitation in the Sierra Nevada," *Quaternary Research* 39 (1993): 249–55. See also A. S. Jayko and S. N. Bacon, "Late Quaternary MIS 6-8 Shoreline Features of Pluvial Owens Lake, Owens Valley, Eastern California," in *Late Cenozoic Drainage History of the Southwestern Great Basin and Lower Colorado River Region: Geologic and Biotic Perspectives*, ed. M. C. Reheis, R. Hershler, and D. M. Miller (Special Paper #439, Geological Society of America, 2010), 185–206, which suggests that, based on research about the level of Owens Lake, precipitation in the Owens drainage has decreased for the past two thousand years.

9. D. A. Graybill and G. S. Funkhouser, "Dendroclimatic Reconstructions during the Past Millennium in the Southern Sierra Nevada and Owens Valley, California," In *Proceedings of the Southern California Climate Symposium: Trends and Extremes of the Past 2000 Years: Technical Report*, ed. M. R. Rose and P. E. Wigand (Los Angeles: Natural History Museum of Los Angeles County, 1999), 239–69. Graybill and Funkhouser found a repeating 300-year cycle for wetter and drier periods, "with lows near 1300, 1600, and 1900, followed by wetter than normal conditions" (258).
10. Average flow of Wyman at its mouth below the Crooked Creek confluence was 2.6 to 4.6 cubic feet per second for 1944–1948, then between 4.0 and 8.0 during the wet cycle in the mid-1980s. The general drought in the American Southwest during the first decade of the twenty-first century, however, saw Wyman stream flows in the 1.5 to 2.5 range. Bruce R. Laverty, email to Jack Newell, January 21, 2008.
11. Sources for this section include Robert L. Bettinger, "Aboriginal Occupation at High Altitude: Alpine Villages in the White Mountains of Eastern California," *American Anthropologist,* New Series 93, no. 3 (September 1991): 656–79; Robert L. Bettinger, "Prehistory of the Crooked Creek Area," in *The Crooked Creek Guidebook*, ed. Clarence A. Hall and Barbara Widawski (Bishop, CA: White Mountain Research Station, 1994), 123–32; and Delacorte, "The Prehistory of Deep Springs." Casual aboriginal passage through Deep Springs may date back to the earliest American Indians in the Eastern Sierras more than 10,000 years ago, but few artifacts bolster such a claim.
12. Sven Liljblad and Catherine S. Fowler, "Owens Valley Paiute," in *Handbook of North American Indians*, ed. Warren L. D'Azevedo (Washington, DC: Smithsonian Institution, 1986), 11:418.
13. J. Robert Macey and Theodore J. Papenfuss, "Amphibians," in *Natural History of*

the White-Inyo Range, ed. Clarence A. Hall Jr. (Berkeley: University of California Press, 1991), 283–84. The black toad has survived the threats of human activity and maintains a healthy though tightly compact population of eight to nine thousand around Corral Springs and Buckhorn Springs. See John F. Murphy, Eric T. Simandle, and Dawne E. Becker, "Population Status and Conservation of the Black Toad, *Bufo Exsul*," *Southwestern Naturalist* 48, no. 1 (March 2003): 54–60.

14. For an examination of the Owens Valley groups, see Sven Liljeblad and Catherine S. Fowler, "Owens Valley Paiute," and Isabell T. Kelly and Catherine Fowler, "Southern Paiute," in *Handbook of North American Indians*, 11:412–34 and 11:368–97, respectively.
15. *United States Indian Census, 1885–1940*, "Nevada Indian Tribes," www.accessgenealogy.com/native/nevada.
16. Julian H. Steward, "Ethnography of the Owens Valley Paiute," *University of California Publications in American Archeology and Ethnology* 33, no. 3 (1933): 233–350. For information on Steward's thesis and contributions, see Delacorte, *Prehistory of Deep Springs*, 2–8. Steward's interest in Paiute culture began when he attended Deep Springs College, 1918–1921. He went on to become a leading authority on American Indian languages and culture. See Virginia Kerns's *Scenes from the High Desert: Julian Steward's Life and Theory* (Urbana: University of Illinois Press, 2003).
17. Bettinger, "Prehistory of the Crooked Creek Area," 126–27. See also Marcia Tate, *The Atlatl Story: An Ice Age Hunting Weapon* (Aurora, CO: Tate Enterprises, 1986).
18. Delacorte, "Prehistory of Deep Springs," 60–64. The transient nature of these camps is evident because of the paucity of obsidian chips that littered the ground around long-used dwellings.
19. R. M. Lanner and H. Lanner, *The Pinyon Pine: A Natural and Cultural History* (Reno: University of Nevada Press, 1981). Also see Bettinger, "Aboriginal Occupation at High Altitude," 656–79.
20. Steward, "Ethnography of the Owens Valley Paiute," Map 2. Steward also found Paiute campsites on Bitterbrush Flat and in Dead Horse Meadow—all within a few miles of the college.
21. Delacorte, "Prehistory of Deep Springs," 79–93, described Deep Springs Paiutes' dwellings.
22. Ibid., 64–67.
23. Paul Reeve, Professor, Department of History, University of Utah, email to L. Jackson Newell, April 15, 2008.
24. For a useful summary of early Euroamerican explorations and occupation, see Jeff

Putnam and Genny Smith, eds., *The Deepest Valley: A Guide to Owens Valley*, 2d ed. (Mammoth Lakes, CA: Genny Smith Books, 1995), 238–45. See also W. A. Chalfant, *The Story of Inyo*, rev. ed. (Bishop, CA: Community Printing and Publishing, 1975), 93–146.

25. Winona Johnson Holloway, *Moving Out: A Sequel to Moving On* (Live Oak, CA: Shadow Butte Press, 1992), 281–84.
26. Putnam and Smith, *The Deepest Valley*, 238–41.
27. The White Mountain voting scam is described in Chalfant, *Story of Inyo*, 143–45.
28. "Letter from the White Mountains," *Alta California*, May 3, 1864 (date of publication). Composed April 15, 1864, "From an Occasional Correspondent, Roachville, Mono County Cal. White Mountain District. LJN Papers.
29. *Inyo Independent*, July 5, 1884.
30. Dorothy Clora Cragen, *The Boys in Sky-Blue Pants: The Men and Events at Camp Independence and Forts of Eastern California, Nevada and Utah, 1862–1877* (Fresno, CA: Pioneer Publishing, 1975), 55–62.
31. The cave is in a direct line with the fence that runs west across the valley. Holloway, *Moving Out*, 134–35.
32. George M. Wheeler, *Preliminary Report Concerning Exploration and Surveys Principally in Nevada and Arizona. Prosecuted in Accordance with Paragraph 2, Special Orders No. 109, War Department, March 18, 1871, and Letter of Instructions of March 23, 1871, from Brigadier General A. A. Humphreys Chief of Engineers, Conducted under the Immediate Direction of 1st Lieut. George M. Wheeler, Corps of Engineers, 1871* (Washington, DC: Government Printing Office, 1872), 49–50 (hereafter cited as Wheeler, *Preliminary Report*). Its Appendix B is "Report of Second Lieutenant D. A. Lyle, Second United States Artillery, March 5, 1872."
33. Variations of the story of the attack on the miners are found in Cragen, *The Boys in the Sky-Blue Pants*, 72–73. See also Chalfant, *Story of Inyo*, 227–28, and Friends of the Eastern California Museum, comp., *Mountains to Desert: Selected Inyo Readings* (Independence, CA: n.pub., 1988), 56–58.
34. Pre-Empt Claims, Volume B, 25, Records of Mono County, CA, February 19, 1869, Courthouse in Bridgeport, CA.
35. Wheeler, *Preliminary Report*, Appendix B, 79.
36. Ibid., 80.
37. Ibid.
38. The other five mines were the San Juan, Julia Dean, San Francisco, Tenant, and Homestead. Lyle did not record their locations.
39. Lyle reported the owner as J. [Jonathan] W. McMurry, Samuel's son. Jonathan was only eleven years old at the time.

40. Wheeler, *Preliminary Report*, Appendix B, 49–50.
41. Ibid., 80.
42. *Inyo Register*, May 23, 1968. Information about the orchard came from an undated map of a proposed picnic area and park at the site. Folder: "County Commissioners," Eastern California Museum, Independence, CA.
43. "Historic Earthquakes: Owens Valley, California, 1872 03 26 UTC Magnitude 7.4." U.S. Geological Survey, http://earthquake.usgs.gov/earthquakes/states/events/1872-03_26.php.
44. "Earthquake along the Eastern Sierra," *Inyo Independent*, Saturday, April 6, 1872.
45. U.S. to Nathan Gilbert. TS 7 Sec. 1: Lot #4 in NW quarter of Sec. 1; 36 and 89/100 acre plot. Inyo County Records, Books of Deeds W, p. 179, Abst. 53, 1872. This ground is within fields 1 and 2 of the modern Deep Springs Ranch.
46. Documenting pre-1886 mines and claims around Deep Springs is a challenge. Some records were destroyed in the 1872 earthquake, while others burned in an 1886 fire at the Inyo County Courthouse. Newspaper articles and family history sources are the only mention of a number of these mines, but their locations often remain a mystery. The information about the Sullivan land transactions are courtesy of local historian David Wright, Great Basin Research, of Big Pine, California.
47. Land, Water, and Mining Claims, Deeds Book, 1873, 58, Inyo County Records.
48. Mount Diablo Meridian, Township No. 6 South, Range No. 36 East, May 12, 1885, Survey General's Office, San Francisco.
49. Julian H. Steward, *Basin-Plateau Aboriginal Sociopolitical Groups* (Washington, DC: U.S. Government Printing Office, 1938), 58–59. The census records did not give the names of Paiute women and children, nor did they list Paiute men unless they were employed by whites.
50. Ibid., 59–61.
51. *Inyo Independent*, May 20, 1876. Washington Mathews became an expert on native plants. He collected plants from the Eastern Sierra and sent them to Asa Gray at the Harvard Herbarium. Gray named two of the plants found in the Owens and Deep Springs Valleys for Mathews: Bushy Bedstraw, *Galium Mathewsii* (Rubiaceae) and Desert Calico, *Loeseliastrum Mathewsii.* Mathews also became known internationally for his interest in American Indian ethnography for which he was recognized internationally. Larry Blakely, "Who's in a Name: People Commemorated in Eastern Sierra Plant Names," *Newsletter of the Bristlecone Chapter, CNPS* 19, no. 5 (September 1999).
52. Chalfant, *Story of Inyo*, 218–19.
53. Bowers filed on April 1, 1878. Land, Water, and Mining Claims, Book C, 316, Inyo County Records.

54. Richard E. Lingenfelter, *Death Valley and the Amargosa: A Land of Illusion* (Berkeley: University of California Press, 1986), 107–8.
55. Bowers and his unnamed wife and daughter are also recorded in the Big Pine census with the same information. His grandchildren were listed "boy" and "Baby."
56. *Inyo Independent*, July 15, 1884.
57. California Highway 168 descends from the top of Westgard Pass down Payson Canyon and enters Deep Springs Valley at its southwest corner. A few hundred yards to the north, travelers can see the trees that mark Antelope Springs where Lewis Payson lived.
58. Deep Springs Mining District, Book 6, p. 50, Inyo County Records.
59. Misha Hoekstra, email to Denis Clark, L. Jackson Newell, et al., January 3, 2010, in my possession. I am indebted to Misha Hoekstra for his help in sorting out the Payson family history and many of the land issues in the valley.
60. Land, Water, and Mining Claims, Book C, 1880, 15, 46, 58, 85–87, 102.
61. Ibid., Book C, 58. Chastain's name appeared as "Chastine" in the 1880 Census.
62. Bonds, Book A, 1880, 162, Inyo County Records.
63. Ibid., Book P, 595.
64. For sale to J. D. Hudgin, 1880, see Book of Deeds, Vol. A, p. 153, Inyo County Records. For U.S. Government land deeded to Nathan Gilbert, see Book of Deeds, Vol. W, pp. 29, 179; Vol. Z, p. 28. Gilbert bought 80 acres in 1890, 37 acres in 1892, and another 160 acres in 1896.
65. *Inyo Independent*, June 21 and July 19, 1884.
66. SPR [Samuel P. Roberts], *Inyo Independent*, February 2, 1884.
67. *Inyo Independent*, November 29, 1884.
68. Ibid.
69. Mortgages, Vol. D, 353, Inyo County Records. The equivalent monetary value today would be over $150,000.
70. *Inyo Independent*, February 2, 1884.
71. *Inyo Independent*, February 9, 1884. The "excursion" to Deep Springs, if it was that, must have taken place the previous fall before winter snows fell, making a return trip across the White Mountains impossible.
72. Walcott's 1896 expedition resulted in the scientific paper: "The Post-Pleistocene Elevation of the Inyo Range and the Lake Beds of Waucobi Embayment, Inyo County, California," *The Journal of Geology* 5, no. 4 (May–June 1897): 340–48.
73. Deeds, Vol. 11, p. 322, 326; Vol. 17, p. 85, 4, Inyo County Records. Also see *Inyo Register*, June 1, 1905, "It is reported that Nathan Gilbert has sold his well known Deep Springs Valley Ranch, water right and other properties to Broughton Bros. of Los Angeles and Lida. This receives confirmation from a real estate transfer

mentioned in the *Independent* last week, Amos W. Broughton having received a deed from Mr. Gilbert for the Boomerang mine, Deep Springs; consideration $15,000." This sum included both the ranch and mine. *Inyo Register*, December 17, 1908.

74. For Gilbert's repossession of this property see Deeds, Vol. 14, p. 432 (Abstract, p. 58). For the 1906 sale see Deeds, Vol. 6, p. 282 (Abstract, p. 50), Inyo County Records.
75. *Inyo Independent*, January 25, 1907; *Inyo Register*, January 24, 1907.
76. *Inyo Register*, December 17, 1908. Some documents misspell his name "Steward."
77. Deeds, Vol. 16, p. 85, Inyo County Records.
78. Misha Hoekstra, email to Jack Newell, January 3, 2010.
79. My conversation with Stan Lloyd, retired Southern California Edison engineer, May 12, 2011. LJN Papers.
80. Deeds, Book/Vol. 12, p. 294, Inyo County Records. Roberts was still working the Index Hill Mine in 1909.
81. *Inyo Register*, March 1, 1917.
82. From Inyo County Records and other sources, Linda K. Newell compiled an impressive list of transactions dealing with land, water, and mining claims in and around Deep Springs Valley. LJN Papers.
83. "Inyo County Toll Roads, 1871–1921," File in Eastern California Museum, Independence, CA. For the stagecoach announcement, see *Inyo Register*, July 22, 1905.
84. "Inyo County Toll Roads, 1871–1921," 69.
85. Robert B. McCoy and John T. Strachan, *Midland Trail Tour Guide, 1916* (Glorieta, NM: Rio Grande Press, 1916), 94. See also "Information on the So-Called Westgaard Pass [*sic*] Road, Known in Very Early Days as The Deep Springs Valley Toll Road," Pamphlet, Eastern California Museum, Independence, CA. Vandals set fire to the toll house and burned it to the ground in the spring of 1964. Toll information appears on the historic tollhouse sign now at the Eastern California Museum.
86. The Deep Springs potash works and company settlement are shown in 1922 photographs, U.S. Geological Survey, /htmllib/btch537/batch537j/btch537z/mgr00608.jpg.
87. Deep Springs College Photo Archive. The battered two-foot-square print is rolled up and in poor condition.
88. *Inyo Register*, July 22, 1905.

Chapter 5. Dawn at Deep Springs, 1917–1925

1. These questions and several others were listed on a single sheet of paper filed with Nunn, Letter to Herbert Reich, confirming his acceptance, September 15, 1917.

Reich Family Papers, a private collection; used by permission.

2. Though rumored earlier, President Jacob Gould Schurman did not request the wartime use of Telluride House until September 1918.
3. Herbert Reich to his father, Jacques Reich, September 30, 1918.
4. Walter Welti, interviewed by Brad Edmondson, July 5, 1983.
5. When the buildings were rebuilt and seismically refitted in the late 1990s, construction superintendent Lee Powell discovered that each structure was uniquely engineered, reflecting the absence of architectural drawings and, as a result, revealing the particular methods and skills of each building's crew.
6. When he completed this work, Kropf moved to Death Valley to supervise construction of Scotty's Castle for Nunn's long-time associate, Albert M. Johnson. See Kropf's biographical sketch in *Death Valley Ranch (Scotty's Castle)*, in *Historical American Building Survey*, No. GA-2257 (Washington, DC: National Park Service, Department of the Interior, Archives, Scotty's Castle, Death Valley National Park), 43.
7. Nunn expressed this sentiment with reference to Telluride Association membership in an undated letter to David Wegg at Telluride House, probably in May 1911, quoted in Orville Sweeting, "The Education Experiment of L.L. Nunn," 839.
8. Deep Springs Student Body Minutes, November 25, 1917, DSA.
9. In 1918, the group changed the title of its presiding officer to "president."
10. Ed Meehan to Dean E. A. Thornhill, December 5, 1917.
11. This company town is pictured in a U.S. Geological Survey photograph taken in 1922, /htmllib/btch537btch537j/btch537z/mgr00608.jpg. In 1921, the California Alkali Company sold its Deep Springs operation. Fletcher Hamilton (State Mineralogist), *Report XVII of the State Mineralogist: Mining in California during 1920* (San Francisco: California State Printing Office, for California State Mining Bureau, January 1921), 296, reports: "Inyo Chemical Company, Detroit, Michigan. Planning to install a plant at Deep Springs Valley Lake for extraction of soda and potash from the lake brines. Ten men employed for construction and in hauling material and supplies for [the] plant." Charles Trimble, is listed as superintendent with a home office in Big Pine, California. The abandoned Hippodrome [horse racing arena] in Goldfield was torn down to provide materials for the operation at the lake.
12. In 1997, Misha Hoekstra, then dean of the college, and I read a file of documents bearing on Nunn's effort to use legal means to drive the potash works from the valley. During the reconstruction of the Main Building a year or two later, this file was lost and has not resurfaced.
13. Harold Waldo, Dictated recollections, November 10, 1973.

14. Ibid., 8.
15. This generator model produced direct current rather than alternating current.
16. Henry Hayes, Oral History, interviewed by Christopher Breiseth, September 1979, 2–3.
17. Ibid., 15.
18. Ibid.
19. A water treatment and filtration system was not added until 1938.
20. James S. Holmes to L.L. Nunn, February 1, 1922. LJN Papers.
21. A decade later, to produce latex for his automobile empire, Henry Ford established a utopian agricultural community in the Amazon basin, with similarities to Deep Springs. See Greg Grandin, *Fordlandia: The Rise and Fall of Henry Ford's Forgotten Jungle City* (New York: Metropolitan Books/ Henry Holt and Company, 2009).
22. Telluride Association considered investing in a start-up company that manufactured tractors in 1916, but decided against the venture as too risky. Deep Springs used teams of draft horses well into the 1930s and gave them up only after a fight.
23. Hayes, Oral History, September 1979, 7–8. Jim Mansfield participated in this conversation, and the two played their memories off each other.
24. Ibid.
25. Ibid.
26. Herbert Reich's "Legends," Subgroup 23, Box 2, fd. 2, DSA, October 5, 1919, 3.
27. One alumnus remembered this man as "Professor Burgin," but it was probably Paul Cadman, who became a charter trustee.
28. Reich, "Legends," January 16, 1918.
29. Ibid., October 5, 1919.
30. Ernest Thornhill, "Classes, 1920," holograph, LJN Papers.
31. Ernest Thornhill, Academic Report to L.L. Nunn, February 27, 1918; see also *Telluride Association Newsletter*, n.d. but autumn 1924 from internal evidence, 6–7.
32. George C. Lyon, "Legends of Deep Springs," Record Group 3, Subgroup 23, Box 2, 1–2, DSA.
33. Professor Ralph Tyler Flewelling (1871–1960) was already a scholar of renown, having published four of his best-known books: *Christ and the Dramas of Doubt* (1913), *Personalism and the Problems of Philosophy* (1915), *Philosophy and the War* (1918), and *Bergson and Personal Realism* (1919). Professor Frank J. Klinberg (1883–1968) was well into his career and had recently returned to what would become UCLA after a year of lecturing at The League to Enforce Peace. He was best known for his work on British humanitarianism and the antislavery movement there.
34. Herbert Reich, "Journal," Photocopy in LJN Papers, courtesy of Herbert Reich, February 8, 1918.

35. L.L. Nunn to Deep Spring Student Body, September 26, 1919, in Sweeting, "Education Experiment," 1058.
36. Reich "Legends," 2.
37. DSSB Minutes, December 18, 1918.
38. Reich, "Legends," 3.
39. Cabot Coville, Interviewed by Bradley Edmondson, April 25, 1985, 458–59, DSA.
40. Ibid.
41. See two oral histories: Harvey Mansfield, Interviewed by Christopher Breiseth, September 14, 1981, 56, DSA; and Herbert Reich, Interviewed by Christopher Breiseth, April 28, 1982, 98, DSA.
42. Henry G. Hayes, "Autobiography of Henry G. Hayes," 44, n.d., typescript; copy in LJN Papers.
43. L.L. Nunn to student body, April 5, 1921. The student dormitory was later built on the tennis court.
44. Reich, Journal, March 13, 1920: "A new gold vein has been discovered in Goldfield, Nev."
45. See Virginia Kerns's prize-winning biography, *Scenes from the High Desert: Julian Steward's Life and Theory*.
46. Ibid., 53. Also of interest is Hervey H. Voge, ed., *The Climber's Guide to the High Sierra: A Sierra Club Totebook* (N.p.: Sierra Club, 1954): "The Thumb" (elev. 13,885) has sometimes been called East Palisade. The first ascent was made December 12, 1921, by W. B. Putnam, 271. Another entry of interest under "Mount Winchell" (13,749) reads: "The first ascent was made June 10, 1923, by H. C. Mansfield, J. M. Newell, and W. B. Putnam by Route 1." These peaks are both visible from Deep Springs.
47. Letter to John W. Aird, August 19, 1921.
48. Polly Aird, Interviewed by telephone by L. Jackson Newell, December 11, 2010. She, too, is a historian. See also Robert B. Aird, *Eighty Odd Years on Borrowed Time: My Academic & Professional Career* (San Francisco: Self-published, 1989), 10, 23–24.
49. Aird, Letter to Brad Edmundson, August 16, 1987, in ADSTA, DSA; Dunn, "An Interview with Chester Starr Dunn"; Reich, Oral History.
50. Carlyle Ashley, Oral History, conducted by Christopher Breiseth, March 18, 1982, in ADSTA, DSA, 80.
51. Ibid., 80–81.
52. L.L. Nunn to Wallace Cook, September 17 and December 20, 1920, L.L. Nunn Correspondence with Wallace Cook, DS 21, LJN Papers.
53. Nunn to Cook, September 3, 1921.

54. Nunn to Cook, dated "Pasadena Xmas 1921."
55. Wallace Cook later married and reared a family. His son, Chandler, attended Deep Springs in the 1950s and later gave his father's correspondence with Nunn to me for archival deposit.
56. Nunn to John W. Aird, August 19, 1921, Photocopy in LJN Papers, 2.
57. Nunn to L.G. Nightingale, June 15, 1918. Nunn letters, LJN Papers.
58. Ross, Oral History, 18.
59. Chet Dunn, Herb Reich, and Robert Aird, Joint Oral History, interviewed by Chris Breiseth, May 1, 1982, in ASTRA, DSA, 128.
60. Robert Aird, Letter to Brad Edmondson, 140.
61. Ibid., 141. The elected position of labor commissioner would later become the most sought-after student body office.
62. L.L. Nunn to Jim Holmes, February 22, 1919, Subgroup 15, Box 1, fd. 3, DSA.
63. Ibid.
64. Ibid.

Chapter 6. The Voice of the Desert

1. Martin Robert Sachse, "Personal History," n.d., Unbound manuscript, DSA; photocopy in LJN Papers, Box 12, fd. 1,34.
2. Ibid.
3. Ibid.
4. Martin Sachse, Letters to Kate Park, January 5, 1924, to July 21, 1924. Their daughter, Heide Sachse Moore, donated these courtship letters to the Deep Springs Archives in 2000.
5. Sachse to Park, June 8, 1924.
6. Sachse to Park, January 5 and 22, 1924.
7. Sachse to Park, February 3, 1924.
8. Sachse to Park, March 2, 1924.
9. Sachse to Park, June 22, 1924.
10. Virginia Thornhill Northrup, Interviewed by Brad Edmondson, December 3, 1982, ADSTA, #224, DSA, 198.
11. Lee G. Davy, Interviewed by Brad Edmondson, January 6, 1983, in ADSTA, DSA, 240.
12. Sachse mailed his log to Kate Park on April 16, 1924. LJN Papers, Box 12, fd. 1.
13. Sachse to Park, April 23, 1924. The plans for the distinctively modern "Desert Cottage, Mr. Sachse, Deep Springs" can be viewed online at "Frank Lloyd Wright, Designs for an American Landscape, 1922–32." These drawings were exhibited at the Library of Congress in 1997 and are part of the permanent collection, Frank Lloyd Wright Foundation, Scottsdale, Arizona.

14. Sasche, Log of Death Valley trip to Park.
15. Ibid.
16. Ibid.
17. This structure housed the Sachses and subsequent college mechanics for decades. It was later assigned to student cowboys, becoming known as the Cowboy House.
18. Sachse, "Personal History," 38.
19. Ibid.
20. L.L. Nunn to Paul Ashworth, June 2, 1914, Accession 7, Box 3, fd. 5, DSA.
21. Reich, Oral History, 100.
22. Herbert J. Reich to Mr. Nunn, April 1, 1919.
23. Nunn to "Gentlemen," April 1, 1919.
24. Nunn to "Gentlemen," March 23, 1920, Constitution of Deep Springs and The Deed of Trust (Gray Book), 6–7.
25. L.L. Nunn to Deep Springs Student Body, March 26, 1920; ibid., 7–8.
26. Student Body to Mr. L.L. Nunn, April 3, 1920; ibid., 9.
27. L.L. Nunn, untitled notes, single page, n.d. but spring 1919.
28. L.L. Nunn to Student Body, September 26, 1919, in Orville Sweeting, "Education Experiment," 1058.
29. Nunn to Simon Whitney, Secretary, January 24, 1921, Nunn Papers; photocopy in LJN Papers.
30. L.L. Nunn to the Student Body of Deep Springs, April 5, 1921.
31. Ibid., 2–3.
32. Ibid.
33. Student Body Minutes, April 6, 1921.
34. Sachse to Park, February 16, 1924. A Victrola was a popular hand-cranked record player for music.
35. Ashley, Oral History, 80.
36. Ibid.
37. Robert Gatje to Newell, February 18, 2012, LJN Papers.
38. Nunn to Lionel C. Nightingale, April 28, 1919, in Sweeting, "Education Experiment," 1408–9.
39. Heide Moore, Letter from Chuck and Bea [surname not given], October 17, 1997, Sachse correspondence, LJN Papers.
40. Mansfield, Oral History, September 14, 1981, 11.

Chapter 7. In Perpetuity?

"To the Trustees, in 1924," in "Jurisdiction a fourteen-page selection of passages from L.L. Nunn's last letters compiled by Wallace Cook (DS'20) and mailed from

Nunn's home to the Trustees of Deep Springs on October 28, 1924.

1. P.N. Nunn to A. M. Marquis c/o *Who's Who in America*, April 17, 1922, quoted in Sweeting, "Education Experiment," 14.
2. L.L. Nunn, Biographical sketch, April 17, 1922, quoted in ibid., 15.
3. Thomas Ewing Sherman, quoted in Bailey, *L.L. Nunn: A Memoir*, 24–25.
4. Quoted in ibid., 32.
5. L.L. Nunn to Fellow Members [Telluride Associates], June 15, 1923, in Sweeting, "Education Experiment," 1293.
6. L.L. Nunn to Fellow Members, March 24, 1915, in Sweeting, "Education Experiment," 910–17.
7. "Deep Springs," *Telluride Newsletter*, 1924, 6.
8. L.L. Nunn to Charles Walcott, June 15, 1918, in Sweeting, "Education Experiment," 1044–45.
9. Harold Waldo, "Transcript of Remarks made by H.R. Waldo at Deep Springs College on November 10, 1973," Subgroup 23, Box 2, fd. 21, DSA, 6.
10. Ibid.
11. Ashley, Oral History, 173.
12. This assessment of Harold Waldo and his place among the original trustees has been voiced by scores of early students and observers, including Eunice Whitney, the wife of Simon Whitney, early alumnus and later Deep Springs director. Eunice Whitney, interviewed by telephone by L. Jackson Newell, November 26, 2011, transcript in LJN Papers. As a student in the late 1950s, I also knew Waldo, then an elderly but still astute trustee.
13. Deep Springs Trustees Minutes, Informal Meeting, May 15, 1923.
14. Davy, Oral History, 457. Before or during this process, Nunn was persuaded to excise his original intent to have the Deed of Trust converted to a corporate structure after ten years. It appears likely that his trustees-in-waiting talked him out of this provision, which effectively granted them lifetime service as trustees.
15. Deep Springs Trustees Minutes, June 25, 1923. Nunn's letter to Waldo was dated June 22, 1923, and was written at Jamieson Apartments, 915 So. Carondelet St., Los Angeles.
16. Ibid.
17. L.L. Nunn to Trustees of Deep Springs, September 22, 1923, in Deep Springs Trustees Minutes.
18. The number of students Nunn planned oscillated between eighteen and thirty. He never explained why he specified one number or another, but the norm during his lifetime was close to twenty.
19. Deep Springs Trustees Minutes, June 25, 1923.

20. *The Constitution of Deep Springs & The Deed of Trust*, published in 1975, is commonly known as *The Gray Book*. This essay appears on pp. 41–42. Nunn was now increasingly emphasizing (and exaggerating) the length of his educational experimentation.
21. Ibid., 42.
22. Sweeting, "Education Experiment," 728; see also 1408–9.
23. Denis E. Clark to L. Jackson Newell, February 20, 2012, LJN Papers.
24. The career reminiscences of Morse Adam Cartwright, 1890–1974, were recorded in 1967 by the Columbia Center for Oral History. He is perhaps best known for his *Adult Education in the United States of America* (1929).
25. The Deed of Trust of Lucien L. Nunn, Gray Book, 28–33.
26. Deed of Trust, Section 1.
27. Ibid., Section 2.
28. Ibid., Section 5. Emphasis mine.
29. Ibid.
30. "L.L. Nunn to SB [Student Body], October 18, 1920, in "Jurisdiction," in *The Gray Book*.
31. Father Thomas Ewing Sherman, quoted in Bailey, *L.L. Nunn*, 25.
32. Henry G. Hayes, quoted in "Recollections of Mr. Nunn and Early Deep Springs," ca. 1986.
33. Virginia Thornton Northrup, Interviewed by Bradley Edmondson, December 3, 1982, p. 185.
34. "Excerpt from RBA Travel Compendium," ca. 1921, Subgroup 23, Box 2, fd. 2, DSA.
35. L.L. Nunn to Lionel Nightingale, April 30, 1919, in Sweeting, "Education Experiment," 1411.
36. L.L. Nunn to Deep Springs Student Body, January 22, 1925, in ibid., 1278.
37. Telluride Association Convention Minutes, originals in the Telluride Association office in Ithaca, NY, copies in LJN Papers.
38. Budget figures assembled by Matt Mandelkern and Terrell Carter from Deep Springs Trustees Minutes, Box 1, fd. 1. Report in Newell Collection.
39. A description of this mailing appears in Sweeting, "Education Experiment," 1262.
40. Nunn had bought those holdings in the name of the association. Telluride Association Convention Minutes, Manager's and Treasure's Report, June 2, 1925. A half-million dollar figure is cited in Telluride Association Minutes, Financial Committee Report, June 20, 1941.
41. Brian Kennedy, email exchange with Jack Newell, March 13, 2012, provided insights about Telluride's view of this conflict at the time.

42. L.L. Nunn to Lionel Nightingale, April 28, 1919, in Sweeting, "Education Experiment," 1408–9.
43. Carroll Whitman, "The Convention," *Telluride Newsletter*, June 1, 1920, 2. Note: Telluride varied from time to time between the title "Newletter" and "News Letter." I have used the term its editor did, issue by issue.
44. Telluride's gifts of $10,000 a year declined significantly as a proportion of Deep Springs' annual budget after the Depression, resulting from inflation and the rising costs of running the college. Brian Kennedy estimated that half of Telluride's members had come through Deep Springs.
45. "The Purpose" appears in *The Gray Book*, 37–40.
46. Ralph Waldo Emerson's 1837 essay, "The American Scholar," seems to have been on Nunn's mind toward the end. This thought echoed Emerson's concern that members of society "have suffered amputation from the trunk, and strut about so many walking monsters—a good finger, a neck, a stomach, an elbow, but never a man" (84).
47. Charles D. Walcott, quoted in Bailey, *L.L. Nunn*, 116.
48. "To the Trustees," in "Jurisdiction," 12. Among other exposures to Eastern thought, Nunn had studied the ideas and practices of Rabindranath Tagore, whose progressive school in India he greatly admired.
49. "To the Dean at Deep Springs," in ibid., 10; L.L. Nunn to Ray W. Fruit, December 26, 1916. Here again, Nunn echoed Emerson's thought: "Character is above intellect. . . . A great soul will be strong to live, as well as strong to think." Emerson, *American Scholar*, 94.
50. Frank Noon, quoted in Bailey, *L.L. Nunn*, 76.
51. Chester Dunn, among others, claimed late in his life that he was in the room when Nunn died.

Chapter 8. Nunn's Tempestuous Wake, 1925–1926

1. Deep Springs Student Body Minutes, April 2, 1925, 44.
2. A medical examination by Dr. Arthur Stanley Granger at St. Vincent's Hospital, Los Angeles, on November 12, 1919, found almost no viability in the left lung. Sweeting, "Education Experiment," 1147.
3. See exchange of letters among Nunn's siblings Fred, Emily, and Ellen in chapter 2.
4. "Nunn, Long Ill, Dies at Home Here: Attorney and Mining Man Native of Ohio: Pioneer in Hydroelectric Work," *Los Angeles Times*, April 3, 1925.
5. "L.L. Nunn Former Salt Lake Business Man Dies on Coast," *Deseret News*, April 3, 1925.
6. "Benefactor Closes Long Useful Life," *Provo Herald*, April 3, 1925.

7. "Hydro-Electric Power Pioneer Dead on Coast," *Telluride Journal*, April 9, 1925.
8. Telluride Association, Death Announcement. Copy in LJN Papers, courtesy of Polly Aird from her father's papers.
9. W. L. Biersach to Harvard Alumni Directory, September 28, 1925, LJN Papers.
10. Charles D. Walcott, memorandum to E. M. Johnson, November 5, 1926, published as "Charles D. Walcott's Tribute to L.L. Nunn" in the *Telluride Newsletter*, January 1929, 3.
11. See chapter 2. I examined and photographed these and other of Nunn's personal effects at the Kroch Library.
12. William Biersach, "Return for Federal Estate Tax for the Estate of Lucien L. Nunn," Schedule E, p. 10, submitted March 27, 1926.
13. In current dollars, these $15,000 bequests had the buying power of nearly $200,000, a $10,000 bequest about $135,000, and so on.
14. Biersach, "Return for Federal Estate Tax." The $750,000 for Telluride may be approximated by combining gifts of $448,000 and $150,000 and adding the $113,000 (possibly $121,000) that Nunn spent to build the Telluride House on West Avenue plus its early operating expenses. See also Sweeting, "Education Experiment," 1061.
15. Telluride's Natrona proceeds of over $550,000 did not represent new money from Nunn, but his timely intervention converted this huge illiquid asset into cash. See chap. 7. As a member of Telluride and its fiscal agent, Nunn alone had the power and the finesse to arrange the sale and secure effective control of the resources for the association. It was his last major task in positioning his two educational institutions for the long haul.
16. The figures cannot be added sensibly because they are investment values at different times. Thus, what Nunn *gave* to Telluride and Deep Springs over a period of fourteen years cannot be added together to show assets that either institution possessed at his passing. Both had been accruing interest and dividends on his gifts, and paying operating expenses from these assets. Further, the gifts Nunn gave to the two institutions were received at different points across their short histories.
17. "The Biography of Mr. Nunn," *Telluride Association Newsletter*, April 1927.
18. Telluride Association Convention Minutes, June 1925.
19. Elmer M. "Johnny" Johnson, ibid.
20. Ibid.
21. Ibid.
22. Stephen A. Bailey's *L.L. Nunn: A Memoir* was published by Telluride Association in 1933 and republished in 1993 with McDermott's Prologue. The quotation is from Bailey's Prologue, xiv.

23. J. Walter Kean to Elmer Johnson, December 3, 1925, quoted in ibid., xv.
24. See Ford, "A Brief History of Homosexuality in America"; American Psychological Association, "Sexual Orientation and Homosexuality."
25. Ibid.
26. See especially chapter 2 for the exchange of letters among his siblings in 1882.
27. New L.L. Nunn holographs that bear on this matter continue to pop up. In September 2009, Chandler Cook gave me two dozen intimate letters from Nunn to his father, Wallace Cook, written from 1920 through 1924. These documents are in the Nunn Papers, Cornell University Library; copies in DSA and LJN Papers.

Chapter 9. The Sway of Affairs, 1925–1940

1. P.N. Nunn delivered his address, titled "Reminiscences of Early Electrical Development," at the Newhouse Hotel in Salt Lake City on February 15, 1927.
2. See Newell, Reynolds, and Marsh, eds., *Maverick Colleges.*
3. Sweeting, "Education Experiment," 1443.
4. P.N. may have been encouraged partly because he was chosen almost immediately to succeed his brother as president of the reorganized Telluride Power Company, later Utah Power and Light.
5. Sweeting, "Education Experiment," 1449.
6. L.L. Nunn, Letter to Mr. Suhr, May 21, 1924, Aird Papers, Box 4, fd. 1, DSA. A paragraph from this letter appears with three other Nunn quotations on a page prepared sometime later by Carroll Whitman.
7. Two of Waldo's sons did matriculate at Deep Springs in the early 1930s, providing him some financial benefit. When his third son applied, however, the student body opposed his application on the grounds of nepotism. He went elsewhere.
8. James R. (Jim) Withrow Jr., Oral History, interviewed by Christopher N. Breiseth, October 1983, in ADSTA, 447.
9. Ibid., 443.
10. Students titled the college literary magazine *The Bonepile* in 1991. Published sporadically, it reached volume 11 in 2014.
11. Ned Bedell, "Notes from Deep Springs," *Telluride Association Newsletter*, April 1939, 5.
12. L.L. Nunn had purchased the silos, one of which was later removed.
13. Thomas E. Fairchild to Dad, October 25, 1929, in Susan Fairchild Chase, transcriber, *Thomas E. Fairchild Letters, 1929–31,* released in digital format on March 22, 2008, e-copy in LJN Papers. All Fairchild letters in this chapter are from this collection and are cited by author, addressee, and date.
14. Email to author from C. N. Breiseth, April 25, 2012, LJN Papers.

15. Johnson's multifaceted support of Deep Springs constituted an important part of Telluride Association's role in Deep Springs' development.
16. Fairchild to Mother, April 14, 1930.
17. The board passed an antinepotism resolution later that spring. Trustees of Deep Springs Minutes, May 18, 1928 (hereafter TDS Minutes).
18. Ibid.
19. Fairchild to Mother, February 14, 1930.
20. Sweeting, "Education Experiment," 1469.
21. W. D. Kumler to Trustees of Deep Springs, May 16, 1930, TDS Minutes, DSA.
22. W. L. Biersach to Gentlemen, January 1, 1932, TDS Correspondence, DSA. The $40,000 figure for income in 1932 would be worth nearly $700,000 today, with the next year's projection pegged about $350,000.
23. W. L. Biersach to Elmer M. Johnson, January 11, 1932, TDS Correspondence.
24. These and other income and expense figure were taken from "Trustees of Deep Springs Estimated Income, Sept. 1, 1933, to Aug. 31, 1934," Trustees of Deep Springs Minutes, May 11, 1934. Deciphering actual expenses during this era is complicated because the cost of the "General Office" for managing remaining Nunnian business enterprises in Utah (which included a salary for William Biersach and his staff) was included in the Deep Springs budget. The figures cited here exclude $8,500 and $7,400, respectively, for the General Office for the two years.
25. TDS Minutes, March 19–20, 1932.
26. Student Body Minutes, September 14, 1931.
27. Ibid., December 12, 1931.
28. Jim Haughey, Interviewed by L. Jackson Newell, July 22, 2002.
29. Ibid.
30. An attorney and accomplished artist who lived in Billings, Montana, Haughey did not reconnect with Deep Springs until 2002, when he returned at my invitation. Saluting the college for its positive influence on his life, he became an enthusiastic supporter and gave it some of his award-winning paintings. I ceremoniously turned P.N. Nunn's portrait face to the wall when Haughey entered the Main Room, a gesture that amused him greatly.
31. John S. deBeers, Interviewed by Bradley Edmondson, June 22, 2005, E-copy in LJN Papers, 6.
32. Helen M. Heckman, Conversations with L. Jackson Newell, November 24, 2009, and November 29, 2010, notes in author's collection, and letter from Helen Heckman to the author, April 26, 2012.
33. Ibid.
34. P.N. Nunn, "What's the Matter with Deep Springs?" in Trustees of Deep Springs,

Minutes June 21, 1929.

35. Ibid., 1.
36. Ibid.
37. P.N. Nunn to Harold Waldo, October 28, 1932, attachment to TDS Minutes, October 28, 1932.
38. Ibid.
39. Student Body Minutes, October 17, 1931.
40. Fairchild to Mother, May 19, 1930.
41. P.N. Nunn to Waldo, October 28, 1932.
42. Ibid., 4.
43. P.N. Nunn, "That New Social Order," delivered to the Student Body at Deep Springs, January 4, 1933, LJN Papers, and Deep Springs Archives.
44. Student Body Minutes, April 13, 1935.
45. Robert Sproull, September 18, 2002, interviewed by Bradley Edmondson, transcript in LJN Papers.
46. William Biersach to Larry Kimpton, May 23, 1936.
47. Student Body Minutes, January 23–April 16, 1937.
48. Francis Tetreault to Mother, n.d., but apparently sent in the fall of 1937. Clearly, Tetreault was misinformed when he said L.L. Nunn would not allow faculty wives to live at Deep Springs.
49. Report of the Student Body Trustee, in Trustees of Deep Springs Minutes, November 5, 1938.
50. Aird, *Deep Springs*, 44.
51. In the 1980s, Telluride sold three of the paintings to an alumnus of Deep Springs who then donated them to the college. Telluride gave the fourth Midjo to the college in 2002.
52. TDS Minutes, March 20, 1932.
53. Ibid., April 1, 2012, also telephone conversations with long-time Fish Lake Valley residents Link Stanley (now of Bishop, California) and Jim and Verna Wallace and Leland Wallace of Dyer, Nevada, April 1, 2012, with L. Jackson Newell, LJN Papers.
54. Wallace Cook to O. B. Suhr, in Trustees of Deep Springs Minutes, May 21, 1931, and October 23, 1931. The last truly wet season had been the winter of 1926–1927.
55. Ned Bedell, "Deep Springs Notes," *Telluride Association Newsletter*, June 1939, 1.
56. TDS Minutes, May 6, 1924.
57. Ibid., October 29, 1926.
58. Ibid., May 24, 1940; also Lawrence A. Kimpton, "Report of the Management to the Board of Trustees," Trustees Meeting, May 12, 1939, DSA and LJN Papers.

59. TDS Minutes, May 21, 1931; also Cook to Suhr, May 21, 1931.
60. Ned Bedell, "Deep Springs Notes," *Telluride Association Newsletter*, February 1939, 1, 5. See description of Meiklejohn in chapter 3.
61. Student Body Minutes, April 28, 1938, box 3, fd 11.
62. Stanley Cloud and Lynne Olson, *The Murrow Boys: Pioneers on the Front Lines of Broadcast Journalism* (New York: Houghton Mifflin, 1996), 111–21. Collingwood also became Deep Springs' first Rhodes Scholar.
63. Sproull, Oral History, Part 1, September 18, 2002.
64. Christopher Breiseth, email to Jack Newell, April 25, 2012, LJN Papers.
65. "Report of Investigation of Range Cattle Transactions for the Period March 1, 1933, to November 20, 1939," Record Grp. 1, Subg. 2, Box 10, fd. 1, DSA.
66. Sproull, Oral History, Part 1, September 18, 2002, 14.
67. *Centennial Catalogues: The Presidents of the University of Chicago, A Centennial View* (accessed online), LJN Papers.
68. Henry G. Hayes, unpublished typescript of "Autobiography of Henry Hayes," 1973, LJN Papers, Box 11, fd. 2.
69. Ibid.
70. Fay E. Ward, *Working Cowboy's Manual* (New York: Random House Value Publishing, 1983), 66.
71. The use of anything but an approved branding iron is illegal.
72. "Report of Investigation of Range Cattle Transactions."
73. C. N. Whitman to Trustees of Deep Springs, May 10, 1940, DST, Correspondence, Box 5, fd. 5. This twenty-six-page "Supplemental Cattle Report" summarized eleven new categories of evidence against MacKenzie. For example, "Item 5, Bulls," concluded: "Acting on [MacKenzie's] advice, we bought 38 bulls during his employment. Including 11 in the May, 1933 inventory, we have owned 49 in all. Our present inventory of such stock is 18. Our books show the disposition of only 15." The former ranch manager had apparently sold sixteen of the bulls and pocketed the cash.
74. P.N. Nunn, Obituary-tribute, *Telluride Association Newsletter*, November 1939, 1.
75. Paul N. Nunn (1860–1939), "Death Claims Pioneer Power Chief," *Salt Lake Tribune*, October 29, 1939. Subgroup 15, Box 1, fd. 8, DSA.
76. Sweeting, "Education Experiment," 7. Agnes died in 1945, Jewel in the early 1960s.
77. Ibid.
78. Kimpton engaged at least three Deep Springs alumni (Waldo Rall, Leo Lavantelli, and Armand Kelley) in the Manhattan Project. He went on to serve as chancellor through the 1950s and was saluted as the chief architect of modern fund-raising at Chicago. He was also excoriated by the faculty for his 1958 decision to suppress

publication of *The Chicago Review* literary magazine because it contained articles by Jack Kerouac and William Burroughs.

79. This sentiment of Lawrence Kimpton was printed with Kimpton's permission in Deep Springs brochures throughout the 1950s and 1960s.
80. Generations of students would savor "Olin's Cabin" as a solitary retreat for an afternoon of reading or a night alone.
81. Paul Swatek, Alumni Essay, September 20, 1964. Swatek became a well-known engineer with the Dravo Corporation, shipbuilders based in Pittsburgh, Pennsylvania.

Chapter 10. Flowering and Root Rot, 1941–1956

1. Alice Bergel, statement filed in "Legends of Deep Springs, 1983–86," Record Group 3, Subgroup 23, Box 2, fd. 2, DSA.
2. Melvin L. Kohn, Oral History, May 8, 2012, tape recording in LJN Papers. Kohn was a student of the Bergels.
3. *Los Angeles Times* articles: "To the Last, Devotion to Schweitzer," January 24, 1998, and "Chapman Professor Bergel, Schweitzer Expert, Dies at 89," March 25, 2001. Claudia Horn, Coordinator of Special Collections Archives at Chapman University, provided information about the Bergels' academic backgrounds.
4. Erik Pell, "Deep Springs, 1941–43," Typescript, n.d. (ca. 2009), LJN Papers, 3–4.
5. Ibid., 3.
6. Adrien Duncan, "Deep Springs Notes," *Telluride Newsletter*, January 1942. The trustees and Saunders agreed on a monetary settlement the next year.
7. Pell, "Deep Springs," 7.
8. "Deep Springs Opens Fall Term," *Telluride Newsletter*, November 1943, 1–5.
9. Pell, "Deep Springs," 14.
10. Ibid., 15.
11. Robert F. Gatje to "Dear Folks," October 17, 1944, LJN Papers. Gatje provided me with copies of scores of letters he wrote home from 1944 to 1946.
12. Kohn, Oral History, May 8, 2012.
13. Gerrard Pook, email to Jack Newell, July 4, 2010.
14. *Telluride Newsletter*, January 1943, 1.
15. R. L. Arnesen, "Deep Springs Notes," *Telluride Newsletter*, April 1943, 5–6.
16. Bob Gatje, email to Will Cowan et al., November 29, 2011, LJN Papers.
17. *Telluride Newsletter*, November 1943, 2.
18. *Telluride Newsletter*, November 1944, 1–10. This issue was devoted entirely to news from Deep Springs.
19. Edwin Wesely, Interviewed by L. Jackson Newell, June 29, 2006, recording and

transcription in LJN Papers.

20. Bill Allen to Jack Newell, May 29, 2012, LJN Papers.
21. Bill Allen, quoted in *Telluride Newsletter*, November 1943, 2.
22. Student Body Minutes, October 28, 1942.
23. Ibid.
24. Deep Springs Trustees Minutes, November 14, 1942.
25. Student Body Minutes, December 16, 1942.
26. Carroll Whitman quoted in Simon N. Whitney, "Memorandum to the Deep Springs Student Body by Simon N. Whitney, Retiring Director," May 31, 1948. Typescript in "Si Whitney: Letters and Notes," in LJN Papers, courtesy of Eunice M. Whitney. Simon Whitney sent copies of this memorandum to nine people, including Acting Director Bonham Campbell and Trustees Jack Laylin, Harold Waldo, and William Biersach.
27. Harvey C. Mansfield (DS'21), "The Jewish Quota at Deep Springs, 1944," LJN Papers and DSA, 5. For a larger view of discrimination in admissions at three leading universities in this era, see Marcia Synnott's *The Half-Opened Door: Discrimination and Admissions at Harvard, Yale, and Princeton, 1900–1970* (Westport, CT: Greenwood Press, 1979).
28. Kohn to Newell, email, May 26, 2012.
29. Mansfield, "The Jewish Quota," 6.
30. Bill Allen (DS'42) later opined: "Even the best of the trustee . . . partook of the 'polite' anti-Semitism of the time." Allen, email to Newell, December 1, 2011.
31. Student Body Minutes, November 15, 1944.
32. "Director's Report," Deep Springs Trustees Minutes, November 27, 1944.
33. "Dear Folks" from Gatje, August 1, 1945. A clipping from a New York newspaper that Bob Gatje saved with his letters heralds Brooklyn Tech High School as the first to produce three members of the Deep Springs Student Body at once: Don Claudy, Bob Gatje, and Edwin Wesely. High schools in Palo Alto, California, Shaker Heights, Ohio, Milwaukee, Wisconsin, Rochester, New York, and Chicago's New Trier also sent many students in this era.
34. Laylin's 1939 appointment as a trustee occurred when Waldo chaired the board, and Cadman and Thornhill were both active trustees. Waldo's moderate stance, with Laylin's support, also carried Monroe onto the board in 1941—just prior to Waldo's resignation as chairman.
35. Whitman to Trustees, February 1, 1945, quoted in Mansfield, "The Jewish Quota," 8–9.
36. Hugh Davy, Oral History, interviewed by Christopher Breiseth, November 13, 1982.

37. "Diary: Simon N. Whitney," October 24, 1942, 155. Copy of diary in LJN Papers, courtesy of Eunice M. Whitney, 2005.
38. Norton Dodge, Oral History, interviewed by Bradley Edmondson, February 1989, audiocassette and transcript in LJN Papers.
39. "Deep Springs Notes," *Telluride Newsletter*, May 1944, 3.
40. Bill Allen to Newell, May 29, 2012; and Gatje to parents, February 17, 1946, LJN Papers.
41. Gatje to parents, June 10, 1944.
42. Ibid., February 13, 1946.
43. On August 14, 2008, the U.S. National Archives released the names of 24,000 Americans associated with the OSS during World War II. Erik Hoover (DS'86) examined the documents and sent me a detailed report on the engagement of Deep Springs alumni by email on July 19, 2010.
44. Alice Bergel, "A Few Vignettes from the 40s," 1–2.
45. Ibid.
46. Kurt Bergel was involved in an automobile accident in which teenaged Ann Brokaw, daughter of Claire Booth Luce, was killed. Though apparently not at fault, his sadness over the event endured.
47. David Werdegar would become one of the early recipients of the prestigious Deep Springs Medal, the trustees' highest award for alumni whose lives have exemplified the ideals of L.L. Nunn.
48. Whitney, "Memorandum to the Deep Springs Student Body."
49. T. H. Heitkamp (DS'46) launched his illustrious career with this work.
50. Humphrey Fisher to Dear Sirs (application), June 3, 1951, photocopy in LJN Papers.
51. F. C. Noon to Trustees of Deep Springs, August 23, 1951, TDS Minutes.
52. Ibid.
53. Humphrey Fisher, Letter to Simon Whitman, September 30, 1951, Fisher file, DSA.
54. Harold Waldo, Letter to Humphrey Fisher, October 5, 1951, DSA.
55. Whitman to Fisher, October 7, 1951, p. 6. Fisher File.
56. "Anonymous Student [probably not Fisher] to Bonnie [Bonham Campbell]," November 13, 1951, Fisher File, DSA.
57. Mr. and Mrs. George Rabin to Humphrey Fisher, October 6. 1951, DSA.
58. Fisher's most recent book, cowritten with Allan G. B. Fisher, is *Slavery in the History of Black Muslim Africa* (New York: NYU Press, 2001).
59. Misha Hoekstra email to Jack Newell, January 3, 2010. Clara's daughter and granddaughter visited Deep Springs in 1997, still perplexed as to why the college had moved the cabin.

60. President Alan Valentine of the University of Rochester, in Whitman's home city, was his model for an academic leader. He was celebrated by the political right for his fundamental conservatism.

Chapter 11. An Unlikely Awakening, 1956–1960

1. "Report of the 1958 Budget Committee." A five-member student committee filed this report with the Trustees of Deep Springs on April 10, 1958. Nearly a decade later, another Planning Committee prepared a new document for the board. Planning Committee Report, April 7, 1967, LJN Papers. The latter effort prompted the board to commission an architectural study of the condition of the physical plant.
2. Edwin Wesely interview, June 29, 2006.
3. Telluride Newsletter, June 1958, 6.
4. "An Oral History Conversation about Deep Springs College, 1958–59, by William C. (Bill) Hoffman and L. Jackson Newell, March 24, 2010," 32, LJN Papers and DSA.
5. Ibid., 14–16.
6. Alumni recollections have differed on this account, with some remembering that Fort had bragged about having FBI ties and others believing that we had inferred such ties and generated rumors about them.
7. "President's Reports," Deep Springs Trustees Minutes, May 7, 1959, and October 15, 1959, DSA.
8. Deep Springs Student Body Minutes, January 19, 1959, Officers' Report (hereafter cited as DSSB Minutes).
9. Michael Putney, "To Members of the Student Body," February 5, 1959, in DSSB Minutes, February 13, 1959. Putney continues to serve as an award-winning news anchor for WPLG-TV (ABC) in Miami, Florida.
10. William E. Fort file, LJN Papers.
11. L.L. Nunn to Harold Waldo, November 24, 1923, in Sweeting, "Education Experiment," 1289.
12. DSSB Minutes, Special Meeting of the Student Body Minutes, March 25, 1959, 20.
13. "Memo, CNW [Carroll Whitman] to Trs. [Trustees], etc., Re: TRENDS," March 11, 1959. Document attached to Michael McGuire, "Year of Turbulence," 1989, LJN Papers, Box 8, fd. 8.
14. C. N. Whitman to Harold Sanders, May 31, 1960, Robert Aird Papers, DSA, Acc. 2, Box 4, fd. 15.
15. DSSB Minutes, April 10, 1959.
16. Ibid., April 16, 1959.
17. Ibid., April 20, 1959.

18. Ibid., April 24, 1959.
19. Ibid., May 1, 1959.
20. Ibid., May 8, 1959.
21. Carroll N. Whitman to Harold R. Waldo, Secretary of Deep Springs College, May 8, 1959, TDS Minutes.
22. DSSB Minutes, May 10, 1959. Trustees' minutes of these proceedings and throughout this whole era contain little information about the controversial issues. The best source is generally the student body minutes, notwithstanding the emotions involved in students' responses to events.
23. DSSB Minutes, May 10, 1959.
24. Roger Seiler, Oral History, interviewed by L. Jackson Newell, August 10, 2009, LJN Papers, 5.
25. Vernon D. Penner, telephone conversation with L. Jackson Newell, March 31, 2012, audio recording, LJN Papers. See also Seiler, Oral History, 5.
26. Carroll N. Whitman to Board of Trustees, Harold R. Waldo, Secretary, October 8, 1959, DST Minutes, DSA.
27. Ibid.
28. Reading in the Robert B. Aird papers in the Deep Springs Archives, Linda Newell came upon a faded carbon copy on onionskin paper of a letter written by William E. Fort dated October 18, 1959. The addressee was identified only as "Dear Sir" with no mailing address. The details of the trustees' meeting come from that letter. Transcribed for legibility, this single-spaced letter runs eight full pages. The passages quoted here are on p. 3. See "Fort's Dear Sir Letter," LJN Papers.
29. Ibid. The original carbon copy on onionskin paper is in DSA, Box 4, fd. 6.
30. Ibid., 8.
31. Seiler, Oral History, August 10, 2009.
32. Ibid.
33. H. R. Roodhouse to Messrs. [Frank] Noon, [Harold] Waldo, [William] Biersach, [Harold] Sanders, and [Robert B.] Aird, December 26, 1959, Aird Papers, Box 4, fd. 8.
34. Ibid.
35. Fort died in 1988 at age eighty-two in Palm Beach, Florida. Keith Wilson, Brigham Young University professor, and his daughter, Kim, assisted in locating Fort's death certificate, obituary, and related information. LJN Papers. Fort published an essay in *The Challenge and the Choice*, ed. Richard Vetterli, published by the Mormon-related company, Bookcraft, 1969. W. Cleon Skousen penned the foreword.
36. Hoffman, Oral History, interviewed by Newell, March 24, 2010, LJN Papers and DSA.

Chapter 12. The Reformation, 1960–1976

1. James Martin taught at Deep Springs until the middle of the decade. He maintained ties with the disciples of political philosopher Leo Strauss in Telluride Association, some of whom later became leading neoconservatives.
2. Aird, *Deep Springs*, 62.
3. Ibid., 67. Noon may have approved the title transfer as a way to supplement Roodhouse's compensation and reward his personal loyalty without other trustees knowing about it.
4. Aird, *Deep Springs*, 63.
5. "In Memoriam WHITE COW November 5, 1964," *Deep Springs Newsletter*, February 1966.
6. Ron Alexander kept a careful record of these events as a student and assisted me in reconstructing this sequence. Alexander, email to Jack Newell, re: "Comments on Chapter 12," August 7, 2012.
7. Randall C. Reid, Oral History, interviewee not identified, March 12, 1989, DSA, 6.
8. Ron Alexander, a close friend of Mossner's at Deep Springs, has quoted this line many times.
9. Reid, Oral History, 4.
10. Stryker is a leading figure in neuroscience and a member of the National Academy of Science, Swanson has occupied important positions with the World Bank throughout his career, and Noll served for many years as president of an Episcopal university in Uganda.
11. Four students were fatally shot by National Guard troops at Kent State University, Ohio, on May 4, 1970; and within a fortnight, two more were killed while demonstrating at Jackson State College in Mississippi.
12. Denis Clark, email to Jack Newell, August 8, 2012, LJN Papers.
13. Alumni Reunion, Deep Springs, September 20–21, 2008, sessions recorded by Ron Alexander, discs in DSA and LJN Papers.
14. Alexander, email to Jack Newell, re: "Comments on Chapter 12," August 7, 2012, 2.
15. I participated in this reunion, having been a faculty member in the mid-1960s, and gleaned this information from the formal recorded sessions and personal conversations with alumni.
16. Ron Alexander, Rick Hansen, and William Pezick each provided valuable assistance by telephone and email to help me piece together this account. Neither they nor their peers agree on some points.
17. *Master Plan: Deep Springs College by HCD Collaborative Architects and Planning*, n.d., Box 56, fd. 4, LJN Papers.
18. These buildings remain the only two that the Trustees of Deep Springs have named

for donors or honorees. They chose not to continue this practice during the 1995–2001 campaign for Deep Springs.

19. Eric V. Swanson, email to Jack Newell, September 19, 2012, LJN Papers.
20. Winona Johnson Holloway's books were titled *Moving On* (1989), *Moving Out (A Sequel to Moving On)* (1992), and *Riders to the Rainbow: Traders to the People* (1998). All three were published in Live Oaks, CA: Shadow Butte Press, as paperbacks.
21. Denis Clark, email correspondence with Jack Newell, June 2012. Clark later married Katharine Reid.
22. McMurtry's novels, essays, and scripts are set chiefly in the Old West or in Texas. Ken Kesey was best known for his 1962 novel *One Flew over the Cuckoo's Nest*, whose protagonist is named "Randle McMurphy." Kesey was a countercultural writer who bridged the Beat Generation of the 1950s and the hippie movement of the 1960s. Robert Pinsky became the Poet Laureate of the United States and a consultant to the Library of Congress for poetry.
23. Clark to Newell, June 2012.
24. Ibid.
25. Michael P. Stryker, email to Jack Newell, September 20, 2012. Reid had also taught at San Diego State College. He wrote *The Fiction of Nathanael West: No Redeemer, No Promised Land* (1967), the novel *Lost and Found*, and several short stories, including "Detritus," which was selected for inclusion in *O'Henry Prize Stories 1973*.
26. Reid, Oral History, 1, 3.
27. Randy Reid, "Dean Reid Finds Himself a Conservative about Deep Springs: Values Union of Intelligence and Character," *Telluride Newsletter*, May 1973, 4–5.
28. Sweeting, "Education Experiment," 676. See commentary on final page of chapter 2.
29. Randall Reid, "Sunday Service by Deep Springs Dean Randall Reid," March 7, 1965, copy in LJN Papers. Reid spoke these words as the visiting dean, two years before the breakdown of decorum and order over recreational drug use. He was in concert with both John Erskine (see chapter 3) and Lionel Trilling, both of whom wrote pieces titled "The Moral Obligation to Be Intelligent."
30. Clark to Newell, June 25, 2012, attachment, 20.
31. The domestic water hill tank was not in the flood's path, but the heavy rain undermined its base, tipping it over and creating "a brief but lovely waterfall." Reid, Oral History, 2.
32. Denis Clark to family, August 1, 1969, LJN Papers.
33. Weather experts use a term like "five hundred year flood" to indicate the probability of an event of that magnitude happening again within the number of years

stated. It is a rough gauge.

34. Jan Vleck, "Deep Springs Student Studies Local Feral Horses." *Deep Springs Newsletter*, July 1972, 4–5.
35. Hiking to the top of that ridge in the winter of 1999, my daughter Heather and I came upon a white mustang with two other healthy specimens. They were probably descendants of those Vleck had studied three decades earlier.
36. In 1996, when Congress mandated the expansion of Death Valley National Monument to become a National Park, much of Eureka Valley was incorporated within its boundaries. Ironically, the Park Service based its new map of the park on an old one that still tagged Chocolate Mountain as Piper Peak. This mislabeled landmark anchors the northwest corner of the official map of Death Valley National Park.
37. Brad Edmondson, email to Jack Newell, September 13, 2012, LJN Papers.
38. Paul Starrs, personal conversation with Jack Newell, June 16, 2012, LJN Papers.
39. Miguel Dozier, interviewed by Jack Newell, Dozier home, Santa Clara Pueblo, New Mexico, May 12, 2008; my notes filed in "1970s Alumni Survey Letters," LJN Papers.
40. Jim Partridge, "In Memoriam: A Tribute from Jim Partridge (DS'66)," September 21, 2008, in "1960s Reunion" file, LJN Papers.
41. The story of Mossner burning his draft card and enlisting in the army came to light in 2000, when the professor with whom he had studied Thoreau found the burned draft card in the book he had loaned David. See James Matlack, "A Graduate's Postscript," *Christian Science Monitor*, June 21, 2000, 9.

Chapter 13. Spiraling, 1976–1994

1. Allan Bloom, *The Closing of the American Mind* (New York: Simon and Schuster, 1987). As a young professor at Cornell University, Bloom had been a faculty guest-in-residence at Telluride House in 1963. Paul Wolfowitz, U.S. Deputy Secretary of Defense for President George W. Bush, was influenced profoundly by Bloom when they both lived at the Telluride House at Cornell.
2. Email correspondence with the author, August 13, 2012, LJN Papers.
3. Edwin Cronk and Merritt Holloway, Promotional flier, n.d., LJN Papers, Box 42, fd. 7.
4. Edwin Cronk, Oral History, interviewed by Brad Edmondson, May 21, 2004, supplemented by "Oral History 2", paragraph 1 of 2, in Brad Edmondson, email to Newell, March 7, 2010. The college reaped over $9,000 from this plan.
5. Edmondson, telephone conversation with Jack Newell, September 3, 2012, LJN Papers.
6. Reich, Journal, January 29, 1920, 18.
7. Deep Springs Trustees (DST) Minutes, May 11–13, 1979, 2.

8. "Deep Springs to Remain Male Only," *Telluride Newsletter*, September 1979, 6.
9. Over two-thirds of living alumni responded to the four-page questionnaire, generating enough data to produce a refereed journal article and a lengthy report for trustees and alumni. See L. Jackson Newell, "Among the Few at Deep Springs College: Assessing a Seven-Decade Experiment in Liberal Education," *Journal of General Education* 34 (Summer 1982): 120–34, and Newell, "Among the Few: A Study of Deep Springs College Alumni, 1917–1980, with Recommendations for Educational Policy. Final Report: September 1980," 156 pages, in DSA and LJN Papers.
10. "Chris Breiseth–New Deep Springs' Dean," *Telluride Newsletter*, May 1980, 6.
11. Christopher N. Breiseth, Autobiography, n.d., draft of "Chapter 13: Deep Springs," 4, which Breiseth sent to me as an email attachment, August 24, 2012.
12. Christopher N. Breiseth, "Learning to Hear the Voice of the Desert," *Change Magazine* (September 1983): 28–35. Also during Breiseth's presidency, English professor David Schuman published "Education and Solipsism," *The CoEvolution Quarterly* (Spring 1981): 132–39.
13. One of the perpetrators told me this story in confidence.
14. L. Jackson Newell, Notes on 1980s Reunion Conversations, May 31, 2010, "Unloading My Brain," Section #1: Random Turner-Jones, 1980s email correspondence in LJN Papers.
15. Dr. Robert Schechter, email to Jack Newell, August 22, 2012, LJN Papers. HPS is transmitted by fresh urine or feces, especially from the deer mouse (*Peromyscus maniculatus*) found throughout North America. Persons taken ill with HPS often have been in close quarters with these rodents. Geoff recalled that mice were especially prevalent around the ranch during the heavy winter of 1984. Sue may also have been exposed, however, in central California where she and Geoff had gone to buy livestock shortly before her illness. Although unidentified, hantavirus has apparently taken victims in North America and around the world for centuries.
16. The Breiseths returned to Springfield, Illinois, where he resumed his duties at Sangamon State University. Wilkes College (now Wilkes University) appointed him president the following year; he and Jane served there together for seventeen years. They moved to Hyde Park, New York, in 2001, where he served as president and CEO of the Franklin and Eleanor Roosevelt Institute until 2008.
17. Charles Abbott, email to Jack Newell, September 17, 2012.
18. The accounts of sexual engagements between adults and students reported in this section are based on recorded reminiscences at the May 2010 reunion of 1980s alumni, and my notes from personal conversations and email correspondence with students from that decade. LJN Papers.
19. Abbott to Newell, September 17, 2012.

20. Faculty Personnel Policy: Deep Springs College, Final: January 25, 1996, LJN Papers, Box 19, fd. 3, and Box 58, fd. 14, 5–6.
21. At least two gay students reported having such an experience with the same faculty woman. This information was provided by one of them and acknowledged by the other. My information is taken from a recorded conversation with Geoff Pope and my detailed notes from a conversation with Random Turner-Jones: Newell, "Notes on 1980s Reunion Conversations, May 31, 2010, Unloading My Brain."
22. Ibid.
23. Misha Hoesktra, email to Jack Newell, September 15, 2012.
24. Ibid.
25. Email correspondence with a presumed participant.
26. "Geoff and Iris Pope: A Conversation about the 1980s at Deep Springs," conducted by Jack and Linda Newell, May 28, 2010, LJN Papers.
27. Bruce Laverty, "Deep Springs College Hydro Project: Fact Sheet," July 26, 2010, LJN Papers. Permission to build a small dam to impound water could not be obtained, so generator output fluctuates constantly depending on rainfall, snowmelt, time of year, and time of day.
28. These words accompanied a pledge envelope for gifts ranging from $100 to $1,000 or more.
29. Deep Springs Student Body Minutes, May 16, 1961.
30. Experts disagree on definitions and information is difficult to gather, but the proportion of men who consider themselves gay appears to be 5–10 percent.
31. Mossner, "Deep Springs," lyrics, David Mossner file, LJN Papers.
32. Tom Hudgens, *The Commonsense Kitchen: 500 Recipes + Lessons from a Hand-Crafted Life* (San Francisco: Chronicle Books, 2010), 608 pp.
33. Cultural bias in standardized tests has been the subject of intense controversy for decades. Revisions to make the exams more culturally neutral continue.
34. Credited with originating the holistic management movement, Allan Savory won the 2010 Buckminster Fuller Challenge with his African Center for Holistic Management.
35. "Withrow's Bequest Exceeds One Million: Conditions Raise Single-Sex Questions." *Deep Springs Newsletter*, Spring 1988, 1, 4.
36. Last Will and Testament of James R. Withrow, Jr., September 7, 1984. William H. Allen, LL.B. (DS'42) gave me the legal file, titled "DS Trustees, Withrow Will," LJN Papers. Withrow's close friend and fellow trustee, Beatrice Renfield, was associated with the Visiting Nurses Association in New York.
37. James R. Withrow Jr. to Philip L. Kennicott, April 8, 1985, in William Allen, "DS Trustees, Withrow Will." LJN Papers.

38. Dale R. Corson, Cornell University president emeritus and trustee of Deep Springs from 1977 to 1985, designed a sundial to honor his friend and Deep Springs' benefactor.
39. "Betty Anderson a Burst of Sunshine," *Deep Springs Newsletter*, Spring 1988, 3.
40. Jeffrey Lustig, Hanna Pitkin, Randall Reid, John Schaar, David Schuman, and Sharon Schuman, Letter to Bruce Laverty, August 9, 1990, with copies to Trustees of Deep Springs and Dr. Saul Benjamin, LJN Papers, Box 19, fd. 14.
41. On January 29, 1991, the *Exponent*, Montana State University's student newspaper, published a lead article about Saul Benjamin and that day or the next, the *Bozeman* (Montana) *Chronicle* also ran a cover story about him. LJN Papers. Benjamin later served as headmaster of the Verde Valley School in Sedona, Arizona, and, more recently, as a professor at the American University of Beirut.
42. I witnessed this conversation.
43. When he was leaving the presidency, one trustee and several other alumni lobbied openly for Hoenicke's immediate election to the board. This effort did not succeed. Disenchanted for a few years, he later expressed great warmth toward the college. Edwin Hoenicke, Oral History, conducted by Jack Newell, October 10, 2006, LJN Papers.
44. These foundations included the Hugh and Hazel Darling Foundation, the H. N. and Frances C. Berger Foundation, and the Sahandaywi Foundation.
45. Chuck Christenson, Letter to Trustees of Deep Springs, January 20, 1994, DSA and LJN Papers. The error that misled the trustees was in categorizing endowment holdings disproportionately in favor of "quasi-endowment" (or liquid assets) as contrasted with "true endowment" resources for which principal could not be invaded. The new FASB standards had sharpened the distinction, which lowered the liquid portion of the remaining $4.37 million endowment from $2 million to $1,286,000. Operating deficits over the previous four years had run between $210,000 and $314,000.
46. One student, Nat Birdsall (DS'95), had nailed a Twister game canvas to the ceiling over his bed to keep plaster from falling on him at night, and most of the bathrooms in the dormitory were unusable because of rusted-out pipes and permanently clogged drains.

Chapter 14. Reckoning, 1994–1995

1. Nunn's chief concern about social relationships in neighboring towns stemmed from expectations of reciprocity that would threaten the solitude he prized for his students.
2. Trustees of Deep Springs (TDS) Minutes, June 24, 1994.

3. Mrs. Donn M. Miller to Jack Newell, July 25, 1994, LJN Papers.
4. L. Jackson Newell, Chair, "On the Brink of Decision: A Letter to the Trustees of Deep Springs," September 1, 1994, LJN Papers, catalogued with the Newell Presidential Journal.
5. TDS Minutes, September 26 and October 11, 1994.
6. Their urgings came as no surprise. Breiseth had been trying to interest me in leading Deep Springs since he had left the presidency himself in 1983; and other trustees or former board members, especially Paul Todd and Erik Pell, pressed me to consider the job in 1987, 1990, and 1992. Our children's ages argued against such a move, although Linda and I seriously considered the tempting possibilities in 1990.
7. Mansfield to Aird, November 2, 1986.
8. Jim Withrow's bequest, received in 1988, was the only seven-figure gift to the college since 1923, although Bob Aird's cumulative support approached that amount.
9. L.L. Nunn, "The Man Required for Deep Springs," 1923, in *The Gray Book*, 41–43. Sweeting dated the statement October 18, 1923, and noted that Nunn gave it to the trustees as he stepped away from formally leading the college.

Chapter 15. Renaissance, 1995–1998

1. Deed of Trust of Lucien L. Nunn, Sect. 5, para. 1, The Gray Book.
2. L. Jackson Newell, Journal (hereafter LJN Journal), December 7, 1995, 103–4.
3. Ibid., 104.
4. Ibid., December 11, 1995, 108.
5. Patrick O'Connor has gone on to become Professor of Hispanic Studies and Comparative Literature at Oberlin College in Ohio. Andreas Kriefall has since left academe for the ministry and is now a social justice activist in Albany, New York.
6. Joe Szewczak conducted research at the White Mountain Research Station (WMRS) for about six years and then moved to a professorship at California State University, Humboldt. I was gratified to write a reference letter to assist him in securing that position and, in the process, restore a friendship that had flourished during my years as a trustee. He and his sons, Nicholas and Dylan, spent a day with Linda and me at Deep Springs before they moved to Eureka for his new post. He achieved academic tenure his second year and quickly advanced to the rank of professor. Susan remained at WMRS for over a decade and then pursued a career as a consultant and independent contractor in Reno, Nevada.
7. LJN Journal, February 1, 1996.
8. While teaching at the college, Smith initiated a project that resulted in his collector-quality book: *The Students of Deep Springs College: Photographs by Michael A. Smith, Essay by L. Jackson Newell, Afterword by William T. Vollmann* (Revere, PA:

Lodima Press, 2000).

9. Robert B. Aird, *Deep Springs: Its Founder, History, and Philosophy with Personal Reflections.*
10. L. Jackson Newell to Richard Cornelison, May 29, 1997, LJN Papers.
11. Note for my file: "Chuck Thompson Problems," September 12, 1999, LJN Papers.
12. Dick Rudolph or Ken Abbott of Rudolph Construction and I conferred several times a week by telephone and they made occasional visits to the construction sites.
13. It had been illegal to collect or cut bristlecone pines for many decades, but Powell knew someone in Owens Valley who kept a stack of decommissioned power poles and was willing to give him one.
14. L. Jackson Newell, Memo to trustees, re: Earthquake, November 17, 1997, LJN Papers.
15. Telluride Association's support of construction at Deep Springs was not without precedent. The association's members had sponsored a 1939–1940 drive that provided almost one-third of the funds needed to build the faculty duplex.
16. Clare Wolfowitz to Jack and Linda Newell, April 21, 1998, LJN Papers.
17. L. Jackson Newell to Clare Wolfowitz, May 14, 1998, LJN Papers.

Chapter 16. Reality, 1999–2004

Nearing death on December 30, 1924, Nunn concluded his final statement on "The Purpose" of Deep Springs with this sentiment. *The Gray Book*, 40.

1. The Harry S. Truman Scholarship Foundation website, http://truman.gov/
2. Deep Springers often view such honors as an enigma, remembering the value L.L. Nunn placed on the dignity of doing any job well regardless of its standing among the many walks of life.
3. Haynes played a key role in releasing the fifty-two American citizens who had been held hostage at the U.S. Embassy in Tehran from 1979 to 1981.
4. Other holders of the Withrow Chair during these years included Ambassador William vanden Heuvel (DS'46), Sir Peter Parker (British civil servant and Shakespearean actor), South African Justice Richard Goldstone (who presided over the war crimes trials following the genocides in Bosnia and Rwanda), *New Yorker* journalist Philip Gourevitch (who had just written *We Wish to Inform You that Tomorrow We Will Be Killed with Our Families)*, and Muzaffar Ali (artist, filmmaker, poet, and social reformer from Lucknow, India).
5. http://www.thebestschools.org/blog/2012/12/04/50-best-colleges-united-states/
6. The term "home ranch" refers to a plot of privately owned land that is required for the award of federal grazing allotments in this area. In this case, the acreage is an

unfenced and undeveloped parcel on the desert floor.

7. Paul H. Todd Jr. founded the highly successful Kalamazoo Spice Extraction Company (now Kalsec) that produces natural flavors and colors. Elected a congressman from Michigan's third district in 1964, he served one term before his appointment as chief executive officer of Planned Parenthood. Todd died in Kalamazoo, Michigan, in 2008.
8. "The Dreadful Day We Hoped Would Never Come: Second Year Student Michael Pihos's Tragic Death at Deep Springs," written September 21, expanded on October 1, 1999, "Postscript" on April 18, 2007. 13 pages. LJN Papers. For a fellow student's memories of Pihos and his death, see "Desert Stories" by Mark Kirby (DS'98), *Harvard Summer Review*, Issue 8 (Summer 2002).
9. Alan Farnham told me this story in person.
10. When we launched the Campaign for Deep Springs in the autumn of 1995, the Dow Jones industrial average lingered around 4,200. When we gathered for the Renaissance Reunion, it had already spiked at 11,338 but remained above 10,000 *en route* to a low near 7,000 a year later.
11. On January 6, 2004, the *Los Angeles Times* carried a front-page article by Peter Y. Hong, "Making Hay with Education," and in its June 2004 issue, *Vanity Fair* published a long article by Evgenia Peretz, "Cowboy Scholars" (pp. 198–210). Over the next couple of years, Deep Springs also received prominent coverage in the September 4, 2006, *New Yorker* with an article by Dana Goodyear, "The Searchers" (pp. 62-71); the *New York Times* on April 23, 2006, in Peter Applebome's "The Final Four" (about the four remaining men's college in the U.S.); and others. French filmmaker Gonzague Pichelin also gained approval from the student body to do an ethnographic film of life at Deep Springs. He captured over 100 hours of ordinary events and special occasions and, although no product came of his efforts, in 2013 he offered the footage to the University of Utah Library's Special Collections, LJN Papers.
12. Nick Gossen, Jacob Hundt, Bryden Sweeney-Taylor, Japhet Weeks, Jack Murphy, Andrew Gossen, and L. Jackson Newell, "Hidden Springs: A Planning Guide for a Second College Akin to Deep Springs," April 19, 2000, LJN Papers.

Epilogue

Richard J. Goldstone served as the first chief prosecutor of the United Nations International Criminal Tribunal for the former Yugoslavia and for Rwanda from August 1994 to September 1996. He wrote *For Humanity: Reflections of a War Crimes Investigator* (2000). The quotation was taken from his personal remarks following a speech at Deep Springs in 2002.

1. Mark Dunn married Callie Mitchell, daughter of Ken Mitchell, then ranch manager, and Karen Mitchell, gardener, and they moved to a farm management position near Warm Springs, Nevada, in 2010. The Mitchell parents retired from Deep Springs in 2011 and undertook a Nazarene mission to Asia with their two younger daughters, Katie and Emily.
2. Superior Court of California, County of Inyo, Case No. SICVPB 12-53232, In re the Matter of the L.L. Nunn Trust for the benefit of Deep Springs College under the Deed of Trust dated November 5, 1923, p. 51. This complete document and all others bearing on the trial are available on the official Deep Springs College website.
3. Email to Rick Coville, Rich Haynie, Bill Hoffman, Jane Hoffman, Bill Turpin, and Jack Newell on November 28, 2014.
4. Michael P. Stryker, email to Jack Newell, October 10, 2012.
5. Andrew J. McCreary, emails to Jack Newell, June 5, 2012, and January 16, 2013. LJN Papers.

Appendix

1. Deep Springs alumni are identified as "DS" followed by their year of matriculation. Telluride Association members are identified as "TA" unless they are also Deep Springs alumni. Others are identified by their most recent career affiliation.

Acknowledgments

1 L. Jackson Newell Collection, University of Utah, Marriott Library Special Collections, Accn. 2342 (LJN Papers).

2 Linda took special interest in researching Deep Springs Valley and drafted a number of passages for chapter 4.

3 In 1984, Doubleday & Company published the prize-winning biography *Mormon Enigma: Emma Hale Smith*, by Linda King Newell and Valeen Tippetts Avery.

BIBLIOGRAPHY

Note: Writings by L.L. Nunn (letters, memos, articles, etc.) are listed separately before the main bibliography, while writings by his brother, P.N. Nunn, and other Nunn relatives are listed in this main bibliography. Items quoted in Sweeting, "The Education Experiment of L.L. Nunn," are not separately cited.

Abbreviations

DSSB Minutes.	Deep Spring Student Body Minutes. Cited by date. In DSA.
DSA.	Deep Springs Archives, Deep Springs College, California.
The Gray Book.	See descriptive entry under Bibliography of L.L. Nunn Documents. Nunn Papers. Lucien L. Nunn Papers, #37-4-1770. Division of Rare and Manuscript Collections, Cornell University Library, Ithaca, New York.
LJN Papers.	L. Jackson Newell Papers (Accn 2342), Special Collections Dept., J. Willard Marriott Library, University of Utah, Salt Lake City.
TDSMinutes.	Trustees of Deep Spring College Minutes, 1929–present. Cited by date in the endnotes.

L.L. Nunn Documents

Deed of Trust. In *The Gray Book.* Deep Springs, CA: Deep Springs College, n.d., [ca. 1975].

The Gray Book. Deep Springs, CA: Deep Springs College, n.d., [ca. 1975]. Though universally known as *The Gray Book*, its official identification is *Constitution of Deep Springs and The Deed of Trust.* Third-year students John Sledd, Carl Rupert, and Christopher Campbell assembled the volume, but their names did not appear on the 44-page publication. An earlier version in 5x7 format was published about 1950 by the Trustees with an introductory essay by the trustees. Both editions include the Deed of Trust, "The Purpose" and "The Man Required for Deep Springs" (by L.L. Nunn), and letters of L.L. Nunn to the student body. I cite only the 1975 version, which omits the trustees' essay and includes more Nunn letters. Its various documents are cited individually if they are quoted in the history. Originals in Nunn Papers, DSA, and LJN Papers.

"Last Will and Testament of Lucien L. Nunn," March 31, 1922. Nunn Papers.

Letter to John W. Aird, August 19, 1921. Photocopy in LJN Papers. Folder: "L.L. Nunn Letters."

Letter to Paul Ashworth, June 2, 1914. Accession 7, Box 3, fd. 5, DSA.

Letter to J. B. Bailey, February 21, 1916. LJN Papers.

Letter to Oliver R. Clark, March 20, 1917. LJN Papers.

Letters to Wallace Cook, September 3 and 17, 1920; also December 20, 1920; September 3, 1921; "Pasadena Xmas 1921"; October 28, 1924. DSA. Subgroup 15, Box 1, fd. 7, 6; photocopy in Folder: L.L. Nunn Correspondence with Wallace Cook (DS'21). LJN Papers.

Letter to Deep Springs Student Body, March 26, 1920. In *The Gray Book*, 7.

Letter to Chet Dunn, May 15, 1917. Nunn Papers; copy in LJN Papers.

Letter(s) to Ray Fruit, December 9, 1915, December 26, 1916. Box 17, #37/4/1770, Nunn Papers, Box 4, fd. 1; photocopy in LJN Papers.

Letter to "Gentlemen" (student body at Claremont), January 27, 1917. Subgroup 8, Box 1, fd. 4, DSA.

Letter to Gentlemen, February 8 and 20, 1917. Subgroup 8, Box 1, fd. 4, DSA.

Letter to "Gentlemen" [the Student Body of Deep Springs College], April 1, 1919. Subgroup 15, Box 1, fd. 3, DSA.

Letter to "Gentlemen," March 23 and March 26, 1920. In *The Gray Book*, 6.

Letter to "Gentlemen," February 17, 1923. Holograph in Nunn Papers; photocopy in LJN Papers; also printed in *The Gray Book.*

Letter to Jim Holmes, February 22, 1919. DSA. Subgroup 15, Box 1, fd. 3.

Letter to C. O. Jandl, February 3, 1917. DSA, Subgroup 8, Box 1, fd. 4.

Letter to Lionel G. Nightingale, June 15, 1918. Folder: "L.L. Nunn Letters." LJN Papers.

Letter to My Dear Brother [Fred], January 23, 1882. Holograph, Nunn Papers.

Letter to Members of the Telluride Institute of Virginia, February 4, 1917. Subgroup 8, Box 1, fd. 4, DSA.

Letter to Ellen Nunn (Telluride, Colorado), February 3, 1882. Holograph, Nunn Papers.

Letter to Herbert Reich, September 15, 1917. In Reich Family Papers, a private collection; used by permission. Photocopy of holograph in LJN Papers, courtesy of Linda L. Nunn.

Letter to Student Body, October 18, 1920, 14 pp. Subgroup 15, Box 1, fd. 7, 6, DSA; LJN Papers.

Letter to the Student Body of Deep Springs, April 5, 1921. In *The Gray Book*, 14; copy in LJN Papers.

Letter to Mr. Suhr, May 21, 1924. A paragraph from this letter appears with three other Nunn quotations on a page prepared sometime later by Carroll Whitman. Aird Papers, Box 4, fd. 1, DSA.

Letter to the Trustees of Deep Springs, September 22, 1923. In TDS Minutes.

"Letter to the Trustees, in 1924." In "Jurisdiction." Dated October 28, 1924. 14 pp. L.L. Nunn.

Letter to Trustees of Deep Springs, September 22, 1923. TDS Minutes.

Letter to C. D. Walcott, April 5, 1915. Nunn Papers, Box 2, fds. 5–6. I viewed and photographed this document circa November 23, 2005.

Letter to Simon Whitney, Secretary, January 24, 1921. Nunn Papers; photocopy in LJN Papers, folder labeled "L.L. Nunn Letters."

Letter to Harold Waldo. June 22, 1923. DSA; LJN Papers.

Letter to Harold Waldo, October 28, 1932. Attachment to Trustees of Deep Springs Minutes, October 28, 1932.

"The Man Required for Deep Springs." In *The Gray Book*, 41–43. Sweeting dated the statement October 18, 1923.

"The Moral Sense." *Mansfield Herald*, March 22, 1880. Nunn Papers; copy in LJN Papers.

Untitled notes, single page. N.d. but spring 1919. Nunn Papers, photocopy in LJN Papers.

Abbott, Charles. Email to Jack Newell, September 17, 2012. LJN Papers.

Adams, Henry. *The Education of Henry Adams*. 1918. Rpt., New York: American Heritage Library, 1961.

ADSTA Oral History Project: Interviews, Speeches, and Letters, 1979–87. Cited in the remainder of the bibliography and in the notes as "In ADSTA." ADSTA stands for the "Association of Deep Springs and Telluride Alumni," a now-defunct joint alumni group of Nunnian institutions. The oral histories were conducted by Christopher Breiseth and Brad Edmondson in 1979–1987. In 2000, Denis Clark digitalized these papers. In 2001, they were printed and ring-bound with the title "ADSTA Oral History Project: Interviews, Speeches, and Letters, 1979–87." This compilation includes three speeches about Deep Springs' early history; a letter from Robert B. Aird in lieu of an interview; and the transcripts of twenty-three interviews with early alumni, pinheads, or others who lived at Deep Springs in its early years. It also includes three later interviews with Virginia Thornhill Northrup and later alumni James Withrow and Ernest Tucker. All of my quotations and citations are from the 2000 digital version (240 pp.).

Aird, Polly. Interviewed by telephone by Jack Newell, December 11, 2010. 05n49

Aird, Robert B. *Deep Springs: Its Founder, History, and Philosophy with Personal Reflections*. Deep Springs, CA: Deep Springs College, 1997.

———. *Eighty Odd Years on Borrowed Time: My Academic & Professional Career*. San Francisco: Self-published, 1989.

———. Letter to Brad Edmundson, August 16, 1987, 140. In ADSTA. Aird wrote this letter in lieu of an oral history. DSA.

Alexander, Ron. Email to Jack Newell. Re: Comments on Chapter 12, August 7, 2012.

Allen, William H. Emails to L. Jackson Newell, February 24, 2010, December 1, 2011, and May 29, 2012. LJN Papers.

———. James R. Withrow Jr., Letter to Philip L. Kennicott, April 8, 1985. In file labeled "DS Trustees, Withrow Will." LJN Papers.

———. Quoted in *Telluride Newsletter*, November 1943.

Alumni Reunion in 1960s, Deep Springs, September 20–21, 2008. Sessions recorded by Ron Alexander. Discs in DSA and LJN Papers.

Anonymous student. Letter to Bonnie [Bonham Campbell], November 13, 1951. In file: "Fisher." DSA.

Arnesen, R. L. "Deep Springs Notes." *Telluride Newsletter*, April 1943.

Association of Deep Springs and Telluride Alumni. See ADSTA.

Ashley, Carlyle. Oral History. Interviewed by Christopher Breiseth, March 18, 1982. In ADSTA, DSA.

Ashworth, Paul. Autobiography, 1956. Nunn Papers, Box 5, fd. 47.

Austin, Mary. *Land of Little Rain*. New York: Dover Publications, 1903.

"Avis." Letter. *American Bee Journal* 10, no. 7 (July 1874): 1.

Bacon, S. N., et al. "Last Glacial Maximum and Holocene Lake Levels of Owens Lake,

Eastern California, USA." *Quaternary Science Reviews* 25, nos. 11–12 (2006): 1264–82.

Bailey, Mark Warren. *Guardians of the Moral Order: The Legal Philosophy of the Supreme Court, 1860–1910*. DeKalb: Northern Illinois University Press, 2004.

Bailey, Stephen A. *L.L. Nunn: A Memoir*. Ithaca, NY: Cayuga Press for Telluride Association, 1933. Rpt., Ithaca, NY: Cayuga Press for Telluride Association, 1993.

Barnes, Wayne. Conversation with Jack Newell, March 23, 2012.

Bedell, Ned. "Deep Springs Notes." *Telluride Association Newsletter*, June 1939.

———. "Notes from Deep Springs." *Telluride Association Newsletter*, February 1939.

———. "Notes from Deep Springs." *Telluride Association Newsletter*, April 1939.

Bergel, Alice. "A Few Vignettes from the '40s: Legends of Deep Springs 1983–86." Record Group 3, Subgroup 22, Box 2, fd. 2. DSA.

Bettinger, Robert L. "Aboriginal Occupation at High Altitude: Alpine Villages in the White Mountains of Eastern California." *American Anthropologist*, New Series 93, no. 3 (September 1991): 656–79.

———. "Prehistory of the Crooked Creek Area." In *The Crooked Creek Guidebook*, edited by Clarence A. Hall and Barbara Widawski, 123–32. Bishop, CA: White Mountain Research Station, 1994.

"Betty Anderson a Burst of Sunshine." *Deep Springs Newsletter*, Spring 1988.

Biersach W[illiam]. L. Letter to Harvard Alumni Directory, September 28, 1925. LJN Papers.

Biersach, William. Letter to Elmer M. Johnson, February 13, 1932. LJN Papers.

———. Letter to Larry Kimpton, May 23, 1936.

———. "Return for Federal Estate Tax for the Estate of Lucien L. Nunn." Submitted March 27, 1926. Photocopy in LJN Papers.

"Biography of Mr. Nunn." *Telluride Association Newsletter*, April 1927.

Blakely, Larry. "Who's in a Name: People Commemorated in Eastern Sierra Plant Names." *Newsletter of the Bristlecone Chapter, CNPS* 19, no. 5 (September 1999).

Bloom, Allan. *The Closing of the American Mind*. New York: Simon and Schuster, 1987.

Bonds, Book A, 1880. Inyo County Records, Independence, CA.

Book of Deeds, Vol. A, 153, Inyo County Records, Independence, CA.

Breiseth, Christopher N. Autobiography. n.d. Draft of "Chapter Thirteen Deep Springs," which Breiseth sent to me as an email attachment, August 24, 2012.

———. Email to Jack Newell, April 25, 2012. LJN Papers.

———. "Learning to Hear the Voice of the Desert." *Change Magazine* (September 1983): 28–35.

Budget. Compiled by Matt Mandelkern and Terrell Carter from TDS Minutes, Box 1, fd. 1. Report in LJN Papers.

California Alkali Company (later Inyo Chemical Company). Photograph of Deep Springs facilities, U.S. Geological Survey photograph, 1922. htmllib/btch-537btch537j/btch537z/mgr00608.jpg.

California Transportation Department (Caltrans). "Leg. Route 168." n.d., circa 1960. Highway History, LJN Papers.

Cartwright, Morse Adam. *Adult Education in the United States of America*. N.p., 1929.

Centennial Catalogues: The Presidents of the University of Chicago, A Centennial View. Online. LJN Papers.

Chalfant, W. A. *Story of Inyo*. Rev. ed. Bishop, CA: Community Printing and Publishing, 1975.

"Chet Dunn, dictation at request of Mike Cravey, 1974," Subgroup 23, Box 2, fd. 5, DSA.

"Chris Breiseth—New Deep Springs' Dean." *Telluride Newsletter*, May 1980.

Christenson, Charles. "Confidential Report of the Presidential Evaluation Committee." N.d. (internal dating establishes that it was distributed to trustees between December 17 and 27, 1990). LJN Papers, Box 36, fd. 1.

Christenson, Chuck. Letter to Trustees of Deep Springs, January 20, 1994. DSA and LJN Papers.

Clark, Burton R. *The Distinctive College*. New Brunswick, NJ: Transaction Publishers, 1992, with new introduction.

Clark, Denis E. *Telluride Power: A Brief Illustrated History of the Early Days*. Ithaca, NY: Telluride Association History Committee, June 2001.

———. Emails to L. Jackson Newell, February 20, June (no day), and August 8, 2012. LJN Papers.

———. Letter to His Family, August 1, 1969. LJN Papers.

———. Letter to Jack Newell, February 20, 2012. LJN Papers.

Cloud, Stanley, and Lynne Olson. *The Murrow Boys: Pioneers on the Front Lines of Broadcast Journalism*. New York: Houghton Mifflin, 1996.

Constitution of Deep Springs & The Deed of Trust. In *The Gray Book*. N.p., 1975.

Coville, Cabot. Interviewed by Bradley Edmondson, April 25, 1985. DSA.

Coville, Frederick V. Email to L. Jackson Newell, April 7, 2011.

Cowan, William W. Letter to Jack Newell, n.d., [ca. April 23, 2008]. LJN Papers.

Cragen, Dorothy Clora. *The Boys in the Sky-Blue Pants: The Men and Events at Camp Independence and Forts of Eastern California, Nevada and Utah, 1862–1877*. Fresno, CA: Pioneer Publishing, 1975.

Cronk, Edwin. Oral History. Interviewed by Bradley Edmondson, May 21, 2004. In ADSTA.

Cronk, Edwin, and Merritt Holloway. Promotional flier, n.d. LJN Papers, Box 42, fd. 7.

Cummins, M. L. "An Industry and an Institution of Higher Learning Are Born at Ames, Colorado—1891." *Pioneers of the San Juan Country*, 4 vols. Libby, MT: Sarah Platt Decker Chapter D.A.R., Big Mountain Publishing, 1961.

Davy, Hugh. Oral History. Interviewed by Christopher Breiseth, November 13, 1982. In ADSTA.

———. Oral History. Interviewed by Brad Edmondson, January 6, 1983. In ADSTA, DSA.

D'Azevedo, Warren L., ed., *Handbook of North American Indians, Vol. 11.* Washington, DC: Smithsonian Institution, 1986.

deBeers, John S. Interviewed by Bradley Edmondson, February 22, 2002, and June 22, 2005. E-copy in LJN Papers.

"Deed of Trust of Lucien L. Nunn," Appendix A in this volume. Printed in *The Gray Book*, 28–33.

Deeds, 1905, Vol. 11, p. 322, 326; Vol. 17, p. 85, 4, Inyo County Records, Independence, CA.

"Deep Springs." *Telluride Newsletter*, 1924.

Deep Springs Mining District, Book 6, p. 50. Inyo County Records, Independence, CA.

"Deep Springs Notes." *Telluride Newsletter*, May 1944.

"Deep Springs Opens Fall Term." *Telluride Newsletter*, November 1943.

"Deep Springs Oral History Project, 1979–87." See ADSTA.

"Deep Springs to Remain Male Only." *Telluride Newsletter*, September 1979, 6.

Deep Springs Student Body. Letter to Mr. L.L. Nunn, April 3, 1920. In *The Gray Book*, 9.

Deep Springs Student Body Minutes, November 1917–present. DSA and LJN Papers.

Deep Springs Trustees. See Trustees of Deep Springs College Minutes, 1929–present.

Delacorte, Michael Gibson. "The Prehistory of Deep Springs Valley, Eastern California: Adaptive Variation in the Western Great Basin." PhD diss., University of California, Davis, 1990.

Dewey, John. *Democracy and Education*. New York: Macmillan, 1916.

Dodge, Norton. Oral History. Interviewed by Brad Edmondson, February 1989. Audiocassette and transcript in LJN Papers.

Dozier, Miguel. Interviewed by Jack Newell, May 12, 2008. My notes are filed in "1970s Alumni Survey Letters." LJN Papers.

"The Dreadful Day We Hoped Would Never Come: Second Year Student Michael Pihos's Tragic Death at Deep Springs," written September 21, expanded on October 1, 1999, "Postscript" on April 18, 2007. 13 pp. LJN Papers.

Duncan, Adrien. "Deep Springs Notes." *Telluride Newsletter*, January 1942.

Dunn, Chester Starr. "An Interview with Chester Starr Dunn." Interviewed by Wm. L. Mills, February 13, 1975. Subgroup 23, Box 2, fd. 5, DSA.

Dunn, Chet [Chester], Herb Reich, and Robert Aird. Joint Oral History. Interviewed by Chris Breiseth, May 1, 1982. In ADSTA.

Edmondson, Brad. Emails to Jack Newell, March 7, 2010, and September 13, 2012.

———. Telephone conversation with Jack Newell, September 3, 2012. Notes in DSA.

Edmondson, Bradley. Oral History. Interviewed by Christopher N. Breiseth, July 1983. In ADSTA and LJN Papers.

Emerson, Ralph Waldo. *The American Scholar*. 1837; rpt., New York: Penguin Book, 1982 printing.

Erskine, John. *The Moral Obligation to Be Intelligent and Other Essays*. New York: Duffield & Company, 1915.

"Excerpt from RBA Travel Compendium." ca. 1921. Subgroup 23, Box 2, fd. 2, DSA.

"Extracts from Letters Concerning the Educational Work at Deep Springs." DSA. Subgroup 15: Unpublished Letters, Box 1, fd. 8.

"Faculty Personnel Policy: Deep Springs College, Final." January 25, 1996. LJN Papers, Box 19, fd. 3, and Box 58, fd. 14.

Fairchild, Thomas E. *Thomas E. Fairchild Letters, 1929–31*. Translated by Susan Fairchild Chase. Digital format, March 22, 2008. E-copy in my possession courtesy of Susan Fairchild Chase.

Feng, Xiahong, and Samuel Epstein. "Climatic Implications of an 8000-Year Hydrogen Isotope Time Series from Bristlecone Pine Trees." *Science* 265 (August 19, 1994): 1079–81.

Fetter, Richard L., and Suzanne Fetter. *Telluride: From Pick to Powder*. Caldwell, ID: Claxton Press, 1979.

Fisher, Humphrey. Letter to Dear Sirs, June 3, 1951. In Application File, Humphrey J. Fisher, Deep Springs Office, photocopy in LJN Papers.

———. Letter to Simon Whitman, September 30, 1951. File: Fisher file. DSA.

Fisher, Humphrey J., and Allan G. B. Fisher. *Slavery in the History of Black Muslim Africa*. New York: NYU Press, 2001.

Fishry, G. T. Letter to L.L. Nunn, October 24, 1891. Photocopy in LJN Papers.

Flexner, Abraham. "A Modern School." *American Review of Reviews* 53 (1916): 465–74.

Fort, William E., Jr. Letter to "Dear Sir" [addressee unnamed], October 18, 1959. DSA. Robert Aird Papers, Box 4, fd. 6, DSA.

———. In Richard Vetterli, ed., *The Challenge and the Choice*. Salt Lake City: Bookcraft, 1969.

Friends of the Eastern California Museum, comp. *Mountains to Desert: Selected Inyo Readings*. Independence, CA: n.pub., 1988.

Gatje, Robert. Email to Will Cowan et al., November 29, 2011. LJN Papers.

———. Letter to L. Jackson Newell, February 18, 2012. LJN Papers.

———. Letters to parents, 1944–1946. Photocopies in my possession courtesy of Robert Gatje. LJN Papers.

"Geoff and Iris Pope: A Conversation about the 1980s at Deep Springs." Conducted by Jack and Linda Newell, May 28, 2010. LJN Papers.

Goldstone, Richard J. *For Humanity: Reflections of a War Crimes Investigator*. New Haven, CT: Yale University Press, 2000.

Goodyear, Dana. "The Searchers." *New Yorker* (September 4, 2006): 62–71.

Gossen, Nick, Jacob Hundt, Bryden Sweeney-Taylor, Japhet Weeks, Jack Murphy, Andrew Gossen, and L. Jackson Newell. "Hidden Springs: A Planning Guide for a Second College Akin to Deep Springs." Typescript, April 19, 2000, LJN Papers.

Grandin, Greg. *Fordlandia: The Rise and Fall of Henry Ford's Forgotten Jungle City*. New York: Metropolitan Books/ Henry Holt and Company, 2009.

Grant, Gerald, and David Riesman. *The Perpetual Dream: Reform and Experiment in the American College*. Chicago: University of Chicago Press, 1978.

Graumlich, Lisa. "A 1000-Year Record of Temperature and Precipitation in the Sierra Nevada." *Quaternary Research* 39 (1993): 249–55.

Graybill, D. A., and G. S. Funkhouser. "Dendroclimatic Reconstructions during the Past Millennium in the Southern Sierra Nevada and Owens Valley, California." In *Proceedings of the Southern California Climate Symposium: Trends and Extremes of the Past 2000 Years: Technical Report*, edited by M. R. Rose and P. E. Wigand, 239–69. Los Angeles: Natural History Museum of Los Angeles County, 1999.

Hamilton, Fletcher. *Report XVII of the State Mineralogist: Mining in California during 1920*. San Francisco: California State Printing Office, for California State Mining Bureau, January 1921.

Haughey, Jim. Interviewed by Jack Newell, July 22, 2002. Transcript in LJN Papers.

Haycock, Obed C. "Electric Power Comes to Utah." *Utah Historical Quarterly* 45, no. 2 (Spring 1977): 173–87.

Hayes, Henry G. "Autobiography of Henry G. Hayes." 1973. In "Recollections of Mr. Nunn and Early Deep Springs," ca. 1986. The file is labeled "Legends of Deep Springs, 1983–86." Record Group 3, Subgroup 23, Box 2, fd. 2. Typescript. Photocopy in LJN Papers.

———. Oral History. Interviewed by Christopher Breiseth, Deep Springs, September 1979. In ADSTA.

———. Unpublished typescript of "Autobiography of Henry Hayes," 1973, LJN Papers, Box 11, fd. 2.

Heckman, Helen M. Conversations with Jack Newell, Apple Valley, CA, November 24, 2009, and November 29, 2010. Notes, LJN Papers.

———. Letter to LJN, April 26, 2012, LJN Papers.

———, comp. "Snippets from Alice Bird's Diaries." Nunn Papers.

Herder, Johann Gottfried von. *The Spirit of Hebrew Poetry.* Trans. James Marsh. Burlington, VT: E. Smith, 1833.

"Historic Earthquakes: Owens Valley, California, 1872 03 26 UTC Magnitude 7.4." U.S. Geological Survey. http://earthquake.usgs.gov/earthquakes/states/events/1872-03_26.php.

Hoekstra, Misha. Email to Denis Clark, Jackson Newell, et al., January 3, 2010. LJN Papers.

———. Emails to Jack Newell, January 3, 2010, and September 15, 2012 (includes quotations from Kinch Hoekstra). LJN Papers.

———. Ship manifest. May 4, 1874. LJN Papers.

Hoenicke, Edwin. Oral History, interviewed by Jack Newell, October 10, 2006. LJN Papers.

Hoffman, William C. Oral History. Interviewed by Jack Newell, March 24, 2010. LJN Papers and DSA.

Holloway, Winona Johnson. *Moving On.* Live Oak, CA: Shadow Butte Press, 1989.

———. *Moving Out: A Sequel to Moving On*. Live Oak, CA: Shadow Butte Press, 1992.

———. *Riders to the Rainbow: Traders to the People*. Live Oak, CA: Shadow Butte Press, 1998.

Holmes, James S. Letter to L.L. Nunn, February 1, 1922. LJN Papers.

Honan, Park. August 11, 1964, Alumni Essays. Subgroup 23, Box 2, fd. 3, DSA.

Hoover, Erik. Email to Jack Newell, July 19, 2010.

Hovey, Kenneth A. "Realizing the Ideal: L.L. Nunn's Educational Theory in Historical Context." Address delivered to the Deep Springs community on May 19, 1987. He published highlights from this address as "The Intellectual Origins of L.L. Nunn." *Deep Springs Newsletter* (Autumn 1987): 5–9. Manuscript in box labeled "Official Publications of Deep Springs College, 1994–2007." DSA.

Hudgens, Tom. *The Commonsense Kitchen: 500 Recipes + Lessons from a Hand-Crafted Life.* San Francisco: Chronicle Books, 2010.

"Hydro-Electric Power Pioneer Dead on Coast," *Telluride Journal,* April 9, 1925.

"In Memoriam WHITE COW November 5, 1964." *Deep Springs Newsletter*, February 1966.

"Information on the So-Called Westgaard [*sic*] Pass Road, Known in Very Early Days as the Deep Springs Valley Toll Road." Pamphlet. Eastern California Museum, Independence, CA.

"Inyo County Toll Roads, 1871–1921." File in Eastern California Museum, Independence, CA.

Inyo Independent. This brief publication is cited by date in the notes but usually without headlines.

Jayko, A. S., and S. N. Bacon. "Late Quaternary MIS 6-8 Shoreline Features of Pluvial Owens Lake, Owens Valley, Eastern California." In *Late Cenozoic Drainage History of the Southwestern Great Basin and Lower Colorado River Region: Geologic and Biotic Perspectives*, edited by M. C. Reheis, R. Hershler, and D. M. Miller, 185–206. Special Paper #439, Geological Society of America, 2010.

"Jurisdiction." See Nunn bibliography. 14 pp. L.L. Nunn. Letter to Student Body, October 18, 1920, 14 pp. Subgroup 15, Box 1, fd. 7, 6, DSA; LJN Papers.

Kelly, Isabell T., and Catherine Fowler. "Southern Paiute." In *Handbook of North American Indians*, 11:368–97.

Kennedy, Brian. Email exchange with Jack Newell, March 13, 2012.

Kerns, Virginia. *Scenes from the High Desert: Julian Steward's Life and Theory*. Urbana: University of Illinois Press, 2003.

Kesey, Ken. *One Flew over the Cuckoo's Nest*. New York: Viking, 1962.

Kimpton, Lawrence A. "Report of the Management to the Board of Trustees." Trustees Meeting, May 12, 1939. DSA and LJN Papers.

Kinney, M[alachi]. "A Sketch of the Pioneer Life of Lucien L. Nunn from June 1880 to November 1887." November 20, 1927, with a "P.S." dated November 27, 1927. DSA. Subgroup 8, Box 2, fd. 11.

Kirby, Mark. "Desert Stories." *Harvard Summer Review*, Issue 8 (Summer 2002), 7 pp. www.dce.harvard.edu/pubs/review/2002/01/kirby.html.

Kirwan, Thomas. Newspaper clipping from *Boston Herald*, November 30, 1890. Nunn Papers.

Kohn, Melvin L. Oral History, May 8, 2012. Tape recording in LJN Papers.

Kropf, Frederick W. Biographical sketch. In *Death Valley Ranch (Scotty's Castle)*. In *Historical American Building Survey*, No. GA-2257. Washington, DC: National Park Service, Department of the Interior, Archives, Scotty's Castle, Death Valley National Park.

Land, Water, and Mining Claims, Book C, 1873. Inyo County Records, Independence, CA.

Lanner, R. M., and H. Lanner. *The Pinyon Pine: A Natural and Cultural History*. Reno: University of Nevada Press, 1981.

Last Will and Testament of James R. Withrow Jr., September 7, 1984. Copy provided to me courtesy of William H. Allen, LL.B. (DS'42). Folder labeled: "DS Trustees, Withrow Will." LJN Papers.

Laverty, Bruce R. "Deep Springs College Hydro Project: Fact Sheet." July 26, 2010. LJN Papers.

Laverty, Bruce R. Email to Jack Newell, January 21, 2008. Folder: "DSV Climate and Weather." LJN Papers.

Lee, Jeffery, Charles M. Rubin, and Andrew Calvert. "Quaternary Faulting History along the Deep Springs Fault, California." *GSA Bulletin* 113, no. 7 (July 2001): 855–69.

"Legends of Deep Springs." DSA. Record Group 3, Subgroup 23, Box 2, fd. 2.

"Letter from the White Mountains," *Alta California*, May 3, 1864. The editor identified the letter writer: "From an Occasional Correspondent, Roachville, Mono County Cal. White Mountain District, April 15, 1864." LJN Papers.

Liljeblad, Sven, and Catherine S. Fowler. "Owens Valley Paiute." In *Handbook of North American Indians*, Vol. 11, edited by Warren L. D'Azevedo, 412–34. Washington, DC: Smithsonian Institution, 1986.

Lingenfelter, Richard E. *Death Valley and the Amargosa: A Land of Illusion.* Berkeley: University of California Press, 1986.

Lloyd, Stan. Conversation with Jack Newell, May 12, 2011. LJN Papers.

Lowenberg, Richard. "Lighting up the Nineties." InfoZone, n.d. http://infozone.telluride.co.us/store/acpower.com. Print-out in LJN Papers, Box 11, fd. 8.

Lukas, J. Anthony. *Big Trouble: A Murder in a Small Western Town Sets Off a Struggle for the Soul.* New York: Simon and Schuster/Touchstone, 1998.

Lustig, Jeffrey, Hanna Pitkin, Randall Reid, John Schaar, David Schuman, and Sharon Schuman. Letter to Bruce Laverty, August 9, 1990, with copies to Trustees of Deep Springs and Dr. Saul Benjamin. LJN Papers.

Lyon, George C. "Legends of Deep Springs." Record Group 3, Subgroup 23, Box 2, 1–2. DSA.

Macey, J. Robert, and Theodore J. Papenfuss. "Amphibians." In *Natural History of the White-Inyo Range*, edited by Clarence A. Hall Jr., 283–84. Berkeley: University of California Press, 1991.

Mansfield, Harvey C. "The Jewish Quota at Deep Springs," 1944. LJN Papers and DSA.

———. Letter to Robert Aird, November 2, 1986. DSA. Subgroup 23, Box 2, fd. 2.

———. Oral History. Interviewed by Christopher Breiseth, September 14, 1981. DSA. In ADSTA.

"Marshal Did Not Serve L. L. Nunn." *Telluride Journal*, June 29, 1911.

Martin, MaryJoy. *The Corpse on Boomerang Road: Telluride's War on Labor, 1899–1908.* Lake City, CO: Western Reflections Publishing, 2004.

Master Plan: Deep Springs College by HCD Collaborative Architects and Planning. N.d. Box 56, fd. 4, LJN Papers.

Matlack, James. "A Graduate's Postscript." *Christian Science Monitor*, June 21, 2000, 9.

McCormick, John S. *The Power to Make Good Things Happen*. Salt Lake City: Utah Power and Light Company, 1990.

McCoy, Robert B., and John T. Strachan. *Midland Trail Tour Guide, 1916*. Glorieta, NM: Rio Grande Press, 1916.

McCreary, Andrew J. Emails to Jack Newell, June 5, 2012, and January 16, 2013. LJN Papers.

McDermott, Scott. "Prologue." In Bailey, *L.L. Nunn: A Memoir*.

McGilvra, Louise Nunn. "Notes Concerning Nunn Family." Information from Paul N. Nunn, ca. 1900. Copy in LJN Papers courtesy of Helen Heckman.

McGuire, Michael. "Year of Turbulence." 1989. LJN Papers, Box 8, fd. 8.

McPhee, John A. *Basin and Range*. New York: Farrar, Straus and Giroux, 1980.

Meehan, J. E. (student body president at Claremont). Letter to L.L. Nunn, May 8, 1917. Nunn Papers; photocopy LJN Papers.

Meehan, Ed, to Dean E. A. Thornhill, December 5, 1917. Photocopy in Deep Springs Student Body Minutes, November 1917–September 1918, Box 1, fd. 3.

Meiklejohn, Alexander. "The Freedom of the College." *Atlantic Monthly* (January 1918): 83–89.

"Milestones: Alternating Current Electrification, 1886." IEEE Xplore Digital Library. IEEE Berkshire Section, Dedication: October 2, 2004.

Miller, Mrs. Donn M. Letter to Jack Newell, July 25, 1994. TDS Minutes for June 1994–March 1995. LJN Papers.

Miller, Gilbert, and Sidney Walcott. "Report on Virginia as a Home for the Central Branch of Telluride Association," circa summer 1916. Subgroup 8, Box 1, fd. 4, DSA. Copy in Nunn Papers.

Miller, William J. "Geology of Deep Springs Valley, California." *The Journal of Geology* (1928): 510–25.

Minutes. Informal Meeting of Trustees, May 15, 1923. See TDS Minutes.

Mono County. Records. ca. 1869. Courthouse in Bridgeport, CA.

Mortgages, Vol. D, 353. Inyo County Records, Independence, CA.

Moore, Barbara. "Bodie Electrifies the World." *The Album* [Bishop, California], July 1988, 29–33. Box 7, fd. 4, LJN Papers.

Moore, Heide. Letter from Chuck and Bea [surname not given], October 17, 1997. Sachse correspondence. LJN Papers. 06n39

Mossner, David. "Deep Springs." Lyrics. David Mossner file. LJN Papers.

Mount Diablo Meridian. Township No. 6 South, Range No. 36 East, May 12, 1885. Surveyor General's Office, San Francisco.

Murphy, John F., Eric T. Simandle, and Dawne E. Becker. "Population Status and Conservation of the Black Toad, *Bufo Exsul*." *Southwestern Naturalist* 48, no. 1 (March 2003): 54–60.

Newell, L. Jackson. "Among the Few at Deep Springs College: Assessing a Seven-Decade Experiment in Liberal Education." *Journal of General Education* 34 (Summer 1982): 120–34.

———. "Among the Few: A Study of Deep Springs College Alumni, 1917–1980, with Recommendations for Educational Policy. Final Report: September 1980." 156 pp. DSA and LJN Papers.

———. "Chuck Thompson Problems." Memo to file, September 12, 1999. LJN Papers.

———. Letter to Richard Cornelison, May 29, 1997. LJN Papers.

———. Letter to Clare Wolfowitz, May 14, 1998, LJN Papers.

———. Memo to trustees, re: Earthquake, November 17, 1997. LJN Papers.

———. Notes on 1980s Reunion conversations, May 31, 2010. "Unloading My Brain," Section no. 1: Random Turner-Jones, 1980s email correspondence in LJN Papers.

Newell, L. Jackson, chair. "On the Brink of Decision: A Letter to the Trustees of Deep Springs," September 1, 1994. LJN Papers, catalogued with Newell Presidential Journal.

———. Presidential Journal. LJN Papers.

Newell, L. Jackson, and Padraic Macleish. "Alexander Meiklejohn (1872–1964)." *Encyclopedia of Education* (2d ed.), edited by James L. Guthrie. New York: Macmillan Reference, 2003.

Newell, L. Jackson, and Katherine C. Reynolds, eds. *Maverick Colleges: Ten Notable Experiments in American Undergraduate Education*. Salt Lake City: Utah Education Policy Center, University of Utah, 1993.

Newell, L. Jackson, Katherine C. Reynolds, and Scott Marsh, eds. *Maverick Colleges: Fourteen Notable Experiments in American Undergraduate Education*, 2d ed. rev. and expanded. Salt Lake City: Educational Policy Center, University of Utah, 1996. Published in OpenCourseWare Program, Massachusetts Institute of Technology, 2009, online for Learning Seminar, Experiments in Education (SP.291/ESG.SP291).

Noon, Frank. A personal reflection, ca. 1960. DSA. Subgroup #23, Series 2, Box 2, fd. 4.

Noon, F[rank]. C. Letter to Trustees of Deep Springs, August 23, 1951. TDS Minutes.

Noon, Frank. Quoted in "Telluride Association Establishes Another Branch," December 6, 1916, DSA.

Northrup, Virginia Thornton. Oral History. Interviewed by Brad Edmondson, December 3, 1982. ADSTA, #224, DSA.

Nunn, Emily. Letter to Frederick Nunn, February 25 and March 12, 1881. Holograph, Nunn Papers.

Nunn, Jennie D. (Mrs. Josiah J.). Letter and attachment to Frank C. Noon, November 23, 1938. LJN Papers, Box 4, fd. 5.

Nunn, Miriam Kendall. Letter to Frederick Nunn, postmarked November 28, 1881. Holograph, Nunn Papers, Cornell University Library.

Nunn, P[aul] N[apoleon]. (1860–1939). Papers. Subgroup 15, Box 1, fd. 8. Nunn Papers, Cornell University Library.

Nunn, P.N. Letter to A. M. Marquis c/o *Who's Who in America*, April 17, 1922. Nunn Papers. LJN Papers.

———. Obituary-Tribute. *Telluride Association Newsletter*, November 1939.

———. "Reminiscences of Early Electrical Development." Address delivered at the Newhouse Hotel, Salt Lake City, February 15, 1927, first joint session of the Utah Society of Engineers, the American Institute of Electrical Engineers, and the Electrical League of Utah. LJN Papers.

———. "That New Social Order." Delivered to the Student Body at Deep Springs, January 4, 1933. LJN Papers.

———. "What's the Matter with Deep Springs?" In TDS Minutes, June 21, 1929. See also an earlier version, which Sweeting copied and edited in pencil, dating it "Probably June or July, 1927." DSA, Subgroup 8, Box 15. Original in Nunn Papers, copy in LJN Papers.

Officers' Report, January 19, 1939. In Deep Springs Student Body Minutes. DSA and LJN Papers.

Olmsted, John. Letter to Brad Edmondson, February 4, 1984. Photocopy in LJN Papers.

"Oral History Conversation about Deep Springs College, 1958–59, by William C. (Bill) Hoffman and L. Jackson Newell, March 24, 2010." LJN Papers and DSA.

Oral History Project. Alumni of Deep Springs and Telluride Association. Uncorrected proofs. September 1987, DSA. See ADSTA Oral History Project.

O'Rourke Paul. "The Telluride Heist: Butch Cassidy's First Bank Robbery." *Telluride Magazine*, Summer 2005.

"Oxford: Former Honors Director Falsified Resume." *Exponent* (Montana State University's student newspaper), January 29, 1991. LJN Papers.

Partridge, Jim. "In Memoriam: A Tribute from Jim Partridge (DS'66)," September 21, 2008. In "Alumni Reunion, 1960s" file. LJN Papers.

Pell, Erik. "Deep Springs, 1941–43." 23 pp. Typescript, n.d. (ca. 2009). LJN Papers.

Penner, Vernon D. Telephone interview with L. Jackson Newell, March 31, 2012. Audio recording. LJN Papers.

Peretz, Evgenia. "Cowboy Scholars." *Vanity Fair* (June 2004): 198–210.

Pezick, Bill. Email to Jack Newell, August 2, 2012. LJN Papers.

Planning Committee Report, April 7, 1967. LJN Papers.

Pook, Gerrard. Email to Jack Newell, July 4, 2010. LJN Papers.

Pope, Geoff. Recorded and transcribed conversation with Ross Peterson and Gareth Fisher. LJN Papers and DSA.

Pope, Geoff, and Iris Pope. "A Conversation about the 1980s at Deep Springs." Interview conducted by Jack and Linda Newell, May 28, 2010. LJN Papers.

Pre-Empt Claims, Volume B, 25. Records of Mono County, CA. February 19, 1869. Courthouse in Bridgeport, CA.

"President's Reports." In TDS Minutes, May 7, 1959, and October 15, 1959. DSA.

"Purpose." *The Gray Book*, 37–40.

Putnam, Jeff, and Genny Smith, eds. *Deepest Valley: A Guide to Owens Valley*, 2d ed. Mammoth Lakes, CA: Genny Smith Books, 1995.

Putney, Michael. "To Members of the Student Body." February 5, 1959. In Deep Springs Student Body Minutes, February 13, 1959. DSA.

Rabin, Mr. and Mrs. George. Letter to Humphrey Fisher, October 6, 1951. DSA.

Reeve, Paul. Email to L. Jackson Newell, April 15, 2008. LJN Papers.

Reich, Herbert J. Journal. February 8, 1918–January 29, 1920, and March 13, 1920. Photocopy in LJN Papers, courtesy of Herbert Reich.

———. "Legends." January 16, 1918, and October 5, 1919. Subgroup 23, Box 2, fd. 2, DSA.

———. Letter to Mr. Nunn, April 1, 1919. Subgroup 15, Box 1, fd. 3, DSA.

———. Letter to Jacques Reich, September 30, 1918. Reich Family Collection. Loaned to Jack Newell.

———. Oral History. Interviewed by Christopher Breiseth, April 28, 1982. DSA. In ADSTA.

Reid, Randall C. "Dean Reid Finds Himself a Conservative about Deep Springs: Values Union of Intelligence and Character." *Telluride Newsletter*, May 1973.

———. "Deep Springs and the Ideal Vision," n.d. [ca. spring 1965]. DSA and LJN Papers.

———. Oral History. Interviewer not identified, March 12, 1989. DSA.

———. "Sunday Service by Deep Springs Dean Randall Reid," March 7, 1965. Copy in LJN Papers, courtesy of Ron Alexander.

"Report of Investigation of Range Cattle Transactions for the Period March 1, 1933, to November 20, 1939." Record Group 1, Subgroup 2, Box 10, fd. 1, DSA.

"Report of the 1958 Budget Committee," April 10, 1958. In DSA and LJN Papers.

Rio Grande W. Ry. Co. v. Telluride Power Transmission Co. Utah 22, 63, 995 (1900), p. 995.

[Roberts, Samuel P.], writing under the initials SPR. *Inyo Independent*, February 2, 1884.

Roodhouse, H. R., to Messrs. [Frank] Noon, [Harold] Waldo, [William] Biersach, [Harold] Sanders, and [Robert B.] Aird, December 26, 1959. Aird Papers, Box 4, fd. 8. 11n33

Ross, Arthur ("Cy"). Oral History. Interviewed by Christopher N. Breiseth, August 1982. In ADSTA. Photocopy of typescript in LJN Papers.

———. Oral History, Interviewed by Brad Edmondson, July 4, 1983. In ADSTA.

Rotberg, Robert I. *The Founder: Cecil Rhodes and the Pursuit of Power.* New York: Oxford University Press, 1988.

Rudolph, Frederick. *The American College and University: A History*. New York: Alfred A. Knopf, 1962. Rpt., Athens: University of Georgia Press, 1992, with "Introductory Essay and Supplemental Bibliography" by John R. Thelin.

[Sachse], Chuck, and Bea [surname not given] to Heide Moore, October 17, 1997. In Sachse correspondence. LJN Papers.

Sachse, Martin Robert. Letters to Kate Park, January 5–July 21, 1924. DSA. Photocopies in LJN Papers, Box 12, fd. 1.

———. Log of Death Valley trip to Kate Park, April 1–16, 1924. LJN Papers, Box 12, fd. 1.

———. "Personal History." n.d. Unbound manuscript, DSA; photocopy in LJN Papers, Box 12, fd. 1.

Schechter, Robert. Email to Jack Newell, August 22, 2012. LJN Papers.

Schuman, David. "Education and Solipsism." *The CoEvolution Quarterly* (Spring 1981): 132–39.

Schuman, Sharon. Letter to Trustee David Werdegar, April 6, 1982. DSA. Subgroup 23, Box 2, fd. 15.

Seiler, Roger. Oral History. Interviewed by L. Jackson Newell, August 10, 2009. LJN Papers.

Smith, Michael A. *The Students of Deep Springs College*. Photographic essay with accompanying essays by L. Jackson Newell and William T. Vollmann. Revere, PA: Lodima Press, 2000.

Smoot, Reed. Telegram to Nunn, September 24, 1916, Nunn Papers. Photographic copy in LJN Papers, taken September 29, 2003.

Sproull, Robert L. Letter to L. Jackson Newell, March 26, 2010. LJN Papers.

———. Oral History, September 18, 2002. Interviewed by Bradley Edmondson, in two parts. In ADSTA. Copy of transcript in LJN Papers.

Stanley, Link. Telephone conversation with L. Jackson Newell, April 1, 2012. Transcription LJN Papers.

Starrs, Paul. Conversation with Jack Newell, June 16, 2012. LJN Papers.

Steward, Julian H. *Basin-Plateau Aboriginal Sociopolitical Groups.* Washington, DC: U.S. Government Printing Office, 1938.

———. "Ethnography of the Owens Valley Paiute." *University of California Publications in American Archeology and Ethnology* 33, no. 3 (1933): 233–350.

Stryker, Michael P. Emails to Jack Newell. September 20 and October 10, 2012. LJN Papers.

Student Body Minutes, November 1917–present. DSA.

Student Body to Mr. L.L. Nunn, April 3, 1920. DSA; Nunn Papers.

Swanson, Eric V. Email to Jack Newell, September 19, 2012. LJN Papers.

Swatek, Paul. Alumni Essay, September 20, 1964. Box 2, fd. 3, DSA.

Sweeting, Orville. "The Education Experiment of L. L. Nunn." Unfinished typescript, 1976. Nunn Papers. Photocopy in LJN Papers.

Synnott, Marcia. *The Half-Opened Door: Discrimination and Admissions at Harvard, Yale, and Princeton, 1900–1970*. Westport, CT: Greenwood Press, 1979.

Tate, Marcia. *The Atlatl Story: An Ice Age Hunting Weapon*. Aurora, CO: Tate Enterprises, 1986.

Telluride Association. Convention Minutes. Manager's and Treasurer's Report, June 2, 1925. Electronic copy in LJN Papers.

———. Death announcement for L.L. Nunn. Copy in LJN Papers, courtesy of Polly Aird from the papers of her father, Robert B. Aird.

———. Financial Committee Report. In Minutes, June 20, 1941. Nunn Collection.

Telluride Association Newsletter. Also *Telluride Journal.* For a time, this newsletter ran a column of items with the standing title "Deep Springs Notes." Cited by date in the notes but without headlines.

Telluride Association. Letter to L.L. Nunn, July 2, 1913. LJN Papers.

"Telluride Power Company, Provo Office: Balance." December 31, 1906. Nunn Papers, Box 4, fd. 23.

Tetrault, Francis, to Mother, n.d., but ca. fall of 1937. Subgroup #23, Box 2, fd. 18, DSA.

Thornhill, Ernest. Academic Report to L.L. Nunn, February 27, 1918.

———. "Classes, 1920." Holograph. LJN Papers.

———. Letter to Committee on Scholastic Standing, January 17, 1917, Subgroup 8, Box 1, fd. 4, DSA.

Trimble, Stephen. *The Sage Brush Ocean: A Natural History of the Great Basin*. Reno: University of Nevada Press, 1989.

Trustees of Deep Springs College (TDS). Minutes, reports, attachments, and correspondence. May 6, 1924–May 24, 1940. Box 1, fds. 1–5. DSA and LJN Papers.

Turner-Jones, Random. "Unloading My Brain." Section no. 1: 1980s. Email correspondence in LJN Papers.

———. Quotations in L. Jackson Newell. "Notes on 1980s Reunion Conversations," May 31, 2010. LJN Papers.

United States Geological Survey, 1922. www.htmllib/btch537/batch537j/btch537z/mgr00608.jpg.

United States Indian Census 1885–1940. "Nevada Indian Tribes." www.accessgenealogy.com/native/nevada.

United States Land Office. Deed to Nathan Gilbert. TS 7 Sec. 1: Lot #4 in NW quarter of Sec. 1; 36 and 89/100 acre plot. Inyo County Records, Books of Deeds W, p. 179, Abst. 53, 1872.

Utah Power and Light Company. *Utah Power and Light: History of Origin and Development. Prepared in Connection with Federal Power Commission Request*. Salt Lake City: UP&L Company, January 28, 1941. Photocopy of typescript in LJN Papers dated May 11, 1937.

Veblen, Thorstein. *The Higher Learning in America: The Conduct of American Universities by Business Men.* 1904; rpt., New York: B. W. Huebsch, 1935.

Vleck, Jan. "Deep Springs Student Studies Local Feral Horses." *Deep Springs Newsletter* (July 1972): 4–5.

Voge, Hervey H., ed. *The Climber's Guide to the High Sierra: A Sierra Club Totebook.* N.p.: Sierra Club, 1954. 05n47

Walcott, Charles D. Memorandum to E. M. Johnson, November 5, 1926. Published as "Charles D. Walcott's Tribute to L.L. Nunn." *Telluride Newsletter*, January 1929.

Walcott, C[harles]. D. "The Post-Pleistocene Elevation of the Inyo Range and the Lake Beds of Waucobi Embayment, Inyo County, California." *The Journal of Geology* 5, no. 4 (May–June 1897): 340–48.

Walcott, Sid. Letter to Robert Aird, April 20, 1977. DSA. Subgroup 23, Box 2, fd. 20.

Waldo, Harold. Dictated recollections at Deep Springs College, November 10, 1973. Typescript. Subgroup 23, Box 2, fd. 21, DSA.

———. Letter to Humphrey Fisher, October 5, 1951. DSA.

———. "Transcript of Remarks at Deep Springs College, November 10, 1973." Subgroup 23, Box 2, fd. 21, DSA.

Wallace, Jim, Verna Wallace, and Leland Wallace. Telephone conversation, April 1, 2012, with L. Jackson Newell, LJN Papers.

Ward, Fay. *Working Cowboy's Manual.* New York: Random House Value Publishing, 1983.

Warren, Howard Crosby. "Academic Freedom." *Atlantic Monthly* (November 1914): 689–99.

Welti, Walter. Interviewed by Brad Edmondson July 5, 1983. In ADSTA. 421, DSA, and LJN Papers.

Wesely, Edwin. Interviewed by L. Jackson Newell, June 29, 2006. Recording and transcription in LJN Papers.

Wheeler, George M. *Preliminary Report Concerning Exploration and Surveys Principally in Nevada and Arizona. Prosecuted in Accordance with Paragraph 2, Special Orders No. 109, War Department, March 18, 1871, and Letter of Instructions of March 23, 1871, from Brigadier General A. A. Humphreys Chief of Engineers, Conducted under the Immediate Direction of 1st Lieut. George M. Wheeler, Corps of Engineers, 1871*. Washington, DC: Government Printing Office, 1872. Contains Appendix B. Report of Second Lieutenant D. A. Lyle, Second United States Artillery.

White, Andrew Dickson. *A History of the Warfare of Science with Theology in Christendom*, 2 vols. 1896. Rpt. in the Great Minds Paperback Series. New York: Prometheus Press, 1993.

Whitman, Carroll N. "The Convention." *Telluride Newsletter*, June 1, 1920.

———. Letter to Board of Trustees, Harold R. Waldo, Secretary, October 8, 1959. In TDS Minutes.

———. Letter to Trustees of Deep Springs, May 10, 1940. DST, Correspondence, Box 5, fd. 5. DSA.

———. Letter to Harold Sanders, May 31, 1960, Robert Aird Papers. DSA. Acc. 2, Box 4, fd. 15.

———. Letter to Harold R. Waldo, Secretary of Deep Springs College, May 8, 1959. TDS Minutes, May 7–8, 1959.

———. "Memo, to Trs. [Trustees], etc., Re: TRENDS," March 11, 1959. Document attached to Michael McGuire, "Year of Turbulence," 1989. LJN Papers, Box 8, fd. 8.

———. Whitman to Fisher, October 7, 1951, p. 6. Humphrey Fisher File. LJN Papers and DSA.

Whitney, Eunice. Interviewed by telephone by L. Jackson Newell, November 26, 2011. Transcript in LJN Papers.

Whitney, Simon N. Diary, January 1, 1942–May 14, 1945. Photocopy in LJN Papers, courtesy of Eunice M. Whitney, 2005.

———. "Memorandum to the Deep Springs Student Body by Simon N. Whitney, Retiring Director," May 31, 1948. 23 pp. Typescript in "Si Whitney: Letters and Notes," in LJN Papers, courtesy of Eunice M. Whitney, December 2005.

Wiens, Doug Stan. "Eoff–Brady–Hon House." Searchable online at Boise Architectural Project.

Withrow, James R., Jr. Letter to Philip L. Kennicott, April 8, 1985. In William Allen, "DS Trustees, Withrow Will." LJN Papers.

Withrow, James R. (Jim). Oral History. Interviewed by Christopher N. Breiseth, October 1983. In ADSTA.

"Withrow's Bequest Exceeds One Million: Conditions Raise Single-Sex Questions." *Deep Springs Newsletter*, Spring 1988.

Wolfowitz, Clare. Letter to Jack and Linda Newell, April 21, 1998. LJN Papers.

Wright, David. Great Basin Research, of Big Pine CA. N.d. Folder: "Great Basin Research Deep Springs." LJN Papers.

———. Report on Inyo County Records. April 2005–May 2008. LJN Papers.

Wright, Frank Lloyd. "Desert Cottage, Mr. Sachse, Deep Springs" (elevation, perspective, and plan). In "Frank Lloyd Wright, Designs for an American Landscape, 1922–32." These drawings were exhibited at the Library of Congress in 1997 and are part of the permanent collection, Frank Lloyd Wright Foundation, Scottsdale, Arizona.

Wu, Frank H. *Yellow: Race in America beyond Black and White.* New York: Basic Books, 2002.

INDEX

Note: LLN = Lucien Lucius Nunn.
Numbers in **bold** refer to photographs.